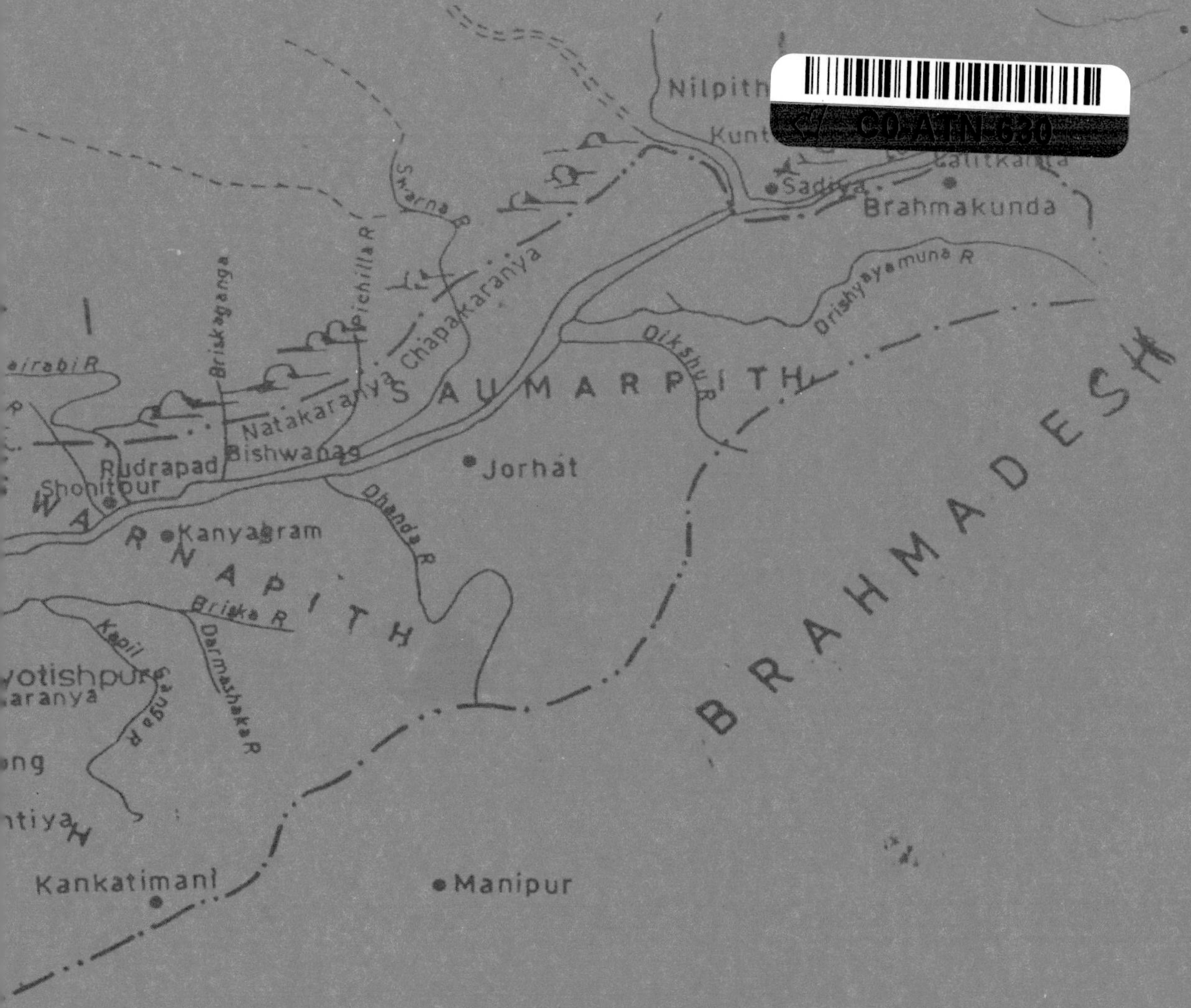

ANCIENT KAMRUP

SCALE

Miles 20 0 20 40 60 Miles

Indian Folk Music

Bhāwāiyā

Ethnomusicological Study

Indian Folk Music

Bhāwāiyā

Ethnomusicological Study

DR. SUKHBILAS BARMA

GLOBAL VISION PUBLISHING HOUSE

20, Ansari Road, Daryaganj, New Delhi-110002 (INDIA)

GLOBAL VISION PUBLISHING HOUSE
F-4, 1st Floor, 'Hari Sadan'
20, Ansari Road, Daryaganj (Near Delhi Book Store)
New Delhi-110002 (INDIA)
Tel.: 30971125, Mob: 9810644769
Email: nsingh_2004@vsnl.net
Website: globalvisionpub.com

Bhāwāiyā: Ethnomusicological Study

First Edition, 2004
ISBN: 81-8220-070-9

PRINTED IN INDIA

Published by Dr. N.K. Singh for Global Vision Publishing House, New Delhi-110002 and *Printed at* Balaji Offset, Naveen Shahdara, Delhi-32.

MUSIC

MUX

Foreword

THE pastoral songs commonly known as the *'Bhāwāiyā gan'* have been very popular with the people of North Bengal and Western Assam for a long time. These are basically love lores containing erotic passions and pangs of separation centred round the life of the poor cattle rearers who had to lead lonely life in the vast pasture lands of the areas mentioned above. In the earlier times these lyrics were looked down upon by the elite sections of the society for their erotic overtones. The singers had to seek secrecy and privacy for their clandestine recitals. Subsequently, these lyrics had been able to attract the encouraging attention of the younger generation of the elite section of North Bengal. By this time, texts of Bhawaiya lyric were included by G.A. Grierson in his Linguistic Survey of India, Vol. V, Part - I, (1903) as a vivid specimen of the northern variety of the Bengali language. Ultimately, Abbas Uddin Ahmed (1901-1959), a renowned folk singer hailing from Cooch Behar recorded in Gramophone discs the Bhawaiya lyrics with the help of Harish ch. Pal, a folklorist of Cooch Behar and Kazi Nazrul Islam (1899-1976), the eminent rebel - poet of Bengal and made this musical variety popular to the whole of Bengal. After Abbas Uddin many folk singers followed his example, the latest, though not the last, of whom is the author of the present book.

Like Abbas Uddin Ahmed, Dr. Sukhbilas Barma also hails from a remote village of Cooch Behar, having spontaneous linguistic competence and wide societal experience related to the local set up of rural North Bengal. Moreover, he has enriched himself with proper academic acumen to conduct a systematic study in some given area in connection with his long career as an able administrator belonging to the Indian Administrative Service. In this respect, Dr. Barma seems to have inherited the time - honoured legacy of John Beames (1837-1902), G.A. Grierson (1851-1914), Ramesh Ch. Dutta (1848-1909), Gurusaday Datta and others who not only served their respective governments in Bengal as able administrators but also served the cause of advancement of learning by pursuing serious academic researches in the respective areas of folk life of Bengal. This aspect of Dr. Barma's career has definitely added a very positive dimension to his doctoral programme and the book.

The present volume is significant from the stand-point of three distinct academic disciplines, viz, musicology, linguistics and folkloristics. In his musicological analysis of the lyrics, I had the pleasure to guide him in the proper linguistic assessment of the texts of the Bhawaiya lyrics from the socio-linguistic points of view. In fact, the present work will serve as a very useful glottopolitical indicator in the contemporary socio-political scenario of North Bengal. Of late, some questions have been raised from some interested quarters regarding the actual linguistic status of the regional variety of the Bengali language which is being used by the local residents of North Bengal through the ages. Although the actual status of this dialect has been infallibly identified by the professional linguists like Dr. Suniti Kumar Chatterji, Dr. Sukumar Sen and so on, some mischievous campaigns have been going on in this regard to create division among the Bengali speaking population of North Bengal. Dr. Barma having been born to this dialect community has been able to dispel all confusions and mis-interpretations regarding the actual status of the local dialect of the Bengali language on the strength of his own experience of being a domestic speaker of this dialect. His work deserves full appreciation in helping establish the prime importance of dialects in determining the strength of a language.

I hope that this volume of immense utility will be widely greeted by the readers all over the world.

Dr. Nirmal Kumar Das
Prof. of Bengali Language & Literature (Retd.)
Rabindra Bharati University, Calcutta
and Guest Faculty of Bengali Deptt.,
Calcutta University

* * *

WE have a rich age-old tradition of 'Sangeet' which covers music, dance and drama. We are rich in study of musicology from the period of 'Vedanta'. But the study of ethnomusicology, a comparatively new discipline, is so to say, a new chapter in our music discipline. It would, perhaps, not be an undue mentioning that the study of this new discipline is yet to attain desired pace.

Music of a particular community, called ethnic or folk whatsoever, not only engrosses the people by its mesmerizing effect but at the same time portrays the socio-economic condition of that particular community through its lyric. This portrayal, in general, is canvassed through feeling of an individual of that particular community. The analysis of note structure and scale enables us to identify a particular form of music amongst innumerable music-streams of the world that flow eternally to one ocean of music which elevates a human being from mundane to celestial level. Again, many ethnic or folk music formats transcending their particular limit touch the soul of neighbouring communities. Thus study of such music can never be complete or, in other words, it fails to transmit complete connotation if it is restricted within analysis of note structure and scale only. The study of socio-economic condition, anthropological and historical back-drop, uses, customs etc. of the concerned community thus becomes unavoidable in understanding the mystery behind creation and sustainability of their age-old music, its impact on society, commonness of feeling and human bondage between different communities and the features of society that created the particular form of music.

All such study under the rubric of ethnomusicology of the area of North Bengal has been done by Dr. Sukhbilas Barma, a born of that area, with deep love and, as an accomplished singer himself, with wisdom in analyzing musicological structure.

Dr. Barma's subject "Bhawaiya' a treasure not only of the Rajbanshis of North Bengal but also a pride of Bengal is no exception from the basic theme of all the age-old sustaining forms of music of the world - **Our Sweetest songs are those that tell of saddest thought.**

Dr. Barma in twelve chapters has covered all the required subjects to reach his conclusion. He, with great expertise, has not by-passed any of the varieties like Chatka, Bisahara, Kushan, Kati, Saitol etc. of Bhawaiya. And it is most praiseworthy to mention that Dr. Barma has not restricted his passage here only for the scholars of the subject.

I am confident that the music loving people of not only West Bengal but also world would be able to enrich themselves from this book and would have to pay their gratefulness to Dr. Barma for this monumental work.

Prof. Utpala Goswami
M.A., Ph.D., Sangeet Saraswati
Ex-Principal: Bengal Music College,
Calcutta University
Ex-Head & Dean: Faculty of Fine Arts
Rabindra Bharati University, Calcutta

Preface

"Folk songs are 'born into a tradition that fits a certain society.... Folk song is the musical and poetic expression of the fantasy of the lower classes.... as the life of the common people is changed, however slowly, through the movement of society, so their folk music alters too".

Folk music is subjected to social and geographical specification, historical change and cultural layering. Also the issue of the interaction between folk music and other music is important. As traditional societies modernise, isolated folk enclaves are assimilated into capitalist cultural relations, old fashioned rural populations are urbanised and commercially organised practices supersede folk practices, the folk music is found to give way to a form of music commonly known as pupular music. Reference may also be made to various twentieth century folk revivals and multiplicity of neo-traditional styles and hybrids developing in 'third-world' countries.

The book has been planned with the object of having an ethnomusicological analysis of the folk form of Bengali song popularly known as *Bhāwāiyā*. Folk song is region based and culture based. It is the mirror of the culture/sub-culture of the region and the people whose song it is. Bhāwāiyā is the folk song of the northern part of Bengal commonly known as North Bengal. This part of the country was greater part of ancient region of Kamrup. Original residents of this region are called Rajbanshis – a group of people believed to belong to Mongoloid race. Ancient Kamrup under the rule of Naraka and Bhagadatta was later on known as Pragjyotispur. The region under the name of Kamtapur was ruled by the Khen dynasty and then by the Koch dynasty under the name of the Princely State of Cooch Behar. The region has, therefore, ancient and quite interesting history.

The original people of the region, initially belonging to the Mongoloid group, by the name Koch-Rajbanshi also have an interesting history. In fact, there is a great deal of controversy about their origin. Some scholars claim that they are believed to belong to Koch-Rajbanshi group, while others are of the view that they are Kshatriyas. Still more amazing is the language, the dialect they speak. Although they are believed to belong to Mongoloid group, their dialect is Indo-Aryan and not Tibeto-Burmese.

The letter written by King Naranarayana of Cooch Behar to the Ahom king is claimed to be the first evidence of prose form in Bengali. But the language has not developed because of the loss of importance of the region in subsequent periods *i.e.* from the British period onwards. It has retained so many features of early phase of Neo Indo-Aryan (NIA). The language has some distinctive features and the distinction between the literary Bengali and Kamrupi is based on four main aspects (*i*) Phonology (*ii*) Morphology (*iii*) Syntax and (*iv*) Vocabulary and idioms. The linguists find enough materials of interest in the analytical discussions of this dialect/language.

Analysis of the folk music of this region naturally demands analysis of cultural ethos of the Rajbanshis and the linguistic analysis of the language in which the songs are composed. Understanding and proper appreciation of the contents of songs demands this. Pronounciation of the words in the lyrics is also important. Some amount of attention has been accordingly given on this aspect. The linguistic analysis has been quite elaborate to make the information available to the readers in English. All these are hardly available in concise form. Whatever materials/information on Kamrupi language are available here and there, are in Bengali or in Assamese. There is hardly any book in English, which has dealt upon this dialect. In fact, I have complied with the demand of a good number of linguists and folklorists including Dr. Nirmal Das and Dr. Pabitra Sarkar, linguist and ex-Vice Chancellor, Rabindra Bharati University who asked me to deal with the language in English, in as much details as possible to make it the principal source of information of this kind. Even 'Origin and Development of the Bengali Language' (ODBL) by Acharya Suniti Kr. Chatterjee, 'The Rajbanshis of North Bengal' by Charu Chandra Sanyal and 'Assamese: Its Formation and Development' by Dr. Banikanta Kakati do not give comprehensive picture of this dialect, a language originally Aryan in its basic grammatical structure, but heavily influenced by extra Aryan characteristics.

The past history and the present status of the region have to be studied. The geographical and natural environment of the area *i.e.,* the rivers, forests, mountains, plains – have tremendous relevance for such studies. The cultural history of the Koch Rajbanshis, their socio-economic life, their social customs, rituals, religious belief are extremely relevant in order to get an insight into their total life. This is why an attempt has been made to include all these aspects while analysing some popular pieces of Bhāwāiyā songs. In short, whatever an ethnomusicological analysis of a particular form of songs demands has been attempted with special reference to Bhāwāiyā.

The present trend of Bhāwāiyā through the evolutionary process and the future of it has been attempted to explain with reference to various song pieces. The study obviously gives an idea about the trend of changes in religious belief and social customs and rituals of the Rajnabshi society explained with the help of song pieces. The problem of retaining the tradionality and genuineness in Bhāwāiyā and prevention of distortions in lyrics, melody, tune, pronounciation in folk timbre has been discussed. An overview of the history of the present day North Bengal, the seat of Kamtapuri movement and the cultural history of the Rajbanshis, the people supposedly involved and associated with the movement has been attempted in the process. Such works already available are very few in number and very much inadequate; they hardly serve the purpose of ethnomusicology. Moreover, whatever is available are mostly in Bengali. The vast groups of people who cannot read and write Bengali do not have access to this field so interesting and varied in nature. The British scholars like Buchanon Hamilton, Dalton, Risley, Grierson, Gait, and O Maley had dealt with the history of the region and its people at some length. Scholars like Suniti Kumar Chattopadhyay also dealt with this field in ODBL and Kirata-Jana-Kriti. But their main concern was history and not cultural history. Culture-represented by songs, dances, drama, socio-religious customs of these people has hardly found place in their studies. Charu Chandra Sanyal in 'The Rajbanshis of North Bengal' included brief analysis of all the aspects but again it does not give adequate idea about the vast field of cultural life of the Rajbanshis. Some more works available in the field are mentioned for the sake of recapitulation.

The first and foremost attempt was the works of G.A. Grierson – the collection and compilation of folk songs in Bengali and Assamese languages for different districts – Rangpur, Cooch Behar, Jalpaiguri, Dinajpur, etc. in the process of collection of samples of local dialects of those districts in connection with the works on 'Linguistic Survey of India', published in 1904 (Vol. V: Indo-Aryan Family, Eastern Group, part I). Side by side, a few scholars like Pt. Jadaveswar Tarkaratna, Purnendu Mohan Sehanobis, etc. associated with Rangpur Sahitya Parishad, took some attempts for collection and publication of folk songs of Rangpur which included *Sonarayer gan, Gorakhnather gan*, etc.

Publication of 'Haramoni' by Mahammad Mansur Uddin in 1930 was an important landmark in the study of folk songs. 'Haramoni' contained good number of folk songs of Rangpur, Dinajpur and Bogra *i.e.* Bhāwāiyā-Caṭkā songs. During 1950's Asraf Siddique of Bangladesh, was influenced and enthused by Rabindra Nath Tagore and also by his teacher Mohammad Shahidulla to collect and study folk songs. Siddique published his works as 'Lok Sahitya' 1963 in two volumes, which contained a good number of Bhāwāiyā-Caṭkā songs with brief analysis. A very important compilation of Bhāwāiyā-Caṭkā songs and Bhāwāiyā-based other songs including some good articles written on the subject by various local collectors of songs and writers, was published in 1971 by Shibananda Sharma under the title "*Goalpara Jilla Sangrakshan Smriti Grantha*".

During 1930's and 1940's Abbas Uddin Ahmed and his associates like Pyarimohan Das, Gangadhar Das, Nayeb Ali, Keshab Barman, etc. collected a considerable number of Bhāwāiyā-Caṭkā songs and performed them in gramophone discs. Haris Chandra Pal of Cooch Behar published the 'Uttar Banglar Palligeeti', Bhāwāiyā part in 1973, with popular Bhāwāiyā songs with notations as recorded on gramophone disc. Similarly 'Uttar Banglar Palligeeti', *Caṭkā* part was published in 1975 with the notations of Caṭkā songs as recorded in gramophone discs. The most valuable work of Bhāwāiyā-Caṭkā songs with their numerous variations was 'Pranta Uttar Banger Lok Sangeet' by Dr. Nirmalendu Bhowmick published in 1977.

Dr. Bimal Chatterjee, following the footsteps of Dr. Nirmalendu Bhowmick authored the work 'Uttar Banger Lok Sangeet' published in 1992, which gives an account of a number of songs with their short interpretations. A little journal 'Kal Baishakhi' published by Shri Ramani Mohan Barma of Dinhata of Cooch Behar district, is devoted to the analytical study of North Bengal's literature particularly Bhāwāiyā-Caṭkā based folk music. The book "Rajbanshi Lok Sahitya" authorised by Shri Barma in 1993, contains analysis of some Bhāwāiyā-Caṭkā songs. Some other little journals in all the districts of North Bengal have been dealing with the analytical study of Bhāwāiyā-Caṭkā based music for the last three decades or so. Particularly important in this respect is 'Madhuparni' published by Ajitesh Bhattacharyya of Balurghat, the district headquarters of South Dinajpur, in its 'Uttar Banga' number published in 1970's and "Cooch Behar District and Jalpaiguri District" numbers published in 1990's dealing with Bhāwāiyā-Caṭkā including the folk dramas based on Bhāwāiyā. Drama has played important role in the cultural life of all ethnic groups. Rajbanshis also have rich drama forms. Very popular folk dramas of Rajbanshis are (*i*) *Kuśān* (*ii*) *Dotorā* and (*iii*) *Bishaharā*. Folk dramas are characterised by the mixture of songs, dialogue and acting. Bhāwāiyā songs, therefore, play quite important part in the folk dramas.

There have thus been important and serious efforts made by a number of scholars in the collection and analysis of Bhāwāiyā-Caṭkā songs. But most of the works done so far lack systematic and scientific analysis of Bhāwāiyā-Caṭkā and as such they are found deficient in some respect or other in so far as ethnomusicological analysis of a form is concerned. The studies seem to be particularly deficient in regard to the analysis of musicology of the form of Bhāwāiyā-Caṭkā. Bhāwāiyā is a melody with specific type of tune developed over time. The tune has some specific features so far as musicology is concerned. Unfortunately, no attempt has so far been made by any musicologist to have musicological analysis of Bhāwāiyā. The reasons are that the music scholars do not have enough knowledge of Bhāwāiyā – in fact such scholars do not consider it necessary to analyse folk forms, whether Bhāwāiyā, *Bhatiali*, *Jhumur* musicologically. On the other hand, Bhāwāiyā singers themselves have hardly any knowledge about musicology. They learn the songs by listening to others and are hardly bothered about the musicology involved. This is, therefore, a pioneer attempt on my part to give a musicological analysis of Bhāwāiyā in this book. The socio-cultural factors responsible for the evolution and continuance of such a form representing the cultural life of a vast area inhabitated by a cultural group under the common name 'Rajbanshi' also have not been addressed to in proper perspective.

As such, any work on this has to deal with all these aspects in quite serious, systematic, scientific manner. My objective is to attempt such a study in this Book. The Book has, therefore, been planned with a view to filling the blank of a good work on the all out information about North Bengal. Knowledge about North Bengal is particularly important today in the face of subversive activities by various ethnic groups like Kamtapuri movement. Intellectuals, both within and outside North Bengal should have proper and adequate knowledge about the region, its people, its dialect and its overall culture. The special feature of the book is that all these informations will be made available while providing explanations of the song pieces.

In planning such a book I have received valuable advice and suggestions from my friends, colleagues and sympathisers. Dr. Nirmal Das and Dr. Utpala Goswami my guide for the doctoral thesis have been a constant source of encouragement and advice in planning the book. Shri Paritosh Datta, Shri Chandan Chakrabarti, Dr. Dibyajoyoti Majumdar have been other sources of encouragement and advice. Dr. Pabitra Sarkar, ex-Vice Chancellor of Rabindra Bharati University and Dr. Pallab Sengupta, former Professor of Bengali, Rabindra Bharati University have regularly enquired when I was going to complte the book. Dr. Shamik Bandopadhyay, a distinguished critic of English literature and film has immensely helped me in English rendering of some of the song pieces. He has taken the trouble of personally doing the English rendering of two very lengthy and important song pieces-*Satyapirer gan* and *Sonarai gan* in the midst of his extremely busy schedule. I have hardly any words to express my gratitude to him for this love and affection. Also I am grateful to his niece Miss Sudeshna, who extended ungrudging help in the translation of some of the pieces. Shri Arup Choudhury and Shri Supriya Roy Choudhury, who happened to be the Personal Assiatants in my tenure of Principal Secretary of the

Backward Classes Welfare department, Shri Dilip Kumar Bhakat, my present Personal Assitant, gave unbelievable amount of labour in typing out the materials of the book in computer. I am especially grateful to them. At home, my wife Dipti and my daughters Tina and Pomy have literally chased and encouraged me in completing the book. Also the assistance extended by Shri Goutam Baine is worth mentioning. I am grateful to Dr. N.K. Singh, Global Vision Publishing House for his help and encouragement in publishing this book.

PLEASE NOTE

	आ Ā/ā	ऋ Ri/ṛ	ं m (anusvara)	ः h (visarga)	
Palatals :	च Ca/ca	छ Cha/cha	ज Ja/ja	झ Jha/jha	
Cerebrals :	ट Ṭa/ṭa	ठ Ṭha/ṭha	ड Ḍa/ḍa	ढ Ḍha/ḍha	ण Ṇa/ṇa
Dentals :	त Ta/ta	थ Tha/tha	द Da/da	ध Dha/dha	
Sibilants :	श Śa/śa	ष Ṣa/ṣa	स Sa/sa		
Aspirate :	ह ha	क्ष kṣa	ज्ञ jña		

CONTENTS

1

Introduction

"Music is closely connected with human life from the very beginning of its creation. Every nation or society made music their means to progress and prosperity in social, political, cultural, religious and spiritual spheres of life." — *Swami Prajnanananda.*

Music is an art: It combines the sound in such a way as to gratify our ears or effect our imagination or both. It is an atmosphere conditioned by a network of conjuring tones or of sensible variety of rhythm or both. It is an aesthetic representation of the artists' inner depth-production of the tonal form or picture, corresponding to that of the mind combined with colour, pitch, grace, harmony, melody, succession of tones and microtones.

The basic element of music is 'sound' which is manifested in the form of tone and microtones. Indian psychologists and philosophers say that the psyche or soul of music is made up of sounds with emotions. The *Nada* or causal sound is the ground of music and upon this primal ground all the phenomena of Indian music are built. The notes originate from the vibrations that evolve from the vital air or *Pran-Vayu*.

In the *Narada-siksha*, Narada describes how the vital air, rising upward from the navel base, gets in contact with the junctions of the canal of the throat and produces sound of different pitches that are *Sadja, Rsabha*, etc. According to Yoga and Tantra philosphies, the primal will of all living beings resides in the navel base or *Muladhara cakra* in the form of *Kundalini* (a coiled/sleeping serpent). *Kundalini* is the symbol of energy and it is the base of causal sound or *Nada*. Cakras are centres of vital forces or *Pranshakti* manifested by vital air or *Pran Vayu*. Other *Cakras* are *Swadhisthana, Manipuraka, Anahata, Visuddhi, Ajna* and *Sahasrana*.

Sensual or sexual pleasures or creations are evolved from this *Kundalini*. When there originates a will-to-speak or will-to-sing, the vital air comes in contact with the will power or *Ichha Shakti* and there originates a vibration or *spandan*, resulting in a subtle audible sound which is called the *Anahata Nada*. *Kundalini* awakens and rises upwards through the canal or passage that passes from the navel base to the throat or mouth.

It becomes *Pasyanti* or visible in the *Swadhisthana Cakra*. When it ascends to the *Anahata Cakra*, it is united with intellect or *Buddhi* and becomes *Madhyama*. Gradually it ascends upward and reaches the *Vishuddhi Cakra* in the throat and becomes *Vakhari*. From there it rises towards the head, spreads over the palate, the tongue, the lips, the teeth, the root of the tongue, and produces articulate sound. It becomes grosser and grosser in the process and at last manifests through the vocal chord in the form of *Ahata Nada* or causal sound. It becomes musical when it is pleasing and soothing. Sarangadeva in 'Sangit Ratnakar' describes it as the indescribable unmanifested will which passes through different plexes or *Cakras* in the spinal column and is manifested in the base of the tongue and ultimately exits as voice through the mouth or nasal cavity.

Indo-musicology opens with *Nada* as the origin-each type of musical sound is a form of *Nada*. *Nada* is the vital concept in Indian music as it is the foundation of *Swara* which again is the basis of *Raga* and the whole world is filled with *Nada*. *Nada* is the originator of music but it is not so much audible as it is worthy of realisation. Musicians of the past, however, have found out some points in the scale of *Nada* that are charming as well as cognizable by naked ears.

Twentytwo such points in an octave were traced before 2000 years and those were termed as *Srootis*, the most important elements of the ancient Indian music. *Srooti* is the minutest form of sound that our ears can recognise. It is our common experience that three parts of our body-navel (abdominal area), throat and nasal area—are differently activated for the production of three types of sounds-low (*Mandra*), middle (*Madhya*) and high (*Tara*), whose Vedic names are Udatta, Mudatta and Swarita respectively.

Early Indian music was *Srooti*-ridden, as the vocal chord was then highly efficient to reproduce the subtle existence of tone. By the passage of time and by natural changes, human voice lost its sharp qualities and gradually became flattened. With the gradual process of innovation, flatter and wider units at larger gaps were discovered at seven stages, spanning equal to twentytwo of the past. Each of the stages is *Swara* and the seven *Swaras* are *Sadaja, Rishava, Gandhara, Madhyama, Panchama, Dhaivata* and *Nishada*. *Nada* is thus like a stream of water while *Srootis* are its drops (only a few rustic or folk voices may spontaneously present the character of *Srootis* and that too unknowingly). So, from *Nada* arises *Srooti*, from Srooti comes Swara or tone and from Swara comes Raga (melody).

From the source of sound, the energy is propagated through the surrounding medium in the form of waves. When these waves reach our ear, we have the sensation of sound.

Sound waves are longitudinal—they are transmitted through air or any other gas. A vibrating body acts as source of sound. A vibration produces disturbance in the surrounding media (usually air); waves are, therefore, generated and these waves-called sound waves-travel outwards from the source. However, average normal ears respond only to those vibrations whose frequencies lie between 20 to about 20000 cycles per second (cps) (*i.e.* limits of audibility).

It can, therefore, be said that any vibrating body whose frequency lies within the limits of audibility may be regarded as a source of sound. Physiologically, vocal organ is the sound producing mechanism in human body. It starts from the lungs where air is stocked. The vocal organ consists of the vocal chord and the wind-pipe through which the wind goes upward. The upper portion of this pipe is a bit inflated and is known as Trachea where the Larynx membranes lie flat on the inner surface.

Above the Trachea is Glottis where there is a valve-like organ named Epiglottis; then is the mouth-cavity at the base of which there is Pharynx. Above the mouth there is nasal cavity. Original sound is thrown out by manipulating with tongue, throat muscle, teeth, lips, top of the mouth and nasal bores. The flow of air initiated and controlled by muscular contraction and expansion is the mechanism of production of human voice, which in other words is *Nada*.

Vibration which gives rise to musical sound can be produced by nail (strings), wind (flutes) and from leather (drums), metal (percussion instruments), besides the human voice which is the most important of them. There are two categories of sound—musical sound and noise. Any sound that seems pleasant to ear is said to be musical; it is noise if it appears unpleasant.

A musical sound is produced when the vibrations are regular or periodic. Sound with irregular and non-periodic vibrations or of abrupt nature is noise. A musical sound having a simple frequency is called a tone. A tone is produced when the source of sound executes S.H.M. (Simple Harmonic Motion). A musical sound generally consists of number of components having different frequencies. Such a sound is called a note. A note is a combination of several tones. Main characteristics of musical sound are intensity, pitch and quality.

Musicology tells us that Will creates music and music allures the mind of all living beings—that sound is like physique with flesh and blood, whereas vital force or *mukhya-pran* is the psyche or soul of music. The sound represents two-fold aspects, causal and gross—the causal being unmanifested is imperceptible, and the gross is perceptible and known as music. The gross sound comes out through the vocal chord, and enriches itself with tones, microtones, modes, melodies, rhythm, tempo and aesthetic sentiments. Its richest ingredient is the melody or *raga*/harmony that evolves from the combination and permutation of notes.

According to Kant, music is the highest form of art, as it plays with sensation *i.e.* emotion. Both aesthetic and philosophic conceptions play important roles in the domain of history of music. Marius Schneider in 'Primitive music' in the *New Oxford History of Music* gives the best short statement about music.[1] The earliest music in man's life was associated with psychological, sociological, religious, symbolic and linguistic elements. Early man has taught the later man that the functions of singing are legion, loving, playing, mocking, greeting, sorrowing, giving thanks, amusing oneself while at work, engaging in worship, medicine or magic, easing birth, lullabying the new child, giving him activities as he grows, dominating wars, public ceremonies, weather and hunting—all these functions.

It is easier to sing than to speak of love; easier to sing abuse than to deliver direct scorn. Dr. Arthur Harvey, an American music therapist who has been conducting research into music psycho-neurology or the effects of music on the brain for over 20 years says,"children who hear music at pre-birth stages turn out to be smarter than those who do not." In other words, music does penetrate unknown realms of the brain.

The eldest son of Albert Einstein recollected that whenever his father had come into a difficult situation he would take refuge in music and that would usually resolve all his difficulties. A passionate violinist Einstein himself, discussing his love of music and his ground-breaking physics research, stated 'Both are born of the same source and complement each other'. John S. Dwight in 1857, Natalia Curtis Burlin in 1917 and Alan Lomax in 1959 stressed the point that singing, as expression is the language of the heart. Lomax added, 'Heart burned clean of pretense'. "As the song spreads from the individual to the folk crowd, carrying secret messages of hope, peace, brotherhood, freedom and love', Lomax continues, 'it transforms the crowd into a unified chorus".

The artistic expression of primitive people can be better found in P. Merriam's *The Anthropology of Music.*[2] It is notable that the primitive people set the tone of the basic cultures. In his chapter on 'Social Behaviour: The Musician', Merriam establishes the place of the individual, especially the individual creator in basic society. He shows how the role and status of the individual creator is determined by the consensus of the society of which he is a part. Music had a special role to play in the primitive society. In the earlier stages of our society when the language was not suficiently developed, man relied more on his vocal tunes for his communication with the supernatural powers whom he had to supplicate for food and drinks, for cure from illness, for protection against the enemies and for so many other daily necessities of life. Music has been playing vital role as medium of communication.

T.C. Berkley observed that in primitive cultures, especially songs of religious or magical character out-numbered secular class of songs like lullabies, work-songs, game and drinking songs, etc; for not only must the gods be served and placated as a part of religious ritual but there were hundreds of other beings whose impact on every day life, on farming, hunting, marriage, burial, war and travel, etc. must also be dealt with properly. Thus music formed an integral and indispensible part of the life of the people.

To Yehudi Menuhin it is music that weilds spiritual and sensual that can convey ecstasy free of guilt, faith without dogma, love as homage. According to him, music is the oldest form of expression, older than language or art.

> "It begins with the voice, and with our overwhelming need to reach out to others, music touches our feelings more deeply than most words and makes us respond with our whole being.......As long as the human races survive, music will be essential to us. We need music, I believe, as much as we need each other."

The combination of music and speech into the single expression of song has unique power, conveying feeling of great elation or almost unbearable poignancy. When we gather for common celebrations, music helps to activate the sharing of feelings to a level of intensity that words alone could not hope to attain.

According to Kant—the history of music is closely associated with human society. It is a product of intelligence and creative faculty of the human society and hence is the importance of sociological factors that are behind the creation of music. Dr. Arthur Harvey has observed that when the volume is regulated, good music can drive away anxiety and depression and even help in concentration by its subtle, pervasive influence. With children especially, music helps to open up the mind enabling them to soak up all kinds of information effortlessly.

Modern research has proved that music stimulates the body to produce endorphins (pain relievers) as also S-IgA (salivary immunoglobin A), which spreads up healing, controls heart rate and reduces the danger of infection. Music therapy plays a special role in the areas of pain, anxiety and depression. In many cases, it reduces blood pressure as well as basal metabolism and respiration rates, thus lessening physiological responses to stress. Music has been described as the 'massager' of the brain.

'Forget mnemonics. Talk about music. It will help you remember'. 'Music holds the key to better memory' is the news item published in the Times, London (Nigel Hawkes) republished in the Statesman, Calcutta on 13th Nov. 1998. The latest study carried out at the Chinese University of Hongkong by Mrs. Agnes Chan and her colleagues has shown that studying music produces a higher IQ, a better grasp of mathematics, science and languages and better reasoning power.

Children getting music lessons before the age of 12 have better memory for words when they become adults. According to a doctor in Thane, Bombay, who has applied music for the treatment of mentally ill patients, the suggestive, persuasive and compelling elements of music bring patients out of their shells and make them receptive to treatment.

According to Mrs. Manjula Bose of Balwant Roy Mehta Vidya Bhavan, Delhi who uses music to educate the hearing impaired and mentally slow children,

> "Music therapy helps to improve the speech as well as the physical problems of the handicapped".

A researcher in Yorkshire, however, found that in some discotheques sound levels went up to 110 decibels (the maximum sound level recommended 90 decibels). A few months of exposure to such noise and they would need hearing aids. Too much noise also increases the pulse rate, causes nervous disorders, emotional imbalances and indigestion.

According to a research carried out in America, plants have been found to grow better in an atmosphere of classical music, while prolonged exposure to heavy metal rock actually kills them. According to Dr. B.C. Dewa who received doctorate for research on the psychophysics and psychoacoustics of music,

> "much of the tension experienced these days is because of bad music. Constant exposure to sexually exciting music can cause sexual neurosis and lead to drug addiction. All this hashish smoking, etc. one hears of amongst yougsters could well be caused by erotic music".

Music thus appears to be food of life but there is definitely a problem of differentiating between good music and bad music.

Evolution of Music

Regarding the evolutional nature of the art of music, Cecil Gray in his "The History of Music" says,

> "In no art, science or other departments of human activity, has the doctrine of evolution been so enthusiastically welcomed, so eagerly adopted and so wholeheartedly endorsed, as in music. Indeed the whole history of the art has almost invariably been conceived and represented as a simple, orderly and undeviating line of progress from the simplest and most primitive beginnings upto the complexities of modern practice; and the account of this gradual process of development which is generally to be met with in musical histories, reads exactly like the account given in scientific textbooks of the origin and evolution of life from the amoeba".[3]

Charles Darwin was of the opinion that music evolved from the imitation of the cries and calls of the animals. Alfred Einstein also holds this view. Primitive men may have been attracted by bird song in the first place and continued to use it as a model of imitation.

Similar belief prevails in India. Naradasiksha mentions—'*Sadjam Mayura Vadati*...etc.' *i.e.*, the call of the peacock is similar to the tonality and pitch of the note *Sadja*, that of the bull to that of *Rsabha*, that of goat to that of *Gandhara*, Crane—*Madhyama*, Cuckoo—*Panchama*, Horse—*Dhaivata* and Elephant—*Nishada*.

Shadjam Mayura vadati, Gavastu Rishabha bhashinah
Ajadi kantu Gandharam, Crounchah kvanati Madhyamam
Pushpa sadharanekale, Pikah kujati Panchamam
Dhaivatam hreshati Vaji, Nishadam vṛmhate Gajah.

The western savants like Rousseau, Harder and Herbert Spencer are of the opinion that speaking with a raised voice was the beginning of song or music *i.e.*, music evolved from the raised voice speech in all nations and a kind of speech-song or chant-like recitation was indeed to be found among the primitive men. Specially, the Spencerian theory is an idealisation of the natural language of passion. According to this theory, music is an extension of the primitive desire to communicate *i.e.* communication of human emotions and passions.

Rowbotham does not accept this view and he points out that impassioned speech is the source of music and it works as a vehicle for everyday emotions. Wallaschek advances the theory that the original musical impulse was purely aesthetic, growing out of the rhythm. Dr. Burney is of the opinion that music is anterior to word and language. "Vocal music is of such high antiquity that its origin seems to have been coeval with mankind, at least the lengthened tones of pleasure and pain, of joy and affection, must long have preceded every other language and music".

Theodore M. Fishery is of the opinion that music emerged into the history as a social art and consequently its history cannot be written without mentioning its social uses. "The types of music may vary immensely, but the forms of its use, the purposes for which any culture retains music as a part of its social heritage remain almost the same."

'Music', says Romain Goldron, writing in 1968 "is traceable to the Paleolithic Age". Most primitive people were familiar with the concept that "sound forms the basis of reality in the universe". Through music man, since his beginning, has striven to emulate his gods and to evoke, again and again, the amount of creation for present benefits. Curt Sachs tells that in primitive man, "music began with singing and song is sound shaped into beautiful form by the desires of the heart and the artful working of the mind."

The evolutionary process of music comprises the musical anthropology or the ethnic history of music, which deals with the origin and growth of music in the race or country through different strata of time and space. The primitive people sang and danced when they felt something positive to express and to enjoy. Music is the oldest form of expression.

Singing and dancing were the spontaneous outbursts of their simple and sweet thought, quite often mingled in the course of their life and social performance. They sang the narrations or stories of their daily life. They observed the rhythm by the clanking of stones, the pounding of wood or by the dashing of stone spearheads against wooden shields. Possibly gathering the idea from the hide-covered shields, they stretched skins across the two open ends to the hollow trunks of trees or covered the open mouth of the earthen ditches and thus invented the musical instruments like drum accompanying their songs and dances.

To keep time and to create stirring emotion they clapped their hands, nodded their heads and moved the limbs of their bodies, and from there they gradually gathered the sense of measure of time giving rise to the idea of rhythm. Initialy the relations and distant measures of the tones were not known. They used to add the notes to the words or speech making them suitable for music. Gradually they observed the forms and beauty of cadences of rise and fall in words and tones, and from the succession of words and tones, they discovered the laws and forms of melody, though in a crude form.

It is the melody that made music so significant in their life. Gradually, harmony came out of the melodic variants in the West. All the rites relating to birth, circumsession, marriage, hunting, war, weather, medicine and death were permeated with musical elements. Often the type of voice used determined the character of melody.

Archaeological evidence suggests that primitive man was using bones, drums and flutes long before the last ice age. One can safely speculate that such instruments were used for the ceremonies and rituals, both sacred and profane. For our ancestors, food gathering was vital work. In the process, both animals and men had to hunt for berries and roots, melons and nuts, even as they might prey on each other. The hunt became as much a part of survival as the harvest and it was the discovery of bow and arrow, which gave man control over the animals from a distance, that altered the balance of power in favour of man.

From the ritual of the hunt sprang music; the bow could produce a mellifluous twang. A widely held view is that the bow and arrow is the ancestor to the violin. Food gathering rituals began by invoking the blessings of the gods for the success of the search. As agriculture and the building of shelters developed, music became associated with work. And as our societies grew, music to honour leadership came into being. Royal processions with musical instruments go back to Egypt and Sumer.

The invention of musical instruments is one of the great human miracles. The oldest traces of specific tools for the making of music have come from excavations in Siberia (3500 years ago). Those included an ensemble of mammoth bones and huge shoulder joints with markings showing the places where the best resonances could be secured. Found with them was a bone curved as a beater and two small flutes also made of bone with four small holes, two above and two below, suggesting that they were held by the thumb and two fingers of both hands. Other sites have yielded carved stone drum shells over which skins appeared to have been stretched.

Resonant sound was produced by striking hollow logs and by placing wood beam across an open pit and striking it. This was perhaps the first natural amplifier. The ground bow was an extension of the log over a pit. A bridge was added at mid-point, and a string of natural fibre or animal gut (plucked or struck) drawn tightly over it. This principle of the amplifying resonator was applied to many kinds of sound production. Gourds served as the foundation for early harps, as did the shells of living creatures from the armadillo to the turtle and conch. Their ready and easy availability might have contributed to the early development of the string instruments through which the early man could also refine the sense of pitch because of the variable tuning of the strings.

The discovery of the principle of flute and horn is again fascinating based on the resonating property of an enclosed vibrating column of air. The earliest flutes and horns were made of hollowed bones, branches and barks. Hollow substances like bamboo served as flutes. With animal horns, the column was made to vibrate by the use of the lips. The horn had great carrying power and widely used as signal. The horn, man-made or animal, has been used as musical instrument since pre-historic.

The vibrating reed mouthpiece, almost as old as the flute and horn, replaces the lips or cutting edge and sets the air-column vibrating. A piece of cane crushed flat by a hammer blow may be the oldest reed mouthpiece. The lips gripped two flat pieces bound together. Yehudi Menuhin says:

> "To me, the structure of music is part of the structure of nature of the very vibrations themselves, the system of overtones. Every voice and instrument produces tones which vibrate at a basic rate, but their characteristic colour is obtained from the overtones generated at the same time".

Evolution of Indian Music

The history of Indian music is an authentic record of the development of music of Indian people. It has extended itself from the antique pre-historic age to the present time. It changed and evolved as inevitable for the shifting phases or the changing circumstances of the Indian society. In the antique Vedic age, the chanters and common people were content with purely sacred hymnal type of *Samaganas*, which were possessed of different numbers of notes, registers, meters and literary compositions. In the beginning of the classical period (600 BC) *Samans* were replaced by the *Gandhara* type of music that evolved in connection with the necessity of drama.

The dawn of the Christian era brought with it a new awakening in the field of Indian music. A systematic and scientific outlook in the form and system of music was first observed in the works of Muni Bharata in his epoch – making '*Natyasastra*'. The genuine type of *raga* came into being with the new names of *Jatiraga* and *Gramaraga* with ten determining characteristics (*dasalaksana*) and psychological value. Then came again a new change in the 3rd-7th century A.D. when Kohala, Yastika, Durgasanti, Matanga and others attempted systematisation of the aboriginal and regional types of tunes in the classical music. The non-Aryan tunes gradually got into Aryan stock and this resulted into the enrichment of the vital force of Indian music.

Most scholars now believe that the Vedic Aryans poured into India in batches from the Northwestern side around 1500 B.C. Before that India was populated by different ethnic groups of people—commonly known as pre-Aryans, aborigins etc. The Vedic people brought with them a powerful language, the Aryan speech. But they, it appears from the Vedic literature, did not have a developed system of music. Vedic music was predominantly seasonal—in the form of *stava, stotra* performed in connection with different *yajnas*.

On the other hand, the pre-Aryan ethnic groups like Gandharvas, Apsaras, Kinnars, Nagas have been referred to as the master musicians in the Jaina literature, classical Sanskrit literature and even in the late Vedic literature. It is worth-mention that some names of the ancient Indian tribes occur in the names of the musical modes listed by ancient authorities like Dattila (2nd century A.D), Bharata (3rd century A.D) and Matanga (5th to 7th century A.D.). The musical mode '*Andhri*' finds places in the lists of Dattila and Bharata. Matanga in his '*Bṛhad-deśi*' mentions musical modes like Andhri, Saka, Bhotta, Andhiri, Gurjari, Kulindi, Pulindi and Dravida *gitis*, after the names of the tribes living in these areas. Some later writers mention Savari, Kodu and Gondkiri *ragas* named after the tribes Savar, Kora and Gond living in Orissa, Bihar and M.P respectively.

Then some of the foreign tribes were absorbed into the Aryan music. Hundreds of *ragas* evolved with their new and novel names and forms. The ancient *gramas* were replaced by the *murchhanas* (series of upward and downward notes), variations were found in the number of notes, as some displaced (*komal*) notes appeared by the side of the sharp notes.

In the 15th-16th century A.D., the groupings appeared with new nomenclature of *mela* or *ṭhāṭa*. In the middle of the 18th century A.D. there came a radical change upon the forms and groupings of the notes (*varjikarana*) of the ragas. This evolutionary process of the Indian music continued with the Indian tradition of preservation of the genuine culture and method of practice (*gharana*) of music, which have been handed down from generation to generation or from the teacher to the student (*Guru-sisya-sampradaya*).

Elements of Music

The basic stuff of music are the elements from which it is composed—rhythm, melody/harmony, tone-colour and the forms created by the interaction of these elements. Dynamics and expression are also elementary to music although they cannot be as decisively indicated as the elements mentioned above. Further, each element is inseparably related to the other.

A. Melody, in the broad sense of organised and rhythmic succession of tones, is the most important element in music and the most pervasive element in the development of music.

B. Rhythm is the only element that has life of its own. Rhythmic factor in our daily life, work and play is so common that it has a life of its own apart from music. Rhythm is concerned with regulating and ordering the time relationship with tones either by accents or by patterns of long and short notes. It is responsible for the flow of music. It is commonly identified with meter.

   Character of a melody is determined by (i) rhythmic features, (ii) range—how high and how low it goes, (iii) interval—arrangement of successive tones – how a melody proceeds from one tone to the next—by step or by skip and (iv) general shape of contour *i.e.* order, direction and rhythmic pattern of the successive intervals.

C. Tone colour, a term derived by analogy from painting, refers to the particular shades (or timbre) of individual voices, instruments, and their many combinations. The timbre of a particular voice or instrument often appeals most directly to the ear.

D. Form is a result of combining elements, rather than a primary element, in the same way that a building is the result of shaping stones, wood and other materials into an organised structure.

E. Dynamics and expression relate to the capacity of the performer. The emotional impact of a melody depends not merely on intervals and rhythms of a melody in the abstract, but more or less tangible factors like tone colour of the voice or instrument, nuances of the loud and soft, all the nuances of touch, the tempo-deviations from tempo, subtleties of phrasing and accent by the singer or player,

> the manner of attack, release and connection of notes—everything that gives personality and individuality to the performance. The subtlest shades of expression are impossible to indicate by the symbols of music. The manner of expression, scoring and marks of expression make the difference between a live and glowing performance and, one that is dull and lifeless.

Elements of Indian Music

Gradual change in the music of Indian tribes generally followed the line of development of classical music of India. Rig-vedic hymns used to be sung in three pitches—Udatta, Anudatta and Swarita. In this tritonic music, the idea of octave was absent. Musical line was unitary with no symmetrical rhythm. Samaveda is just the musical version of the *Rigveda*. Seventyfive verses of the *Rigveda* were recited in the *Samaveda* in the form of liturgical melodies. By the time Bharata wrote his *Natyasastra* around the 1st century B.C, Indian music seems to have developed the heptatonic scales with different semi-tones, idea of *srooti*, different *jatis, talas, layas* and four musical lines-*asthayee, antara, abhog* and *sanchari.*

Indian classical music based on the combinational expressiveness of the *swaras* or notes is called the *raga*-music or modal music. A *raga* is a musical mode produced by formulaic combination of a group of notes around a tonic, each mode conveying some idea or expression.

Raga

"*Ranjayati iti ragah*" – that which colours is a *Raga*. The earliest definition of *Raga* as provided by Matanga—"A *Raga* is called by the learned that kind of sound composition which is adorned with musical notes in some peculiarly stationary, or ascending or discending or moving values (*varna*), which have the effect of colouring the hearts of men". The four varnas involved are values of duration (*sthayee*), values of ascent (*arohana*), values of descent (*avarohana*) and values of movement (*sanchari*).

The other definition quoted in the 'Sangita-Narayana' ascribed to Bharata is somewhat more subjective and vague. "Those are called *Raga* by Bharata and other sages by which the hearts of all the beings in the three worlds are coloured and pleased". The third version goes like this—"By which all people are coloured or elated as soon as they hear it, and by reason of giving pleasure to all, that is known as *Raga*". In all these definitions, the word '*Raga*' is derived from the root '*ranja*', meaning 'to colour', 'to tinge'.

The definition given by Herbert A. Popley in 'The Music of India' is worthmentioning in this connection. "*Ragas* are different series of notes within the octave, which form the basis of all Indian melodies, and are differentiated from each other by the prominence of certain fixed notes and by the sequence of particular notes. We may perhaps find in the term 'melody-type', the best way to transcribe *Raga* in English". The comment of Alain Danielou is also relevant in this connection.

> "The expression of a mode is the sum of the expressions of its different notes, each depending upon its individual relation with the tonic. According to the theroies of the *srutis*, many notes cannot have the same kind of expression and, therefore, in a scale, there are necessarily contrasts. This is why the most intense *ragas* have often incomplete scales, for they suppress as far as possible that would not support the predominant expression"....."Thus a very sad *raga* will leave out the fifth (*Pa*) because a fifth always expresses sunshine, joy. A very passionate raga will have no natural fourth (*Suddha Ma*), since that always expresses peace, serenity".

The *raga* music has accepted a fixed note as the tonic (usually 'Sa'). There are also a dominant note, the sonant or *vadi*, and the consonant (*samvadi*), assonant (*anuvadi*) and dissonant (*vivadi*) notes, all of which contribute to give shape to the *raga*. The interrelationship between the tonic and the remaining notes, and between the *vadi-samvadi-anuvadi* notes, is very important, for only the correct combination of them can lead to the right expression.

Besides the clear and sweet utterances and the formulaic combinations of *swaras*, the other factors that increase and diversify the expressive power of music are language, rhythm and tone colour (*timbre*).

Rhythm in music can be distinct and indistinct or symmetrical and asymmetrical, depending on the degree of regularity of the rhythmic patterns, *laya* and *matra* being two important concepts in this connection. The unit adopted for measuring the duration of a musical line is called *matra. Tala* refers to symmetrical rhythm. Two basic *tala* divisions are made of 2 and 3 *matras*. In Indian classical music, rhythm plays very vital role. There are very many complicated talas of 7 *matras*, 10 *matras*, 12 *matras*, 14 *matras*,16 *matras* and so on. Music can be with *vilambita layas* (slow type) and *druta layas* (fast type) of various *talas*. Most interesting and fascinating are *dhrupad, dhamar* and *vilambita kheyal*.

Tone colour (*timbre*) in the classical music mostly depends on the skill of the performers. This leads us to the discussion on the musical scale. In regard to the musical scale, the earliest theories of classical music give the following information:

(i) Mention of the word grama-two such gramas being *sadja* and *madhyama i.e.* two different starting points,

(ii) Mention of the pentatonic (*odava*), hexatonic (*shadava*) and septatonic (*sampurna*) scale,

(iii) Mention of the theory of consonance – *vadi, samvadi, anuvadi* and *vivadi*, and

(iv) Mention of *srooti.*

Discussion on tone colour and musical scale takes us to the interesting field of folk music in the Indian music system. Matanga in 'Bṛhad desi' classified Indian music into seven types called *'gitis'* of which *raga-giti* is one. According to him no classical melody can be composed from four notes or below. He further mentioned that melodies with notes less than five were used by tribes such as Savaras, Pulindas, Kambojas, Vangas, Kiratas, Andhras and Dravidas. It appears from his writings that some of these forest tribes who used melodies with less than five notes, gradually became advanced accepting the Hindu culture, improved upon their own melodies and produced new classical modes which have been named after them.

It is quite likely that non-*raga* gitis referred to by Matanga were, actually speaking, the different types of folk music prevalent in different regions of this subcontinent. Some of the folk melodies might have gradually developed into minor *ragas* but most of them continued to represent the folk music of the rural areas.

Folk music has actually occupied an intermediary position between primitive (tribal) music and the cultivated Indian classical music. It has gradually become the music of social groups that are part of intermediary and higher cultures but are not themselves musically literate. The observation of Alain Donielou is worth-mention in this connection. 'Besides, there remain in many regions, in certain valleys of the Himalayas in particular, archaic forms of music with an upper tonic and a descending scale, the study of which would be of great interest for the understanding of ancient music'.

Folk Music

The phrase 'folk music' is a German compound applied exclusively to peasant songs originally. The connotation has now undergone changes in the hands of experts of various fields. In anthropoligical parlance, 'folk', as defined in the Dictionary of Anthropology by Charles Wirck, is "a group of associated people, a primitive kind of post-tribal social organization—the lower classes or common people of an area." Encyclopaedia of Anthropology, gives the definition of folk as:

> "A less ethnocentric and broader definition of folk would be any group of people who share at least one common factor (for example, common occupation, religion or ethnicity)".

Regarding the definition of folk song, the famous statement of Righard M. Dorson in 'A Foreword on Folklore' in 'American Folklore', 1962 is worth-mention: "Folklore is a word with short but turbulent history". Perhaps the same is true about folk song also. It is a simple terminology with very many interrelated complex issues.

In 1907, Cecil Sharp defined folk music as the spontaneous music of the unspoiled, unlettered classes created out of their pure natural instinct. Based on Sharp's principles, the International Folk Music Council at its conference in Sao Paolo, Brazil in 1954 defined folk music as the product of musical tradition that has been evolved through the process of oral transmission. The factors which contribute to shape this tradition are:

(*i*) continuity which links present with the past,

(*ii*) variation which springs from the creative impulse of the individual or the group, and

(*iii*) selection by the community which determines the form or forms in which the music survives.

This definition of folk music has now been widely accepted. Folk music, Sharp says, reflects feelings and tastes that are communal rather than personal. The music of these common people is always genuine and true "for instinct is their only guide and the desire for self-expression, their only motive." In folk music, the individual invents while the community selects. The racial character of a song, therefore, is due to communal choice, not communal invention.

Folk music is usually seen as the authentic expression of a way of life now, past or about to disappear (or in some cases, to be preserved or somehow revived). Unfortunately, despite the assembly of an enormous body of work over a long period, there is still no unanimity on what folk music is. With the complexity of social interaction and stratification increased over time, with the urbanisation of rural music, the various conditioning criteria like 'traditon', 'continuity', etc. have come under attack. Nevertheless, the concept of folk has not been relinquished by most of the folklorists. In the modern world, the folklorists like A.L. Lloyd criticise the characteristics traditionally ascribed to folk music-orality, community of response, continuity, variation of formulae, etc. but having attacked Sharp's concept of folk, they stick to the 1954 International Folk Music Council definition of folk song.

Henry Edward Krehbiel says, "folk songs are echoes of the heart beats of the vast folk and in them are preserved feelings, beliefs and habits of antiquity". Grimm says, "folk song composes itself." Ralph Vaugham Williams has added some useful distinctions. The folk song grows straight out of the needs of the people, and the people find a fit and perfect form for satisfying those needs.

The folk singer is bound by no prejudices or etiquette. In his rhythmical figures he is free. There is no original in traditional art; no virtue in the earliest known version. Later versions are development, not corruptions. Bruno Nettl, one of the greatest ethnomusicologists who has contributed lot to the collection and analysis of folk music states, "folk music both old and contemporary, is representative of the people's ancient traditions as well as an indicator of their current taste".

The songs and instrumental pieces in folk and non-literate culture must be accepted by a substantial part of the population; otherwise they will not live. Music is preserved and transmitted in these cultures by way of oral traditions. Music is passed by word of mouth; songs learnt by hearing; musical instruments making and playing learnt by watching. In sophisticated culture, a piece of music which was conceived by its composer, written but not performed even for once, might be discovered centuries later by a scholar and resurrected.

But in case of folk, a song must be sung, remembered and taught by one generation to the next. Surely, then a piece of folk music must in some way be representative of the musical taste and aesthetic judgement of all those who know it and use it. A folk song must be accepted or it will be forgotten and will die. If not accepted, it may be changed to fit the needs and desires of the people who perform and hear it and changes made over the years tend to become integral parts of the song. Most of the folk songs are old but they have changed.

This music, no matter how far back its roots, has probably undergone a great deal of changes because people wanted to improve it or they forgot parts of it or they felt it necessary to make it sound like other music that they were hearing. For every folk song, verse and melody is the product of a folk community. Folk community is a people of common backgrounds—social, economic, ethnic, sectional, urban, rural, mountainous, occupational. The background must have developed over a period of generations so that they are well set in the minds of the group. To common grounds are added common goals, interests and values and most of all common pressures of which evolves a common psychology. The community supplies its themes and its subject matter. Its unique language has grown in the community's own soil and under the community's atmosphere and weather conditions. From its community a body of folk song derives its natural history, its anthropology, its mythology, its subtle implications.

Within the community, there must be a need for expression—a common language whether in words, instruments, dances, art pieces or some other device. The folk song wears group clothes when it needs to, and personal clothes when they are more appropriate. When calling for rain or warding away pestilence it is a group song; when dealing with loneliness with love, betrayal by a lover or the pain, it is supremely personal. Folk song should not be read 'literally' without reference to the peculiar language of the folk community. When family members communicate with each other it is full of oral shorthand, symbol, meaningful but peculiar accent, irony and significant silences.

But with the folk community, the complexity of the language is accentuated even more, since there are many people to communicate with. In its art, as Nutia points out, it uses "mask, irony, human values, dimension". The quality of a folk song which should be judged in the context of the relationship to its community, depends upon the depth of involvement of the folk group and the success of the artistic devices employed. The purpose of folk song is to highlight matters of deep concern to its community. As Tagore said:

> "it speaks of intense yearning of the heart for the divine in man. It is often the people's only form of worship".

When a talented individual with the philosophy, style and emotions of the community he belongs to, creates a song and gives it to the group, the group may accept it in toto, may strike off portions, even add a phrase or a line. Over the period of range of transmission, it may add stanzas. These individual creators know what they need to sing, what they want to sing, what will solve their emotional complications, what will lift their spirits. In a body of folk songs from a given folk group there will be a variety of philosophies and styles expressing a single community attitude.

The earliest dramas, based on folk pieces, are intermix tunes of singing, playing of instruments and dancing both in the West as well as the East. The basic folk singer who creates song to express something definite may borrow from a foreign song when he finds its adaptability. Folk music is both old and contemporary. It is a product of individual composer and of the creativity of masses of people. Folk music composed by individual have been improvised and changed by many and then a song re-created in effect.

The main characteristic of folk song is transmission by oral tradition, not written down and as a result it develops variants and the original form is rarely known. Folk music normally is created by untrained, unprofessional musicians and performed by singers and players with little or no theoretical background. Song is old; style is archaic. But folk cultures do have a history; they allow their music to change, their compositions to be altered and their repertory to be turned over. It is the musical expression of a whole people or tribe or a significant portion of a culture; folk song must be performed and accepted in order to remain active.

Folk music comprises songs and dances that have attained common currency among the mass of people in communities, regions or nations. Who composed the music may or may not be known; even when the composer is known, a tune often attains the status of being of a community origin by virtue of changes and adaptations over the years in folk usage. Songs were handed down for years by oral tradition and in the process many of them were lost. Most of the folk songs we hear today are of recent origin.

Music researchers think that the earliest known folk songs are not older than the 12th century and there are very few of those. Folk songs and dances owe their long life to the simplicity and beauty of their melody, and to the fact that they express the emotions and sentiments deeply and intimately felt by regional and national groups of people. The character of folk music varies as widely as the nationalities or communities from which it comes.

The musical variety of folk music is emphasised still more by investigations through the phonograph which have shown that many folk songs use intervals of less than half tone or intervals that do not correspond exactly to the western system of half or whole tones. The addition of many ornamental tones is also a feature of folk songs. Inspite of such wide variety, however, most folk songs have in common singable qualities and the use of refrains or stanza forms. At the same time, folk music has sometimes been influenced by composed music as it has always been a treasury of melody for the composers.

Music arose because of some need for expression and communication. Like language, music is a means of communication. Music, however, transcends language in that it can communicate emotions more directly and sometimes it can transmit emotions and intensities of emotions of which language is incapable. As stated by Alan Lomax, 'singing is a specialised act of communication akin to speech, but far more formally organised and redundant.' Musical and linguistic sounds are both the results of vibrations of air in the vocal region.

Whereas in music, the breath is at first produced in the vocal region with the help of the regular and periodic vibrations, and then instead of being articulated by the tongue and lips, as in language, it is diversified with varying height or depth caused by the difference of the rapidity of vibrations. This is called the pitch of the sound, which is the chief material for music. Satisfactory musical effect requires (*i*) a variety of pitch and (*ii*) rhythm produced by the duration of sound and accent. A musical sound or a combination of them may act as a medium of communication in two ways— (*i*) they have inherent potentiality of creating particular ideas or feelings; (*ii*) the expressive power of musical sound can be increased by skilful persons while performing with or without the help of meaningful words.

Both these possibilities have been recognised and exploited by the Indian classical musicians. From the very beginning of classical music, *i.e.* from the Vedic age itself, music has been considered as an effective means of communication with god. Signalling power of music has been indicated by the mythology of Krishna's playing on the flute to attract Radha and such other stories like Gorakhnath, the famous guru of Nath sect wherein his disciples played drums with such precision that Gorakhnath (in the guise of

King) understood the signal and woke up from his slumber of mundane pleasure. Various *mudras* of classical dances–Odissi, Kathak and Bharat-natyam have special meanings to be communicated. Drum, trumpet, conchshell, horns are still used all over India as signalling instruments for various purpose

Any communication system is highly structured network of signs or it is a system of signs. When we study signs and their relations, we virtually study a communication phenomenon. The nature of these signs and the relationship between these is also highly structured. Music of any culture is a highly ordered sign-system. It is a system of signs through which cultural meanings, by and large arbitrary in nature, are communicated and understood. For example, a marriage song cannot be confused with a 'wail' in any culture because the textual content, the style of singing, the rhythm, the intonation and other musical qualities, statistically measurable, are different in both the cases.

This power of music as a means of communication is much more pronounced and evidenced in folk music. Alan Lomax, the great ethnomusicologist states–Folk song is a multi-levelled communication that combines the signals carried by many systems into a single evocative message. Elements of the dance, of special melody, of role–playing, of social organisation, of ritual practice and of emotive communication blend together in a performance so that none of the components is individually perceptible. It is this view about the importance of folk songs as a media of communication that takes us to the broad subject of ethnomusicology. Traditionally, folk songs have served the purpose of communication. But only recently, the ethnomusicologists have brought out this role of folk songs more clearly and explicitly.

In the earlier stages of our society when the language was not sufficiently developed in man. He relied more on his vocal tunes for his communication with the supernatural power whom he had to supplicate for food and drink, for cure from illness, for protection against the enemies, for so many other daily necessaries of life. In civilised societies, music is considered as an art whose primary function is to please the audience. Music as a medium of commnication is not given much importance in such societies. But it has been well observed that music particularly folk music can be used as an unambiguous signal for expressing human thoughts.

The idea, that folksong is closely associated with a people, a nation or a culture and its characteristics, has long been widely accepted. Songs can be passed from culture to culture. The same is true of musical characteristics—stylistic traits. A type of scale, a kind of rhythm, a way of singing can be passed from one people to another without a simultaneous passing of songs. Each culture has a primordial musical style of its own.

Indian music can be broadly divided into two categories— uncultivated and cultivated. Tribal and folk music fall under the category of uncultivated, while cultivated music means the classical music. The ancient pundits have classified Indian music into two divisions— '*Marga*' and *'Desi'*

Alapadinibaddho jah sa ca Marga prakirtitah,
Alapadivihinastu sa ca Desi prakirtitah.

That which is sung with *alap*, etc. is called Marga while that which is sung without them is called Desi. To make it still clearer they clarified—

Abalabalagopalaih Kshitipalairnijecchaya,
Giyate Sanuragena Swadeshe Desirucyate

That which is sung by women, lads, cow-herds and kings on their own accord is called 'Deśi' music, implying thereby that the Desi music is for all strata of the society.

On the different stages of cultural evolution- economic, spiritual, material culture, language, etc, the tribes have been classified into three broad groups—primitive tribes, semi-tribes and semi-castes by the great ethnomusicologist Sudhibhusan Bhattacharyya.[4] The characteristic features of music of the three classes of tribes are broadly mentioned below.

(*i*) Primitive tribes—Diatonic, tritonic or tetratonic composed in single musical line and without any regular rhythm or *tala i.e.,* they were asymmetrical. They were mostly ritualistic or functional and restricted to particular tribes or culture groups.

(*ii*) Semi-tribes—Music gradually became tritonic and tetratonic–additional lines occasionally introduced—both symmertrical and asymmetrical—mainly functional but non-functional also got some place.

(*iii*) Semi-castes–-Influence of regional folk music is perceptible and music became tetratonic and pentatonic-symmetrical with 3 or 4 *matras* predominating-functional music still predominant-greater use of meaningful words and literary ideas—not always confined to particular tribes or culture groups.

Music being an integral part of tribal culture, their music undergoes changes and acquires more and more the features of folk music in course of their cultural evolution moving onwards to the next higher stage of semi-tribe and semi-caste. Folk music thus occupies an intermediary position between primitive music and the cultivated music. According to Bruno Nettl, the great ethnomusicologist in his "An introduction to Folk Music in the United States" "Folk music occupies a kind of middle ground between the primitive and the cultivated".[5]

They are composed anonymously and passed from singer to singer by oral tradition. Two broad types of folk music are—functional and non-functional. Functional songs are connected with festival, ceremony or religious rites falling in the magico-religious category of tribal music. Non-functional music is performed solely for the purpose of entertainment, though in the process they bring out the essence of the cultural traits.

Folk songs have been there in all the societies. Interest of the city-bred intellectuals in folk songs is of recent origin—an event of this century only. The existence and importance of a whole body of folk songs was not recognised in Europe till Cecil Sharp (1859-1924), the greatest English collector of songs and expert on folk songs who published with notations a considerable number of folk songs and dances strikingly similar to those still lingering on in the west of England, although several centuries had passed since the British had emigrated to America and got interested in collecting and studying them.

Industrialisation posed a threat to folk music at the beginning of the 20th century. Efforts were made to collect and record these songs before they got vanished forever. The Folk Songs Society had been founded in England in 1898. Cecil Sharp founded another society in 1911 for the encouragement of English folk dance. Cecil Sharp's society was amalgamated with the Folk Songs Society in 1932 to form the Folk Dance and Song Society as an important and successful collecting agency.

Before Cecil Sharp, the other great musician inspired in folk songs was Johannes Brahms in Germany (1833–1897). Another great musician of the world almost contemporary to Cecil Sharp who took keen interest in folk songs was Bela Bartok (1881-1945) of Hungary. With serious interest in folk songs, he travelled widely and collected numerous folk songs. He created 'a harmonic idiom, a new musical language out of the intrinsic qualities and possibilities of the folk song.' The other great widely known musician enthused by folk songs was Paul Robeson (1898) of Princeton. He was particularly interested in Negro songs and won a name for the fearless demands for a solution of the Negro problem.

Ethnomusicology

Agreeing with Bruno Nettl, music must be understood as a part of culture, a product of human society and so also the process of musical change. Face-to-face confrontation with musical creation and performances by the people, who conceive of, produce and consume music, is essential. Analysis of music, particularly the folk music in the context of socio-cultural behaviour falls within the subject 'ethnomusicology', which I feel, needs some detailed introduction for our understanding.

The term 'ethnomusicology' is attributed to Jaap Kunst, who used it in the sub-title of his book "Musicologica, a study of the Nature of Ethno-musicology, its Problems,

Methods and Representative Personalities" (Amsterdam, 1950).[6] Subsequent editions were entitled Ethnomusicology, first with, and later without the hyphen. He considered this term preferable to comparative musicology. Ethnomusicology is the systematic study of music both in its historical and cultural aspects, a scientific study both of the form and matter of music. As defined in the Harper's Dictionary of Music, 'Ethnomusicology' is the study of music in relation to culture that produced it. The subject of such studies is frequently outside the western traditon, such as the music of China, Japan, the Arab countries or various peoples of Africa.

Ethnomusicology thus lays stress on the traditional and uncultivated music of the world—social and cultural aspects of music, particularly of folk music. In his article 'Ethnomusicology' in the Havard Dictionary of Music, Mantle Hood states:

> "Ethnomusicology is an approach to the study of any music, not only in terms of itself but also in relation to its cultural context."[7]

The characteristics of the music include melodic range, level, direction and contour; melodic intervals and interval patterns, ornamentation and melodic values; formal structure, scale, mode, duration, tone, and tonic; meter and rhythm; tempo and vocal style. Some other characteristics are added by the individual performers and almost every body of song demands unique attention in some respects.

There remain, however, a number of difficulties in the technical analysis of music. The first of these concerns transcription itself and the accuracy that can be achieved through the human ear. Closely connected with this, is the unresolved question of how accurate a transcription must be. The third problem concerns sampling. How large a sample does yield reliable results? It must also be decided whether one type of song in a given culture is significantly different from another and if so, whether these types have to be treated separately or lumped together into a general set of results for the entire body of music. There is also the major problem of which elements of a musical style are significant and characteristic. All these issues are important besides the basic problem of notation.

Associated with the study of musical structure is the study of musical instruments taken from both the technical and the distributional points of view. Ethnomusicology has provided for detailed studies of the manufacturing and tuning of instruments as well as a precise classification of instruments according to the mechanism of sound production (aerophones, chordophones, idiophones and membranophones). Despite these questions the technical analysis of musical style has reached a point at which a reasonably high degree of precision is possible and the experts have done it with reasonable amount of accuracy.

Music as Human Behaviour

Musical sound does not and cannot constitute a system that operates outside the control of human beings. It is a product of the behaviour that produces it. Behaviour includes a wide variety of phenomena. The first of these refers to the physical behaviour of the musician and his audience. The performers' body posture, tensions, attitudes are correlated with musical styles. Also correlated are the physical and physiological ways in which the audience responds to the music.

The second form of behaviour is the social behaviour that accompanies music. In response to his social behaviour, the individual musician behaves in specific ways according to his own concept and attitude as well as in response to the pressures placed upon him by society at large. To him, the attitudes and expectations of the society as well as his own attitudes towards himself define what is considered to be 'musicianly'. The third aspect of music behaviour concerns learning both on the part of the specialist and the layman.

The musician needs training whether it is through initiation, apprenticeship, formal schooling and some other device. Moreover, initiation and training of layman matters. Beneath the level of behaviour as such lies a deeper level, that of the conceptualisation of music. The ethnomusicologist deals with why music sounds the way it does, as well as with 'musts' and 'shoulds' of music. The underlying concepts in terms of which the behaviour is shaped are the nature of distinctions made between music and non-music, the sources from which music is drawn, techniques of composition, the inheritance of musical ability and other questions of similar nature. There exists, then, a continuance of levels of analysis in the study of musical behaviour.

Music must begin with basic concepts and values, which in turn are translated into actual behaviour; this in turn is directed towards the achievement of a specific musical product, or structural sound. There remains one further aspect of the continuance—the acceptance and rejection of the final product by the musician and by the members of the society at large. If the product is not adjudged acceptable, then the concepts must be changed and translated into different behaviour in order to adjust the structural sound to what is considered proper.

The entire study of music as human behaviour, of course, lies well within the sphere of social scientists. The important aspect is the study of music as symbolic behaviour, both in itself and as it relates to the broader areas of culture under study. Political, social, legal, economic and religious concepts can all be symbolised in musical sound and behaviour. The functions of music in any given culture tell much of the organisation and processes of the culture at large, and reference is made here not only to 'use' but to 'integrative' function as well. Music operates for specific purposes in all cultures and analysis of these processes reveals much about both specific and general behaviour.

Importance of study of song texts comes to the picture in this context. Song texts are a badly neglected area of study both in connection with music itself and with the wider culture. Studies have shown that language behaviour in song may differ sharply from everyday discourse, with the stress in song often being placed upon the expression of otherwise unculturable feelings, thoughts, attitudes and ideas. Texts are thus very often extremely important index to basic values.

By its very nature ethnomusicology is inter-disciplinary using the techniques, methods and theories of both musicology and ethnology; from the fusion of the two it gains new and unique strengths. Ethnomusicology has thus developmed in two directions. On the one hand, music is treated as a structure that operates, it is presumed, according to certain principles inherent in its own construction. On the other hand, since music is produced by and for people, it must also be regarded as a product of human behaviour operating within a cultural context and in conjunction with all the other facts of human behaviour.

The quality of music as a human phenomenon is thus emphasised in ethnomusicological studies; while musical sound has structure-that structure is produced by human behaviour and operates in a total cultural context. The only way to comprehend music is to analyse all of the parts of music-not only sound but material objects and instruments, the people who make music and what they do, the desires and wishes and knowledge of the audience who listen to music.

Ethnomusicology has been shaped through various historical processes. Arising at a time when virtually nothing was known outside Western and to a certain extent Oriental culture, ethnomusicology placed heavy emphasis on the unknown areas of the world-Africa, aboriginal North and South America, Oceania, inner Asia and Indonesia. The development of ethnomusicology to a considerable extent paralleled that of anthropology; both disciplines forced to deal with all these areas- the anthropologists with the total cultures of the so-called 'primitive' peoples and the ethnomusicology with the total study of their music.

It is, however, worth-mentioning that as a discipline, ethnomusicology may have arisen after World War II from the ashes of comparative musicology. Dynamic developments possibly played a greater role in its rebirth. For scholars of the western industrialized nations, remote parts of the world had become more swiftly and easily accessible and sound recording, even filming became vastly improved and less costly than before. With this context, some musicologists lost patience with their bondage to a historical study of western art music based on written notes. At the same time some anthropologists felt the urge to study music as fully as possible in the context of its life in society, and as a process the Society for Ethnomusicology, founded in 1955, provided a chance for such interests to be disucssed and shared with others with its journal Ethnomusicology.

The annual conferences and the journal of the International Folk Music Council founded in 1949, presently known by the name International Council of Traditional Music (ICTM) provided an important forum especially for leading folk music specialists but also for ethnomusicologists working in other subjects. A few scholars of the school of comparative musicology of Berlin, who had immigrated to America, played an important role in the development of the field in the western hemisphere. The American Charles Seeger has had an incalculable influence on ethnomusicology in the USA. We can have an idea how ethnomusicological studies have been used to analyse the relation of song style and culture.

Ethnomusicological Process in the Advanced Countries

Collection and Documentation: Technological innovations have played a large part in ethnomusicological collection of primary source since World War II. Most important was the portable tape-recorder, battery-operated in the early 1950's. Somewhat later it became possible to synchronise film cameras and recording equipment. Polaroid cameras became available by the 1970's; videotape and multi-channel recording were in frequent use. There have been spectacular advances in the collection of traditional music as documents basically in the form of printed music collections and/or gramophone records.

Documentary longplaying records of traditional music have become indispensable tools for study and teaching of ethnomusicology. They are particularly useful in conveying characteristics of performance that cannot be notated, such as voice quality, pitch variation. Recording of the music has come to be accompanied by photographs, filming and interviews with performers and audiences. Studies of dances and rituals have used film documentation extensively. Labanotation has been adopted increasingly for dance notation. Musical instruments have been collected and films made showing how they are manufactured. In the later years, the growth in the recordings of musical forms all over the world and the rapid development of high quality recording equipment have added new dimensions to the notion of ethnomusicology.

The ethnomusicologists are now not only interested in the technicalities and the structure of the music of various cultures, but they also use discoveries of structures or patterns and various musical paradigms to explain such important cultural behaviour as social structure, governmental complexity, degree of class differentiation, severity of sexual restrictions, gender relationship, degree of social solidarity and important aspects of world view. This development in ethnomusicology are attributed to the highly ambitious

'Cantometrics' project of the Columbia University directed by Alan Lomax and assisted by ethnologists, musicologists, linguists, performing art specialists and computer experts.

A 'song-style' is the recurrent juxtaposition of a set of such qualitative formulas that define the precise limit for tempo, loudness, emphasis, interval, width, etc. Style is a potent culture classifier because it goes to the level where people actually experience and shape culture patterns. Four different advanced analytical techniques applied for studying song style are:

(*i*) Cantometrics to overall song performance style;

(*ii*) Choreometrics to overall dance and movement style;

(*iii*) Phonotactics to overall phonetic patterning in song verse;

(*iv*) Concept analysis to overall conceptual patterns of song verse.

'Cantometrics' is descriptive technique that statistically measure song-style or singing-style (both textual and musical) of the recorded data by testing the musical expressions of various nations, cultures, or human groups on a kind of hypothesised scale, correlating the pattern thus discovered into regional, zonal or continental patterns and establishing the relation between the discovered musical patterns and social behaviour of the region, zone, culture or the nation concerned.

For example, after subjecting the musical styles of many cultures all over the world to the cantometrics test, a scheme of music families of the world, somewhat akin to the language families or ethnic families, was outlined. It was found that actually all the singing-styles of mankind could be described in terms of the two basic models designed as a result of the above testing. These two basic models are:

Model A	*Model B*
(Individualised – solo)	(Integrated, Groupy)
Textually Complex	Choral, multi-levelled, cohesive
Metrically complex	Repetitions in text
Melodically complex	Melodically simple
Ornamented	Metrically simple
Usually noisy voice	Usually clear voice
Precise enunciation	Slurred enunciation

'Cantometrics' is a word coined to mean a measure of songs or song as a measure. It is a method used for systematically and historically describing the general feature of accompanied or unaccompanied song performances. With the cantometric system the listener can evaluate a song performance in ways that supplement the conventional measures of melody, rhythm and harmony.

A recorded song can be played again and again for judges and their observations can be compared to those obtained from repeated auditions of other recordings. This provides good opportunity for a comparative study of social communication. The system sets up a behavioural grid upon which all song-styles can be ranged and compared. The grid was not designed to replicate the music already accurately recorded on tape, but to rate it on series of rating scales (loud to soft, tense to lax, etc.) taxonomically applicable in all cultures.

The 'cantometric method' measures the total song-singing repertoire of the whole globe on the above mentioned two modes and musical inventories listed under them. With the help of computers the infinite data is then reduced to finite categories and 'patterns' and finally on the basis of psychological or psychoanalytical principle, each 'pattern' is related to ethnographically 'proved' social behaviour of the culture in which a given musical pattern was found. The following observations of Alan Lomax are worth-mention in this connection.

> "Cantometrics finds then that no branch of human family, no matter how well or ill-equipped technically, fails to symbolize its social norms in a suitable song-style. Each culture raises its voice in a way that speaks for its economy, its social mores, its degree of stratification, its ways of organising groups, etc. Therefore, the main song performance profile in a culture will match an important behavioural profile made up of many general features of social structure. Both song and social profiles are models for human behaviour, the former organising some sort of collective, public exercise in phonation, the latter a framework of relations between people in everyday life...."

Analysis with Contometrics method has brought out certain significant information. The important findings about song-styles are that song-styles shift consistently with (1) productive range, (2) political level, (3) level of stratification of class, (4) severity of sexual mores, (5) balance of dominance between male and female, and (6) level of social cohesiveness.

From these correlations a song-style seems to summarize, in a compact way, the ranges of behaviour that are appropriate to one kind of cultural context. Song presents an immediate image of a culture pattern. Song-style is also a reflexion of economic level. Complexity of song texts varies directly with productive complexity. On the other hand, position of women in the production system seems to control the level of integration in a song style. It was found from the cantometric experiment that the more piercing, high pitched, squeezed and narrow the musical pattern of a given culture, the more stringent their sexual sanctions are and vice versa. The experiment related music to politics and other cultural behaviours such as solidarity and stress.

It has been observed that the folk, the primitive, the non-industrial societies account for most of the cultural variety. Though rich in the expressive and communicative arts, these folk communities seldom have the means to record, evaluate or transmit their songs and tales except by word of mouth. The folk song texts, if analysed in a systematic fashion, give clear expression to the level of cultural complexity and a set of norms that differentiate and sharply characterise culture. Folk song is far more redundant than folk tale, since not only does it recur in steady functional relation to the daily lives of a people and is composed of stock literary devices and favoured subject matter, but it is also redundant in its intonation patterns (musical form) and its vocalisation patterns (vocal timbre).

Folk song may be recognised in the discourse of a culture simply because it is more redundant at more levels than any other forms of utterances. This feature of high redundancy confines folk songs in two respects, both augmenting its value as a diagnostic tool. First, the formalities of melody and meter tend to limit the choice of the singer and the song maker to a set of stock phrases, devices and poetic forms. Ballad scholars point to incremental repetition as a main characteristic of the medieval ballad. Further restrictions are imposed by other redundancy features present; such as melody, rhythm, and phonotactic structure.

Given the high redundant nature of folk song and the fact that the folk song is usually a group communication device serving to focus the attention of groups, to organise them for joint response, and to produce consensus, it seems obvious that the texts of folk songs will be limited to those matters, attitudes, concerns and the feelings on which the community is in maximum accord. If it is not the case, the song is not likely to hold its audience and it probably will not pass into oral tradition, where acceptance means that consensus has taken place over and over again through time. Thus, in theory folk song texts ought to be highly loaded with normative cultural indicators.

Social Solidarity: In order to achieve a 'good blend' or 'total cohesiveness', a singer has to conform his pronounciation of vowels and consonants, use of pitch, rhythmic attack, and many other aspects of phonation to a model shared by the group. Teamwork of any sort demands that idiosyncrasies or personal conflicts be subordinate to the requisites of common goal. Singing the same melody, dancing to the same rhythm, utilising the same pitch and levels of accent or any of the shared regularities of behaviour essential to song or dance performance arises from and enhances a sense of commonality.

A principal function of music and dance is to augment the solidarity of a group. The manifold levels of phonation essential to produce a unified choral sound—the syllables, intervals, glides, attacks, releases, levels of emphasis, many voice qualities, etc. are a difficult task. Nevertheless singing with blended voices like marching in step is found in all six continents.

Style Analysis: Song performances can characterise a culture in terms of basic structural elements such as complexity and subsistence level, political structure, stratification, complimentarity and sexual mores, besides other complexity indicators. It must be pointed out that some form of musical complexity may occur at every level of social and technological development. Some ethnomusicologists have observed that complex vocal polyphony and polyrhythm are far more common among primitive gatherers than any other groups. Dance performance looks at culture in terms of dynamic components of its interaction patterns. It locates regions of comparative complexity and synchrony and differentiates those in terms of varying sets of movement qualities.

With textual analysis, one turns from these somwhat abstract aspects of culture to concrete verbally stated themes that can give substance to the description of life style. In the texts, one discovers what is valued or disdained, where pain and satisfaction lie; one finds some of the principal dimensions of the psychic constellation that bounds a sector of the human universe. The textual analysis is a part of dynamic constituent to stylistic analysis.

In a sense, style analysis turns the task of developing a much-needed dynamic taxonomy of human things over to mankind itself—to the varied families of man, each of which has set forth its pattern of preferences, though sometimes cryptically, in its songs, tales and traditions. From a recent informal survey of folk song texts it came out that love songs seem to be the major type in areas such as Mediterranean and the Near and Far East, where sexual sanctions are severe and reinforced by religious sanction. The sighing yearning lover who feels that he is dying from his passion is rarely found among the simple, less alienated culture of the world, or at least has left few traces in traditional song.

Many Japanese peasant songs are extremely erotic in content with vivid reference to sexual organs, but their overall import is frequently aggressive, hostile or melancholy. Relaxed vocalising not only stands for permissive sexual standards for women, but for another basic source of feminine independence as well—importance of women in basic subsistence. Vocal tension (narrow nasal vocalising) is far higher in non-complimentary societies, where men perform all or most of the subsistence tasks. On the other hand, wide relaxed voices seem to be the norm in complimentary societies. People tend to sing in wide voices in societies where women are most secure in their productive and sexual roles. So, for good vocal blend complimentarity is essential. When feminine labour is crucial in production, tension between the sexes is reduced, voices are relaxed, leading emergence to vocal solidarity.

There is also some relation of music to age. A kind of generation gap exists in music appreciation, besides other kinds of social behaviour. For instance, the youth and younger generations seem to have liking for the fast, high-pitched film music, western rock, disco and similar forms. The older generation seldom seems to enjoy this kind of music. May be, it has some biological base in the sense that after the passage of youth, the body rhythm undergoes certain changes and rejects high-pitched music, while among the youth high-pitchedness remains popular because of the fast body rhythm.

We do not have at our disposal the advanced methodology of study such as Cantometric analysis. We will, however, observe from our traditional analysis of ethnomusicology that almost same characteristics are found in *Bhāoiā-Caṭkā* songs of North Bengal.

Ethnomusicology and Indian Music

The process of ethnomusicology started with musicology as usual. Music in India never occurs in isolation. It is almost always embedded in song, dance, drama, religion, rituals, etc. This is a unique phenomenon and is highly important for the growth of Indian ethnomusicological theories and methodologies. This embeddedness is more in folk and tribal musical forms than in classical form. While dealing with this kind of embeddedness, one cannot afford to isolate the musical element and record it or study it because all aspects of the phenomenon seem to be equally important and responsible for the phenomenon itself. For instance, the musical patterns of Teyyam of Northern Kerala or Teesta-Burir gan (*Bhādoi khelā*) of Jalpaiguri district of West Bengal would be meaningless for any kind of interpretation unless the other patterns pertaining to religion, ritual, dance, drama, myth, etc. associated with them are simultaneously collected and interpreted. Each aspect of this performance seems to derive meaning from the other aspects. Narrative pattern and pattern of ritual provide pattern for the music and vice versa.

Musical pattern of a given song cannot be interpreted differently from the content of the song when both, structurally speaking, depend on each other. How can one deliver a marriage song in a musicalness meant for a funeral song? Indian ethnomusicologists have, however, mostly been studying the system of which music forms an integral and inseperable part. Music being essentially a form of communication has to be comprehended in terms of la langue and la parole. Individual competence to produce music and the social norm in which this competence is channelised are essential dimensions of music and both deserve consideration.

Indian classical form of music, though always interacting with certain other forms such as folk, etc., seem to have confined itself traditionally to the temple, palace, fort and now to the city. This form of music is highly individualised and does not enjoy acceptability as langue beyond a highly specialised group of people. Folk music and music of tribal groups, on the other hand, irrespective of their linguistic or ethnic affiliations, seem quite opposed to the classical form. They are more group-oriented and enjoy much wider social base. By and large, classical dance and music are female-dominant, while in folk music and dance systems both males and females participate. Two forms can be expressed in the following paradigm:

Classical (music and dance)	= Individualised	$\frac{\text{low}}{\text{slow}}$	$\frac{\text{female}}{\text{dominant}}$	city based
Folk and Tribal (music and dance)	= Group-oriented	$\frac{\text{high}}{\text{fast}}$	$\frac{\text{male-female}}{\text{dominant}}$	wider base

A look at the Indian scene reveals that for a clear ethnomusicological position *vis-a-vis* Indian music, one has to wait till the late 18th or the early 19th century. The onset of ethnomusicology in British India can be dated to Sir William Jones' paper entitled '*On the musical Modes of the Hindus*' (1784). However, the reality is that ethnomusicology lagged behind Indology. Jones had no connection with the performing tradition and he attempted to comprehend music through books.

With his knowledge of Sanskrit metrics he could translate the word '*Sangeet*' more aptly and literally as 'symphony'. He could see the close relationship between the Persian system of music and the Indian one. Yet he failed to see in reality that *raga* is not mode which is closer to 'ṭhāṭ'. Also he did not realise that classical music was a crystalisation of a long interaction between Persian and other musics on the one hand and the indigenous tradition on the other. Jones' paper was representative of an Indological look inherently ill suited to grapple with the musical reality.

But it is true that the Indologists showed the path of ethnomusicological studies. The other important works were by Capt. Willards, Francis Fowke, J.D. Paterson, Capt. James Tod, etc. Capt. Willard's fascinating work entitled "A Treatise on the Music of Hindustan" (1834) was a landmark in this respect. Fowke's short presentation entitled "On the Vina or Indian Lyre" (1788) was important because of its brief objective and precise description of 'been', a major plucked string instrument in Hindustani music. Its informants were two active performers – Jeevan Shah and Pyar Khan. Tuning, playing technique and manufacturing details of instrument were also provided.

Sir William Ousley in "Anecdotes of Indian Music (1797)" threw light on the Persian sources of Indian music. He showed how a Bengali '*tappa*' represented a very important trend of marrying regional languages to Hindustani musical formats. His brief mention of notational indications of some playing techniques in the Persian manuscript was also important. J.D. Paterson dealt with the technical problem of Grama-s or musical scales of

Hindus (1805–6). He quoted *grama* and not *raga* with the western modes. His presentation on Hindu Mythology and Tradition also brought out the ethnomusiclogical liberalism.

John Crawford's writings (1820) are important because of their focus on important ethnomusicological situation connected with Indian culture and music. Java and Bali both received Hindu and Islamic influences in the early days but the resulting cultural mix meant a radical change in the original influences. He pointed out how dancing pervaded the Javanese life, unlike that in western India. Javanese culture and society-'rude' compared to the western society-have a music and dance that are not so 'rude'. Lt. Col James Tod's references to music in his "Annals and Antiquities of Rajasthan" (1829-32) are very important works on the subject. Tod seems to have adopted the effective technique of sending assistants in the interior to collect informations.

Ethnomusicology Versus Bengali Music

Bengal played the role of pioneer in the matter of ethnomusicological-rather musicological studies so far as Indian classical music is concerned. The most important and valuable contribution made in this regard was by Raja Sourendramohan Tagore. His patronage made possible quite a large number of musicological compilations, although some of them contained fair amount of wrong informations and analysis. The first major work in Bengali language was, of course, 'Sangeet Tarang' (1818) by Radhamohan Sen Das. The methodology adopted by him was the same as that adopted for the Sanskrit works on music. The other important works prior to Raja Sourendramohan Tagore were 'Brahma Sangeet' (1828) by Raja Rammohan Roy, "Sangeet Rag Kalpadruma" (1842), Vol. I by Krishnanand Vyas Ragsagar, 'Concerted Instrumental Playing and Notation' (1858) by Kshetramohan Goswami, 'All India Music Conference' (1867), by Thakurs of Pathuria ghat, 'Ingraji Swaralipi Paddhati' (1868), by Kaliprasanna Bandopadhyay, 'Sangit Siksha' and 'Hindustani Airs Arranged for the Piano Forte" by Krishnadhan Bandyopadhyay in 1868.

The comprehensive works on musicology were, however, done by Raja Sourendramohan Tagore. He started writing in 1870 with 'Sastriya Sangeet Vishayak Prastab' and his main works were 'Banga Sangeet Vidyalaya' (1871), 'Sangeet Samalochoni' (Periodical 1872), 'Sangeet Sar Sangraha' (1872), 'Yantra Kshetra Deepika – Setar Siksha Vishayak Granth' (1872), 'Mridang Manjari' (1873), 'Harmoniam Sutra' (1874), 'Yantrakosh' (1875), 'Six Principal Ragas with a brief view of the Hindu music' (1876), 'Bengal Music College' (1881) 'Nrityankur' (1885), 'Indian Ragmala' (1894) and 'Universal History of Music' – together with Various Original Notes of Hindu Music' (1895). 'Sangeet sar Sangraha' was a good work on all aspects of Indian classical music. Similarly, 'Yantrakosh' gives descriptions of various musical instruments—western and classical including those used with folk songs.

The other important works were 'Indian ragas and the western orchestration attempted' by Dakshina Ranjan Sen, 'Gita Sutrasar' (1885) by Krishnadhan Bandopadhyay.[8] 'Gitasutrasar' is a very comprehensive work on Indian classical music. The application of staff notation on classical music was the main contribution of this work. Ramdas Sen also wrote a number of articles on music in the last century and they were 'Hindudiger Natyabhinoy', 'Bharatbarsher Sangeet Sastra', 'Swar Vijnan', 'Rag Nirnay', etc. Brajendra Kishore Roychowdhury contributed a number of essays on Indian musicology.

The most notable works on musicology are, however, by Swami Prajnanananda. His discourses in 'Sangeet O Sanskriti' 'Historical Development of Indian Music' 'Rag O Roop' give highly enlightening picture of Indian music. Bimal Roy also wrote a number of essays on Indian music, 'Ragas and Raginis' of O.C. Ganguly, 'Ragas and Raginis' and 'Prachin Bharater Sangeet Chinta' of A.N. Sanyal are other important contributions in this regard. Dilip Kumar Roy's works on musicology in various essays in 'Gitasree', 'Sangitiki', 'Tirthankar', 'Sur Bahar', etc., are thought provoking contributions about musicological consciousness. Dhurjati Prasad Mukhopadhyay, Indira Debi Choudhurani, Santidev Ghosh are other important names. The other works deserving mention are 'Sangeetkosh' of Bimalakanta Roychoudhury, 'Bishnupur Gharana', 'Ganer Asor', 'Sangeet Kalpataru' of Dilip Kumar Mukhopadhyay, 'Bangla Sangiter Roop' of Sukumar Roy, 'Sangeet Parikrama' of Narayan Choudhury, 'Banglar Geetikar' of Rajyeswar Mitra, 'Rabindra Sangeet' of Priyabrata Choudhury, etc. In the later years, many more scholars have written volumes of critical materials on musicology of Indian music and light musics based on classical form such as Rabindra *Sangeet, Nazrul Geeti, Kirtan* and other devotional songs, patriotic songs as also modern including film songs.

Most of these writings have, however, been restricted to musicology and have not extended their scope to what is termed ethnomusicology. As explained earlier in details, ethnumusicology involves two modes of discourse – music and the language (English or Bengali), the first dealing with musicology *i.e.,* form, style of music, etc. and the second with the cultural perspective in which the music has grown over the period. The second aspect *i.e.* analysis of music in cultural perspective has been mostly found to be lacking in the works mentioned.

Ethnomusicology Versus Bengali Folk

It has been observed that there has been very little effort made by the scholars to deal with the other form of music *i.e.,* folk and tribal music, although it is folk music which should have been the appropriate field of ethnomusicology. What has been the trend and development of ethnomusicological study *i.e.,* collection, systematisation, dissemination and institutionalisation of folk music in Bengal? For this, we have to deal with various forms of folk music of Bengal. As stated, folk music can be divided into two broad types – functional and non-functional. Functional songs are connected with festival, ceremony or religious rites falling in the magico religious category. Non-functional music is performed solely for the purpose of entertainment. Further, in Bengal there are three types of folk songs based on faith, belief and philosophy of the religious sects – Devotional (*Shakta* and *Vaishnavite*) folk songs, Baul folk songs and Fakiri folk songs.

The most important feature of folk music in Bengal is that it is not confined to any culture group but to a culture area where it is practised by different groups of people. On the basis of culture areas major folk forms in different areas of Bengal can be broadly classified under (1) *Bhatiali* of the then East Bengal and now Bangladesh, (2) Bhāwāiyā of North Bengal and adjacent districts of Assam, (3) *Gambhira* of Malda and Rajshahi districts, (4) *Jhumur* prevalent in western part of Bengal *i.e.* Burdwan, Bankura, Purulia, Midnapore and Birbhum districts and (5) *Baul* of some East Bengal districts and Birbhum district of West Bengal.

It was Rabindra Nath Tagore who initiated the ethnomusicological studies in Bengal during the concluding years of the 19th century. There was practically no interest taken by any scholar/musicologist on the folk songs of Bengal – collection, systematisation, analysis, etc. – before Rabindra Nath Tagore. The importance of folk songs was recognised by Rabindra Nath Tagore through his contact with the singers of rural Bengal, particularly the *Bauls*. He collected a number of such songs, enthused and involved others to collect and adopted the folk tunes of *Baul* and *Bhatiali* and their themes for his own composition. Almost along the same time period, G.A. Grierson, in the process of his monumental work on the Indo-Aryan languages collected considerable number of folk songs of various districts of Eastern Bengal and North Bengal to study the characteristics of the local dialects in which the songs were composed of.[9]

Attracted by an article 'Matir Jogan' on Kabigan written by Chandra Kumar De of Mymensingh in 1912, Dinesh Chandra Sen made contact with Mr. De and collected the ballads of East Bengal and Mymensingh through him. He then published the same as the Eastern Bengal Ballads-Mymensingh in 1919-23 with the financial support of Calcutta University under the patronisation of Sir Asutosh Mukhopadhyay. Being encouraged by Rabindra Nath Tagore, Mahammed Mansur Uddin collected substantial number of Bengali songs and published by the name 'Haramoni' in a number of volumes. Dr. Asraf Siddique of Bangladesh attempted analysis of different types of folk songs of East Bengal in 1963 in his work 'Lok Sahitya'. There was virtually no development on the subject during the late 40's and 50's because of the political turmoil and settlement in the country.

At the beginning of the 60's, Dr. Sudhir Karan collected folk songs and tribal songs of Purulia-Bankura and published them in "Simanta Banglar Lokjan" in 1964.[10] This is a major work on the analysis of various types of folk and tribal songs – Bhadu, Tusu, Nachni, Karam, etc. sung in that area under the general folk form 'Jhumur'. This work was perhaps the pioneer attempt towards ethnomusicological study on a folk style in Bengali. In 1960, Calcutta University included 'Lok Sanskriti (Folklore)' as a subject to be studied at post-graduate level as special paper in Bengali at the initiation of Dr. Asutosh Bhattacharyya. Through his students Prof. Bhattacharyya collected folk songs of different style and published in "Lok Sangeet Ratnakar" in 1966 with brief descriptions and explanations. Bengali department of the Calcutta University under his able leadership provided a good number of folklore researchers/students who in the later years devoted their attention to the study of folklore in general and folk music in particular. Some other scholars were also taking interest in folk songs of Bengal. Imporatant names amongst others in this connection are Purnima Sinha, Hemanga Biswas, Nirmalendu Bhowmick, Tushar Chattopadhyay, Subodh Basu Ray, Sudhir Chakraborty, Chittaranjan Deb, Barun Chakrabarty, Sanat Mitra, Sisis Majumdar, Pallab Sengupta, Nirmal Das, Manas Majumdar, Benoy Bhattacharyya, Dulal Chowdhury, Bankim Mahato, Benoy Mahato, Binapani Mahanta, Pashupati Mahato, Bimal Chatterjee, Tripti Brahma, Arun Kumar Roy, Dibyajyoti Majumdar of West Bengal and Asraf Siddique, Majaharul Islam of Bangladesh.

Thus considerable amount of studies appear to have been undertaken by a number of scholars and researchers but very few of those works have actually satisfied the criteria of ethnomusicology. All of them are restricted to either collection or brief analysis of content of the songs, not necessarily socio-cultural aspects. They do not deal with the musical style/forms and detailed cultural perspectives and atmosphere under which the particular song styles have grown over the ages in the particular areas. Ethnomusicological study involves detailed analysis of a particular folk song style/form—analysis of musicological style and analysis of content in its cultural perspectives.[11]

Ethnomusicology versus Bhāoiā (Bhāwāiyā) Caṭkā

Ethnomusicological study on Bhāwāiyā involves such a detailed study on this form of folk song. What ethnomusicological studies have been undertaken in the field of Bhāwāiyā-Caṭkā is, therefore, a pertinent question to ask. The first and foremost attempt was the works of G.A. Grierson on collection and compilation of the folk songs in Bengali and Assamese languages for different districts such as Rangpur, Cooch Behar, Jalpaiguri, Dinajpur, etc. in the process of collection of samples of local dialects of those districts in connection with the works on "Linguistic Survey of India", published in 1904 (Vol.V Indo-Aryan Family, Eastern Group part I).

Side by side, a few scholars like Pt. Jadaveswar Tarkaratna, Purnendu Mohan Sehanobis, etc. who were associated with Rangpur Sahitya Parishad made serious attempts for collection and publication of folk songs of Rangpur. Pt. Jadaveswar Tarkaratna collected the famous 'Jager Gan' of Rangpur from the village Itakumari of Rangpur and presented before the Sahitya Parishad in 1908. The songs were subsequently published with details about the lyricist Ratiram Das and descriptions about the contents of the songs.

Similarly, Purnendu Mohan Sehanobis collected the Bhāwāiyā songs of Rangpur which were subsequently published in the Sahitya Parishad Patrika. Shri Sehanobis collected and published Sonarayer gan also. The other personalities who collected 'Sonarayer gan', 'Gorakhnather gan' and other Bhāwāiyā-Caṭkā songs were Brindabon Ch. Bhattacharyya, Basanta Kumar Lahiri, Panchanan Sarkar (Barma), etc. As stated earlier, publication of 'Haramoni' by Mahammad MansurUddin in 1930 was an important landmark in the study of folk songs, 'Haramoni' contained good number of folk songs of Rangpur, Dinajpur and Bogra *i.e.*, Bhāwāiyā-Caṭkā songs.

During 1950's Asraf Siddique of Bangladesh was influenced and enthused by Tagore and also by his teacher Mohammad Shahidulla to collect and study folk songs. Siddique published his works in 1963 in "Lok Sahitya" which contained a good number of Bhāwāiyā-Caṭkā songs with brief analysis. A very important compilation of Bhāwāiyā-Caṭkā songs and Bhāwāiyā-based other songs including some good articles written on the subject by various local collectors of songs and writers, was published in 1971 by Shibananda Sharma under the title 'Goalpara Jilla Sanskriti Sangrakshan Smriti Grantha'.

During 1930's and 1940's Abbas Uddin Ahmed and his associates like Pyarimohan Das, Gangadhar Das, Nayeb Ali, Keshab Barman, etc. of Cooch Behar collected considerable number of Bhāwāiyā-Caṭkā songs and performed them in gramophone discs. This was landmark in the history of documentation of folk songs in Bengal, perhaps in India. There was, however, no written publication of those songs. Haris Chandra Pal of Cooch Behar fulfilled this want in 1973. He published the "Uttar banglar Palligeeti", Bhāwāiyā part in 1973 which contained some important Bhāwāiyā songs with notation recorded on gramophone discs by the reputed artists of North Bengal.[12] "Utar Banglar Palligeeti", Caṭkā part was published in 1975 with the notations of Caṭkā songs recorded in gramophone discs.

Perhaps the most valuable work on the Bhāwāiyā-Caṭkā songs with their numerous variations was "Pranta Uttar Banger Lok Sangeet" by Dr. Nirmalendu Bhowmick published in 1977.[13] This work contained the lyrics of Bhāwāiyā-Caṭkā songs on various subjects including the folk dramas based on Bhāwāiyā-Caṭkā style of singing. The songs have, however, been collected mainly from Jalpaiguri distict and Terai areas. Hemanga Biswas in his "Lok Sangeet Sameeksha-Bangla O Assam" has dealt with brief analysis of musicology and ethnographic content of a number of Bhāwāiyā-Caṭkā songs.[14] Another important work was "Uttar Banger Lok Sahitya O Bhasa" by Dharma Narayan Sarkar Bhaktisastri of Lalmanirhat, Bangladesh published in 1987. This contains short descriptions of a few Bhāwāiyā-Caṭkā songs on different subjects. Dr. Bimal Chatterjee, following the footsteps of Dr. Nirmalendu Bhowmick worked on the collection and interpretation of Bhāwāiyā-Caṭkā songs on different subjects. The work "Uttar Banger Lok Sangeet" published in 1992 gives an account of a number of songs with their short interpretations.

A sincere attempt of ethnomusicological analysis of Bhāwāiyā-Caṭkā musical system is available in this work Ramani Mohan Barma of Dinhata has been an enthusiastic personality in the pursuit of collection and study of Rajbanshi literature including Bhāwāiyā-Caṭkā songs, for quite a long time. Shri Barma has been publishing a little journal "Kal Baishakhi" which is devoted to the analytical study of North Bengal's literary pursuits particularly the Bhāwāiyā-Caṭkā based folk music. Shri Barma has published a book "Rajbanshi Lok Sahitya" which gives analysis of some Bhāwāiyā-Caṭkā songs in 1993.

Some other little journals in all the districts of North Bengal have been dealing with the analytical study of Bhāwāiyā-Caṭkā based music for the last so many years. Particularly important in this respect is 'Madhuparni' published by Ajitesh Bhattacharyya of Balurghat, the district headquarters of South Dinajpur.[15] In its 'Uttar Banga' number published in 1970 and "Cooch Behar District and Jalpaiguri District" numbers published in 1990's quite fruitful discussions and analysis have been attempted by a number of authors on the folk music of this area *i.e.* Bhāwāiyā-Caṭkā including the folk dramas based on Bhāwāiyā.

There have thus been some serious efforts made by a number of scholars in the collection and analysis of Bhāwāiyā-Caṭkā songs. But most of the works done so far lack systematic and scientific analysis of Bhāwāiyā-Caṭkā and as such they are found deficient in some respect or other in so far as ethnomusicological analysis of a form is concerned. The studies seem to be particularly deficient in regard to the analysis of musicology of the form of Bhāwāiyā-Caṭkā. The socio-cultural factors responsible for the evolution and continuance of such a form representing the cultural life of a vast area inhabitated by a cultural group under the common name 'Rajbanshi' do not also appear to have been addressed to in proper perspective.

REFERENCES

1. M. Schneider, *Primitive Music, New Oxford History of Music, Ancient & Oriental Music,* ed. by E. Wellesz, London, 1957.
2. A. P. Merriam, "The Anthropology of Music", (Evanston. IL), 1964.
3. Gray Cecil, *The History of Music,* Reprint Services Corp., 1935.
4. Sudhibhusan Bhattacharya, *Enthomusicology and India,* Indian Publications, Kolkata, 1968.

5. Bruno Nettl, *Folk and Traditional Music of the Western Continents,* (Englewood Cliffs, NJ), 1965.
6. Jaap Kunst, *Musicologica, a Study of the Nature of Ethno-musicology, its Problems, Methods and Representative Personalities*, Amsterdam, 1950.
7. Mantle Hood, *The Ethnomusicologist,* McGraw Hill Text, 1971, rev. edn., New York, 1982.
8. Krishnadhan Bandopadhyay, *Geeta-Sutrasar*, A. Mukherjee & Co., Kolkata, 4th edn. 1382 B.S.
9. G.A. Grierson(ed.), "*Linguistic Survey of India"*, Vol. V, Motilal Banarsidas, New Delhi, 1904.
10. Sudhir Karan, *Simanta Banglar Lok Jan,* A. Mukherjee and Co., Kolkata, 1371 B.S.
11. Purnima Sinha, *An Approach to the Study of Indian Music,* Indian Publication, Kolkata, 1970; Bhowmik, Nirmalendu, *Pranta Uttarbanger Lok Sangeet,* Chirayata Prakashan, 2nd edn., Kolkata, 1997; Biswas, Hemanga, *Lok Sangeet Samiksha – Bangla O Assam,* A. Mukherjee & Co., Kolkata, 1978; Mahato, Pashupati Prasad, *The Performing Arts of Jharkhand,* B. B. Prakashan, Calcutta, 1987; Siddique, Asraf, "Lok Sahitya", (Folk-Literature) *The Student Ways,* Muktadhara, 1963; 2nd edn. Dhaka, Bangladesh, 1980.
12. Harish Ch. Pal, *Uttar Banglar Palligeeti, Chatka Khanda,* Chandrasekhar Pal, Kalika Press, Kolkata, 1975.
13. Nirmalendu Bhowmik, *Pranta Uttarbanger Lok Sangeet,* Chirayata Prakashan, 2nd edn., Kolkata, 1997.
14. Hemanga Biswas, *Lok Sangeet Samiksha – Bangla O Assam,* A. Mukherjee & Co., Kolkata, 1978.
15. Ajitesh Bhattacharyya (ed.), *Madhupurni-Cooch Behar Number and Special North Bengal Number,* Shibtali complex, Balurghat, West Bengal, 1396 B.S., 1990.

■■■

2

Bhāwāiyā: A Folk Form

There are various viewpoints on the meaning of Bhāwāiyā (Bhāoiā). Some say that the term Bhāwāiyā has come from 'Bhāwā'; others say it has come from 'Bāo' and still others refer to 'Bhāo'. There is another viewpoint according to which it has been derived from the terms *Bāudiyā* or *Bāurā*. Low lying places left behind by the change of course of the rivers which remain inundated during most part of the year and which are full of watergrown shrubs and bushes (mainly *kush/kasiya*) are called 'Bhāwā'. These are good grazing lands for buffaloes. The buffalo-keepers (maisal) used to sing these Bhāwāiyā songs while grazing buffaloes on these Bhāwās and the songs waved through the nearby villages.

It is argued by some that Bhāwāiyā has thus been derived from Bhāwā. They speak of huge number of songs connected with buffalo and its keepers in Bhāwāiyā in support of their argument. Others opine that Bhāwāiyā is the changed form of Bāwāiyā. The 'bāo' means breeze/wind. The tunes of the songs sung by the buffalo-keepers on the 'Bhāwā', by the farmers on the working fields or open wide fields waved through the villages carried by bāo (breeze) and the song was therefore called Bāwāiyā from which came the changed form Bhāwāiyā. This is, however, a minority view.

We get the widely accepted view about the derivative meaning of Bhāwāiyā from Suren Ray Basunia, one of the sincersmost devotees of Bhāwāiyā in the early part of this century. According to him, the song full of emotional feelings that urges the people to think deeply is called Bhāwāiyā. The derivative is *Bhāv* > *Bhāo* + *Iyā* = *Bhāoiyā*. The derivative meaning of Bhāwāiyā is one who is emotionally charged. It is a song of the emotional one. In this region one who eats is called *khāoiā*, one who sings is *gāoiā* and similarly one who thinks is *Bhāoiā*. The song is so simple in its tune and theme that the feeling and meaning it conveys can be understood easily and it is without any complications. This is the reason why this song has been named Bhāwāiyā—a media of automatic expression of the subtle feelings in simple tune and rhythm. According to Abbasuddin, the magic-singer of Bhāwāiyā—Bhāwāiyā song is the wealth of North Bengal. Its movement is like that of wind blowing at random and so it is called Bhāwāiyā. Sibendra Nath Mondal of Gouripore, a devoted researcher of Bhāwāiyā had the opinion that the term is a '*desi*' word and it should be Bhāv + Iyā = Bhāwāiyā. Bhāwāiyā is the song that makes one unattached and indifferent to the world and is full of emotions; it is the song whose tune stirs up the mind and fills it with emotions.

According to Dharma Narayan Sarkar Bhaktishastri of Lalmonirhat, Bangladesh, a researcher of this form of song, the term Bhāwāiyā means growing out of *Bhāv* (feelings). The letter 'v' is a semi-vowel and its pronounciation should be somewhat like'oa', such as 'dev' being pronounced as 'deo'. Thus 'Bhāv' has become 'Bhāo' and Bhāvāiyā has become Bhāwāiyā. Because they are the expressions of spontaneous feelings of mind, they are called Bhāwāiyā. Pyarimohan Das, the first recipient of Lalan Award from the Government of West Bengal as Bhāwāiyā singer and lyricist subscribes to this view. Kumar Nidhi Narayan, a proponent of Bhāwāiyā, supports this view of 'Bhāo' from 'Bhāv' also. Dr. Haripada Chakraborty, retired Head of the Dept. of Bengali of the North Bengal University and a researcher in North Bengal folk culture has a different view. He is supporter of the viewpoint of Bhāwāiyā from 'Bhāwā'. According to him, Bhāṭiāli—the song of the boatman is from the term 'Bhāṭi' and similarly Bhāwāiyā, the song of buffalo-keepers is from 'Bhāwā'. 'Āli' and 'Iā', these two affixes are used to mean relations. Bhātiāli is related to 'Bhāṭi' and Bhāwāiyā is related to 'Bhāwā'. To him, this is the most acceptable view.

Prof. Hiten Nag of Dinhata College in the district of Cooch Behar, a researcher of folk culture of North Bengal, while analysing various viewpoints has discarded all of them. According to him, in the rural areas of North Bengal especially in Cooch Behar, adding the affix 'Iā' indicates people's profession and professional familiarity. For example, one who plays instruments is Bājāiyā, one who eats is Khāwaiyā, one who tills the land is Hāluā, one who sells is Bechāiyā, one who buys is Kenāiyā. The words with such affix 'Iā' indicate the immediate or permanent work and profession. Prof. Nag's argument thus follows the viewpoint of Suren Ray Basumia. Prof Nag, however, does not stop here. He proceeds further and says that based on the above argument, the word Bhāwāiyā implies the profession in it. According to him during the years of the evolution of Bhāwāiyā, the singers were in moving spree. They had no opportunity of staying for long in a particular place. Constant moving was the truth of their life. They moved sometime on the buffalo-back, sometime on boat, on the bullock cart or with the ploughing bullocks. The songs of such singers on move are Bahāiyā. They are the songs for removing the fatigue of life on constant movement and hence they were called Bāwāiyā. Bāwāiyā has gradually become

Bhāwāiyā through oral transmission. Life on move has thus remained engrossed with Bhāwāiyā.

All these viewpoints we will analyse now. But before that we should see what the common people, particularly the rural singers and listeners of Bhāwāiyā who are the part and parcel of this Bhāwāiyā culture, think about it. It may be mentioned in this context that I conducted a field survey in connection with a project on Bhāwāiyā, sponsored by the Folk cultural and Tribal Cultural Centre of the Government of West Bengal.

The information emitted from the survey can be a good source of opinions of the cross section of people interviewed including the performers with education level from illiteracy to graduation belonging to both the sex. Only a few of them spoke in favour of the viewpoint that Bhāwāiyā has come from the word 'Bhāwā'. Few others favoured the viewpoint that the song is called Bhāwāiyā because it is sung in loud open voice with the mind free from attachment. All others spoke in favour of the viewpoint that Bhāwāiyā has come from Bhāo > Bhāv, whatever might be the meaning of this word—whether it is deep feelings or love or melancholy feeling or disinterested feeling We can now analyse the viewpoints one by one.

My initial reaction was to accept the viewpoint of 'Bhāwā'. After talking to so many performers and researchers I am now inclined to discard this viewpoint. The people do not accept this interpretation of Bhāwāiyā in general in the Bhāwāiyā region. 'Bhāwās' are not there everywhere in this region. Moreover, Maisal is not the only hero in Bhāwāiyā songs. There are others playing this role—particularly the heroines coming from all walks of life. Above all, the songs relating to Maisals as the heroes are commonly known as Maisali Bhāwāiyā. From all these angles this viewpoint is not acceptable.

It is worth noting that almost all the Bhāwāiyā singes have said that Bhāwāiyā has come from 'Bhāo'. Bhāv > Bhāo + Iā = Bhāwāiyā. The questions therefore arise what is the actual word—Bhāwāiyā or Bhāoiā? If we notice carefully the viewpoint of Suren Ray Basunia and the way it is pronounced by the older generation people of Bhāwāiyā region the term appears to be Bhāoiā. For example, they will say 'Calo re, Bhāoiā gān śunir jāi". Let us go to hear the Bhāoiā gan. There is a popular saying in the villages—"Dotorār ḍāng ār Bhāoiyā gāān, Pāgal kairce kainār mon".

'Bhāv' is a basic emotional state. According to Viswanath, the famous writer of Sahitya Darpan, 'Bhāva' turns into *Rasa* in the minds of truly sensitive persons. 'Rasatāmity rātyādi sthāyee āsacetasam.' Further, *Rasa* cannot be appreciated without an aesthetic propensity—*vasana* and impressions (*Sanskara*). This is true of enjoyment of Rasa from literary as well as musical forms. The observation of Jadaveswar Tarkaratna of Rangpur, the collector of 'Jag gan' and 'Bhāwāiyā gan' towards the end of the 19th Century is worth mentioning in this context. The songs collected by him have been published in the Rangpur Sahitya Patrika in 1908. His observations about Bhāwāiyā are as below: "Abikāratmake Citte bhāva prathama bikriyā".

This 'bhāv' is probably the source of the word Bhāwāiyā. There are good many Sanskrit, Prakrit and Pali words in the language of the Rajbanshis of Rangpur. According to the principles of Prakrit grammar, 'v' of most of the Sanskrit words takes the form of 'o'. Prakrit of the word 'Dev' is 'Deo', which is again the Rajbanshi word for 'Dev'. Most of the Bhāwāiyā songs relate to courtship. That is why Bhāwāiyā in Rajbanshi language has been named Bhāoiā from the Prakrit 'bhāo' of the word 'bhāv'. Pangs of separation, destitution, etc. have found place in it subsequently. The connotation of the word 'Bhāvikam' as 'bhāo' by Dr. Sukumar Sen is also of relevance in this connection. While commenting on the promptness and expertise of Malabika in the lessons on acting 'Chalik' in the drama 'Malabikagnimitra' of Kalidasa, Ganadasa says,

> "*Jadjadprayoga viṣaye bhāvikam upadiśyate mayā tasyai*
> *Tadtadviśeṣa karanāt pratyupadiśatiba me bālā.*"

Dr. Sukumar Sen has given the Bengali meaning of 'bhāvikam' as 'bhāo'. This also suggests that Bhāoiyā is from the word bhāv > bhāo. The critics find this viewpoint unreasonable on the gound that each and every type of songs is pregnant with bhāv *i.e.* feelings/emotions. Songs without feelings are bodies without life. If Bhāwāiyā is derived from the word bhāv, then all the songs (Rabindra Sangeet, Nazrul Geeti, modern songs, etc.) can be called Bhāwāiyā, they argue.

This leads us to discussions on the issue with some deeper thinking. The custom of christening in the Bhāwāiyā region may give us some clue in this connection. In this region of Rajbanshi culture one who is born on Thursday (*Bisadbār*) is given the name Bisādu, one is Somāru if born on Monday (*Sombār*), Budāru if born on Wednesday (*Budbār*). Similarly, the names *Manglu, Sukāru, Saniyā, Rabican* (Abican), given from the days of birth on Tuesday (*Mongalbār*), Friday (*Sukurbār*), Saturday (*Sanibār*), Sunday (*Rabibār*) respectively. The children born in the early morning hours are given names such as 'Pohāti', 'Sakālu', 'Pohātu', some one born in the month of *Āsādh* is christened as 'Āsāru', born in the month *Bhādra* is named Bhādu. Name is given on the basis of the child's apparent nature, physical appearance, colour, etc. A female child apparently clever looking gets a name 'Cālki', one who is weeping type is named 'Kāndurā' (m) or 'Kānduri' (f), one having big belly because of spleen is named 'Dheprā' (m) or 'Dhepri' (f), one who looks very fickle and active type gets a name 'Naṭkhaṭu', somebody quite indifferent and unattached to family keeping on wandering hither thither gets a name 'Bāurā' or 'Bāudiā', one with black skin is named 'Kālācan' and with brown colour is named

[*Note:* m = male, f = female]

'Gorācan', etc. While giving such names to the newly born babies, they never bother to think that there are other children too with the same and similar characteristics and nature. These simple folks are hardly cocerned with such thoughts and complexities.

While naming the songs Bhāwāiyā from the word Bhāv > Bhāo, they had, therefore, hardly bothered about the fact that every song is pregnant with feelings/emotions (*bhāv*) and as such *bhāv* is not the special characteristic of Bhāwāiyā alone, although it is true that Bhāwāiyā is heavily pregnant with feelings and emotions. Moreover, during the period when this song was named Bhāwāiyā (15th or 16th century), there was hardly any other form of songs like Rabindra Sangeet, Nazrul Geeti or Modern Songs. Classical music, Kalikirtan and other religious songs sung to the gods and goddesses had hardly emitted feelings and emotions in that sense. Also there was hardly an opportunity of any familiarity of the performers, musicians and lyricists of Kamrup with the types of songs prevalent in other areas, whetever they might be. Their own song was, therefore, quite naturally full of feelings and emotions to them and so they named it Bhāoiā.

As mentioned earlier the word was Bhāoiā that has been transformed into Bhāwāiyā in the transcription/pronounciation of the urban-bred. This has happened particularly when the term got written form by the city-based scholars and researchers. Bhāv is a compounded word of particular sense (*jogrurha* word) such as, Pankaj. Pankaj means that which grows in mud (*pank*). So many things grow in mud but pankaj means lotus only. Bhāwāiyā is of the same nature of the word 'Pankaj'. Bhāoiā has come to us as Bhāwāiyā in printed form. Such refinements have taken place in so many cases of Rajbanshi words. For example, Rajbanshi word Kestapur has been transformed to Krishnapur, Duska to Dukha, Jaivan to Jauvan, Pyāmerdāngā to Premerdāngā, Bāsā to Bhāsā, Bātān to Bāthān, Pātār to Pāthār, Dotorā to Dotarā, Khāoiā to Khāwāiyā, Gāoiā to Gāwāiyā, and similarly, Bhāoiā to Bhāwāiyā.

In Rajbanshi language, the other meaning of Bhāv is love and attachment. 'Bhāver bandhu, bhāver deorā'–these phrases are quite common in Bhāwāiyā songs. Even with this meaning of bhāv, the viewpoint about the Bhāwāiyā from the word 'bhāv' sounds reasonable. Bhāwāiyā is firmly seized with love—love between man and woman, love for nature, animals, birds, etc.

According to Alan Lomax, the famous anthropologist and musicologist, "Singing as expression is the language of the heart," According to P. Merriam, another anthropologist, "Besides being an expression of deep seated values, song texts are an expression of thoughts and ideas, not permissibly verbalised in other contexts". It is therefore, quite clear from the above discussions that the viewpoint of Bhāwāiyā being derived from the word bhāv > bhāo is much more reasonable and acceptable.

Bhāoiā or Bhāwāiyā, one of the most popular forms of folk songs of Bengal has been prevalent in the vast area spread over the districts of Cooch Behar, Jalpaiguri, Darjeeling (in the plains), North Dinajpur of West Bengal, Rangpur and Dinajpur (Northern part) of Bangladesh and Dhubri and Goalpara of Assam for years together. The songs have been composed in Kamrupi or Rajbanshi dialect that has remained the *lingua franca* of this vast area from the ancient times. They have been sung in traditional manner both in solo and chorus forms.

Solo songs relate to love, affection, union, separation, happiness and sorrows of individuals, description of nature, etc. Chorus songs relate to social and ritual functions, marriage ceremonies, folk-dramas, etc. Side by side with Bhāwāiyā one finds Caṭkā, the brisk form of Bhāwāiyā. It is quite relevant to ask the question—Are the Bhāwāiyā-Caṭkā songs characteristically real folk songs?

Folk music is usually seen as the authentic expression of a way of life now, past or about to disappear (or in some cases, to be preserved or somehow revived). Unfortunately, despite the assembly of an enormous body of work over some two centuries, there is still no unaminity on what folk music (or folklore or folk) is. The Romantics who organised the concept, often thought of 'the people', in the sense of a national essence or they thought of a particular part of the people, a lower layer or even class. As the complexity of social stratification and interaction became clearer and increased, various conditioning criteria, such as 'continuity', 'traditon', 'oral transmission', 'unanimity', 'uncommercial origins' became more important than simple social categories themselves.

For folk music, authenticity plays a central role. The concept has undergone substantial changes with the urbanisation of rural music. Nevertheless, the folk concept has not been relinquished by most of the folklorists. The golden age of folk myth is still there, even though it has been moved and extended, and it is still seen as under attack from today's corruptions. These songs have been sung by the people by way of oral transmission for years together, ages together and have attained the tradition of continuity and sustained the onslaught of evolution and revolution in the process.

As they have not been printed in any books or documents, some variations have crept in lyrics in the process of oral transmission and this is the reason why for the same song one notices variations in lyrics. The particular groups of people who sing them have retained them through proper scrutiny and selection process only because they have found in them the medium of expresion of their feelings, happiness and sorrows, love, affections, their philosophy of life. Therefore, the songs have been orally transmitted and sung by people generation after generation, year after year.

If we analyse the inherent qualities of Bhāwāiyā, we are convinced that these basic characteristics of folk song are very much found in Bhāwāiyā. It is assumed that this form of songs was evolved in the fifteenth or sixteenth century and the same have been sung and transmitted orally for centuries together. The written form of lyrics of Bhāwāiyā was available first in the Linguistic Survey of India published by Sir Grierson in 1904.[1] Grierson collected a few songs from the districts of Cooch Behar, Jalpaiguri and Rangpur towards the end of the last century in course of his study and field survey of the Bengali dialects and subdialects in different districts. Some more examples of lyrics of these songs are available in printed form from the Rangpur Sahitya Parishad Patrika published in 1908-1912.

But nothing can be known as to when and who composed these songs. Only in the case of a few 'Jag gan', it can be reasonably derived, from the introduction of Pandit Jadaveswas Tarkaratna of Rangpur who collected the song from various sources and also from the introduction given by the lyricist in one of the songs, that they have been composed by one Rati Ram Das of Rangpur. In case of other songs the names of composers could not be known. It, therefore, appears that only a few songs have been available in written form at the beginning of this century. Till then, all these songs have been orally transmitted from generation to generation, place to place, singer to singer.

Actually, most of the popular and important Bhāwāiyā-Caṭkā songs have been sung and orally transmitted before the 30's of this century. Quite a good number of such songs were rendered into gramophone records in the 30's at the initiative taken by Harish Ch. Pal of Cooch Behar, a devoted folklorist of the district. Some lyricists like Pyarimohan Das, Abdul Karim, Gangadhar Das, etc. composed Bhāwāiyā-Caṭkā songs who came in the picture sometime in the last century. The number of such songs however, were negligible compared to the number of most popular traditional Bhāwāiyā-Caṭkā songs.

Moreover, most of these songs have been just the shadows of the traditional popular ones. Quite a number of lyricists came to the picture in the subsequent years after the Independence. Some of them pulished the songs in various local journals and in booklet forms.

Bhāwāiyā-Caṭkā songs, therefore, have no longer remained a genre orally transmitted, as it has usually happened to other forms of folk songs also. It is, however, still a fact that the compositions of unknown lyrics that have been transmitted and accepted by the people are the ones that are mostly sung by the traditional singers and as such very popular. Songs of new and known composers, except for a few, have not gained much popularity. As the popular songs have been orally transmitted and have not been transcripted to the written form, they have had variations in wordings quite often. An example of a very popular Caṭkā song will be of help to explain such variations.

Variation-1 *Oki bāp re bāp māo re māo, kām karibār nā pāon muin*
Ai komorer biṣe nā re.
Hāl boyyā āsilen pati bhāle karilen kām
Chāgal bāndhilen pati bhāle karilen kām
Urun gāinṭā bir kariyā dhān pāc syār bān.

Variation-2 *Chāgol duiṭā bāndhi āsilen bhāle karilen kāj*
Ghar cāirṭā sāmṭi elā bhārā khorā māj
Bhārā khorā mājlu pati tui re āmār prān
Urun gāin joṭeyā āni dhān pāc syār bān

Variation-3 *Oho bāp re bāp, oho māo re māo, nā pāon mui kāmāi karibār*
Kāmāi karir nā pāon pati oi kamarer biṣe
Hākkāt kariyā ki hail kabār nā pāon kise
Hāl boyyā āsilu bāri jhāpi māthāt diyā
Hutti tho tor nāngol jongāl bārā bānek āsiyā.

Variation-4 *Hāl boyyā āsilu musā bhāle karlu kām*
Nāngol jongāl atti thuiyā bārā cāirṭā bān.

There are more variations available for this song but no variation in the inner meaning of the song. This is the way the variations have been transmitted. In course of our field survey, we have noticed that all the songs are not equally transmitted and equally popular. Some of the songs have lived for a short while, some others have disappeared after being sung just once or twice because the audience, that is, the community has not accepted them as their own. In other words, the community rejected them through the process of selection.

In this context, reference can be made of the Bhāwāiyā-Caṭkā songs composed by the famous lyricist Nivaran Pandit. Nivaran Pandit settled in a village of district Cooch Behar for some years after he came from East Pakistan, now Bangladesh and based on such limited experience and knowledge about the language and way of life of the Rajbanshi Community, composed quite a number of songs following the style of Bhāwāiyā-Caṭkā. Shri Pandit is considered to be a good composer. His songs have found place in the book published by the Government of West Bengal under the title "Nivaran Panditer Gan". One could reasonably expect that the community would have accepted some of his songs. This has however, not happened in practice. Lack of intimate relation with the community, lack of intimate knowledge about the language/dialect of the community's speech might have been the reasons for which Shri Pandit was not in a position to give vent to the feelings and psyche of this community and so his songs have not been accepted by the community as their own. Here lies the role of selection by the community.

In the analysis of folk songs, continuity, variation and selection- these three elements have to be studied properly and all of them are quite noticably present in case of Bhāwāiyā-Caṭkā. In the language of Hemanga Biawas, the noted folk singer and researcher, a person who is recognised as an artist in the village has to pass this test of acceptance and rejection in that village environment itself. There are people to amend his ways, his style of singing in the village itself. The process of continuity-variation-selection contained in the definition of International Folk Music Council takes effect in the overall production process of the village life of the art and the artists. Tune, music and style or form of folk song is the expression of the community life intertwined with the production process. And the production process involves the factors like the geographical, physical and natural environment in which the community lives and grows.

The knowledge of intimate relation between a specific musical scale and a specific group of people is quite important. Rurality, mode and style of singing, articulation of music mode are regulated by regionality. Regionality is the life-breath of folk songs. Again, mode and style of singer are intimately associated with the phonetics of regional dialect. The melodic pattern of folk song of any particular community composed with the interaction of ascend, descend, candence and the related qualities of notes, is closely connected with the special characteristics of that community—the social, cultural life of the community.

Whatever forms of songs may exist in that communal life, they cannot go beyond that melodic pattern. That becomes the main tune of the community defined by the particular geographical boundary and dialectical boundary. All the songs of Assam have their life source in Bihu. Similarly, the main melodic pattern of North Bengal and Western Assam is Bhāwāiyā. Every nation, every tribe and every community carries in its melodic structure some elements that can be called the 'Pakar' of the community feelings of the region. In the language of Hemango Biswas—the main characteristics of folk songs are regional mode of singing, timbre of the notes, regional pattern of movements, metre and phonetics of the dialect and the intonation, etc. Regionality grows out of the intonation and the mode of pronounciation and articulation related to the dialect of any specific geographical area.

Judged from the above-mentioned important characteristics, Bhāwāiyā is one of the popular folk songs of Bengal. In the language of Hemanga Biswas—Besides the beautiful lyrical qualities, even from the viewpoint of melodic structure and sharpness, Bhāwāiyā is a rare wealth of not only Bengal but also the entire nation. We find the same reactions from Shri Khaled Chaudhury, the noted artist and collector of folk song. While speaking as to why folk songs attract him Shri Chowdhury says that element of simplicity is ingrained in folk songs-simplicity in its language (lyrics), and simplicity in its expression.

Its lyrical syntax is associated with the specific mode of its dialect and that mode is effective. That will not suit our city-based literary Bengali (language). Shri Chaudhuri has noticed tremandous amount of similarity between folk art and folk song because both suggest the roots of our existence. In his opinion, it is the folk song, among all kinds of artistic pursuits, where lies the genesis of our existence. We collect folk songs not because they are wonderful creation but because they are the songs reflecting the entire folk life, folk psyche. They have limitations but their perfections are characterised by those limitations. While discussing about various forms of folk songs of Bengal, Shri Chaudhuri places Bhāwāiyā above all of them. He says:

> "One aspect in folk songs that has influenced me more is the nature..... and the same is suddenly revealed to me when I listen to the folk song of North Bengal".

In Bhāwāiyā the nature takes the fore front place. Buffaloes, Elephants, Birds, Rivers of this area, all find place in this song. Some times they are reflected directly and some times obliquely through comparisons. This intimate relation between the folk and the nature is the specialised characteristic of folk songs and so this is found in other places too. But amongst the songs of Bengal, this is most revealed in North Bengal songs.

In the opinion of Abbasuddin, the famour singer of Bhāwāiyā, these songs composed by unknown unlettered poets have attained love and popularity not because they are the beloved wealth of North Bengal but because they have real lyrical qualities and these tunes with wonderful passionate feelings have created waves in the minds of the whole of Bengal. They are not merely the imaginative luxury; they are the reflections of eternal truth of human heart; natural reflection of life with happiness and misery. In his opinion, anybody willing to critically appraise Bhāwāiyā of North Bengal shall have to take into account the physical map of North Bengal.

In the midst of fickle and naughty behaviour of the playful nature, these songs are sung by the voices of thousands of buffalo keepers riding on the buffaloes in the electrifying sharp tones. Tuned with that melody are played so many flutes and dotaras. In the opinion of noted folklorist and researcher Dr. Sudhir Kumar Karan, Bhāwāiyā-Catkā songs of North Bengal region, the habitation of the Rajbanshis, are definitely uncomparable and uncommon in the category of folk songs of Bengal. Jhumur and Bhāwāiyā are such forms of songs adorned with folk characteristics that we cannot but boast of.

Origin and Evolution of Bhāwāiyā

The natural corollary to the analysis we had so far is to ask how old the Bhāwāiyā is. How has it originated and what course of evolution has it taken? It is very difficult to get exact replies to such queries. The scholars and musicologists have arrived at certain decisions on the basis of circumstantial evidences from sociological and anthropological findings. As such, it is assumed that the embryo of such songs was intrinsic to various rites, customs, worships of deities prevalent in the primitive society and the same has spread into various walks of life in later years.

Right from the dawn of the creation, the simple minded primitive men dwelling in the woods tried to have some perception about the creation and the creator from his experience about the life and the world surrounding him. He has noticed that men are born and they die; the sun comes out piercing into the deep dark night; stars twinkle in the sky. He has further noticed that the mountain peaks get devastated by the torrential winds; the quite peaceful earth gets cracked by the fearful earthquake, rivers and the sea swallow up their banks, etc. That some kind of irresistible force does work behind all such events was deeprooted in his mind. If there were an earthquake, he would think that someone was teaching him some lesson out of deep anger on some counts.

The conception of worship of nature and gods started from this stage itself. Storm, fire, sun, moon, stars, river, sea, etc. have become the objects of worship and out of the fear has grown what is called religion. The leader of the tribe or the society also had tried to convince his ignorant people about the secrets of the creation by narrating various probable/improbable episodes. Thus have come various popular stories about the creation, which is generally known as myth. The subject matter of myth, according to Jameson, is "A story presented as having actually occurred in a previous age explaining the cosmological and supernatural tradition of the people, their gods, heroes, cultural traits, religious belief, etc." Particular animals, natural and geophysical objects, secrets of creation have thus found place in the myth.

There is some difference between the *Purana* and the myth in the sense that the *Purana* is religion dependent while the myth is not bound by religion that way; faith, conviction, and episodes are the main elements of myth. According to Dr. Asraf Siddique, the folklorist of Bangladesh–english concept 'myth' can be called the *Loko-Purana* (popular *purana*) because of all these reasons. *Loko-Purana* is the episodes orally transmitted from generation to generation. The factors working behind the *Loko-Purana* are ancient faith and belief, perceptions, magic belief, etc. The magic rites have gradually taken the form of rituals. According to the Psychologists and Anthropologists, myth or *Loko-Purana* has grown out of the wonder, admiration or dream of the ancient people. Again from this feeling of admiration and wonder have come the concepts of religious rites, customs, worship and magic. According to some Anthropologists,

> The basic feature of the religion of the tribal order may be reduced to three points—animism, magic and ancestor worship…these were inheritances from the religious ideology of earlier

stages of pre-class formation. Animistic representations of the nature which surrounded men, the creation of the spirit of fire, earth, vegetation, water, …became fused with the representation of ancestors who were the protectors of man in his activity in the field, in the forest and in the water.

Out of such psychology based on faith and belief has grown the intense desire to win over the force of nature or to propitiate them. How to do it? Man has used the medium of music as the basic weapon to achieve this desire of winning over or propitiating the nature and its irresistible forces.

In the Vedic period, the mantras of the sacrifices and Vedic rites used to be sung in various musical tunes. As a result, the songs, which were sung in a particular occasion, used to be transmitted orally with the aid of memory and hearing for the next occasions. These were the Samaganas. In the post Vedic period, when the Vedic forces were replaced by the notion of gods and goddesses who were now to be worshipped and propitiated, the prayers and stavas were reduced to songs by applying various tunes on the basis of mantras of the words. In the still later period, these were called Marga Sangeet, Raga Sangeet or ritual and classical songs. In the later stages in the age of Gatha Saptasati, these songs took the new form of ballad songs and were sung from place to place by turns or in succession as *Pālā Gān* (ballad). These were called 'Jagarani' as they used to be sung by awaking through the night.

The Buddhist Siddhacharyas reduced their prayers, rituals, customs and religious rites to the musical tunes following the footsteps of Samaganas and Hindu classical songs and brought about a revolution in the Indian music system named *Caryāgitis*. After the *Caryaganas* came *Kirtans*. The songs relating to the narratives and glories of the publicity-oriented gods and goddesses of the Mangal period continued side by side. Thus continued through the media of songs the various branches of Hindu religious sects such as Vaisnava, *Śakta*, etc. in the form of *Kirtana*. Besides, the various folk religious sects belonging to the Vaisnava cult and *Śakti* oriented Nathayogi cult used the media to preach their ideals. Ashutosh Bhattacharyya, the famous folklorist of Bengal has observed in the 'Lok Sangeet Ratnakar' that it is easier to know Bengal through its music than other aspects because right from the ancient days to the modern period the greatest wealth Bengal has run after and nourished is its music.

Let us discuss the evolution taking shape in the actual social set up. Deductive logic suggests that initially the social leader individually or jointly composed certain songs mainly as prayer songs to propitiate the deities (gods and goddesses). These have undergone many changes with the passage of time under the influence of the so called folk traditions with music variety in the themes. The songs, which used to be sung at the sowing season as parts of sympathetic magic have most probably been converted into the work songs, which are being sung as means of pleasure to the peasants today.

Thus a particular singer, composer or a group of composers must have composed a song to meet the social needs. Again out of the social needs and through oral trnasmission process, different versions crept into that composition. Out of these versions/readings only those, which were capable of entertaining people and hence accepted by them, continued to be sung and others went into oblivion. Memory was the main instrument of education and training of folk songs. They are learned by ear and transmitted in this fashion from generation to generation. Nor is there a conscious awareness of form or construction on the part of a folk singer. Also, the body of folk song grows rather through a process of recreation on materials already in existence. The observation of Verrier Elwin in 'Folk Songs of Chhattisgarh (Bombay, 1936)' is worthmentioning in this context. According to him:

> "It is just a simplified concept that folk literature is the composition of a group. Widely popular, performed and loved compositions are the creations of a genius of that society. In the traditional society, the creator has never associated his name with his creation. As a result, his creation has become the wealth of the whole society through publicity and performance. ...It is true that a great many of the songs are the possessions of the people as a whole; nobody knows when they are composed, they are repeated again and again, and the only change is often for the worse."[2]

In every region a particular type of song is sung by a particular group of people. In general, children like couplets, youths like love-songs and the older people like mystic songs relating to the other world, while the women like songs suitable for them, particularly for their rituals and ceremonies. Folk songs march forward through the process of repeated performances. Sometimes, the themes, popular words or lines or parts of some songs give a particular song new form and vigour.

As the tunes of folk songs are traditional, common people do not have to bother about its tunes. Lyrics are mostly simple and not difficult to memorise and remember. The folk composers hardly bother about the various grammatical and musicological characters relating to metre, pitch, lexicography, etc. He sings the songs, which have been sung from generation to generation with little variation here and there. Because they are so close to the soil, nature and are nurtured by the open wide environmental conditions, these compositions are full of unlimited simplicity and liveliness. And that is the reason for their sustenance through the ages. Folk songs have, therefore, grown out of socio-religious-economic needs coupled with the needs of enjoyment and entertainment. It is worth-explaining the needs in brief. The needs can be classified in five dimensions: (*i*) Magico religious, (*ii*) Instruction and moral, (*iii*) Athletic oriented competition, (*iv*) Aid to work, and (*v*) Aesthetics.

(*i*) *Magico-religious*

We have already had some discussions on this. Faith and belief is a mental condition. The concept of magic is associated with faith. Many a times things become the objects of faith and belief without cogent reasons and faith becomes the central point. This is called magico-religious belief, which is a folk conception. All kinds of religious rites, rituals, customs, mantras, nice *Tulsi*-base (*tulsi* is a sacred plant for the Hindus, especially the Vaisnavas), earthen horses placed at the worship sites, songs based on worship-prayers, instrumental music-all these have the principal driving factor in magic. They are based on the belief that performing the ritual, chanting of the mantras, worshipping a particular image (deity), singing the prayers will meet some of the worldly needs/ will make favourable provision for the other world / will cure some diseases and mental agony or will do good to the spirit of the deceased relatives in the other world. Bhāwāiyā-based popular songs like *Kātipujār gān, Sāitol pujār gān, Tistāburir gān, Sonārāyer gān, Bishaharā gan, Hudum pujār gān*- all fall under this category.

(*ii*) *Instructional and Moral*

One of the principal objectives of folk performance is to educate the future generation. The long-cherished traditions and customs of the community are to be learnt and acquired by the new generations; they have to know what is good and what is bad from the viewpoint of the community and they have to acquire the practical knowledge about what to be done, when. The present generation imparts this education to the new generation on oral instructions, besides the practical demonstration. Mother and grandmother teach their children how to cook, how to perform various rituals (vratas) with their titbits and various other home works. Father and grandfather teach their children the details of the profession they are in for the livelihood. The oral compositions relating to these lessons contained in stories, couplets, proverbs and songs of the community and region get transmitted and play the role of distance education on many cases.

(*iii*) *Atheletic Oriented Competition*

The competitive spirit of winning over the other parties and participants in the *Noukā Bāich* (boat race) has given vent to *Noukā Bāicher gan*. Similarly, the incidences of competitive spirit expressed through songs for narrating the beauty and virtues of *Bhādu* and *Tusu* by the competing groups of performers, the expression of competition and rivalry in *Kabigān* and *Tarjā*, the spirit of winning over each other between the sides of bride and bride-groom in the marriages are examples under this category.

(*iv*) *Aid to Work*

The song of boat race (Noukā Bāicher Gān), as mentioned above is sung not only with the spirit of competition among the race-participants but also to make the laborious work of rowing enjoyable and attractive. Various calls, rhymes, couplets, songs have traditionally been used in course of laborious works to make them tolerable and attractive. *Sari gan, Chad Petanor gan, Dhan Katar gan*, etc. fall under this category. Beside the specific songs relating to specific laborious works, the workmen, particularly the farmers use songs as the source of energy and sympathy even in day-to-day works. The boat-man, while rowing, sings the songs like:

> *"Sāgar kuler nāiyā, apar belāy tumi kothāy, jāo bāiyā re;*
> *Or, "Hār kālā karlām re, āmār dyāha kālār lāigyā re*
> *Antar kālā karlām re duranta parabāse"*

Similarly, the farmers sing in course of ploughing—

> *"O dhan mor Kānāiyā re,*
> *Eluā kāśiyār phul nadi haice Kānāi hulāsthul re"*

Or, the farm labours sing while prunning the crops—

> *"O mor kāgā re kāgā, Jakhan Māo mor rāndhe bāde*
> *Patra nā dyān kāgā māyer hāte, Mairbe Māo mor āgūnot pariyā re"*

In fact, the number of songs relating to aid to works is so vast that it is quite often argued by some experts that songs have been created just to get inspiration in work and to keep rhythm in works.

(*v*) *Aesthetics*

According to the well-known definition by Kant, the aesthetic valuation consists of a 'disinterested well being'. There are, however, intrinsic problems involved in both the terms 'disinterested' and 'well-being'. Precisely because of these problems, Dr. Jan L. Broeckx, the Professor of Music History and Aesthetics of Music and also the Director of the Seminar of Musicology at the State University of Ghent (Bengium), preferred to hold the opinion that it would be better to speak of 'being intrinsically enthralled', *i.e.* being enthralled by the properties of music in itself without considering the question whether that music is technically simple or complicated, nor the question whether it provided knowledge, nor its possible utilitarian applications.

In Sanskrit, aesthetics is concerned with forms of 'beauty' only. Sanskrit aesthetic has a number of apparent synonyms expressive of beauty, *e.g.* 'saundarya', 'mādhurya', 'lāvanya', etc. 'Saundarya', according to Vaishnavacharya Sri Roop Goswami of Bengal, arises in the case of human forms from a proportionate setting of different limbs of human frame. 'Madhurya', according to Viswanath, the famous author of Sahitya Darpan is abiding charm in all situations. Another aspect of beauty is 'Lavanya', which presents a magnetic, animated personality. In the language of Sri Roop Goswami, it is akin to the lustrous shine of a pearl of high quality. Certain combinations of musical notes yield to aesthetic forms of beauty of music. These aesthetic forms have their own essential nature called *swaroop, swabhāv*, and *prakṛti* in the form of *jāti, ākṛti* and *vyākti*, *i.e.* type, figure and individuality.

Indian music has evolved such various aesthetic forms expressed in terms of *Rāgas*, and this is its greatest contribution in the domain of music. *Jāti* of a *Rāga* is the theoretical formula which includes a specific combination of musical notes with its *Poorvāng-Uttarāng*; its *Vādi, Samvādi, Anuvādi, Vivādi*, its *Graha, Amśa, Nyāsa;* its ten categories of *Jātis i.e. Sampoorna*, etc. and even its *Āvirbhāva* and *Tirobhāva*. This theoretical scheme of a *Rāga* is realised in concrete form in its various renderings by an artiste. This is the *Vyākti* or Individuality of a *Rāga*. This is related to the personality of the artiste, situation, atmosphere in which it is sung. The *ākṛti* of a Rāga comprises in *śabdakṛti, layakṛti, tālakṛti, swarakṛti*; its *sthāyee, antarā, sancāri, ābhoga*, etc. The *ākrtis* generate and develop different styles of a *Rāga e.g. Dhrupada, Dhamar, Khayal, Ṭhumri, Ṭappā, Bhajans*, etc. Folk songs also can fit in such *ākrtis*. The excellence of various styles of music depends on the purity of its *Jāti*, the perfection of its *ākrti* and the impressiveness of its *Vyākti*. This in short explains the aesthetic forms of beauty of music.

Man globally has aesthetic motivations and commitments. Music, whatever else it is, is a social phenomenon. Any system of musical aesthetic that will deal adequately with the perception of musical values then must have a social foundation. Systems of musical aesthetics in the past had to condemn or to condone, to include one kind of music but exclude other kinds. We should, however, realise that musical aesthetics should be a system not bound by moralising nor circumscribed by political ideology. The system of musical aesthetics should not be concerned with praise or blame but should rather explain how groups and societies through social interactions acquire, hold and change their musical values and search out the socio-musical principles which underlie the foundations of musical judgement. Aesthetic musical experience can take place only during the course of a musico-social information situation in which the music communicates some feeling, emotion or idea related to the individual's musical and/or social experience. Three main actors of the musical aesthetics are then—the music, the individual and the society. The nature of all musical aesthetic experiences is determined by the inter-relationships between them.

Every social interaction situation involves communication. There can be no aesthetic experience if the music fails to communicate. Communication through music will not take place unless the music heard has relevance to the musico-social experience of the individual. The musical experience of the individual depends upon the social groups with which he identifies himself. The music to which the group gives attention, the music which is relevant to the group's social experience, the music which constitutes meaningful communication through its gestures, is the music which a group will accept as meaningful.

The group acceptance of music is different in various social situations, and at different socio-cultural levels. In the sense that some music is accepted by certain social groups and rejected by other groups, it reflects the aesthetic values of the group. It then becomes obvious that the bases of aesthetic experience are two-fold—social awareness and musical awareness. By the first is meant an awareness of and sensitivity of human experience, religious, social and political ideas together with sympathy and/or empathy for man and society. It involves both rational and emotional involvement to a greater or less degree. By the second is meant an awareness of and sensitivity to the musical sound in all its aspects- melody, harmony, rhythm, form, pace, timbre, dynamics, the relationship between the lyric and the music in the case of vocal music, etc.

The needs out of which has grown the music that is, magico-religious, atheletic, competitive, aesthetic, etc. can be explained in terms of values too. Thus, the values that can be attributed to are musico-technical value, knowledge value, practical values (march songs, rowing songs, etc.), ethnic values, didactic values and aesthetic values. Music as part of non-material culture has a system of values or norms. The value judgements are developed in terms of social consequences. The differences in value judgement reflect the group attitude, the social, economic, political, religious and educational levels or milieu in which the group lives and interacts.

The social interaction that took place in the citadel and temple, and in the home and the market place provided the situations through which music grew and developed into communicative art. The use of music was socially purposeful. The aggrandizement of the ruler, the dignity and awe of the temple priest were enhanced by the use of music. It communicated to the audience a feeling of authority and respect, if not fear. The use of music was in that sense means of social control. Music was used as an adjunct to the dance, the fertility rites and the celebration of births and deaths that accompanied family life from the earliest times. The various uses of music to communicate in diverse social situations have been well explained by Leonard B. Meyer in 'Emotion and Meaning in Music' in the following words:

> "Finally, perhaps most important of all, this analysis of communication emphasises the absolute necessity of a common universe of discourse in art. For without a set of gestures

common to the social group, and without common habit response to those gestures, no communication whatsoever would be possible".

In the discussions of music and communication in his dissertation, 'Sociology of Music and Musical Aesthetics' Dr. Allen Stuard Rumbelow of Canada argues that there was a considerable sophistication of musical style long before literate times and that many of the refinements of more recent periods have arisen as a result of the emancipation of the art from strictly purposeful and utilitarian communication to artistic communication commonly called aesthetic expression. The universe of discourse in music has its foundation in tone system, the ordering of sounds to which any particular social group subscribes. It is significant to note that the scalar or step-wise divisions of a tone-system would appear to have been derived from the folk music of a society. Ethnomusicology presents evidence that most primitive folk songs contained relatively narrow variations in pitch. On the other hand, the sounds produced by open horns consist of widely space intervals. Dr. Rumbelow observed in this connection,

> "It remained therefore, for the stringed instruments and the flutes to achieve a rationalisation between these two extremes. The consolidation of tones into a single system was undoubtedly a long process".

In course of time, not only the pitches, which formed the song patterns were regularised but also the pace, the rhythms and the range of the tunes were conventionalised. Growth and change in a universe of musical discourse is due to the introduction of innovations. Such innovations, which are termed as deviants by Meyer, must be socially accepted if they are to remain as part of the musical tone system. A social acceptance is again contingent upon the innovation serving its purpose in the communication of the musical idea. In religious music particularly, innovations were resisted on the grounds that the magical properties of the music would be lost by such innovations and deviations.

Communications in music take place by means of musical gestures which Meyer calls 'Sound terms'. All the constituents of music gesture are involved in its importance as a significant symbol. The melodic, modal, rhythmic, harmonic dynamics, pitch range and timbre in vocal and in instrumental music have a bearing on its ability to communicate. The melodic organisation of a musical gesture has great importance in the communication of musical meaning. Tones, which are widely spaced, especially on the common chord, communicate a feeling of positiveness, aggressiveness, optimism, dominance and happiness. The social pattern of behaviour that heard the common chord blown on the bugles and horns of the military has ascribed this meaning to such an organisation of sounds. On the other hand, a narrow melodic line in the sense of stepwise progressions reveals the vocal, the folk, the religous chant as its source. The communicative aspect of this type of musical gesture implies supplication, submission, sorrow and comfort. The roots of these melodic patterns have given them their meaning as significant symbols in the communication of musical ideas. The rhythmic organisation of a musical gesture adds its significance to meaning in the communication of musical ideas. The unequally divided beat is attention getting, aggressive, powerful.

In combination with other factors such as a slow pace, it implies mysterious power, super-natural events, even evil and doom. The modal organisation of a tone-sytem developed on similar basis, the purpose, custom, and the significance of the poetic text that was to be accompanied. The form of the scale organisation was determined by the socio-religious and socio-political use of the music. Ethnomusicology gives evidence that heterophony both accidental and deliberate is to be found in music of primitive peoples. The generally high range given to the communication of grief can be attributed to the fact that wailing on the occasion of death or other calamity was a function of the women of the family or tribe. The timbre or tone-colour of the different classes of instruments took on communicative significance through their association with different social situations.

The foregoing discussion explains how different forms of songs-folk, tribal, classical have evolved to meet various kinds of needs felt at different levels of evolution by the various social-cultural groups. Growth and evolution of the folk form of Bhāwāiyā-Caṭkā has followed the same course, influenced by the same set of motivations by a large social and ethnic group of people called the Rajbanshis in the region of the then Kamrup, presently North Bengal and Western Assam. The evolution of various music and dance forms in Eastern India can also be explained, at least partly, in terms of the history of the various social-religious movements taking place in this part of the country from time to time. It has been mentioned that magic rites have in course of time been converted into religious rites. The religious psyche, which gave vent to various religious movements in Bengal/Kamrup, has found its reflection on the various forms of folk song, evolved in this region.

Man as a social being has to observe the rules and regulations of the social life and restrictions and customs imposed by the society in the form of Do's and Don'ts. The rules and regulations and restrictions arising out of the social life and the needs of livelihood have gradually become part and parcel of the performance of religious rites. These observed rites can be classified into two broad divisions: (i) ceremonial and ritualistic, (ii) popular and customary (*loukik*). Worship, chanting of *stotras* and *mantras*, sacrificial rites, *bhajans* and prayer songs to the gods and goddesses, etc. are religious ceremonial rites where the *Sastrik* (scriptural) rituals are to be strictly observed; whereas in the popular customary *(loukik)* rites there are no such strictness and rigidity.

The Aryans are supposed to have come to Bengal in the 5th century. *Smṛti, Shruti, Purana* which are the indicators of Brahminism and Brahminic culture had got due publicity and preaching in the Gupta era itself. The rulers in Bengal brought Vedic Brahmins from the Aryavarta during the time from the Gupta period to the Sena era. Worshipping of gods and goddesses belonging to the Vaisnava, Saiva and other cults has been preached among the common people during this period. The Pala kings, although belonged to Mahayana Buddhism did not oppose the Vedic rites. Along with the process of Aryanisation the process of Jainism and Buddhism continued in parallel and side by side for long in Bengal. After the heavenly ascension of Lord Buddha, Buddhism spread out into various branches. The Sahajyana of Carya had its influence in Bengal and Kamrup area in 10th to 12th centuries.

After the Muslim invasion, *Āul, Bāul, Sāin, Guru*, Vaisnava Saḥajiya had direct or indirect influence on the popular rites (*lok dharma*). Due to various reasons, the Brahminic rites got restricted to the upper echelons of the society. Rise and downfall, ups and downs of Hindu-Buddhist- Brahminic culture on the one hand, and the wayward Buddhism with its pervert faith and associated customs and rites on the other, along with the life-long faith, belief, magic-tormented religious mind of the common people of the lower echelon, led to the growth of a mixed type of religious rites and religious belief.

This religious belief got into various ramifications and had influenced the people of higher echelons too in the latter years, as a result of which the deities (goods and goddesses) worshipped by the people of lower echelon, so long, gradually got entry into the higher society with firm positions. This gave rise to various religious sects-*Nātha dharma, Sahajiya dharma, Mangala dharma, Śakta dharma, Vaisnava dharma* and customs and rituals associated with such *dharmas*. The followers of such religious sects and their associated customs and rituals came to be known as *Āul, Bāul, Sāin Darvesh, Kartābhajā, Kisoribhajā, Caran-dāsi*, etc.

Yoga-dharma as an atheistic philosophy was being practised for many centuries in this part of the country. The popular/secular (*lokayata*) stream of this *Yoga-dharma* is probably known as the *Nātha dharma*. The motto of the *Nātha dharma* is to achieve the unachievable by virtue of the *Yoga*. The preceptor (*Guru*) is the saint in the *Nātha* system. *Guru* is all in all. He is the eternal power. *Guru* and God are inseparable in this system. One of the most known literatures of the *Nātha dharma* is 'Maynamatir Gan' collected by George A. Grierson from Cooch Behar-Rangpur area.

According to some scholars, people belonging to the lower castes who had been so long oppressed and exploited by the people of higher ladder of the Hindu society found ways and means of ventilating their grievances and gradually got converted into the Islamic religion under the Muslim rule. The result of such entry of people with such religious convictions and faith into the Islamic faith was that some of the deities worshipped earlier by these people continued to show their strength and glory with the converted form of Islamic mendicants. For example, Ganes became Gāji, Kārtik Kāji, Ban Durga Banbibi, Dharma Ṭhākur, the last relic of Buddism too got converted into Pir Ṭhākur, and Satyanarayan became Satyapir. Combination of Satyanarayan and Satyapir of course, continued to be worshipped by the higher caste people too.

Tantrik faith of the 13th century added some more spice to this. People used to cherish both faith and fear in the miraculous power of *Tantra*. The Muslim *darvesh* (mendicants) took possession of the Monasteries of the *Tantrik sadhus* and showed their supernatural power which attracted the common people of the lower castes towards them and who ultimately embraced the Islamic faith to meet their desire for achieving such supernatural powers.

Again, the religious faith of these people mingled into the forces and counter forces of the society led to the growth and rise of the *Mangala dharma*. Obedience to any higher power—natural, super natural or human, willingly or not, is the resultant effect of fear from such power. Side by side with Muslim religion, the *Mangala dharma* and the associated faith and belief grew out of such fear psychosis and assumed a definite form in the composition of the *Mangala Kāvya*.

Through the *Mangala Kāvyas*, the post-Vedic deities got themselves established and the Vedic gods and goddesses got converted appropriately. Saivism abandoned the Vedic character in this non-Aryan environment and Siva became a popular god of the common people. In Bengal, particularly in North Bengal, Siva became a popular peasant, rather a lazy, work-reluctant, *ganja* (hemp) addict peasant. Similar is the case of *loukik* (folk) goddesses like Manasa and Candi. Manasa is perhaps the most important of all the female deities. Rural Bengal is full of various kinds of poisonous, non-poisonous snakes. Fear of snakes is the innate feeling. Out of this fear psychosis has come the idea of propitiating the snake-goddess Manasā. Worshipping Manasā has thus become quite prevalent in all parts of Bengal. All the *loukik* (folk) gods and goddesses are considered to be wrathful and passionate by nature and Manasā and Kali top the list in this regard. The belief that their anger can harm them has prompted people to worship the folk deities like Manasā, Kāli, and Śitalā, etc.

Tree-worship and worshipping of tree and snake together is the expression of the same psychology although it has an additional aspect of fertility cult. Visually the folk belief in magic is the monopoly of the women as it is the monopoly of the males on the Vedic rites. This is the reason why there are so many types of folk songs and dances centering round the belief in magic and female rites (*vratas*). Songs attract people and dances add new dimension to it. It is easy to express the passions and feelings through the nuances of dances and music. Female rites (*vratas*), rhymes, couplet songs and dances have, therefore, been the traditional ways of expressing the wishes and desires of the common people in India, particularly in Bengal.

The picture delineated above regarding the evolution and development of folk songs and dances is largely true for Bhāwāiyā-Catkā also. There are lots of songs based on rites and customs connected with the worship for various gods and goddesses in Bhāwāiyā form. Some of them are sung in the form of ballads (*Pāncāli*). Analysis of lyrics of these songs makes it quite clear that they have been composed to meet the day-to-day ordinary requirements of the social life; to win over the nature's power by propitiating the deities and/or to protect oneself from the wrath of various supernatural forces. The long journey of the Bhāwāiyā form of songs started with these kinds of songs.

This becomes evident from the analysis of musicological characters of these songs besides the thematic characters. Musicological analysis of *Kātipujār gān, Sāiṭol pujār gān, Sonārāyer gān, Gorakh nāther gān*, etc. shows that there are only 3/4 notes used in these compositions. The tunes are very simple with very simple rhythmic character. Evolution of Indian music subscribes to the viewpoint that music in ancient times was composed with 2/3 notes. More notes were added to the compositions in course of time. In Indian classical music system, no *Rāga* can be composed with less than 5 notes. But in tribal and folk songs there is no such restriction. The illiterate simple people used to sing with 3/4 notes in very simple tunes, although in the later years, the application of 6 or 7 notes have come in usual manner in the folk songs in course of time. For example:

Kāti pujār gān:

> *Kāti re tor māthā bānāice ke*
> Ānu janamere byāl bilāicang re, Māthā bānāice Basudeve.

Sāiṭol Pujār gān:

> Āeko nā cāndote āeko nā māsote,
> *Hoyā geil mor sāto byāṭār biāo re.*

Sonārāyer gān:

> *Bhālore, saity ṭhākur Sonārāy gāirasthak de tui bar*
> *Dhane banśe bāruk giri Sonārāyer bar.*

Gorakhnather gan:

> *Kāndere Goāloni hāte niā dāo*
> *Godhaner badale kyāne nā moil mor Māo*

Madan Kāmer gan:

> *Āilo āilo re, khelār gosāin āilo re*
> *Āilo re madaner Māo, Madonok bariā neo.*

Amongst the songs based on rituals and festivals, the most important are those relating to marriage ceremonies.

REFERENCES

1. G.A. Grierson (ed.), "*Linguistic Survey of India*", Vol. V, Motilal Banarsidas, New Delhi, 1904.
2. Verrier Elwin, *Folk Songs of Chhatisgarh*, Bombay, 1936.

■■■

3

The Folk Community 'Rajbanshi's Ethnic Culture

Cultural reflection of the wider group of people of the particular region is the main characteristic of folk song. Folk song grows out of the folk community. It is the reflection of philosophy of the folk community. In the case of Bhāwāiyā this folk community is the Rajbanshi community of the then Kamrup. This area is nourished by the Rajbanshi cultural milieu. However, it has to be made clear that not only the Rajbanshi but the Brahmin, Khen, Yogi, Koch, Mech, Rabha, Muslim—all these people who have traditionally resided in the greater area of the then Kamrup are patrons as part of this Rajbanshi culture. It can, therefore, be stated that the people of this area—their ideas, manners and behaviour, philosophy of life, happiness and sorrow, religious belief, attitude to art and culture, the geographical features of the area, the river, nature, the language spoken in the area—all these have contributed to the growth of Bhāwāiyā. The people are primarily the Rajbanshis and region is the then Kamrup. We must therefore, have some idea about the Rajbanshis and Kamrup, their place of abode, and the cultural area under study.

There are more than one viewpoint about the Rajbanshis. Some say, the Rajbanshis are of Kshatriya origin, and they have subsequently become degraded/degenerated Kshatriya on account of various reasons and made themselves known as Rajbanshi, the term denoting their association with the *Raja* (king), the Kshatriya. Others are of the opinion that they are included in the Koch tribe of Bodo origin. The basis of this viewpoint is that the Cooch Behar dynasty that ruled in Kamrup had their origin from the Koch tribe. The kings and the subjects being of same stock in this region, the Rajbanshi belongs to the Koch. Both the viewpoints deserve some amount of discussions.

As suggested above, the anthropological and cultural histroy of the Rajbanshis is intimately connected with the history of Kamrup-Kamta, Pragjyotispur, Pundravardhan, and then Cooch Behar. History of the Rajbanshi can be available from various sources. The principal sources are – *Ramayana*, *Mahabharata* and diffferent *Puranas*, *Tantra-*

scriptures on the one hand, and investigative survey reports, discussion papers, census reports, linguistic research and survey reports published from time to time by the English anthropologists, linguists and indologists, on the other.

Entrusted with the responsibility of collecting information on the various sects of population of the Eastern India, Sir Buchanon Hamilton did a survey in the years between 1807 and 1817. Based on Buchanon Hamilton's findings, Montgomary published "The History, Antiquity, Topography and Statistics of Eastern India" in 1838. Buchanon's report "Account of the District of Rangpore, 1810" inserted in that book gives an account of the history of the Rajbanshis.[1] As such it is the principal source of this history. According to this report, Koch Rajbanshis, both being part of the larger Bodo stock, belong to the same caste. The report, however, says that not all the Rajbanshis are Koches, although most of them are. Those who have become degenerated by adopting the profession of palanquin bearer are Koch and amongst them, those who have become further degraded by taking to the habits of eating pork, chicken, etc. are Dahoi or Garol.

Most of the scholars in the latter years followed this research work of Buchanon Hamilton. But all of them have restricted their discussion around the central point whether the Rajbanshi and the Koch are same. Some half-literate natives who had very little idea about the Rajbanshi people of this region worked as assistants to these scholars and as such their findings suffered from various kinds of limitations. After Buchanon, it was B.H. Hodgeson who in the "Journal of Asiatic Society of Bengal 1849" observed that Koch sardar Hajo was the founder of the Koch dynasty.

According to him, Koches are part of Tamulian population and they have been there in North Bengal even before the advent of the Aryans. Biswa singha, the grandson of Hajo adopted Hinduism and became known as Rajbanshi. To him, Koch and Kuvaca are synonyms. Koches of Assam have been divided into three groups—Kamkhali, Madai and Kolita by him. Koches of Rangpur on the other hand, are divided into two groups –Koch and Rajbanshi. In other words, he has described Koch and Rajbanshi as belonging to the same stock from the viewpoint of origin. After Hodgeson, E.T. Dalton in "Descriptive Ethnology of Bengal – 1872" has described the Rajbanshis as belonging to non-Aryan stock and large Bodo population on the basis of their physical appearances. According to H. Beverley (Census Report of Bengal, 1872), the Rajbanshis are Dravidians. To him, the name Rajbanshi is baseless and a part of these Rajbanshis are probably people belonging to some other caste.

The Rajbanshis of North Bengal are of same lineage with Koch and Paliya. According to Hunter (Statistical Account of Darjeeling, Jalpaiguri and Cooch Behar, 1876), the Koches are related to the Mech and the Kacharis of the adjacent region and are descendant

Instruments used in Bhâwâiyâ
(1) Sârindâ (2) Mukhâ Bânshi (3) Benâ (4) Dotorâ

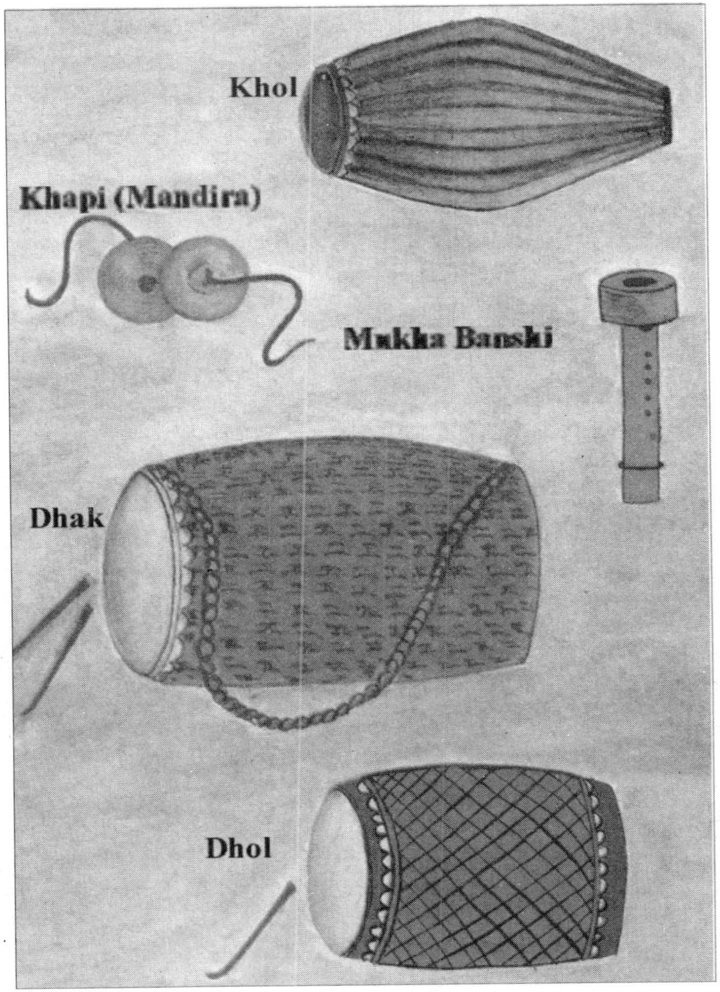

Instruments used in Bhâwâiyâ
Songs and Dances

Jogin Roy Playing Sârindâ

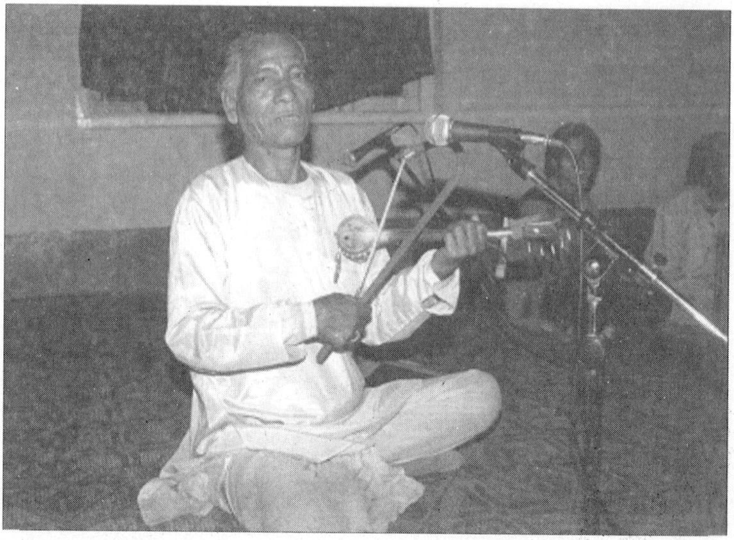

Lalit Roy (Kushâni) Playing Benâ

A Scene of Chhokrâ Dance in Dotorâ Folk Drama

A Scene from Dotorâ Folk Drama: Chhokrâ, Doâri and Gidâl

Fulti Gidâli and Party Performing Shâitol Dance

Rajkumar Gidâl and Party Performing 'Bishahara'

of the Himalayan groups.[2] They have become Rajbanshis after adopting Hinduism. H.B. Rawney (Wild Tribes of India, 1872) has stated that as a result of intercaste marriages of the Koches with the Hindus, their ancient behaviour, manner, culture and religious rites have undergone substantial changes. A part of the tribes thus Hinduised and converted is Rajbanshi. H.F.J.T. Megayer (Census Report of India, Rangpur, 1891) differs a little in his views. There are differences in the ways of thinking amongst the Vaishnava and Saiva sects of Rajbanshis. The Saiva Rajbanshis are Koch Mongolian whereas the Vaisnavas are the Dravidian agriculturists.

O. Donnel has viewed the whole of the Rajbanshi community to belong to the Mongolian stock (Census Report of India, 1891) from the standpoint of origin. According to him, the Rajbanshis are a part of the third batch of Mongolian people coming through the eastern parts. H.S. Risley (The tribes and Castes of Bengal, 1891) has not lent support to this view.[3] According to him, the Rajbanshis are the descendants of larger Dravidians and they have probably had intermixture with the Mongoloids. Rajbanshis are in actuality the Koches. According to George Abraham Grierson (Linguistic Survey of India, 1904) the Rajbanshis are the Hinduised Koches, who belong to the same stock as the Bodos.[4] According to E.A.Gait (Census Report of Bengal, 1901), Rajbanshis are Koch by caste and the influence of the Mongoloid is more pronounced on the Rajbanshis.

According to the Imperial Gazetteer of India, 1908, Koches are not the Rajbanshis although they call themselves so. The sources of origin of both the castes are different. The Koch kings are descendants of Mongoloid stock; the Ranbanshis on the other hand are the descendants of Dravidian and they adopted the name 'Rajbanshis' much before the establishment of the Koch Kingdom. The Rajbanshis of Cooch Behar, particularly the close relatives of the Maharaja, whose physical appearances vividly reveal Mongolian characteristics are either pure Koch or the intermixture of the Koch in power with some other castes (mostly higher castes), whereas the others do not have the Mongoloid features so pronounced. This report therefore, has made distinction between the two groups of Rajbanshis—one originating from the Mongoloid stock and the other from the Dravidian stock, the former representing the royal family and the latter the subjects and commoners. According to O. Maley (Census Report, 1911), whatever might be the sources of their origin, there is no doubt that Rajbanshis and Koches are two different castes at present.

There are some other sources here and there about the history of the Rajbanshis in addition to the reports, research papers and Census Reports mentioned above. 'Tabaqat-E-Nasiri', a Persian history written by Minhaz in 1261 mentions that Baqtiar Khilji invaded Tibet in 1206. The land-track between Lakshanavati and Tibet was full of forest, jungles and hills at that time. And in that kind of land lived three tribes-Koch, Mech and Tharu. Based on the description by Minhaz, Acharya Suniti Kumar Chattopadhyay has observed—

The local residents of North Bengal are the descendants of the Bodo stock of people or the intermixture of Austric-Dravid and Mongolian stock. Here they can principally be called Koch. These Koches are Hinduised or semi-Hinduised Bodo. They had left their own Tibeto-Burman language and adopted the dialect of the northern part of Bengal. Since they have become concious about the Hindu religion and cultuıe (mainly from the time of Biswa Singha and Naranarayan), they started claiming themselves to be *Kshatriyas* on the basis of their obscure false glory of the past; although at that time they accepted the status of scheduled caste, the lowest rung of the Hindu society with a view to having political advantage.

On the other hand, referring to the description by Hiuen Tsang, Acharya Chattopadhyay has observed that the whole of Bengal including the northern part adopted the Aryan language and culture by the 7th century. While assigning reasons for some difference between the language of Kamrup and that of middle India, as mentioned by Hiuen-Tsang, he has commented that Kamrupi language has Tibeto-Burman elements and as such the Aryan language has been a bit distorted by Kamrupi pronounciation.

In other words, Acharya Suniti Kumar accepted that the language of North Bengal was principally the Aryan language in the 7th century itself. Unfortunately, he had adopted two contradictory positions as reflected from his observations mentioned above. From the description of the track followed by Baqtiar Khilji for his Tibet invasion in 'Tabaqat-E-Nasiri', as mentioned by Sukumar Das in "Uttarbanger Itihas", it is clear that Baqtiar Khilji and his men came in contact with the mountainous tribes and their language and there was no opportunity of their contact with the people of the plains *i.e.* the Rajbanshis.[5] It, therefore, follows that the observations of Acharya Suniti Kumar about the Rajbanshis on the basis of the Tabaqat-E-Nasiri are not well founded and hence not acceptable.

The other set of sources about the history of the Rajbanshi are Purnana, *Upa-purana, Tantra, Ramayana*, and *Mahabharata*, etc. The materials available from such sources differ from the findings of the English and Indian researchers and scholars. According to Bhramari Tantra the five sons of Bardhan fled from Poundra-Vardhan being scared of the son of Nandi and lived in the Ratnapith. Due to lack of association of the Brahmins there, they got deprived of the Kshatriya rites. These degenerated Kshatriyas are known as Rajbanshis.

Nandisuta Bhayādbhime Poundradeśāt samāgatāh
Bardhanasya pancaputrāh swaganairbāndhabaih saha.
Ratnapiṭham bitistate kālādbiprarasangamāt
Kshātradharmādapakrāntā Rājbanśiti khyātāh bhubi.

Kalikapurana says,

> *Jāmadagnya bhayabhitāh Kshatriya purbamebahi*
> *Mleccha chadmānupādāya Jalpisam śaranam gatah.*

Being scared of the son of Jamadagni, the Kshatriyas took shelter of Jalpesh in the guise of impure ones (*mleccha*) and after being used to mleccha rites and manners, adopted the *mleccha* language. But they continued the worship of Siva in secret. Thus, according to *Bhramari Tantra*, the Kshatriyas took shelter in Ratnapith being scared of the son of Nandi, while according to Kalikapuran they took shelter of Jalpesh being scared of the son of Jamadagni. Some scholars are of the opinion that the son of Jamadagni referred to in Kalikapuran and Nandisuta (son of Nandi) referred to by Bhramari Tantra are the same and one person only. It does not seem unjustifiable to argue that the historical figure Nandisuta (Maha Padma Nanda), who was infamous for annihilation of the Kshatriyas has been described as the Pauranic figure Jamadagnya (Parasurama), particularly when the Bishnupurana and Srimadvagvata supports this surmise. *Bishnupurana* states that the covetous Mahapadma Nanda is to be born of the lawfully begotten Sudra wife of Mahanandi. This Mahapadma Nanda will annihilate the Kshatriyas like Parasurama and from then onwards the Sudras will reign here. Srimadvagvata also reiterates this.

The question therefore, arises whether Ratnapith and Jalpesh are situated in the same area. One has to go through the ancient history of Kamrup to know the history of the Rajbanshis because their living place was a part of Kamrup only. Ancient Kamrup had four parts—Kampith, Yonipith, Manipith and Ratnapith. The most Western part of the kingdom was Ratnapith. This is supported by Yoginitantra. The report of Buchanon Hamilton also mentions this. Judged by the facts of the boundary of ancient Kamrup and the present location of Jalpesh in Moynaguri police station of Jalpaiguri district, there is no problem to accept that the location of Ratnapith and Jalpesh is the same.

Now, where is the location of Paundrabhumi, referred to in Bhramari Tantra? According to Ramesh Chandra Majumdar, the historian—Poundra is the name of a people. Because they lived in North Bengal this area was famous as Pundradesh and Pundravardhan. The capital of Pundradesh was also named Pundravardhan. It was a famous city in the ancient time. Mahasthangarh located at a place with distance of 7 (seven) miles from Bagura has been accepted as the ruins of Pundravardhan city by the pundits (scholars), because this place has been mentioned as Pundranagari in a stone inscription of the Mauryan age. This opinion of Ramesh Chandra Majumdar is well accepted now. According to Manusamhita, Paundra, Odra, Kamboja, Yavana, Saka, and Kirata—all these Kshatriyas have been degraded to Sudra because of the non-use of sacred thread and non-association with the Brahmins. In the annotation of Sloka 44 of chapter 10 of Manusamhita, Kulluk commented that the Kshatriyas who used to live in Paundravardhana abandoned the Vedic rites and got degenerated to Sudra.

As per Manu's proscription the pure Brahmins, Kshatriyas or Vaisyas, if and when transgress the rules of Varnashrama dharma, become degenerated ones. It can be deducted from the above discussions that some Paundra kshatriyas, being scared of and chased by the King Mahapadma Nanda, crossed the river Karatoya, took shelter in Ratnapith located in Jalpesh area and settled there. They gradually became degraded and converted to *Mleccha* because of their non-association with the Brahmins and close association with the *Mlecchas*, adopting thereby the *Mleccha* language too.

After going through the opinions and comments expressed by the indigenous and foreign scholars and researchers it is clear that they have not been able to arrive at any definite conclusion about the origin of the Rajbanshi community of North Bengal. As we have observed, the viewpoints in brief are that they are (*i*) from the Dravidian stock (*ii*) from the Mongolian stock (*iii*) from the intermixture of Austric-Dravid and Mongolian people. One of the main issues of controversy was whether the Rajbanshi and Koches are the same caste. The indigenous researchers also followed this controversy but to no end. The matter, therefore, needs detailed examination and the ancient history of Kamrup the place inhabited by the Rajbanshis deserves thorough analysis.

This locality has been mentioned as Pragjyotishpur in the *Ramayana, Mahabharata, Bisnupurana, Harivamsa, Yoginitantra* and *Kalikapurana*. The western part of *Pragjyotis* acquired subsequently the fame as Kamrup. The ancient proverb regarding Kamrup or *Pragjyotis* is that Sri Krishna gave this kingdom to Narak out of grace. He appointed Narak the protector of Devi Kamakhya temple of Kamrup. But Narak was killed by Sri Krishna because of his rude behaviour with Mahadev of Kailash, Sri Krishna appointed Bhagadatta, the son of Narak in his place. Bhagadatta fought for the Kauravas in the battle of Kurukshetra and was killed by Arjuna. But his descendants reigned in Kamrup for long. The last of the kings of this dynasty were Subahu and Suparura.

It is guessed that after the dynasty of Bhagadatta, a few Sudra kings reigned in Kamrup. Sudra descendant Deveswar was the likely king in the first or second century. It is further guessed that a king named Prithu of Deveswar's lineage reigned in Western Kamrup. In this connection the Fort of Prithu (Prithu Rajar Garh) near Jalpaiguri is worth-mentioning. A king called Nagsankar reigned in the Eastern Kamrup in 378. Kamrup sent its representative to the religious assembly organised by Asok, the emperor of Maurya dynasty. Sangaldev became a strong king of Kamrup towards the fourth or fifth century. The history of Kamrup during the period from the fourth century to the twelfth century is based on sound footing. The sources of history of this period are available from the descriptions of Hiuen Tsang, Banvatta's Harshacharit, etc.

Pusyavarman (Pusyavarma) a king of Narak dynasty placed Kamrup on an important footing in the ancient Indian map. He assumed the title 'Maharajadhiraj' also. This Varman dynasty reigned in Kamrup till the senventh century. In the seventh century Hiuen-Tsang came to Kamrup at the invitation of Bhaskar Varman, popularly known as Bhaskar Varma, the great king of Kamrup. Good accounts of Kamrup can be available from the descriptions given by Hiuen-Tsang. Bhaskar Varma was contemporary to the emperor Harsavardhana and he defeated Sasanka, the king of Karn-Suvarn. After Bhaskar Varma, Salastambha acquired Kamrup kingdom. The kings of Salastambha dynasty ruled in Kamrup till the tenth century. Tyag Singha was the last king of this dynasty. After the death of issueless Tyag Singha the subjects of Kamrup decided to nominate a leader from the Narak dynasty and Brahma Pal of the Pal dynasty assumed the power. After Brahma Pal, his son Ratna Pal became king in the eleventh century. Dharma Pal of the twelfth century was a famous king of this dynasty. According to Kanaklal Barua, a researcher of Assam, Kalikapurana was composed during the reign of Dharma Pal. Ram Pal the fourteenth king of the Pal Dynasty regained the possession of Kamrup after subjugating the Kaivarta rebellion. Kumar Pal, the son of Ram Pal made Vaidyadev, the son of his minister, a king of a part of Kamrup. Vaidyadev got independence in Kamrup in latter years and Ballavdev descended him.

With the end of the twelfth century, began the history of fighting between the Hindu kings and the Muslims in Gaur. After the conquest of Naodia, the famous Ikhtiar Uddin Mahammad Baqtiar Khilji proceeded for conquering Tibet through Kamrup and dreamt of conquering Kamrup too. But his dream did not meet the success. It is guessed that in 1227 Giasuddin, the administrator of Bengal gained possession of Brahmaputra valley upto Sadia; but he could not retain the possession for long. The next invasion by the Muslim was by Ikhtiar Uddin Ujbak Tugril Khan but he too could not retain the possession. He was defeated by the Kamtapur force and killed and only a few of his soldiers could manage to run away. Again in 1337 Mahammad Shah sent a huge army twice to conquer Kamtapur but could not succed. In the 13th century, the Kacharis dominated in both the Eastern and Western Kamrup. Subsequently the Chutias spread their kingdom in East Kamrup. Bir Pal, Sonagiri Pal, Ratna Pal were some of the kings of this dynasty.

Almost the same time period with the Chutias, Chuka Pha, the first king of Ahom dynasty entered into Assam with a large following. His descendants dominated over East Kamrup. Some descriptions about the control of landlords (Bhuinyas) are available during this time period. One gets descriptions of rule by twelve (*Baro*) Bhuinyas in this area as in Bengal and from this it is inferred that there might have been the growth of some regional rulers due to absence of any heroic ruler in this part of the country during the period. Among these twelve Bhuinyas, one Durlabh Narayan is described as the King of Kamta.

His occupation is considered to be firmly establishd in the region between Karatoya and Bar Nadi towards the end of the 13th century.

Guru Charit and Sankara *Charit* give the account that Durlabh Narayan, the Raja of Kamtapur went to war with another Raja Dharma Narayan who styled himself Gaureswar, the Lord of Gaur. This title was at that time claimed by quite a number of petty chiefs and in the eighth and ninth centuries there were as many as six Gaureswar in North Bengal. Gaur was also the ancient name of part of Sylhet. May be, Durlabh Narayan had war with Dharma Narayan the ruler of Sylhet. The story goes that he sent seven families of Brahmins and seven families of Kayasths to Durlabh who settled them on the frontiers as wardens of the marches and gave lands and slaves to them. The ablest of them was Chandibar. He subsequently settled at Naogong where his great- grandson Sankar Dev was born. Ahom Burunjis also mention of a war between the Ahoms and the Kamta Raja, in which the latter was worsted and forced to give a daughter in marriage to Ahom monarch. Mriganka was another such ruler.

The history of the rulers of Kamrup from the 15th century is well known. During this period, the kings of Khen dynasty reigned in Kamta. The Khens claimed themselves as the Kayasth but most of the scholars do not accept this claim. It is said that the first king of this dynasty Niladhwaj was a cowherd. Following the prophecy made by his Brahmin master that he would become king, Niladhwaj, helped by the Brahmin, overthrew the last degenerated descendant of the Pal family, ascended the throne, made the Brahmin his minister and embraced the Hindu religion. He is reputed to have imported many Brahmins from Mithila. His capital was at Kamtapur on the left bank of Dharla. He was succeeded by his son Chakardhwaj who was an insignificant king of this dynasty. After Chakradhwaj, Nilambar ascended the throne, attained great power and extended his rule eastwards to the Bar Nadi and westwards as far as the Karatoya. He gave attention to the improvement of communication in his State. He constructed a road from Kamtapur to Ghoraghat, a portion of which later formed part of the main road between Cooch Behar, Rangpur and Bogra.

The story about the fall of Nilambar is interesting and well known. The son of his Brahmin councilor had an illicit relation with the queen and the king, hearing of this, caused him to be killed. His father was invited to a banquet and served with the flesh of his son. The councilor came to know this, left the country under the pretence of making a pilgrimage but actually went to Hussain Shah, the ruler of Gaur and persuaded him to send a large army to attack Kamtapur. Hussain Shah laid seizes to Kamtapur for quite a number of years but could not succeed to get possession. He then announced his intention to go back but begged for permission to allow his wife to meet the queen before returning to Gaur. By means of this subterfuge some armed men were sent to the city in litters and the city was captured with their aid. Nilambar was taken prisoner. Nilambar, however, made his escape on the way but was never heard of again. This was in the year 1498.

After some years Hussain Shah made an attempt to annex the Ahom country and this led to the destruction of the entire Mohammadan army and the loss of the whole of the conquered country. After the departure of the Mohammedans there was, for a time, no king in the entire region that was ruled by a number of petty independent chiefs. Among them, two brothers Chandan and Madan became quite famous. From this starts the socalled Koch dynasty. The history of the Koch is available from various sources—Bansavali of Darang Rajas, Assam Burunji, Kamrup's Burunji, *Gurucharit katha*, etc. According to these sources a Mech Sardar named Hariya Mandal married two sisters Hira and Jira, the daughters of Hajo and had two sons by them—namely Bisu, the son of Hira and Sisu, the son of Jira. Bisu was a man of extra-ordinary courage and enterprise. He defeated the chiefs of that area one after another and gradually extended his rule as far as the Karatoya in the West and the Bar Nadi in the East. He rose to power in around 1515 A.D.

The Brahmins discovered that these tribesmen were Kshtriyas who had thrown away the sacred threads when fleeing before the wrath of the Parasuram, the son of Jamadagni, a Brahmin ascetic. Also Bisu himself was declared to be the son of Lord Siva, who assuming Hariya's form had had intercourse with Hira, herself an incarnation of Siva's wife Parvati. Bisu assumed the name of Biswa Singha and his brother Sisu became Sib Singha, while many of his followers discarded their tribal designation and called themselves Rajbanshis. Not only this. Biswa Singha became a great patron of Hinduism. He became devotee to Siva and Durga. He revived the worship of Kamakhya, rebuilt the temple on the Nilachal hill near Gauhati and imported numerous Brahmins from Benaras, Kanauj and other centres of learning. He moved his capital from Chiknagram to Kuch Bihar, where he built a well-planned city and made his brother Sib Singha, the *Jubraj* (Crown prince). In 'Sangram Singh Chilarai' Ambikacharan gives somewhat different account:

> "During the first decade of the 16th century Visu, son of Hariya Mandal, a Boro-Kachari leader rose to power after subjugating the local chiefs *e.g.* Bhuinyas of Khuntaghat, Bijni, Bausi, Karnapur, Pandu, Karaibari, Barnapur, Chaygaon, Rani, Luki, Athiabari and few other landholders. He proclaimed himself as the king of Kamrupa and Cooch Behar. After performing the coronation ceremony as per Hindu custom, he assumed the title Viswa Singha and established his capital at Chikangram (near Goalpara) first. Later having defeated Nasiruddin Hossain Shah of Gauda, he shifted his capital to Kamtapur in Cooch Behar. He had 18 queens from different countries like Nepal, Kamrup, Kashi, Sonitpur and Mithila."

In the Cultural History of Assam, H.K. Barpujari gives the following account:

> "Viswa Singha was a man of exceptional enterprise, courage, military and administrative ability. With the assistance of his brother Siva Singha, he crushed the Bara Bhuiyan and set up a strong, united and independent monarchy. When the Muslims were supplanted by the combined pressure of the Ahoms from the east and the Koches from the west, Viswa Singha

organised a vast army and established his unquestioned authority over his newly built kingdom bounded by the Karatoya on the west and Barnadi on the east. In 1932-33 the Ahom forces attacked the kingdom of Viswa Singha. But he very intelligently, made peace with the Ahoms giving them some presents and agreeing to pay an annual tribute of horses.

In return, the Ahom General handed over to the Koch king the territories west of the Sankosh and assured him of protection against enemies. Gradually Viswa Singha extended his territory to Bhutan who agreed to pay him tribue. He left his kingdom in a strong and flourishing condition. During his time the kingdom came to be known as Koch Bihar (simply Behar in Assamese chronicles) instead of Kamrupa and Kamta. He shifted his capital from Chikangram to Koch Bihar. Biswa Singha governed his kingdom with the help of his brother Sisu (Siva Singha) who was made the Yuvaraj and Raikat and twelve Qazis (Karjis) or Ministers, all of them drawn from the twelve important Mech families. Following the Muslim system, he grouped his soldiers under the officers with names as below: Thakurias having control (over 20 men); Saikias (over 100); Hazaris or Hazarikas (over 1000); Umras (over 3000) and Nawabs (over 22 Umras). Quite possibly he appointed officers titled Wazir, Lashkars, Bhuyas, Baruas, etc. as wardens of the frontiers.

At the time of Viswa Singha's death, his two eldest sons Malladev and Sukladhwaj were in Benares where they had been sent for study under a learned Brahmin. Taking advantage of their absence, Nar Singh, the third son proclaimed himself king. As soon as the news reached them Malladev and Sukladhwaj rushed to Koch Bihar and raising an army defeated Nar Singh. It is said that Nar Singh subsequently became ruler of Bhutan. Although there is no confirmation of this, it is not impossible too. The statement of Sir Ashley Eden in his Report on his mission to Bhutan may be of interest in this connection:

> "Apparently, the Bhutias have not possessed Bhutan for more than two centuries: it formerly belonged to a tribe called by the Bhutias Tephu. They are generally believed to have been people of Koch Bihar. The Tephu were driven down into the plains by some Tibetan soldiers, who had been sent from Lhasa to look at the country".

After the escape of Nar Singh, Malladev ascended the throne and assumed the name Naranarayan. His brother Sukladhwaj was appointed his Commander-in-Chief. Thus after the death of Viswa Singha, his son Naranarayan ascended the throne. Naranarayan was a great king. With the help of Chila Ray, his brother who was one of the greatest warriors in the world, Naranarayan extended his rule to Manipur, Jaintia, Tripura and Sylhet. He introduced 'Narayani Sena' and 'Narayani Mudra'. Thus the Koch kingdom came into history towards the beginning of the 16th century under the leadership of Biswa Singha.

Naranarayan soon came into conflict with the Ahoms. The exact reason for the quarrel is however, not known. In 1546, a battle took place on the north bank of the Brahmaputra and the Koches armed with bows and arrows, under the able leadership of Sukladhwaj, defeated the Ahoms. Less important battles took place in some other places but the results were same. In the process of this, Naranarayan got a 350 miles road constructed with the help of his brother Gosain Kamal from Koch Bihar to Narayanpur near North Lakhimpur. Suklenmung, the Ahom king struck him on this front and cut off the road and thereby cut off their supplies. The result was disastrous defeat for Naranarayan. The hostility ceased for the time being. In 1562, again in a battle the Ahoms were worsted. Ahom Raja sued for terms and peace was concluded at the dictated conditions of Chilarai. Naranarayan then sent an expedition against the Kacharies who purchased peace by agreeing to pay adequate tribute.

The Raja of Manipur also submitted to this strong power. Naranarayan then attackd Jaintia, Tippera and Sylhet, and won victory everywhere. This was possible mainly because of his brother and General Sukladhwaj who was famous for display of such dash and rapidity that he was nicknamed Chilarai or the Kite king. Being encouraged by success everywhere, Naranarayan invaded the stronger power the Padshah of Gaur. The result was obvious. The army under Chilarai was defeated and the latter himself was taken prisoner. He was kept in captivity for sometime but returned home having gained the favour of the Padshah's wife or having married the Padshah's daughter, according to the other version. Naranarayan now became anxious for good relation with the Ahoms and achieved it by releasing the prisoners. At the same time he tried to maintain good understanding with Akbar, the Emperor of Delhi. According to the *Ain-I-Akbari*, Naranarayan "renewed his demonstration of obedience to the Imperial throne" and sent 54 elephants and other presents to Akbar. In the course of the second expedition against the Mahammedans of Gaur, Chilarai was attacked by smallpox and died on the bank of the Ganges, leaving his son Raghu Dev. Naranarayan died in 1584. The power of this dynasty reached its zenith largely due to the skill and valour of Chilarai.

The advent of *Mahapurusa* Srimanta Sankardeva into the Koch Kingdom marked a golden chapter in the history of this area. Sankardeva's continuous stay in this Kingdom for more than two decades resulted in a literary and Cultural Revolution called the 'Sankari Rennaissance'. This was possible primarily due to the patronage of Chilarai and Naranarayan, the greatness of Naranarayan and Chilarai. Sankardev and Madhavdev envisioned to carry on the propagation of Neo-Vaishnavism together with literary, social, cultural activities in the Ahom kingdom only. But they were totally shaken by the inhuman treatment meted out to their disciples by the Ahom king Suklenmung. So, they decided to move towards the west of Kamrup. Accordingly Sankardev with his disciples set out for the Koch kingdom, settled at Patbausi near Barpeta, then under the king of Koch Bihar in 1543. There he laid the foundation of a *satra*, ercted a *namghar* and started propagating his faith.

Here Harideva, Damodardeva and many others joined as disciples. Many Brahmin pandits also came there to have debates with Sankardev on the religious *sastras,* ancient

Sanskrit literature, etc. However, all pandits lost in the debates and left Patbausi. Having lost the battle of debates and also having seen the growing spontaneous popularity of '*Ek Saran Namdharma*' preached by Sankardeva the pandits became extremely worried about their own future. The Brahmin pandits receiving patronage of Naranarayan and Chilarai for so long, spread all types of false rumours and submitted various kinds of malicious complaints against Sankardev to the king. They levelled the complaint that Sankara was propagating a religion called *Ek Sarania* which is actually anti-religious; he does not comply with the dictates of the *Vedas*, the *Gita* and other scriptures; does not respect the holy *tulsi* leaves; he has prohibited *jagna* and *shraddha* ceremonies. Also they used the weapon that the king is likely to lose reputation and longevity, if Sankara is allowed to continue his activities.

The king was naturally furious and ordered arrest and destroyal of Sankar. Knowing about the order of the king, Sukladdhaj became extremely sad and decided to protect Sankar. By his clever maneouvering Sankar escaped arrest and was brought to the palace of Chilarai. The king came to know the move of his brother Chilarai and asked him to produce Sankardev before the court. Having obtained the assurance that no harm would be caused to Sankardev, Chilarai requested the *guru* to appear before the court. The king Naranarayan got spellbound hearing the Hymn composed by Sankardev about Hari and other poems in praise of the king such as:

> *"Jai Jai Malla Nṛpati Rasa-vān*
> *Jākeri guna-gāna nāhike samān."*

On being informed about the grand victory of Sankardev in the Royal court, both Chilarai and his wife Kamalpriya were overwhelmed with delight. At the request of Chilarai, Sankardev stayed at the house constructed for him. It is said that Naranarayan wanted a gist of the Twelve Books of *Bhagwat* in Assamese verse. No Brahmin pandit did show the courage to do it. Sankardev did it with 376 verses in all and presented a copy to the king. He rendered Book-1 and Book-11 with the distinct purpose of making the *Bhakti* cult widespread so that even women and lower classes of the society could follow them. Among his major works the most important are the compilation of the treatise, *Bhakti-Ratnakara* from the *Bhagwata-Purana,* the *Bhagwatgita* and other *Bhakti* and *Vedantic* texts, the compositions *Ramayana-Uttarakanda, Vipra-patni-prasada, Kirtan-ghosa* and the lyrics of the *Bargeeta* and *Bhatima* types.

Sankardev stayed in this kingdom for more than 20 years till his *Maha Prayan* in 1568. Overwhelmed by his *Bhakti* philosophy, Chilarai with his one hundred wives got initiated by the saint. The king himself used to have serious discourses on spiritual matters and *shastras* with the saint.

Chilarai was a great warrior. With a view to strengthening and improving upon the military organisation set up by his father Viswa Singha, Chilarai organised the armed forces into a number of divisions each put under a Chief Cmmander or a General. He constituted certain new divisions, *e.g. infantry, cavalry, elephantry and naval.* Later, the first three divisions were grouped under land forces and the naval division as naval forces. To ensure high sense of love and patriotism amongst the armed forces he arranged settlement of free hold land with the soldiers, according to the ranks, so that the maintenance of their families does not become a problem and demotivator. Simultaneously with the modernisation of the military machine he constructed well designed forts, embankments, ramparts etc for the protection of the forces. Also he deployed an efficient network of spies to collect advance information. The novel strategy adopted by Chilarai was that of attacking the enemy camps at night by using highly trained limited number of soldiers commanded by his ownself and taking the enemy by total surprise. He attained great success through the strategy of guerrilla warfare that which is known as commando actions in modern parlance.

Chilarai was an embodiment of generosity and lofty ideals. He demonstrated the highest standard of patriotism, military dexterity and warriorship, organising ability, leadership quality, erudition, administrative capability, religious tolerance and exemplary loyalty. Although initially he was a follower of Saivism-Shaktism, he later became a Vaishnavite- a profound devotee of Lord Krishna and accepted Sankardev as his *guru*. But he had never discriminated against people of any other religion, creed or caste. Above all, he was a great music lover. The two brothers are reported to have married the two daughters of the powerful landholder of Pandu, Pratap Rai Bhuyan. This marriage brought about a cord of relation between the two families. In those days the princes used to marry many times for political and diplomatic reasons and Chilarai also did so. But he married Bhubaneswari (Kamalpriya) out of love and this love grew mainly for music. One day Chilarai heard Kamalpriya singing a Bar-*geet* composed by Sankardev to the accompaniment of Sarangi and was enthralled by her song as also by her beauty. When he came to know that she was the cousin of Sankardev, he expressed his desire to marry her and the latter too was pleased to agree to such exceedingly welcome proposal.

Chilarai was a secularist too. Apart from rebuilding the famous Kamakhya temple, he cnstructed a number of temples of other gods and goddesses- Siva, Durga, Kali, etc. and some *satras*. By introducing the worship of Madan Mohan at a single place in Koch Bihar, he brought about a certain kind of harmonious co-existence of the *Saktas,* the *Saivas* and the *Vaishnavas*. In fact Chilarai was everything in the kingdom of Naranarayan and this is the reason why he was called the *Chhota Raja*. Naranarayan also used to love him like anything. Being himself a great warrior and virtuous king, he could know the real worth of his great brother. Thus the combination of two outstanding warriors and administrators made possible the consolidation of the kingdom in such manner. The history of the Koch kingdom after the death of Naranarayan is full of incidents of rise and fall. The entire kingdom got divided with the quarrel between the brothers. Invasion by the external forces (Muslim and Bhutan) led them to ask for help and assistance from the East India Company which ultimately got the kingdom converted to a tributary state of the Company.

Maharaja Naranarayan was succeeded by Laksminarayan in 1587 after his death. The glory of the Koch dynasty started fading from this period only. Assam, Tripura, Manipur went out of the hands. Lakshminarayan was succeeded by Maharaja Birnarayan (1627-32). The period was not significant in any respect. After this Maharaja Prannarayan ascended the throne and ruled the state for long 33 years (1632-1665). Taking advantage of the weakness of Shahjahan, Prannarayan attacked the Mughal power centre Ghoraghat and Goalpara and took possession of both. Immediately after ascending the throne, Aurangjeb made Mir Jumla the Subedar of Bengal. With a view to gaining the country of Prannarayan, Mir Jumla attacked the Koch Kingdom and defeated Prannarayan. He left the State in charge of a general and proceeded towards Assam. Prannarayan, taking advantage of this situation, regained the possession of Cooch Behar. Prannarayan was succeeded by his second son Modanarayan (1665-1680). During his time, the powerful Nazirdeo Mahinarayan tried to dislodge him.

Taking advantage of internal squabbling in the State, the Bhutans made several attempts to attack Cooch Behar in collusion with Mahinarayan and his son Darpanarayan. Jagdev and Bhujdev, the Raikats of Baikunthapur (descendants of Sib Singha) came foward to help with the force and established Basudev Narayan (1680-1682), the third son of Prannarayan in power. He was disturbed repeatedly by Jajnanarayan, the descendant of Mahinarayan and the Bhutias. He was succeeded by Mahendranarayan (1682-1693), the minor grandson of his elder brother. Jajnarayan again attacked the kingdom with the help of Bhutias. Ultimately a truce was made between them by which Jajnanarayan was made the general.

During this time, Kochraj had to fight with the Muslims who took possession of Boda, Patgram and Purbabhag parganas. Mahendranarayan was succeeded by Maharaj Rupnarayan (1693-1714). He made truce with the Mughals and got back Boda, Patgram and Purbabhag. He shifted the capital from Atharokotha (which was the capital since Lakshminarayan's time) to Guriahati (Cooch Behar). The existing Madan Mohan temple of Cooch Behar town was built by him. After him, Maharaj Upendranarayan's period (1714-1763) was again characterised by external invasion of Muslim power and Bhutan. The Northern part of the Koch Kingdom was occupied by Bhutan. Next two years was the period of a minor king 5-year old Debendranarayan, who was slain by his enemy while he was playing. Bhutan occupied various parts of the State and the system of a permanent representative of Bhutan Raj in the court of Cooch Behar Maharaja was introduced.

Dhairjendranarayan, the son of Dewan Deo Kharganarayan succeeded him in 1765. He was taken prisoner by the Bhutan Raj over dinner invitation in Buxa. 1970-72 was the period of Rajendranarayan, though the real power was with the representative of the Bhutan Raj 'Pen-Sutma'. After the death of Rajendranarayan, the puppet king, the Nazir Deo with the help of the courtiers and relatives made Dharendranarayan, the minor son of Dhairjendranarayan, the king inspite of stiff objection from the Bhutan's representative. Naturally there was a fight between the two forces. Pen-Sutma was defeated. On receipt of this information, the Bhutan Raj sent huge force and the Koch force was humiliated with defeat. The queen mother fled to Rangpur with the minor king and took shelter of the British administration and asked for help.

The East India Company and their Governor Hastings agreed to extend military help on payment of annual tax to the Company. Cooch Behar kingdom was made a protected state (Protectorate) of the British Power. The Koch kingdom thus lost its sovreign character in 1772. The period between 1772 and 1775 was a period of war and truce. In 1772 the Bhutan power was defeated by the combined force of East India Company and Cooch Behar under the leadership of Mr. Purling. In 1774, the Bhutan Raj made a truce with the Company under which the sub-Himalayan tract from Tista to Sankosh was severed from the Koch kingdom and given to Bhutan. Not only that, the Company raised the annual tax payable by Cooch Behar from Rs. 50000/- to Rs. 100000/- in 1774. From 1775 onwards, the kings who ruled in Cooch Behar, a protectorate of the British power were:

1775-1783	—	Dhairjendranarayan
1783-1840	—	Harendranarayan
1840-1847	—	Shibendranarayan
1847-1863	—	Narendranarayan
1863-1911	—	Nripendranarayan
1912-1913	—	Rajendranarayan
1913-1922	—	Jitendranarayan
1922-1936	—	Regency Council

(The queen mother Indira Devi was the President of the Council)

1936-1950	—	Jagaddipendranarayan

Amongst all these kings Harendranarayan and Nripendranarayan made significant contributions to the socio-economic cultural development of the area. The Koch dynasty played significant role in the growth and development of religion, language and culture in the middle age. They built numerous temples and helped the growth and propagation of Hindu religion in the entire region of Kamrup. They were very liberal in their religious attitude, which has been amply reflected by the peaceful co-existence of Saivism, Vaisnavism and devotion to *Sakti*. Cooch Behar State was under the Regency Council during 1922-36 because the heir Jagadippendranarayan was a minor and he had to complete his education and military training. With the Independence of India, Cooch Behar State continued as a protectorate till August 1949. The Maharaja signed the Cooch Behar Merger Agreement on 28th August 1949 by which Cooch Behar merged with India as a centrally administered land and became part of West Bengal from January 1950 by the Cooch Behar (Assimilation of State Laws) Act, 1950.

The scholars in support of their argument that the Koch and the Rajbanshi is the same caste refer to this history of Koch dynasty. It is from this history they argue that the progenitor of the Rajbanshis of Kamrup Kamta, that is, modern North Bengal and Western Assam was Koch and hence Koch and Rajbanshi is the same caste. The subjects of Koch kingdom are the descendants of Biswa Singha and Sib Singha, the sons of Hira and Jira belonging to Koch family begotten by the Mech sardar Hariya Mondal. Subsequently, the Koch became Hindu and adopted the name Rajbanshi. It should be mentioned that even the origin of the Koch is a subject of controversy. Although there is a general agreement to the fact that the Koch includes the Meches, Kachari, Bodo, Rajbanshi, Garo, etc. there is still a difference of opinion about their racial origin. In the *Jogini Tantra*, the Koch is termed as Kuvaca, and in the *Padma Purana* as Kuvacaka who are said to have taken dirty food and spoken a barbarian tongue. According to Acharya S.K. Chattopadhyay,

> "The word Koc (or rather Komc), comes from a Middle-Indo-Aryan source from Kawomca written Kamoca which can be properly sanskritised as Kamboja".

He further states that the Kambojas of Bengal are apparently the ancestors of the Koch people of North Bengal. Scholars like D.C. Sirkar also supported this view. Thus it is held by some pandits that the appellation Koch is a corrupt form of the Sanskrit *Kamboja* to which there are number of references as a group of people.

Racial Origin of the Koch

According to Risley, Koches were a large Dravidian tribe of North eastern and eastern Bengal with probable admixture of Mangolian blood. Oldham and Dalton subscribe to this view. The other group of scholars like Hodgson, Waddel, Buchanon, Gait subscribe to the view that Koches are definitely of Mongolian stock, rather than Dravidian stock. S.K. Chattopadhyay, D.C. Sirkar, B.M. Das support the Mongolian origin of the Koches. After due examination of all such viewpoints, it has now been more or less accepted by the scholars that the Koches are of Mongoloid origin having their home land in the Himalayan region, most probably in Tibet wherefrom they powered into India following probably the courses of the Teesta and the Dharla. They settled first in North Bengal and then spread gradually towards the east as well as south and west where they mixed themselves up with the Dravidians. Acharya Chattopadhyay divided the Bodos into two groups—the western branch included the Koches of Koch Behar, Kamata and Hajo; and the eastern branch, the Kacharies and the Chutias. Thus the Koches having close affinities with Bodo tribes of Mongoloid origin, in course of time and in some limited areas, intermarried with the Dravidians and gave birth to a mixed Mongolo-Dravidian race but having preponderant Mongoloid characters. Let us now examine how strong is the base of the argument in support of the opinion that Koches are same as Rajbanshis.

All the scholars have claimed that Hariya Mondal was a Mech. This being so, how is it that Biswa Singha, his son became a Koch king? The descendants of Mech are recognised as Mech only. In fact, there are numerous Mech people in North Bengal and Assam. Some scholars try to reconcile this with the argument that both Mech and Koch were non-Aryan, non-Hinduised castes belonging to Bodo tribes. As such, it is hardly material whether the dynasty was named Koch or Mech. What mattered was that Biswa Singha united both and mobilised their strength for laying the foundation of a kingdom. Why could not the dynasty be termed as Mech dynasty then? There is no cogent reply to such question. One of the probable reasons is that the scholars could not afford to take such risk of identifying the Meches with Rajbanshis. Meches are the people quite distinct from the Rajbanshis in their manners, rituals, food habits and particularly in respect of the language they speak. It is very difficult for anybody to say that the Meches are same as the Rajbanshis. Koches on the other hand, are very few in number in this area.

There are Koches in Khasi, Jaintia and Garo hills but their number even today is insignificant. Identifying those few with the Rajbanshis was therefore, not very difficult and also it was quite convenient to pass on the conclusion that the Koches got converted into Rajbanshis after they were Hinduised. No scholar has ever gone into the question of language spoken by the Koches. Hemanta Kumar Ray Barma of Cooch Behar, a retired bureaucrat of the Cooch Behar Maharaja's administration has analysed this point and shown that the language spoken by the Koches of Khasi, Jaintia and Garo hills is completely different from that spoken by the Rajbanshis. Their manners, food habits, rituals also differed significantly. In spite of this, the scholars came to the conclusion that Koches and Rajbanshis are same. Close examination however raises doubts about such hasty conclusions.

It is difficult to accept such conclusion for some other reasons too. It is argued that the Koches had adopted for them the designation of Rajbanshi after their conversion to

Hinduism and that too long after their leader Biswa Singha had established a strong political power to reckon with. The adoption of the designation was believed to be so complete that in the Census 1881, not a single person was returned as Koch in Koch Behar, the cradle of the community itself.

It is interesting to note that neither in the Persian records and foreign accounts, nor in any of the dynastic epigraphs of the time the Koches are mentioned as Rajbanshis. Even the Darang Raj Vamsavali which is supposed to be the genealogical account for the Koch royal family and which was written in the last quarter of the 18th century, does not refer to this term. Instead, all these sources call them Koches and/or Meches. The contention that this term was applied to them immediately after their Hinduisation at the time of their State formation, as held by Gait, Acharya Chattopadhyay and others, is therefore, not well-founded. The third and most important point against such simplistic hasty conclusion is that the Koch dynasty has come into power in Kamrup only since the beginning of the 16th century with Biswa Singha forming the state power in 1515.

We have seen in our discussion that this entire tract of land under various names such as Pragjotispur, Kamrup and Kamtapur, etc. had been inhabited by a group of people or groups of people since the prehistoric period. Who were the people residing here before 1515? No scholar except those belonging to the Rajbanshi community appears to have gone into this relevant issue. We have seen that people from different stocks had ruled this land at different periods, the most important and largest group of people being the Paundras as mentioned earlier in our discussions. This is perhaps the reason why the scholars have differed in their viewpoints about the origin of the Rajbanshis. Some have opined that the Rajbanshis belong to Ausrtic-Dravid group while the others speak of their Mongolian origin. From the physical characteristics also, all the Rajbanshis do not have the same characteristics. The royal family and their close relatives who are called 'Rajgan' by the local Rajbanshis have the Mongolian features much more distinct, much more pronounced—particularly their features of jaw, nose and body colour are much more Mongloid than those of common rural Rajbanshis.

The probable reason is that from the ancient days, people belonging to different communities have come here and stayed in this region some of them permanently and some for temporary period. Even those, who had stayed here for short period, had left something that has contributed to the socio-cultural development of the area. Those who have been left behind have come in contact with the next groups of people and thus a combined people have gradually come into existence. The group of people, the Rajbanshis were quite liberal in their attitude and quite receptive too. Because of this nature, they could assimilate the Aryan religion, language and culture and made themselves a developing group of people.

There has been intermingling of blood between different groups. That is why they had in them the Austric-Dravid and Mongolian blood. They have faith in Saivism, Vaisnavism, Saktism, Tantricism, Sufism, Pir-Satyanarayanism. There has been large scale Aryanisation, Brahminisation and Hinduisation as in other parts of India. Various tribes have become Hindu through Brahminisation at the direct instance of the Brahmins to meet their own need. They had no alternative but to do this to combat the Muslim influences. Moreover, the Brahmins had to do this to obtain favour of the tribal Kings, *Sardars* and *Zamindars*.

According to Acharya S.K. Chattopadhyay before the advent of the Paundras the central part of North Bengal was inhabited by Monkhmer group of people. Tibeto-Chinese people did not come till then. During that period the Dravidians came to the central North Bengal from Banga and Kalinga and in course of time became the ruler. Later on these Dravidians claimed themselves to be the descendants of Aryans. It can be reasonably accepted that these Dravidians are the Paundra Kshatriyas mentioned in the *Purana* and *Tantra*. According to Acharya Chattopadhyay, Aryanisation in Bengal commenced during the reign of the Mauryas *i.e.,* in the 4th Century B.C. and got completed in the Gupta era *i.e.* 7th century A.D. To him, Aryan religion, language and culture spread over the entire North Bengal by this time.

Taking clue from this, it can be deducted that Aryanisation took place in North Bengal too during the same period as in other parts of Bengal. That the Rajbanshis adopted the Aryan language by the 7th century A.D. is supported by the Chinese pilgrim Hiuen Tsang's travel document. Regarding the languae spoken by the inhabitants of Kamrup, Hiuen Tsang observed that the language sounded a little different from that of the middle India. This is explained by Acharya Chattopadhyay's observation that Hieuen Tsang might have heard the language of Western Assam or Kamrup with a little different mode of pronounciation (of the same Indo-Aryan) which has made Assamese look and sound different from Bengali, as a result of which Kamrup's language appeared to him somewhat different from the middle Indian language.

Based on the informations and reasons discussed above, it may not be unreasonable to conclude about the origin of the Rajbanshis that a group of Dravidians or Paundra Kshatriyas of Paundra Vardhana came to Kamrup and resided there towards the end of the 4th century B.C. Later on Tibeto-Burman tribes Koch, Mech, Bodo, Kachari, Rabha, etc. of the Sino-Tibetan group entered North Bengal and Assam in the 1st century B.C. The conservative ones of these tribes maintained their separate entity. The less conservative and liberal ones, however, had gradual intermingling with the Dravidians and formed a combined people. This combined/compound people are perhaps the Rajbanshis, who in the subsequent periods had admixture of blood with the socalled Aryans.

From the ancient period itself, this community of people tried to assimilate the Aryan language and culture and even in the initial stages of assimilation by the 7th century itself adopted the Indo-Aryan language as their own. But from the standpoints of religion and culture the process of assimilation is still continuing. It is from this angle that the Rajbanshis claim themselves as the Kshatriyas. They claim that Koch and Rajbanshis are not the same caste and they try to prove their Kshatriyahood and get rid of the degradation by taking to the sacred thread.

With a view to identifying themselves as the descendants of Aryan Kshatriya and establishing the claim in Government records the Rajbanshis organised mass agitation from time to time. That the agitation took quite well organised shape towards the end of the 19th century and the beginning of the 20th century is reflected from the reports of the census officials. Late Panchanan Sarkar alias Panchanan Barma of the village Khalisamari of Mathabhaga sub-divition of Cooch Behar district and a pleader of the Rangpur court was the principal leader of this agitation towards its final stage.

With the objective of placing the claim before the census officials for identifying the Rajbanshis as the Kshatriya caste in 1911 Census, the Rangpur Assembly of the Rajbanshis on the 1st May of 1910 under the leadership of Panchanan Barma demanded that while the Rahbanshis and the Koch will have to be enumerated separately, the Rajbanshi will be enumerated as the Kshatriya. Rangpur Kshatriya Samity in the mean time got the recognition for the Rajbanshis as the Kshatriya by the Pundits of Nabadwip in one of the proscriptions. On the basis of this proscription, Rajbanshi has been mentioned as the Kshatriya in 1911 Census although they have not been enumerated as Kshatriya. As a follow-up measure of their efforts, the Rajbanshis took up the purificatory measure by organising an assembly at Perolbari of Domar P.S. of Dinajpur district on the 27th Magh of 1319 B.S. where twenty one thousand Rajbanshi men of North Bengal and Assam went through the purificatory rites and got rid of degradation by putting on the sacred thread. In 1913, O. Maley, the then Census Officer recognised Rajbanshi as different from Koch.

At present the Rajbanshis of North Bengal are Scheduled caste, whereas the Rajbanshis of Assam and Purnia (Bihar) are not. During this year 1995-96, there was an attempt to include the Rajbanshis of Assam under scheduled tribe list. A section of the Rajbanshis put up stiff opposition to this attempt. A parliamentary committee under the chairmanship of Shri Amar Ray Pradhan, MP has gone into the question and submitted a report. The findings of the committee have, however, not yet been made public.

From the history of the movement by the Rajbanshis of North Bengal and Assam for identifying themselves as the Kshatriya, it becomes evident that in the process of

Aryanisation and Brahminisation, this liberal minded receptive group of people were not satisfied by mere assimilation of Aryan language and culture; it gave rise to a mass intention of acquiring the same social status as the Aryans and the intention ultimately gave vent to the acquiring of Kshatriyahood. This is in brief the history of Rajbanshi community. This Rajbanshi community of ancient Kamrup is the folk community whose life-breath is the folk song 'Bhāwāiyā-Caṭkā'. Analysis of Bhāwāiyā-Caṭkā, its lyric and music gives illustrations of the socio-cultural, economic and political life of the great community, the Rajbanshis.

REFERENCES

1. Francis Buchanan Hamilton, *Account of the District of Rangpur 1810,* Appendix III of the District Census Handbook, Jalpaiguri and Cooch Behar, West Bengal, 1951.
2. W.W. Hunter, *Statistical Account of Bengal,* Vol. X, Turner and Company, London,1876; rpt. D.K. Publishing House, Delhi, 1974, rpt. West Bengal State Gazetteer, Higher Education Deptt. Govt. of West Bengal, Kolkata, 1997.
3. Herbert H. Risley, *The Tribes and Castes of Bengal,* Vol. I, Bengal Secretariat Press, Kolkata, 1892.
4. G.A. Grierson (ed.), *"Linguistic Survey of India",* Vol. V, Motilal Banarsidas, New Delhi, 1904.
5. Sukumar Das, *Uttar Banger Itihas,* Kumar Sahitya Prakashan, Kolkata, 1982.

■■■

4

Geo-Physical Conditions of Kamrup: Sub-Himalayan Zone

We have since discussed about the Rajbanshis–the folk community whose song the Bhāwāiyā-Caṭka reflects the total life of the Rajbanshis. Before that we have to deal with the environment and nature in which the song Bhāwāiyā has grown and got nourished in the sub-Himalayan zone. Nature, the topography, the mountains, mountainous rivers, open wide fields, agricultural fields all these have given wide dimensions to Bhāwāiyā. Here in this chapter we will deal with the environment and nature that has influenced Bhāwāiyā in its evolution so significantly.From the mention of various rivers as the boundary of the kingdoms in the mythologies, it is quite clear that the rivers played significant role here. The principal rivers that have been referred to in the *Kalika Purana* are Trisrota (Teesta), Jotoda (Gadadhar), Sitaprabha (Dharla), Nabatoa (Torsa), Kshirpakhya (Dudhkumar), Nila (Nilkumar Torsa). The geographical boundary of Kamrup was as mentioned earlier—Mahananda in the west, Brahmaputra in the east, Himalayas in the north and Brahmaputra in the south.

According to the geologists, Bengal has grown out of alluvial soil carried by the rivers. They have divided this land into two distinct areas lower Gangetic delta and north Gangetic sub-delta. The sub-delta has been composed of the materials carried by Ganga and Brahmaputra. The western, southern and eastern parts of this area are old alluvial soil. North- western and western parts of the old alluvial tracts are composed of materials carried over by Koshi-Mahananda-Karatoya rivers. North- eastern part of this area is composed of the materials carried over by Dharla-Sankosh-Gadadhar. The soil of the lower part of the sub-delta has more alluvial mud than sand, which is found in higher portion in the soil of northern part.

The soil of the sub-Himalayan Terai area has been composed of heavy materials like stone, trees and shrubs, wastes, etc. carried by the rivers. Terai area is full of massive forests and quick growing plants, and weeds always cover its foothills. These are high dry lands and not suitable for agriculture. Two river tidal basins-Teesta-Jaldhaka-Torsa-Kaljani basins-have been the mode of connection between the Terai area and the plains. The nature of soil of the lower part of this basin is suitable for agriculture and as such habitation has come up in this area. The area from the foothills of the northern mountains upto a certain point has the characteristic of a plateau.

After that the land has had gradual sloping. Depending on the degree of gradient, big stones, pebbles, wastes on the riverbed have been carried to quite a distance. Heavy stones have rolled upto the point of steep slopes of the rivers. The places with the slopes quite insignificant have been full of small sized pebbles, waste materials and soil. The gradient of the rivers like Teesta, Chel, Ghesh and Chalsa are spread over quite a distance; gradient of Jaldhaka and Torsa on the other hand is not significant. Below this lies the area of very low gradient.

Numerous streams arising from the Himalayas having converted themselves into short and middle length rivers flow over this area—the southern portion of Jalpaiguri and northern portion of Rangpur. The rivers of this mid region carry with them lots of sand and the sand grains get collected as silt of the slow-flowing rivers of this tract. Within a few years the riverbed gets filled with sands; shallow riverbed cannot sustain the water streams of the rains and get spread on both sides. The river banks thus get swollen by the sand deposits and the land close to the banks get covered with sand. The soil is known as sandy, as it contains sand mainly. There being no natural drainage facility, the lowlying areas in between the water streams have remained water logged and the soil has gradually been converted to 'Dola' (low land/cradle).

However, by nature itself the rivers of this region keep on changing their courses; the courses which have been left over get dried gradually and with the passage of time the riverbeds get filled with mud, sand, etc. The abandoned riverbeds thus get converted into low agricultural land (Dola). The mid-region thus got composed of high dry sandy lands and low (Dola) lands. The lower region starts from the southern part of the mid region. The speed of the rivers is still slower here. This region is composed of light sand and silt. The eastern part of this region is the place of confluence of old alluvial lands and has become the centre of old habitation and growth of political power.

Kurigram, Bhurungamari, Nageswari of Rangpur district and the southeastern parts of Dinhata sub-division of Cooch Behar district are full of innumerable swamps and abysses. They bear evidence to the fact that the rivers have changed their courses on regular frequencies. As discussed above, the waterlogged areas gradually got filled with sediments and converted into agricultural lands. In the 12th centuary, most of these arable lands suitable for agriculture fell within the north eastern part of district Rangpur, south western part of Cooch Behar district, northerrn part of Dinajpur district and also the north western Mahananda-Koshi basin. Large-sized tanks and water areas of this region bear the evidence of once prosperous habitation. The tanks with all probability were excavated for creating irrigation facilities and drinking water during the drought.

Autumn rice (*Aush*) was the principal crop. This variety of rice was suitable for cultivation in low lands with its characteristic to withstand heavy rainfall and waterlogging. The cultivation of *kharif* came into practice much later. After the autumn rice, the lands were used for mustard and pulse cultivation and the high sandy lands used for cultivation of ginger, pepper, etc. Both bulls and cows were used as draught animals for tilling the lands. Cows were also meant for supply of milk. Bulls were used for carrying commodities on their backs. The bull-drivers were called 'Baladiya' or Baldiya. Baldiya-*hat* is a famous name in this region. Bullock cart was probably introduced as the improvised form from the system of carrying goods on bull-backs. Buffaloes are stronger than bulls and so buffalo-carts got introduced gradually. Use of buffaloes as draught animals, for supply of milk and also for drawing carts was quite widespread.

The widespread practice of keeping cattle herds came into existence out of immense necessity of cattle in the agro-based economy, side by side the abundant availability of fodder for them in the river islands and uninhabitated open wide fields. Well-off households used to keep sufficient number of cows and buffaloes and these were looked after by the salaried cowboys (Maishals in case of buffalo herds) in the cattle-herds (*bathans*). Lots of places have been named as Gorubathan named after cows and Mahis-bathan named after buffaloes in this region. Those who used to travel from one market (*hat*) to other with goods and commodities on the bullock/buffalo carts were called 'Gariyal' (cart-driver).

There was not much of habitation in the vast areas of the entire region, being infested with jungles, wild beasts and being unsuitable for agriculture. Population was much less in comparison to the land availability and as such there was no concept of ownership of land. Farmers were encouraged to grow crops after cleaning the jungles. Farmers trying their fortune started agriculture with their limited manpower and strength after reclamation of waste and fallow lands. Habitation of agricultural labour and associates grew centring round the house of the principal farmer. Thus grew unplanned scattered habitation over various places.

There was no concept of any right of possession of the ownership of land. It was not clear as to who owned how much of land. There was no system of measurement of land

and the area of land in possession of any household used to be determined by natural borders or by the amount of crops grown. There was virtually no taker of waste-fallow lands even as gift. A farmer could occupy and start cultivation any time anywhere. Land revenue was determined on the quantum of land cultivated and the amount of crops grown thereon. The unit of revenue collection was thus created with a large area in this process.

In the later years, with the regular system of revenue collection the unit became Taluka. Taluka system was in practice during the Mughal period. Villages were named like 'Asharur Taluk', 'Jatiar Taluk', etc. The British Government introduced the concept of Mouza in place of Taluka. From the viewpoint of ownership, land was divided into two categories in this region-rent-paying and rent-free. Rent-free lands used to be bestowed on particular persons (special category) as reward for their special services. Thus came the systems of Brahmottar, Debattar, Lakheraj, Petbhata, etc. along with the system of *Jaigir* (grant of rent-free land).

The system of tenure-holder or leaseholder (Izaradar) was introduced in Cooch Behar in 1790 at the intervention of the British Government. It is through this system and as a result of this process that the concepts of *Jotedar*, *giri* (owner) versus *adhiar* (*bargadar*), landless farmer, etc. came into being subsequently. Under the leasehold system, the entire State was divided into some small areas (parts). *Jote* consisted of few such areas, and the owner of a *Jote* was *Jotedar*. With the increase of population in course of time, farmers unable to get lands on ownership started cultivation of lands belonging to the *Jotedars* with right to the share of crop. Thus came into practice the *bargadar* (share cropper) system.

People's food-habits of a particular region are developed depending on the natural and geographical situation and environment. For this specific reason, food habits of the people of Kamrup have some specialities although the principal food items are rice, fish and animal and bird meat. In the off-seasons and famine period, a large part of population had to live on Cheena, Kaun and Poyra sattu (grinds) *i.e.* some inferior staple food. Milk, because of its abundant availability, found a significant place in the list of food articles. Butter and curd (*doi*) were natural corollaries. The Bhutias used to deal in butter with their purchases from this region. *Ghee*, of course, came into the system much later. One of the popular milk products was curd made in the earthen pot (*ghatiya doi*). There was also a system of making curd in the bamboo spout (hollow). *Chira* (flattened rice), *Muri* (puffed rice), *moya* (sweetened balls of puffed rice) with *ghatiya doi* (curd) were very popular kinds of food. *Doi-Chira* (flattened rice with curd) is still a speciality of the Rajbanshi culture. It is used as *prasada* for deity worship. *Atiya kala* (banana with lots of seeds) sometimes called *Bichi kala* (seedy banana) is added to *doi-chira* when used as *prasada.* Otherwise also *doi-chira* is a must as part of any ceremonial feast-particularly marriage related feasts.

At the time of marriage, *doi-chira* used to be sent on yoke used for carrying the gift articles to the new relative as a token of respect. Fish-small or big which was available in plenty in the innumerable ponds, beels, rivers, paddy fields was an important item of food. The main instruments for catching fishes from such natural sources of water were *Jhoka, Palo, Jakai, Kocha, Jalanga, dhorka, deru, hook, burung, khalai*, etc. After the rains in the months of September and October, lots of fishes, particularly small fishes used to be caught in the ponds, *nalas* and beels, most of which, except the deeper ones, got dried after the winter because of the nature of soil with low water retention capacity. Both the factors led to the idea of dry fish and eating dry fish became a part of food habit in this region. *Sidal*, a food variety made out of dry fish is still a speciality. *Sidal* is made by grinding dry mixed with *mankochu* (arum) in the pestle, thus making a pulp and getting that pulp of fish grind, oil and turmeric scoured and then dried. This is preserved properly so that it can be used any time of the year as a substitute for fish.

One of the important items in the list of food articles is *Guapan* (betel nut and betel leaf). Betel nut grows in plenty in this region. Betel leaf also grows as a creeper claimbing up the betel nut tree. Betel nut was eaten in two forms – green and over ripe. Dry nut was not in much use earlier. Ripe nuts with fibre used to be kept underground in such manner that they can absorb the moisture and get over ripe. This over ripe nut with betel leaf is a speciality and some sort of addiction too. Betel nut and leaf is an important item of this culture even today. Deity worship, marriage, any kind of reception, even ordinary hospitality, is incomplete without betel nut and leaf.

Amongst the vegetables and pulses, the locally cultivated and available brinjal, bitter gourd, bottle gourd, gourd, potato, *kakrul*, shim and *thakuri, musuri, khesari, mug, khulti kalai*, etc. pulses were the main varieties. *Khuriya, bathua, kalmi, dheki, kachu sak, pata sak* (jute leaves), *nafa sak* were main leafy vegetables. *Sukati* made of dried leaves of jute and bathua is one of the delicacies. It may be mentioned that the necessity of salt used to be met by alkaline liquid. This alkaline salt was the alkaline water prepared out of ash obtained by burning the fibrous roots of plaintain trees put through the distillation process. This kind of alkaline fermentation was used for cleansing the hair (specially by women) as substitute of soap and also for washing clothes as substitute of soda. The process of boiling clothes in earthen vessel with the help of alkaline water was given a specific name 'Chyakapara deoa'. Alkaline water, slightly purified, was used for preparing human food called 'Chyaka' also. Alkaline water put in the preparation of gourd and kachu (arum) makes delicious 'Chyaka'.

Houses were constructed mainly with the help of natural resources like bamboo, straw, kush grass, shrubs and wood available in plenty in the naturally grown forests and jungles. In the northern portion of the region which was infested with wild animals, houses were mainly made of forest wood. Comparatively well-off people had the roofs constructed of tin. There was hardly any use of bricks, cement and iron rods. Poles, hedges, truss, etc. were mainly of bamboo. Sometimes jute sticks were used for making hedges.

Their dresses had the regional speciality. The original residents of the region had to become self-sufficient in spinning and making clothes. Spinning was the part time profession of the women in their leisure period. In the Terai, lots of poor women had their livelihood by spinning cotton yarn. Cotton used to grow extensively in Goalpara and Kamrup districts. It has been mentioned in the 'Gurucharit' of Assamese literature that Hariya mandal, the father of Biswa Singha used to cultivate cotton by digging lands with the help of spade. The regional name of cotton is 'banga'. Because the Meches mainly used to do the cultivation of this cotton, this was given the name mech-banga, being carried on the bullock back. The weaving instruments on which the women had to weave were very crude and they had to tie the yarn on their waste and as such the length of the woven cloth was very short.

Women used to wear these short-width and short-length clothes (called Fota or Patani) wrapped over their waste to cover lower portion of the body upto the knee and upper portion covering the breasts. Separate pieces of clothes were worn for covering their head and body. Men also had to wear short clothes for the similar reasons. Poor farmers and labourers used to wear loin clothes covering the buttock and the upper portion of the thigh, whereas the rich class put on the knee-length *dhotis*. Besides the cotton wrappers, relatively well-off people used Bhutia *rags*. Mekhala sheets and heavy kantha were main winter protection. Poor labour class people had to depend on jute made dhokra and sacks. Dishes and water jars made of gourd, earthen vessels, jars, pots, bamboo tubes, etc. were the main household utensils. Zinc bangles, coral beads, silver jewelleries were in use. There was hardly any use of gold ornaments.

There was hardly any facility for education and medical treatment. People were mostly illiterate. Any kinds of sickess used to be considered as a result of being possessed by an evil spirit or deity and treated by *ojha* (exorcist). People had much more confidence in mantra than in medicine. They had profound belief in spirit, witches, etc. Amongst the wild animals tiger, bear, deer, bison, zebra, rhinoceros, snakes, wild boar, elephants were the main species. Hiuen Tsang, the Chinese pilgrim, has specially mentioned elephant of Bhagadatta. The system of catching elephants and taming them for use was quite well known in Kamrup, as mentioned by the pilgrim.

It is quite evident from the natural and geographical environment of the region that the rivers of the rigion have played vital role on its environment. Courses, speed, gradient, depth, width, navigability of these rivers had affected the habitation, growth and development of agriculture, trade and commerce on the areas adjoining the riverbanks. The rivers had unlimited influence on the socio-economic and cultural aspects of the region. Brief description of the rivers will, therefore, be quite relevant. This is however, a very difficult job, because of the nature and course of the rivers. The observation of Dr. Francis Buchanon Hamilton in the Account of the District of Rangpoor, 1810 is worth-mentioning in this context.[1]

> "Since the survey was made by Major Rennell, the rivers of this district have undergone such changes that I find the utmost difficulty in tracing them. The soil is so light and the rivers in descending the mountains have acquired such force that frequent and great changes are unavoidable; so that whole channels have been swept away by others and new ones are constantly forming. The nomenclature is therefore exceedingly difficult...After tracing the name of a river from some distance you all of a sudden lose it and perhaps recover the same name at a distance of 20 miles, while many large rivers intervene and no channel remains to assist in discovering the former connection. The old channels have not only lost a current of water but have been entirely obliterated by cultivation or by beds of sand thrown into them by newly formed rivers. In some instances different portions of the same river remain, while others have been lost and new channels fill the intervals, so that aparently the same river has various names in different parts of its course.... In the transient view which I had an opportunity of taking, my difficulties have, of course, been greater so that in my description I am afraid that there are numerous errors; yet I enter into it with minuteness, the changes to which rivers are liable in a country of this nature, being a subject upon which naturalists have as yet but slightly touched".

The above observation of Buchanon-Hamilton made in case of the rivers of Rangpur, applies to all the important rivers of North Bengal.

Rivers

Karatoya: Karatoya is considered to have been the most important river of the ancient Kamrup. It was the separating line between Kamrup of Bhagadatta and the kingdom of Virat. Coming from the Brahmakund of Sikim hills this river has traversed to Rangpoor through Sikim, Bhutan and Jalpaiguri. In the ancient days, this river played a vital role in the economy of this vast region—its agriculture, trade and commerce, water supply, etc. and as such this river has been described as Karatoya the holy river, Karatoya the sacred river. Even in 1913, the Rajbanshis held their pious ceremony of wearing sacred thread and sacrificial rites with a view to getting rid of degraded status in Perolbari village on the bank of Karatoya. Boda, Debiganj, Pachagarh, etc. small ports developed based on the

Karatoya only. Karatoya was navigable and boats carrying 300/400 quintals of goods used to ply through this river. Karatoya has joined with Teesta, Ghoramara, Atreyee, and Talma etc. at different places. At many places this river is known as Buri Teesta, Mora Teesta, etc.

Teesta: In comparatively modern age, the most important river of this region was Teesta whose Sanskrit name is Trishna or Trisrota. *Kalikapurana* mentions this river. Teesta is believed to have risen from the ice-melted mountain of Tibet. After crossing the Rangdhang hill of Bhutan it has entered into Jalpaiguri district. It had tremendous influence over the socio-economic development of Jalpaiguri, Cooch Behar and Rangpur districts. Teesta is treated as old mother by the Rajbanshis and Teesta-burir gan is an important part of the Rajbanshi culture. *Kalikapurana* version regarding the evolution of Teesta is as below:

> "A demon but devotee of Siva got thirsty during his fighting with Parvati, the wife of Siva and prayed to Siva for water. Siva ordered his wife Parvati to give him water. Parvati gave water to the demon from her breasts in three streams. Trishna or Trisrota, which was subsequently known as Teesta, came into being in this way".

The characteristics of a capricious mountainous river are quite noticeable in its frequent changing courses and that is why it has three streams-Teesta, Buri Teesta and Mara Teesta. This river had played important role in the trade and commerce of agricultural commodities of this region. Commercial boats from Dhaka, Chittagong used to ply through Teesta. As a result small ports and trading centres like Kaliganj, Mekhliganj and Dewanganj developed on the bank of Teesta.

Jaldhaka: Rising from the Bhutan hills, Jaldhaka has entered the district of Cooch Behar at a point near Mekhliganj, flowing by the boundary line of Darjeeling district and through the western Duars on way. In the Duars, the rivers Murti, Diana, etc. have joined this river at different places. The name Jaldhaka is believed to have come from the word Jal-dhakka, which means the water forces. In Cooch Behar district, this river is known as Mansai, Singimari, Dharla at different places. Mathabhaga town is on the Mansai and Changrabandha and Jamaldaha are on the Dharla. The ruins of the ancient Kamtapur are on this river known here as Singimari. It has entered the district of Rangpur after Gosanimari. This river also has changed its course quite frequently and has met other rivers on the way.

Dharla: The source of the river is again the Bhutan hills. The river has played vital role in the socio-economic life of Jalpaiguri and Cooch Behar. In the 15th century, it has been used for protecting the Kamtapur city. The Census report, 1951 gives some descriptions about the river. "The entire bed is very irregular being a series of curves and abrupt bends all along the course. It becomes almost dry during the hot weather months. Even during the rains, the waters do not rise high except after heavy fall of rain when it cannot be crossed without boat or raft."

Torsa: Toa-rosa, which means the angry river. Rising from the southern part of Tibet, the river has traversed through the Bhutan hills, Duars, Cooch Behar and Rangpoor districts and joined the Brahmaputra in Rangpoor. On the way it has created lots of islands, sandy lands, water areas, beels, wastelands. Innumerabe number of thickly populated habitations, markets have been devastated by the onslaught of this river. Cooch Behar town is on the Torsa. It has helped a lot in the protection of the capital town of Cooch Behar.

The devastating restless nature of this river can be reasonably guessed from the names of the villages, which were developed on the banks of this river from time to time. They are Dudher Kuti, Charaker Kuti, Sudhaner Kuti, Maranadir Kuti, Nilkuti, Jajnanarayaner Kuti, Mahisbatan hat, Dodeya hat, Sahebganj, Maruganj hat, Pundibari hat, etc. Kuti refers to char land grown on the area left over by the river while changing the course. Ganja, hat, etc. grew on the banks of the river.

Kaljani: According to Sunder, the Settlement Officer of the western Duars, "This Kaljani is the combined water of the Alaikuri and Dima rivers, which first take the name of Kaljani after their junction at Alipur, the present Headquarters of the Buxa subdivision. At a place Ambari this river has joined Gadadhar where on the occasion of Baruni Astami a big fair takes place every year and the religious minded people take bath on this holy occasion".

Gadhadar: According to Sunder, "The Gadadhar river takes its rise in the Bhutan hills, east of Buxa, where it is known as the Jainti river. It takes the name of Gadadhar from the junction of the Sachuphu and Jainti rivers and falls into the Kaljani below taluk Chalnipak. It is fordable in every part during the winter months." The river has traversed vast areas of Cooch Behar, Rangpur and Goalpara districts and has joined Raidak in Goalpara district.

Gadadhar-Sankosh: In the northern part of the region, the eastern stream of Gadadhar is known as Sankosh or Swarnakosh. In the 16th century during the reign of Maharaja Naranarayan, when Kamrup was bifurcated into two kingdoms, this Sankosh became the boundary line. It has traversed the districts of Cooch Behar and Goalpara and has joined the Brahmaputra. Its lower part is known as Gangadhar.

Raidak: Raidak is a sub-stream of Gadadhar. The western stream of Sankosh is also known as Raidak. Two parallel Raidak Rivers have traversed the northeastern region of Cooch Behar and Goalpara districts with various names such as Dipa, Raidak, and Mara Sankosh, etc. and have joined the Brahmaputra in Goalpara district.

From the description of the natural characteristics and courses of the rivers above, it can be easily guessed why there have been so many beels, water bodies, and nalas in this region. The regional names of these water bodies of various sizes are *Chara, Dara, Beel, Doba*, and *Kura*, etc. *Chara* is a long water body with stagnant water extended over two/three kilometers, sometimes even more. *Dara* is a narrow stagnant water body. *Beel* is the stagnant waterbody of a few hundred hectares. *Kura* is a small but very very deep waterbody. *Kura* can be found within the *beel* and *chara* also.

Moreover, the quality of land and soil quality in the region has been affected by the courses of these rivers. The lands are divided into *danga, payosthi, char, auyal, dola*, etc. on the ground of their quality. Besides, extensive areas of shrubs and jungles of *nalkhagra, pundi* (common reeds), and bamboo have grown in the stagnant waterbodies and wet lands. Car (beach) lands have become the grazing lands for cattle with Kush grass (reeds) and other shrubs. District Census Hanbook of Cooch Behar, 1951 gives good description of the topographical and natural position of this region.

> "The country is a network of rivers and small streams .... the majority of them take their rise in the Himalayas .... and flow into the districts of Rangpoor on their way to join the Brahmaputra, sometimes branching out in different channels but often flowing into each other in their downward course. The banks are generally abrupt giving proof of the wily nature of the stream, and the beds sandy mostly with a beach on one side of the stream. Boulders, rock and gravel are common in the beds of river as they were washed down from the hills. Generally tame and shallow in the dry season, they become very turbulent and fierce during the monsoon. They are subject to floods or sudden onrushes of water due to heavy rain in the hill slopes. A little more than ordinary rainfall in the hills is followed by a sudden rise of waters, which overflow the banks and drown the country for miles around. Crops and cattle are often destroyed. Changes in the course of rivers occur during heavy floods, when the loose sandy soil easily gives way to the force of the current. Generally, however, the banks being steep and the beds deep, the stream keeps within the banks and swifts along with great velocity.... In the monsoon, navigation becomes risky owing to the treacherous sands that lie concealed under the water level. The soil being loose, alluvion and diluvion, land making and land destroying go on constantly on a large scale and sand banks are numerous near big rivers. Towards the end of October, the rivers begin to dwindle, and by March, even the mightiest of them except the Tista, are nothing but tame, narrow, shallow and limpid streams, meandering through innumerable sand banks. The water, sweet and refreshing in summer, becomes muddy and unwholesome during the monsoon. Large market villages are situated on river banks."

It is quite evident from the above discussions that the rivers of this region had their rise from the lower Himalayas and under different names such as Teesta, Torsa, Jaldhaka, Dharla, Kaljani, Raidak, Gadadhar had traversed over the region and have had tremandous influence on the natural environment as well as socio-economic environment of the entire region.

REFERENCE

1. Francis Buchanan Hamilton, *Account of the District of Rangpur 1810,* Appendix III of the District Census Handbook, Jalpaiguri and Cooch Behar, West Bengal, 1951.

■■■

5

The Lyrical Dialect of Bhāwāiyā

It has been mentioned earlier that the Rajbanshis had adopted the Indo-Aryan language before the Seventh century itself. The language, however, appeared a bit different from the language of Mid-India to Hieuen Tsang because of the regional characteristics in its pronounciation. The language, therefore, needs detailed discussion, particularly when our purpose is to analyse the folk songs, which are composed in the language of the region. The regional way of speaking, word throwing, pronounciation, voice modulation are the cherished wealth and properties of folksong. It is, therefore, quite reasonable and relevant to deal with the language used by the Rajbanshis at some length. Sir George A. Grierson in his Linguistic Survey of India has first mentioned the language used by the Rajbanshis of Rangpur, Darjeeling, Cooch Behar, Jalpaiguri, and Goalpara as a separate dialect.[1] He named this dialect as Rajbanshi since this is spoken mostly by the Rajbanshis, but he considered it a dialect of Bengali itself.

After Grierson, the distinguished linguists like Dr. Suniti Kumar Chattopadhyay, Dr. Sukumar Sen followed by Dr. Nirmalendu Bhowmick and Dr. Nirmal Das, etc. had dealt with the linguistic and literary analysis of this language. Suniti Kumar Chattopadhyay and Sukumar Sen preferred to call this language 'Kamrupi', judged by its regional characteristics. Dr. Nirmal Das while dealing with the naming of the language, preferred to follow them. Dr. Das has pointed out that the name 'Rajbanshi' for this language would lead to two errors—error of exclusion and error of inclusion. Lot many other residents of the then Kamrup region such as the Muslims, Khens, Yogis and even the Brahmins of Khagrabari area do speak this language as their mother tongue and hence these people will be excluded by naming the language as Rajbanshi. On the other hand, there are Rajbanshis in Midnapur, 24-Parganas, Hooghly and Nadia districts who may not be of the same stock and do not speak this language but they will unreasonably be included. Dr. Das had, therefore, preferred to call it Kamrupi.

Dr. Satyendra Nath Barman of Mathabhaga of district Cooch Behar, a Rajbanshi himself speaking the language from his childhood and later on, undertaking a scientific study of the language for his Ph.D. thesis accepted the name 'Kamrupi'. Some other distinguished persons belonging to the Rajbanshi community had different views on the issue of naming the language.

Upendra Nath Barma, a learned politician and social leader of this community was in favour of the name of 'Rajbanshi'. Panchanan Barma, the most dominant socio-political leader popularly known as the father of the Kshatriya movement called it 'Kamta Bihari'. Purnendu Mohan Sehanobis, a veteran writer in Rangpur Sahitya Parishad also followed him. Very recently Dharma Narayan Barma has termed it as 'Kamta Bihari' in his book entitled 'A step of Kamta Bihari Language'.[2] They have justified this by the argument that the region is Kamta Bihar or Kamtapur and as such its language should be 'Kamta Bihari'.

As mentioned earlier, the linguistic pundits have not accepted this position. Dr. Nirmal Das while giving critical analysis of the book of Shri Dharma Narayan Barma has found no justification for naming it as 'Kamta Bihari'. This is to mention in this context that some research scholars and writers have termed this language as 'Bāhe'. They have partially followed Grierson who had given this name 'Bāhe' to the variation and form of the dialect as spoken by the Rajbanshis of the Terai area of Darjeeling which numbered 47435 only at that time; but the scholars following him wrongly indicted this name 'Bāhe' to the language (dialect) itself spoken by the entire Rajbanshi population of Cooch Behar, Jalpaiguri, Rangpur, Goalpara which numbered 3509171 at that time. This is almost a case of naming the 'Genus' on the basis of 'Species' and hence quite fallacious.

Moreover, there are inherent fallacies in the naming itself from the viewpoint of the meaning of the word 'Bāhe'. Bāhe is the shorter form of the vocative "Bā-Bā-He". One should consider if it is judicious and proper to call a language group 'Bāhe' and also to call the speakers of the language 'Bāhe' caste just because they use the vocative word 'Bāhe'. That too, this word 'Bāhe' is not used universally to address anybody and every body. The word 'Bāhe' is used by the Rajbanshis to address the persons of paternal/maternal and son/daughter relations of affection and love. It is not used for addressing the persons of brotherly or sisterly relations. For example, a person with the relation and status of uncle will address the nephew-like person; "O, Bāhe, how are you? What is all going on?", etc.

Similarly, the nephew will address or reply in the same manner, "No, Bāhe, the situation is not all right", etc. But a person with brotherly relation will never address his brother or sister, "O Bāhe, how are you?" This is the most important grammatical characteristic of the word 'Bāhe'. Not only that; the word when used conveys a sense of respect and honour. Use of the word 'Bāhe', particularly when used by any unfamiliar or less familiar person with undefined relationship, demands proper use of the verb conveying due respect. For example, "*Ki Bāhe, chāul bechbā nā ki*?" will be a wrong form. The appropriate form of the verb will be 'Bechaiben' instead of 'Bechba', conveying due respect and honour to the addressee. These subtle features of very many words in Kamrupi speech form are not known to the people belonging to the communities other than those speaking the language for ages.

Unfortunately, the outsiders often venture to use these words on inappropriate occasions with inappropriate verbs and create problems. That the words 'Bāhe', 'Bāu', 'Bāpoi', etc. used only for addressing the filial and paternally related affectionate ones may not be known to them. They think 'Bāhe' can be used for addressing anybody. Grierson called the sub-dialect 'Bāhe' because of his ignorance about the characteristic and actual meaning of the word. Moreover, the informants collecting and supplying the informations for him suffered from the same deficiency. The Government employees through whom Grierson collected the informations were mainly from the South Bengal and East Bengal, having scant knowledge about the language. It is seen from his report that the informant for Jalpaiguri district was one Baboo Murlidhar Roy Chaudhury, and Baboo Prasanna Chandra Dutta was the informant for Terai area of Darjeeling.

This Baboo class of people used to look down upon the Rajbanshi poor peasants and the language used by them and naturally having little respect for the language never cared to know the actual inner meaning of the word 'Bāhe'. The implication of such an imagination also did never occur to their mind. The wrong information supplied by them and subsequently followed by the scholars blindly, probably because, the same has been quoted by an English scholar, had led to so much of social tension in the area. On a number of occasions, the literate, educated class of the Rajbanshis organised protests and demonstrations on this issue. This disturbed the communal amity amongst the Rajbanshi and non-Rajbanshi people, particularly immigrants from East Bengal.

The Rajbanshis took exception specially when the word '*Bāhe*' was found to have been misquoted and misused by the scholars to call the Rajbanshis belonging to 'Bāhe' caste, on the argument of their using the word '*Bāhe*' and this had generated controversies, arguments, fighting on many occasions. Misquotations used in literary works by the eminent writers like Samaresh Basu, Prabhat Kumar Mukhopadhyay had caused tension in the Rajbanshi dominated areas. The amount of tension thus caused can better be assessed from an incident narrated hereinafter. Late Jatin Chakraborty, the then PWD Minister of the Government of West Bengal caused tremandous furore by misquoting and misusing the word 'Bāhe' in his address delivered in connection with the laying of foundation stone of Panchanan Setu on the river Mansai near Mathabhaga, Cooch Behar so much so that Shri Dines Chandra Dakua presently Minister in the Government of West Bengal had to clear the stand of the State Government on the issue in an essay with the details of the Rajbanshi/Kamrupi language published in the Gana Shakti. Shri Dakua dealt with the word *'Bāhe'* quite extensively and commented,

> "I have noticed untoward incidents and quarrels taking place in hats (market places), work fields and many such places as a result of gross misuse of such a sweet, beautiful respectable word because of the ignorance of the users, though unintentional".

He narrated an incident where a non-Rajbanshi gentle man asked a Rajbanshi woman who was hawking vegetables *"Ki Bāhe Sāg Bechbā Nā Ki"?* But he got no response from the vegetable hawker and the question being asked repeatedly the woman responded with anger in an irritating tone- *'Ḍyāker nā pān to ḍyākān kyāne*?' Why do you call in such way if you cannot address properly? What was the fault of the gentleman? His fault was that he used the word 'Bāhe' without knowing its concomitant grammar. Grammar of the language demanded that the gentleman should have asked *"Ki Bāhe, Sàg Bechāiben Nā Ki?"* The verb '*Bechāiben*' (honorific form) carries the respect the use of the word 'Bāhe demands, while '*Bechbā*' implies the inferiority of the addressee and this is the reason why the hawker woman responded in such manner.

Unfortunately, the scholars and researches seldom keep these things in mind and intentionally or unintentionally create social tension by wrong, inappropriate use of such words and phrases. In this regard the latest incident refers to the comment of Dr. Asit Kumar Bandopadhyay in his book where he made improper and inappropriate use of the word 'Bāhe' which hurt the sentiment of the Rajbanshis of North Bengal. Not only this; Shri Bandopadhyay, going a step forward, commented that the Rajbanshis and the Santhals are not the 'Bengalee' even.[3] Such comments of Shri Bandhopadyay about a large community of West Bengal gave rise to widespread commotion, meetings, slogans, signature campaign organised by the scholars, teachers, students and socio-political workers of north Bengal irrespective of caste and creed.

The damage was however, done in the mean time. Taking clue from the comment of Shri Bandopadhyay, a retired Professor of Calcutta University, the separatists of Uttarkhanda movement of North Bengal started organising and reviving their activities on the old issue that the Rajbanshis of North Bengal are not Bengalee and as such they should not be with West Bengal and must have a separate State for their own economic, social and political development *i.e.*,better existence. The word 'Bāhe' has thus been very very sensitive one leading to various kinds of socio-political problems in the past but even then some of the scholars and researchers use this word indiscriminately and cause disturbances in the social amity amongst various communities in the area and help fomenting the sentiments which are otherwise taken advantage of by unscrupulous political and so called social leaders.

The history of the origin and development of Rajbanshi or Kamrupi speech form is related to that of Bengali. The linguists have more or less accepted the view point of Grierson and Suniti Kumar Chattopadhyay that Bengali has originated from the Magadhi Apabhramsa. Grierson noticed the linguistic unity of North Bengal and Assam and pointed to Magadhi as the common source of all the Eastern dialects.

> "Magadhi was the principal dialect which corresponded to the old Eastern Prākṛta. East of Magadha laid the Gauda or Pracya Apabhramsa, the headquarters of which was Gaud in the present district of Malda. It spread to the South and Southeast and there it became the parent of Modern Bengali. Besides spreading southwards Gauda Apabhramsa spread to the east keeping to the north of the Ganges and there it is represented at the present day by Northern Bengali and in the valley of Assam by Assamese. North Bengal and Assam did not get their language from Bengal proper but directly from the West Magadhi Apabhramsa, which in fact, may be considered as spreading out eastwards and southwards in three directions. To the Northeast it developed into Northern Bengali and Assamese, to the South into Oriya and between the two into Bengali. Each of these three descendants is equally directly connected with the immediate common parent and hence we find North Bengali agreeing in some respects rather with Oriya, spoken far away to the South than Bengali of Bengal proper of which it is usually classed as a sub-dialect."

Based on the materials of the *Linguistic Survey of India,* Suniti Kumar Chattopadhyay has divided Eastern Magadhi Prākṛta and Apabhramsa into four dialect groups (1) Rāḍha-the language of West Bengal and Orissa (2) Varendra-dialect of North Central Bengal (3) Kamrupi-dialect of Northern Bengal and Assam and (4) Vanga-dialect of East Bengal. It has also been widely accepted that the Apabhramsa from which Bengali has originated is one of the Middle Indo-Aryan languages of the third stage. Lastly, the linguists have accepted the conclusion that Magadhi Apabhramsa has originated at the subsequent stage of the Mangadhi Prākṛta in the eastern branch of Middle Indo-Aryan language.

Since the conclusion of the seventh century, this Apabhramsa started taking certain characteristics quite independent of each other in Bhojpur, Mithila, Magadh, Bengal, Orissa and Assam. These characteristics became quite dominant and clear near about the tenth century and based on these characteristics, several regional forms of the Magadhi Apabhramsa got originated in the abovementioned areas. According to the linguists, these regional forms are Bengali, Assamese, Bhojpuri, Maithili and Oriya, etc. languages. It is, however, true that this evolution of Magadhi Apabhramsa in different regional languages was not complete in a short time. The process took still some more time to get completed.

There are several factors responsible for the evolution of one or more dialects or evolution of variety of regional forms of a dialect. Two main reasons are (i) quite scanty or absence of communication in the social and cultural life of an area and (ii) political separation. Lack of regular close communication and mutual understanding in the social life, want of opportunities of mutual exchange of ideas amongst the people of a community residing in various parts of an area, lead to the growth of various forms of the language *i.e.* dialect. According to Otto Jesperson, a famous linguist, the main reason for the growth of a dialect from a language is not purely physical but want of communication for whatever reason and linguistic unity depends always on intercourse on a community of life. C.F. Hocket also admitted the significance of mutual communication and closeness amongst various branches and areas of the language group to be at the root of the language form and phonetic uniformity. Again an integrated language group gets divided with the political division of a geographical area, giving rise to separate administrative set up. The same language spoken by different groups earns separate distinct characteristics in different areas of such a divided language group. According to Leonard Bloomfield:

> "It is contained that under wider conditions, new political boundary led in less than fifty years to some linguistic differences".

Again, some sort of commonness in language gets consolidated when the area is under the same government and administrative set up. So Bloomfield says:

> "Apparently common government and religion and especially the custom of inter-marriage within the political unit led to relative uniformity of speech".

It has been noticed in our discussion on the history of the Rajbanshi community that the Dravidians or the Paundra Kshatriyas coming to North Bengal towards the end of the fourth century B.C. got mingled with a branch of Tibeto Burmese Mangolite group in the first century B.C. or so. They gradually became a uniform group facing the onslaught of Aryansation in language, religion and culture. In the process of Aryanisation, this coordinated people gave up their old religious belief and adopted the Aryan religion, customs, belief and culture; similarly, they accepted the Indo-Aryan language in place of their own language. Following the comments of Hieuen Tsang, the Chinese traveller, Suniti Kumar Chattopadhyay, after detailed analysis, has come to the conclusion that these people, the predecessors of the Rajbanshis adopted as their own the Magadhi Apabhramsa, the third stage of Middle Indo-Aryan by the seventh century. Magaddhi Apabhramsa, however, took a distinct regional form by their use in its phonetics, declension and conjugation. That this process of adoption and rejection started long back had its proof in the existence of some primitive features of Middle Indo-Aryan in the Rajbanshi language. The Aryan language adopted by the predecessors of the Rajbanshis followed the same rule of evolution of regionality as followed by Bengali in different regions with different characteristics.

But the political and geographical limitations did not allow this evolution to proceed beyond the Middle Indo-Aryan stage. In the nineteenth century, Calcutta assumed significant importance as a political, commercial, economical and cultural centre of Bengal and regional language of the areas in and around Calcutta, combined together gave rise to Bengali as a language of literate people, a language of literature too, with an integrated characteristic which has been accepted as the language of refinement, decorum and civility. The Northeastern part, on the other hand, lost its importance and glory as a result of which the language of the Rajbanshis, the inhabitants of the area also lost its importance and could not march forward in the process of evolution. This is why Rajbanshi dialect has retained so many features of early phase of Neo Indo-Aryan (NIA).

It is worth mentioning that had the principal part of Kamrup, *i.e.* Cooch Behar, Jalpaiguri, Rangpur been included in Assam instead of Bengal, then the evolution of Kamrupi would have been speedier, easier and smoother and it could perhaps develop as the language of literature too. This can be easily derived from the place and glory as noticed for the language of Goalpara and its adjacent areas. The language of Goalpara and a part of Kamrup district was Kamrupi as this part of the territory was included in ancient Kamrup. There was never any linguistic uniformity between the Ahom dominated East Assam and Goalpara-Kamrup region. Sir G.A. Grierson in his Linguistic Survey of India has mentioned lack of such uniformity. While discussing about Assamese and Rajbanshi, the languagte of North Bengal, Grierson said,

> "North Bengal and Assam did not get their language from Bengal proper but directly from the *West Magadhi Apabhramsa*, which in fact, may be considered as spreading out eastwards and southwards in three directions. To the North-east it developed into Norther Bengali and Assamese, to the south into Oriya and between the two into Bengali."

Based on this difference (variation) Banikanta Kakati, the noted linguist of Assam has called the language of Goalpara and Kamrup 'Western Assamese'.[4] Upendra Nath Goswami also has admitted this difference and marked 'Western Assamese' as Kamrupi. This implies that the language of Cooch Behar, Jalpaiguri, Goalpara, Kamrup, Rangpur, Dinajpur which was known as Kamrupi had the prospect of developing into a modern prosperous language had these areas been in a single political entity whether it was Bengal, Assam or Pakistan. Because it did not take place, the language of this vast area did not develop much and so many features of early phase of NIA are contained in it even today.

Acharya Suniti Chattopadhyay has commented that Assam was practically an extension of North Bengal, 'from its geographical position, so far as its speech and early history were concerned'. Dr. Sukumar Sen says,

> "Oriya and Assamese have intimate relations with Bengali. All three were the same language initially.... There is not much difference between Kamrupi dialect of Bengali and Assamese....

Assamese has differed from Kamrupi in the modern period because of inclusion of innumerable Deshi words."

The Assamese researchers have different opinions for reasons quite obvious. Banikanta Kakati has commented that the whole of North Bengal including Cooch Behar, Rangpur, Jalpaiguri, and also perhaps Dinajpur, should have been included with Assam..... if the territorial readjustment were to be made on the basis of linguistic homogeneity. For these obvious reasons the literature developed with the patronisation of Cooch Behar palace has been included in Assamese literature too.

Now let us cite the letter written by Naranarayan, the king of Cooch Behar to the Ahom king in 1555 which has been given recognition as the oldest Bengali prose.

"*Lekhanang karjancha, Etha Amar Kusal, Tomar Kusal Nirantare Bancha Kari, Takhan Tomar Amar Santosh-Sampadak Patrapatri Gatayat Haile Ubhayanukul Pritir Bij Ankurita Haite Rahe. Tomar Amar Kartabye Se Bardhitak Pai Puspita Falita Haibek. Amra Sei Udyogate Achi. Tomaro E Got Kartabya Ucit Hoi Na Kara Tak Apone Jano. Adhik Ki Lekhim, Satyanada Karmi, Rameswar Sarma, Kalketu O Dhuma Saddar, Udvanda Chaunia Shyamrai Imrak Pathaitechi Tamrar Mukhe Sakal Samachar Bujhia Chitap Bidai Diba*".

On the other hand, this letter has been claimed to be the oldest Assamese prose. Of course, this claim of the Assamese Pundits has not been accepted by the Bengali Pundits. Dr. Sukumar Sen's comment is relevant in this context:

"Separate clear cut characteristic of Assamese language was not noticed before the Seventeenth Century."

Ahom Raj's reply to Naranarayan's letter above is also worth mentioning. "*Likhanang karjanca atra kusal. Tomar kusal barta suniya paramapyati hailo. Aru ji likhicha pritibrksa seye tomar amar sahladet brddhik paya falita puspita haibar khan ji kahicha i got bisesh. Kintu tomar amar priti got ji hata hante ghatiche samaste jano. Seirup marjada byavaharat jadi rahiba falita puspita kisak na haiba. Amra purva abhiprayate achi. Aru ukiler sange ji sakal drabyadi pathaichila i sakal sabhat dekhaibar ucit na hay, kintu ji sakale ji hak acari thake a-niti haileo acaraniyak lai take niti swarupe dekhi eteke dibar poya aru samucay sei sei drabyat pravartaniya lokar dwaraye ji bujuva gaiche seirupe bujiba. Tomar ukilar sange amar ukil Sri Candibar o Sri Damodar Sarmak pathova gaiche; emrar mukhe sakal somacar bujhiba. Tomar arthe sandes'nadu kapad than gajadanta 4 ganthiyan 2 mona pahuchaba.* (Sak 1478 mas ahar din.") (Published in Asamvanti Patrika, 27th June, 1901)

While discussing about the similarities of Kamrupi with Assamese, Dr. Nirmalendu Bhowmick has observed that in spite of some similarities in regard to morphology, there is no similarity found from the viewpoint of phonology, although some common words are found in both the languages. Both the Bengali and Assamese Pundits have accepted the letter written in Kamrupi as the oldest prose form of their languages. It is, however, quite funny that the same language has unscientifically been called "Bāhe' in despise by some of the Pundits, as discussed earlier.

Professor Mohammad Abu Talib of Bangladesh, while analysing the political, physical, social, cultural and linguistic factors, came to the conclusion that the language Bengali has evolved from the part of North Bengal adjacent to Magadh.[5] Based on Suniti Kumar Chattopadhyay's views that Bengali has evolved from *Magadhi Prakrta,* it has to be accepted that the Neo-Indo Aryan has spread towards Brahmaputra valley and Assam from North Bengal only.

Nirmalendu Bhowmick has found acceptable reasons in this view. According to him the history of Bengali language and the stages of evolution it followed can be clearly analysed from the study of Kamrupi dialect. This is the reason why there are so much of similarities between the languages of Cooch Behar, Jalpaiguri, Rangpur districts and Goalpara, Kamrup districts. And for the same reasons so much similarities are found in the forms of songs, dances and other cultural traits of this vast area. Bhāwāiyā, of Cooch Behar, Jalpaiguri and Bhāwāiyā-based dance are the main forms of song and dance of Goalpara and Rangpur districts too.

Although some people have made attempts in recent years to give the name of 'Goalpariya' to Bhāwāiyā in Goalpara district, their efforts did not have much success. They have found it more confusing after the bifurcation of Goalpara district with the creation of Dhubri district, because the song has to be called 'Dhubriya' now if it is to be named after the district. The fact, however, remains that Bhāwāiyā is the form of folk song for the entire area as discussed. There are some definite scientific reasons behind the naming of any particular form of song or dance. It cannot be named after any particular place, because, in that case, the same will have to be called Kuchbihariya, Jalpaiguriya or Goalpariya, etc.

We can now discuss the distinctive features of Rajbanshi or Kamrupi language. The distinction between the literary Bengali and Kamrupi is based on four main aspects (i) Phonology (ii) Morphology (iii) Syntax and (ii/) Vocabulary and Idioms. According to Dr. Nirmalendu Bhowmick, analysis of a dialect means the analysis of characteristic features of pronounciation and determination of the extent of distortion of the actual form, wherein lies the regional characters. From the viewpoint of phonology the characteristics of North Bengal dialect are worthmentioning. From the view point of morphology, the distortion or change in colloquial Bengali is vital. The post positional words which were in use in ancient and middle ages but not used in modern Bengali, the forms of cases and inflexion which are used only in poems and are not prevalent in colloquials, the words, syntax, idioms and indeclinables which though available sometimes in the chaste and refined Bengali, are not prevalent in every day use—all such charactristics are available in Kamrupi dialect. It follows from the above that this dialect has intimate relation with the ancient and middle Bengali.

Widespread characteristic use of words, indeclinables and idioms is the unique feature of this dialect. Too much use of sonorous/resounding words is another characteristic. The tendency of using nasals on sonorous words, change of meaning of some known *Tatsama words* (words equivalent to Sanskrit) and derivatives from Sanskrit are specially noticed in this dialect. Numbers of words of this dialect are *Semi-tatsama* (words equivalent to Sanskrit getting corrupt by virtue of pronounciation) and derivatives from Sanskrit. There are, of course, some Desi, Arabic-Persian and Hindi words. Some Bodo words are also there in the dialect. Phonological distinctions:

(*i*) In the process of evolution, Bengali has reached the stages of epenthesis and anaptyxis. But in case of North Bengal dialect this has hardly been reached although epenthesis is found in limited cases. Anaptyxis is also rarely noticed. This means that the vowels of earlier stages have remained unchanged. For example, 'Kalye' in Sanskrit, 'Kalling' in Prakrt, 'Kāli' in ancient and middle Bengali, 'Kāil' in Bengali and 'Kal' in Raḍhi. The word has remained 'Kāli' in Kamrupi.

(*ii*) Although the number of phoneme (vowels and consonants) is same in both Bengali and Kamrupi, their distribution is not the same in Kamrupi. In Bengali, Ra and La-these two phonemes are found in all the three places of word *i.e.* initial, medial and final but in Kamrupi these two phonemes are often absent in initials. In Kamrupi, initial 'Ra' is represented by the vowel associated with it and 'La' is represented by 'Na'. Examples:

Bengali	**Kamrupi**
Rājya	*Āijya*
Rākshas	*Āikshos*
Ras	*As*
Lajjā	*Naijjā*
Lāl	*Nāl*

There is a very popular joke on the pronounciation of 'ra' as 'a'. "Ājā Ājā Tomār Kapālot Kyāne Akta, Noāy Āni Noāy Oṭā Ang Ang." O king, I find some bloodstains on your forehead. O queen, it is not blood but a colour.

But some times 'a' is pronounced as 'ra'. There is a popular joke on this also. "*Ām Ṭhākurer Bāri Genu Rām Khābār Rāśe. Seo Rām Rāgālot Rādā kācā Rādā Pākā.*" (I went to the house of Ram Thakur to eat mango. That mango on the top of the tree was half ripe).

The other examples in this category are: *Aghaṭan* > *Raghaṭan*; *Abhiśāp* > *Rabhiśāp*; *Abatār* > *Rabatār*. *Akshar* > *Rakshar*, etc.

(*iii*) Initial 'a' in the word is often pronounced as lengthened 'a' *i.e.* 'ā'. This lengthened 'a' is articulated as inbreathing aspiration. In the process of articulation and inbreathing, 'a' sounds like 'h' (on way to aspiration). For example:

Akāran > *Ākāran* > *Āhkāran; Parān* > *Pārān* > *Pāhrān*
Abhāgini > *Ābhāgini* > *Āhbhāgini; Kathā* > *Kahthā; Sagāy* > *Sāgāy* > *Sāhgāy*
Ancal > *Āncal* > *Āhncal, etc.*

This characteristic is specially noticed in the articulation of expressive words of Bhāwāiyā songs.

(*iv*) 'A' sound gets different characters because of inbreathing aspiration.

For example:

'A' becomes 'a' in some cases;
Kathā > *Kahthā* > *Kāthā*
Kalāi > *Kahlāi* > *Kālāi; Hatās* > *Hahtās* > *Hātās*
Panjār > *Pānjār; Sandhyā* > *Sāinjhā*, etc.

(*v*) 'A' often becomes 'O'. For example- *Abhāgini* > *Obhāgini; Parān* > *Porān; Gandhāy* > *Gondāy; Sandhāy* > *Sondāy*

(*vi*) Again 'ā' becomes 'a' and 'o' sometimes.

For example:

Pāntā > *Pantā; Māngā* > *Mangā; Māsi* > *Mosi; Sāvan* > *San; Duār* > *Duor.....*

(*vii*) 'ā' sometimes gets obliterated. For example:

Ghrinā > *Ghin; Cinā* > *Cin; Diśā* > *Diś....*

(*viii*) Similarly, the vowels e, i, o, u, ou undergo changes. Examples of such cases are given below:

'i' to 'e' : *Sindur* > *Sendur; Hindu* > *Hendu; Him* > *Hem*
'u' to 'i' : *Pākud* > *Pākidi; ājuli* > *ājili* (affectionate)
'u' to 'ru' : > *Udāsini* > *Rudāsini; Uttar* > *Ruttar; Upāy* > *Rupāy*
'e' to 'ae' : *Deben* > *Dāeben; Rel* > *āel; Cetan* > *Cāetan; Chedan* > *Chāeon*
'e' to 'i' : *Siben* > *Sibin; Nripen* > *Nipin* > *Nirpin*
'e' to 'o' : *Nārikel* > *Nārikol*
'i' to 'u' — *Maric* > *Maruc; Pulis* > *Pulus; āśirbad* > *āśurvad; Kalmi* > *Kalmu*
'o' to 'a' : *Komar* > *Kamar* > *Kamor; Corā* > *Carā; Golām* > *Galām; Dhokrā* > *Dhakrā; Sona* > *Sanā; Kodāl* > *Kadāl*, etc. (particularly in Jalpaiguri district)

'o' to'u' : *Kon > Kun; Kaṭhor > Kaṭhur; Kokil > Kukil > Kukilā.*
'Ou' to 'a': *Coukidār > Cakidār*
'Ou' to 'u': *Poush > Push*
'Ou' to 'ai': *Gourav > Gairav; Jouvon > Jaivon*
Sometimes the vowel 'ri' becomes 'air', 'iri', 'ir', 'o'

For example: *Grihastha > Gāirhastha; Srijan > Sirjan > Sijjan*

Trisnā > Ṭirsa; Brikṣa > Birikh; Jāmātrik > Jāoin

Vowels in contact and residual vowels do show some special characteristic behaviour in this dialect.

Prabhātu > Pahātu > Poātu; Lom > Loā> Noyā
Gubaka > Guāā > Guā (betel nut); *Kup > Kuā > Cuā*
Bidhavā > Biduvā > Biduā (Widow); *Pānikaudi > Pānikoādi*
Debar > Devrā > Deor (brother-in-law); *Devbār > Deovār* (sunday)
Jival > Jial > Jiol; Kak + uā = Kaauā > Kāuā (crow)

Dipthongisation is a special feature of this dialect:

a + i = ai, Example : *Karil > Kail, Maril > Mail*
Mahishpāl > Mahishāl > Maishāl (Buffalo-keeper), *Sarishā > Saisshā*
Pahilā > Pailā, Kabutar > Kautar > Kaitar (Pigeon)
a + u = au, Examples : *Rahuk > Rauk, Mayur > Maur*
Navtan > Nautan

Sometimes one of the vowels in contact get changed instead of dipthongisation:

a + o = ao, *Nava > Naa > Nao*
ā + a = āo, *Mātā > Mā > Māo, Gātra > Gāta > Gā > Gāo*
Tāpa > Tā > Tāo, Rāva > Rā > Rāo (speak), *Pāda > Pā > Pāo*
Nāva = Nāa = Nāo (Boat), *Śāpa > Śā > Śāo* (Curse)
i + a = u, *Ghrita > Ghia > Ghiu*

This dialect has got some special characteristics of consonantal articulation. There is a tendency towards aspiration. Incidence of changes in place of articulation in series or class of the consonants is quite high. Assibilisation, cerebralisation and nasalisation are also quite common. Articulation of 'ca' and 'ja' of this dialect is particularly important. 'C' is not pronounced as Ch or tch; similarly aspirated 'c' *i.e.* ch takes the sound of 's' (mute aspirated, fricative). 'J' is pronounced as dz or z and 'jh' as depressed dzh.

Some distinct examples:

Caukidār > Cakidār > Cakhidār,
Jāygā > Jāgā > Jāghā; Kuā > Cuā; Khosā > Cosā > Cocā > Cochā

Kit > Kyārā > Cyārā; Jwālā > Jhāla; Dasjan > Dajjan > Dajjhan
Donajane > Donojhane; Kācuā > Kāchuā; Tal > Thal.

Inbreathing aspiration is noticed in the t-series, d-series and p-series of consonants:

Katā > Kathā; Panta > Pantha; Jantranā > Janthanā
Udāsi > Udhāsi; Bāudiā > Bāudiā > Bāudhiyā
Pekham > Phyākam (Peacock tail); Alpa > Alpho; Galpa > Galpho
Bāsā > Bhāsā, Beś > Bheś, Khabar > Khapar

Articulation of the semi-vowel (y) as 'ai' and sometimes as 'i' is an important feature of the dialect-

Kaylā > Kailā; Paylā > Pailā; Maylā > Mailā; Paysā > Paisā > Pāisā

In some cases (y) gets obliterated:

Jāygā > Jāgā; Bayas > Bas

Following the principles of Magadhi Apabhramsa, l often becomes 'n'.

Lāl > Nāl; Lāu > Nāu; Lāngal > Nāngal

All three 'S' i.e. Ś, Ṣ, and S are pronounced as (S) in the dialect as in the standard colloquial Bengali (SCB). 'S' however, is sometimes pronounced as 'C'

Śāvan > Śāvon > Chāvon; Sajāru > Chedā; Satya > Sacā > Chācā; Snān > Sinān > Chinān > Chān.

Another main characteristic of this dialect is gemination of consonants-

Buke > Bukke; Sukhe > Sukkhe,
Prajā > Parjā > Pajjā; Hāti > Hātti; Kalkātā > Kailkāttā
Pradhān > Pardhān > Paddhān; ĀĀlāp > Āllāp; Rasātal > Assātal

Changes in vowels and consonants in this dialect thus follow some special rules:

Anaptyxis: Introducing the vowels a, e, i, o, u in-between to ease the pronounciation of compound conjunction.

Mard > Marad; Śarm > Śaram
Kriyā > Kiriyā; Harsh> Harish; Barsh > Barish
Snān > Sinān; Srijan > Sirjan; Sloka > Chollok
Sukra > Sukur; Ushma > Ushum; Pākhnā > Pākhenā
Gāmchā > Gāmochā

In some cases initial 'r' in compound consonants follows the case of anaptyxis

Krodh > Korodh; Grām > Gārām; Prem > Perem > Pem; Prajā > Parjā > Pajā; Pratham > Partham; Brahmacāri > Barhamcāri

Vowel harmony: *Khesāri > Khisiri; Maśāri > Muśuri; Sonā > Sanā; Śobhā > Śabhā.*

Epenthesis:

Geli > Geil; Bāhir > Bāir; Maliān > Mailān; Kalijā > Kailjā
Cāri > Cāir; Khalisā > Khailsā; Bhāsurāni > Bhāusāni
Hādiāni > Hāidāni; Sādhu > Sāudh; Anya > Ainya; Janya > Jainya; Ajna > Aijna; Sandhyā > Sainjhā

Umlaut: There is virtually no case.

Prothesis: Occurence of prothesis only in a few cases.

Binā > ābāne (without); *Tultul > ātultul* (soft)

Aphesis: There is hardly any case of aphesis.

Apocope and Syncope: Incidence of apocope and sýncope is, however, quite high. In fact these are special characteristics of this dialect-

Alābu > Lāu > Nāu
Karila > Karil; Khāila > Khāil; Gela > Geil; Dharila > Dharil; āsila > āsil > āil
Ṭhākuri > Ṭhākri (pulses); *Tāmāsā > Tāmsā; Dotorā > Dotrā; Dārogā > Dārgā*

Kumurā > Kumrā; Chukuri > Chukri; Bāburi > Bābri

Introduction of 'i' and 'e' in- between is worthmentioning in this connection.

Mākdi > Mākidi; Nātni > Nātini; Pāgli > Pāgili
Ghāgrā > Ghāgerā; Cāmrā > Cāmerā; Chyāblā > Chyābelā
Pāglā > Pāgelā; Pātlā > Pātelā; Kātlā > Kātelā

Assimilation:

Progressive	Regressive
Ātmā > Āttā	*Dharma > Dhamma*
Sambandha > Samanda	*Kharcā > Khaccā*
Padma > Padda	*Bharti > Bhatti*
Bākya > Bāikka	*Gharjāmāi > Gharjāoin*
Rājya > āijjya	*Corni > Conni > Cunni*
	Hordyākh > Hoddyākh

Sometimes 'r' in compound consonant cases changes into the consonant following it: For example:

'rn' into 'nn', 'rs' into 'ss', etc. *Purnimā > Punnimā; Kursā > Kussā; Torsā > Tossā; Barshā > Bashshā > Bassā; Kārtik > Kāttik; Durbā > Dubbā; Dharlā > Dhallā.*

Dissimilation: *Lilā > Nila; Lāl > Nāl; Lālasā > Nyāloc; Śarir > Śaril; Jarur > Jaruri > Jarul*

Metathesis: *Jyotsnā > Jonāk; Bugcā* (Turkish) > *Bockā; Box > Bāksa > Bāsko; Māmsa > Masong; Jhongolā > Jholā > Jholongā; Nokṭo > Noṭko; Uṭkon > Ukṭon; Gobisṭhā > Ghaisā; Mahish > Bhais*

Haplology: *Galpa > Gappo > Gap; Bābā > Bā; Bābāhe > Bāhe; Cauparrāti > Cauparāti*

Voiced: *Kāk > Kāg > Kāgā; Śakun > Śagun; Sakal > Sagul*

Unvoiced: *Rāg > āk; Jog > Jok; Khārāb > Khārāp; Gulāb > Gulāp*
Bishub > Bishumā; Coksu > Cokh > Coukh

Aspirated: *Stabak > Thokā; Puccha > Ficā; Barkar > Bhokrā* (he-goat)
Bāsā > Bhāsā; Jakhan > Jhakhan; Jyālā > Jhyālā; Jeman > Jhyāman; Je > Jhe > Jhāy; Jato > Jhato

Unaspirated: *Byāghra > Bāgh > Bāg; Lāṭhi > Nāṭi; Gusṭhi > Gusṭi*
Kathā > Katā; Bāchā > Bācā; Sāthe > Sāte; Māthā > Mātā
Mejhe > Mājiā; āndhār > āndār; Śṛnkhal > Śikol; Śobhā > Śobā

Assibilisation: *Khāinchu > Khāinsu; Paṭāiche > Paṭāise; Nāgāiche > Nāgāise*
Nāgiche > Nāgise; Śobāiche > Śobāise

Nasalisation: *Hamsa > Hāns; Panka > Pānk > Pyānk*

Spontaneous Nasalisation: *Pecak > Pyāncā; Pad > Pāo > Pāon*

Cerebralisation (Spontaneous): *Daksin > Ḍāin; Tirjok > Ṭyārā; Dansak > Ḍāns; Dārimba > Ḍālim; Danḍa > Ḍanḍa; Danḍabat > Ḍanḍabat.*

Morphological Distinctions

Two main factors playing vital role in the morphology and variations of words in this dialect are (i) formative affixes (ii) inflexions and cases.

Affixes: Nouns, Verbal nouns and Adjectives are formed by adding the 'Kṛt' affixes with the roots (verbs). For example:

Āi > Jhār + āi = Jhārāi; Mār + āi= Mārāi; Nar + āi = Narāi
Āit > Syāb + āit = Syābāit
Āni > Fir + āni = Firāni; Ghur + āni = Ghurāni
Āiyā > Dyākh + āiyā = Dyākhāiyā; Dho + āiyā = Dhoyāiyā
Āru > Jujh + āru = Jujhāru, Ḍub + āru = Ḍubāru
Iyā > Byācā + iyā = Byācāiyā, Carā + iyā = Carāiyā
Urā > Hāg + urā = Hāgurā; Mut + urā = Muturā
Oāl > Gār + oāl = Gāroāl; Ghāṭ + oāl = Ghāṭoāl

Ti > Uṭh + ti = Uṭhti; Kam + ti = Kamti
Ri > Ghyāngā + ri = Ghyāngāri; Ḍoḍā + ri =Ḍoḍāri; Sosā + ri = Sosāri
I > Nyādā + i = Nyādāi; Gurā + i = Gurāi; Gochā + i = Gochāi

'Taddhit' affixes when added to noun and adjective form noun, verbal noun or adjective,

Ā > Pascim + ā = Pascimā; Bhaṭi + ā = Bhaṭiā; Haldi + ā = Haldiā
Āti > Cāul + āti = Cāulāti; Hākim + āti = Hākimāti
Ā āni > Ṭhyāng + āni = Ṭhyāngāni; Nāk + āni =Nākāni
Ār > Bādi + ār = Bādiār; Muci + ār = Muciār
Āru > Bāgh + āru = Bāghāru; Budh + āru = Budhāru

Persian affixes:

Khor > Hārām + khor = Hārāmkhor; Casom + khor = Casomkhor; Ghush + khor = Ghushkhor;

Dār > Caki + dār = Cakidar; Bāinā + dār = Bāinādār; Gāyan + dār = Gāyandār

Deśi affixes:

Kāṭā > Cyāderā + kāṭā = Cyāderākāṭā
Pārā > Nādān + pārā = Nādānpārā; Khāngṭiā + pārā = Khāngṭiāpārā
Nāgā > Sorpoṭā + nāgā = Sorpoṭānāgā; Cyāmurā + nāgā = Cyāmurānāgā
Bāri > Garu + bāri = Garubāri; Pātār + bāri = Pātārbāri
Muā > Māiyā + muā = Māiyāmuā; āndār + muā = āndārmuā
Haṭi > Dhān + hāṭi = Dhānhāṭi; Kāur + hāṭi = Kāurhāṭi; Guā + hāṭi = Guāhāṭi

The prefixes used in the formation of words of this dialect:

Ni > Ni + Lāj = Nilāj; Ni + Puttiri = Niputtiri; Ni + Māyā = Nimāyā
A > A + Kumāri = Akumāri........... A case of pleonastic use
Sā + Bālok = Sābālok; Hā + Bhātiā = Hābhātiā

Declension: Variations in Noun

Noun in the dialect gets changed on the basis of cases, inflexions and number and sometimes gender too.

Nominative: Without inflexions and with 'e' inflexions. For example:

Garu dhān khāyyā geiche (The cow has eaten the paddy)
Hānse dhān khāyyā geiche (Goose has eaten the paddy)

Accusative and Dative: With 'k' in words ending with vowel and 'ok' in words ending with consonants. For examples:

Jonākuk khābār ḍyākāo (Call Jonaku for meal)
Ābok cun diā āisong (Let me come after giving some lime to the grandma.)

Accusative: The Case is sometimes expressed without any inflexion. For examples:

Mui bhāt khāim (I will eat rice)
Maish carān mor maishāl bandhu (Buffalo keeper, my friend, grazes the buffaloes)

Instrumental: With 'dwārā' and 'diā' inflexions.

Inflexions 'dwārā' is used with the possessive case form of the main word; and 'diā' used without any inflexion and objective case form of the main word. For example:

Mor dwārā eilā kām haibe nā (These jobs will not be possible by me)
Mok diā eilā kām haibe nā (These jobs will not be possible by me)
Garu diā hāl bai (We cultivate the land with the help of cows)

Ablative:

With 'hyāte' and 'thāki'
Example: *Dyāoā hyāte barsan pare* (It rains from the sky)
Gach thāki phal pare (Gruits fall from the tree)
Konṭe hyāte (thāki) *āsilu*? (Where did you come from?)

Possessive:

With 'r' and 'er' as in literary Bengali; general rule is, vowel + r, consonant + er
Example: *Tor Bābār nām ki*? (What is your father's name?)
Gacher ṭhyālot pakir bhāsā (Birds' nests are on the branches of the tree)

Locative: By adding 't', 'ot', 'te', 'the'. For examples:

Nadit māch āche (There is fish in the river)
Gachot paki thāke (Birds reside on the tree)
Narenerṭe ṭākā āche (Naren has got money)
Jale Jale bhāsi berāi (We float on water)

Locative sometimes without any inflexion. For Example:

Bāri bāri ghuri berāi (We wander from house to house).

Discussion on preposition and post-position words is relevant in this context. A few post-positional words that were in use in old and middle Bengali and that ceased to be used in modern Bengali are found to be retained in this dialect. For example:

Āgot (in front of): *Mor ḍhyānāṭār dukher kathā tore āgot kaong*
Āre/āre (Across): *Bānśer āre āre berān re bandhuyā*
Ābān (Without): *Tui ābāne monṭā mor ṭikṭikiyā thāke*
Bagal (by the side of): *Gāo hākāi! hay bagalot basiyā.*
Badal (in place of): *Nadiro badalere bārite dhon gāo re.*
Bāde (for): *Tor bāde kainyā ghuriyā berāng.*

Byāgol (separate): *Bāpe byāṭāy byāgol khāy.*
Bhiti (to): *Byālār bhiti cāyyā dekho.*
Gor (Root, Bottom): *Kalār gore gore nāgeyā diche pāno re.*
Gun (For): *Kon gune nāgibe tor gān?*
Hāte/Hyāte (From): *Hāṭ hyāte mor janye ki ānichen?*
Kāinṭā (Vicinity): *Gharer kāinṭāt śuti āche*
Kāran (For): *Dharmay pāṭhāiche mok māṭir kārane*
Kul (To): *Dhallā nadir kule jāyyā dila daraśan.*
Kol (Flank): *Gadādharer kole kole o mor maishāl gān kare.*
Nagat (with): *Mor nagat nā paribu.*
Nāgi/Nāgiyā (Towards): *Rājār bārir nāgi karilo gaman.*
Pāk (direction): *Bārir Uttar pāke jor hansāy kāndere.*
Thāki (Since): *Kat khan thāki ghyānghyāner dhairchang.*
Tan (For): *Ām kāṭol khābār tane ghur ghur kari berāy.*
Ṭe: Morṭe, Uārṭe, Torṭe, Khokārṭe, etc.
Te (From): *Bhāle te bhāl āche dyāś ghurile dyākhā jāy.*
Ti: Kutti, Hitti, Etti, Otti, Patti – Patti dube śāluk pābu? (Can every attempt be fruitful?)

Characteristic use of hyate: *Morṭe hyāte, Torṭe hyāte, Bābārṭe hyāte, Kākārṭe hyāte*, etc.

Number: In this dialect, singular number is expressed simply by the noun or by adding 'ṭa' or 'khan' with the nound and 'lā', 'gulā', 'gilā' and 'ghar' added to the noun to express the plural form.

Mānshiṭā (the man), *Cyāngrāṭā* (the boy), *Garuṭā* (the cow). For Example:

Singular	Plural
Cyāngrāṭā (the boy)	*Cyāngrāgulā/gilā* (Boys)
Kāṭārikhān (the knife)	*Kāṭārigulā* (Knives)
Karim	*Karimer ghar* (Karim's *i.e.* Karim and others)
Nāuyā (barber)	*Nāuyār ghar* (Barbers)
Bāpoi (the little boy)	*Bāpair ghar* (little boys)

But sometimes, plural forms are made by duplication of words. For example:

Singular	Plural
Kāy (who)	*Kāy kāy* (who)
Ki (what)	*Ki ki* (what)
Kon (which)	*Kon kon* (which)
Jāy /jhāy (that/who)	*Jāy jāy/jhāy jhāy* (these, who)
Tāy (he)	*Tāy tāy* (They)

Gender: Gender is changed from masculine to feminine by changing 'a'into 'i' and 'u' into 'i' and by adding 'ni' or 'ani' with the word. For example:

Masculine	**Feminine**
Byāṭa (Son)	*Byāṭi* (Daughter)
Pāglā (Mad man)	*Pāgli* (Mad woman)
Burā (Old man)	*Buri* (Old woman)
Bhondā (He-cat)	*Bhundi* (She-cat)
Cākor (Servant)	*Cākorani* (Maid servant)
Myātor (Sweeper)	*Myātorāni* (Female sweeper)
Nāuyā (Barber)	*Nāuyāni* (Female barber)
Jonāku (Male name)	*Jonāki* (Female name)
Kālṭu	*Kālṭi*
Nālciā (Greedy man)	*Nālciāni* (Greedy woman)
Cor (Thief)	*Curni* (Female thief)
Dhaolā (White male)	*Dhauli* (White female)
Dhāgrā (Characterless man)	*Dhāgri* (Characterless woman)

Also there are cases of change in gender by completely different words. For Example:

Masculine	**Feminine**
Gāburu (Bride groom)	*Kainā* (Bride)
Dādā (Elder brother)	*Bhāuji* (Elder sister-in-law)
Golām (Servant)	*Bāndi* (Maid servant)
Bhātār (House lord)	*Māiyā* (Wife)
Soāmi (Husband)	*Banuś* (Wife)
Āju (Grand father)	*Ābo* (Grand mother)

Some of the words in this dialect do not have masculine forms. For example:

Sadhoā (a woman with husband living), *Bairāti* (woman with living husband who is engaged for reception), *Bidhuā* (widow), *Poāti* (a woman giving birth to child only recently), *Bhukāni* (a woman who lives on conversion of paddy into rice), *Cāulāti* (woman dealing in rice), *Molāti* (woman dealing in moa, sweetened preparation of rice), *Bokāli* (baby seating woman).

Number of Pronouns:

Singular	**Plural**
Mui/Muin (I)	*Āmra/Hāmrā* (We)
Uyāy/Umāy (He)	*Umrā* (They)
Tomrā / Tui/ Tuin (You)	*Tomrā* (You)

Given below the form of case endings, inflexions and number of the Pronoun 'mui/ muin' meaning I (myself) as an example of the morphology of Pronoun.

Singular	Plural	Re-inforced plural
Nominative: *Muin*	*Āmrā/Hāmrā*	*Āmrālā/Amrāgulā Hāmrālā/Hāmrāgulā*
Accusative: *Mok*	*Āmāk/Hāmāk*	*Āmrālāk/Āmrāgulāk Hāmrālāk/Hāmrāgulāk*
Instrumental: *Mok diā/ Mor dārā*	*Āmāk/Hāmāk diā Āmār/Hāmār dārā*	*Āmārgulāk/Hāmrāgulāk diā Āmārgulār/Hāmārgulār dārā*
Dative: *Mok*	*Āmāk/Hāmāk*	*Āmrālāk/Āmrāgulāk Hāmrālāk/Hāmrāgulāk*
Ablative: *Morṭe hyāte/thāki*	*Āmārṭe hyāte/thāki Āmārgulārṭe/Hāmārgulārṭe hyāte/thāki*	*Hāmārlārṭe hyāte/thāki Āmārlārṭe hyāte/ thāki*
Possessive: *Mor*	*Āmār/Hāmār*	*Hāmārlār/Āmārgulār/Hāmārgulār*
Locative: *Morṭe*	*Āmārṭe/Hāmārṭe*	*Hāmārlārṭe/Hāmārgulārṭe*

N.B: 'Gulā' in reinforced form is used to indicate large numbers. Re-inforced form of ablative and locative case is, however, rarely in use.

Verb-morphology or Conjugation

Verbs in this dialect take completely different forms from the literary Bengali. Particularly important is the manner of articulation and pronounciation of the verbal forms in the singing in this dialect. Given below the conjugation of the verb *Kar* (Do) as an example:

Kar:

Present Tense

	Singular	Plural
First Person	*(Muin) Karong*	*(Āmrā) kari*
Second Person	*(Tuin) Kar/karis*	*(Tomrā) karo/karen*
Third person	*(Uāy) Kare*	*(Umrā) kare*

Present Continuous Tense / Perfect Continuous

First person	*(Muin) Karir/karibār dhairchung*	*(Āmrā) karir/ karibār dharchi*
Second person	*(Tuin) karir/karibār dharchis*	*(Tomrā) karir/karibār dhairchen*
Third person	*(Uāay) karir/karibār dhairche*	*(Umrā)* (same as singular)

Present perfect Tense

First person	*(Muin) Karchung/Kairchong/Karichang*	*(Āmrā) Kairchi/Karichi*
Second person	*(Tuin) Kairchis/Karichis*	*(Tomrā) Kairchen/Karichen*
Third person	*(Uāy) Kairche/Kariche*	*(Umrā)* (Same as singular)

Sometimes 'nāig' is used in place of 'dhar', such as kairbār nāigchong in place of kairbār dhairchong.

Present Imperatives

Second person (general	*(Tuin) Tui Kar/ karek*	*Tomrā/Tomrāgulā karo/karen*
Second person (honorific)	*(Tomrā) Tomrā Karen / karo*	"
Third Person	*Umrā karuk*	*Umrā/Umrāgulā karuk*

Past Tense (Indefinite)

First person	*(Muin) Karnu/Karinu/ Karlung*	*(Āmrā) Kairlong Karilong*
Second person	*(Tuin) Karlu/Karilu*	*(Tomrā) Kairlen/Karilen*
Second person (Honorific singular)	*(Tomrā) Kairlen/Karilen*	(Same as singular)
Third person	*(Uāy) Karil/Kairlek/Karilek*	*Umrā* (Same as singular)

Past Tense (Probable)

	Singular	**Plural**
First person	*(Muin) Karnu/Karinu hay*	*(Āmrā) Karilong/Kairlong hay*
Second person	*(Tuin) Karlu/Karilu hay*	*(Tomrā) Kairlen/Karilen hay*
Third person	*(Uāy) Karil/Kairlek/Karilek hay*	*(Umrā)* (same as singular)

Future Tense (Indefinite)

First person	*(Muin) Karim*	*(Āmrā) Karmo/Karomo*
Second person	*(Tuin) Karbu/Karibu*	*(Tomrā) Kairben/Kariben*
Third person	*(Uāy) Kairbe/Karibe*	*(Umrā)* (same as singular)

Future (Imperatives)

First person	Nil	Nil
Second person	*(Tui) Karis*	*(Tomrā) Karen/Kairben/Kariben*
Second person (honorific)	*(Tomrā) Karen/Kairben/Kariben*	
Third person	*(Uāy) kairbe/karibe*	*(Umrā) kairbe/karibe*

Note: 'Tomrā' the plural form of 'Tui' is used to mean singular form 'you' in honorific sense. There is no use of 'Tumi', as in Bengali to mean singular 'you' in this dialect.

Future Perfect (will have to)

First person	*Mor karā khāibe*	*Āmār karā khāibe/Āmārgulār karā khāibe*
Second person	*Tor/Tomār karā khāibe*	*Tomār/Tomārgulār karā khāibe*
Third person	*Uār/Umār karā khāibe*	*Umār/Umārgulār karā khāibe*

N.B. 'Nāig' is also used in place of 'khā'. For example- *Karā khāibe* or *Karā nāigbe*)

The above illustration shows the characteristic feature that the verb changes with the change in number for first person and second person. This does not happen in literary Bengali. Example:

Bengali		Kamrupi (Rajbanshi)	
Singular	**Plural**	**Singular**	**Plural**
Āmi jāi	*Āmrā jāi*	*Muin jāong/jāng*	*Āmrā/Hāmrā jāi*
(I go)	(We go)	*Tuin jā/jāis*	*Tomrā jān*
Tumi jāo	*Tomrā jāo*		
(You go)	(You go)		
	Āpnārā jan		*Tomrā jān*
	(You go)		(Honorific)

Again, we get nominative objective in passive voice of speech in Kamrupi in the same circumstances under which nominative possessive is used in literary Bengali.

Bengali	Kamrupi (Rajbanshi)
Āmar dudh bhālo lāge (I like milk).	*Mok dudh bhāl nāge.*
Āmār khide peyeche (I am hungry).	*Mok bhok nāgiche.*
Āmār ghum peyeche (I feel sleepy)	*Mok nin dhariche.*
E sab kathā āpnāder bhālo lāgbe nā. (You will not like this conversation)	*Eilā/hillā katā tomāk bhāl nā nāgibe*

Compound Verbs

Using a verb as an aid to a verb with infinite affixes as in literary Bengali composes compound verbs. But the infinite affix 'ite' of literary Bengali takes different forms in this dialect.

For example: In place of 'ite' are used ibār, 'ibā', or 'ir'.

Example: *Mukh phuṭi mui kāndibār/kāndibā/kāndir nā pāong. Kadam Ṭhākur pujā karibār/karir mon chāy.*

The infinite affix 'e' or 'iyā' of Bengali takes the forms of 'iyā' or 'i'.

Example: *Mariā geise* or *Mari geise, Bhāngiā felāil* or *Bhāngi felāil, Khasiā* or *Khasi paril, Bujhia* or *Bujhi dekhek*. Bengali colloquial forms will be *Mare geche, Bhenge fello, Khase parlo, Bujhe dekho*; Bengali literary form will be *Mariā giāche, Bhāngiā felilo*, etc.

Conjunctives

Conjunctive 'iyā' of literary Bengali takes some characteristic forms in this dialect.

(*i*) Sometimes 'iyā' remains unchanged.
Kāṭiyā kalār pāt, bāriyā neo garam bhāt.

(*ii*) Sometimes due to vowel harmony 'ā' of the immediate prior lower vowel becomes 'i' and gets conjuncted with 'i' of 'ai' that is, 'ā' of 'āi' gets dropped.
Śukāiyā > Śukiyā, Bhirāiyā > Bhiriyā, Lukāiyā > Lukiyā, Ulṭāiyā > Ulṭiyā

(*iii*) 'Iyā'- often becomes 'i'
Kāṭiyā > Kāṭi, Kariyā > Kari, Hāliyā > Hāli, Pindiyā > Pindi, Basiyā > Basi

(*iv*) 'Iyā': becomes 'eyā' in some cases.
Helāiyā > Heleyā, Bārāiya > Bāreyā, Bhyālṭāiyā > Bhyālṭeyā, Pālāiyā > Pāleyā, Khasāiyā > Khaseyā, Becāiyā (Beceyā) > Byācey, Bānāiyā > Bāneyā

In a few cases, however, 'eyā' becomes 'ey':

Pālāiyā > Pāleyā > Pāley, Becāiā > Byāceyā > Byācey
(Kaināṭā pāleyā/pāle geiche), (Bāpo māy byāceyā/byāce khāiche)
Garāiyā > Gareyā > Garey, Khasāiyā > Khaseyā > Khasey
(Bidhātāy gareyā/gārey diche), (Jāmā kāpor khaseyā/khasey phelāo)

On some occasions, 'iyā' becomes 'ā' and with emphasis on vowel 'hā'

Verbs ending with 'h' and 'i' are subject to this.

Bah- Bahiyā > Baiyā > Bayyā, Rah > Rayyā, Kah > Kayyā > Kayhā, Cāh > Cāyyā > Cāyhā

Sometimes the use of 'ite' is noticed to convey the meaning of 'iyā'.

Kāti mās gelo kainār hāsite khelite; Ghare thākite nidayā māut āulāilen parān.

Only in rare cases, however, epenthesis is noticed in the use of 'iyā':

Hāliyā (Hāilā) paril sonār jaiban

Adjectives

Adjectives in this dialect follow the same principles as in literary Bengali.There are, however, some differences noticed in both the phonological and morphological characteristics. Examples:

Bhāl (good), *Bayā/Kharap* (bad), *Gulgulā* (very soft), *gyālgyālā* (Soft like liquid), *Dhaolā* (white), *Nāl* (Red), *Phārā* (Torn), *Moilā* (dirty), *Khamkhamā* (Plump), *Khirkhirā* (thick), *Khongkhongā* (deep), *Kambaktā* (worthless), *Khalāipeṭi* (woman having big bulging belly like a kholoi, a bamboo made long pot for keeping small fishes), *Jhālāpari* (talkative woman), *Dasāparā* (person in distress), *Pāniā_marā* (ill and sickly person with water bash).

Adverbs

Adverbs in this dialect represent and show the influence of Tibeto-Burmese (TB) language and other language groups.

Adverb of time: *Aelā/Aelāy* (now), *Syālā/Syālāy* (then), *Jyālā/Jhyālāy* (when), *Kon Byālā* (which time), *Āji* (Today), *Kāli* (Tomorrow), *Udinkā/Udumkā* (Day after tomorrow or that day), *Āgot* (previously), *Pāchot* (Afterwards), *Pach kari* (hurriedly), *Dināon* (on the day), *Saday* (Every day), *Nagote* (Recently), *āijkail* (These days)...

Adverb of place: *Eṭe/Eiṭe* (here), *Oṭe/Oiṭe/Oṭi/Seṭi/Seṭe* (there) *Koṭe/Konṭe* (where), *Jeṭe/Jheṭe* (where), *Etti* (this side), *Otti* (There, That side), *Jhitti* (that side), *Jhidi* (that way), *Adi* (that way), *Adiyā* (along that way), *Bhitarat/Bhitira* (inside), *Bāirāt/Bāirā* (outside), *Maiddhot* (in-between), *Āgot* (in front), *Pāchot* (afterwards)............., etc.

Adverb of manner: *Ang Kari* (This is how), *Kyāngkari* (how), *Jhyāng Kari* (that is how), etc.

Adverb of quantity: *Alop* (little quantity), *Byāśi* (good amount), *Āetolā/Aetulā* (so much), *Āetogulā* (so many), *Kạtolā/katulā/katagulā* (how many, how much), *Jhatolā /Jatolā* (as much as), *Āeknā* (one little), *Āetoṭā* (such a long one)........., etc.

Adverb of affirmation/negation: *Hay* (yes), *Hay Hay* (yes yes), *Nohāy/Noāy* (no), *āekebāre* (at a time, at all), *Saitye Saitye* (truely), *Michang Michang* (untruly), *Michay Sachāy* (mixed with truth and untruth).

Adverb of cause: *Kyāne* (why), *Kibāde* (what for), *Eibāde* (For this reason), *Seibāde* (for that) Compound form of adverbs: *Eṭe/Oṭe* or *Heṭe/Hoṭe* (here and there), *Jyālāy* or *Jhyālāy Syālāy* (now and then), *Itti-Utti* or *Hitti/Hutti* (heither-theither), *Jidi Sidi* (wheresoever), *Jyāmon* or *Jhyāmon tyāmon* (whatsoever), *Saug Samāy* (always).

Conjunctions and Interjections (Indeclinables)

Indeclinables are very importan in this dialect, particularly in poems and songs. Nā, I, Bā, Ki, Ar, O, To, etc..... are used as in literary Bengali. But they take the regional form. For example- Nā-ki becomes *Nākin*, Haile pare becomes Hāle pare..., etc.

Conjuctions:

1. (i) Connectives: *Āro, Ge, Nā, Bā*, etc. *Ām kāṭhol necur gach, āro dighir poshā māch. Totā kānde moynā ge kānde.*
Āshāro nā śāvan māse, deoā jhare madhu rase. Hāt dharong tor pāon bā dharong

(ii) Alternatives: Main conjunction is 'ki' to convey this sense.
Āsil ki nā āsil bar, kainā tui sitā pariā mar.

2. Adversatives: *Āro, Kintuk, Tabu, Tāhon/Tāo, Te, To, Nāten ki*, etc.
Tok ki āro kabār/kobā nāge. Tomrā kintuk jāiben.
Tobu/Tāhon/Tāo Kālār dyākhā nāi.
Nāi khāis' te/to/khāyā ne. Kāndibu to kānd.
Ghar āche to duor nāi
Dhān kāṭim nāten ki?

3. Exceptions: *Nāten te, nā hale, Jhadi nā*, etc.
Pāṭā ṭhik samay kāṭiben, nāten te śuki jāibe,
Nā hale tor kathā kāy śunibe?
Jhadi tui nā karis' biāo.

4. Conditionals:	*Jadi kāle, Jadi nā hay, Nā hale*.........., etc. *Jadi kāle jābār nā pān.* *Morṭe āsis, Jadi nā hay tor dhān.* *Nā hale tui ṭākā pābu nā.*
5. Concessives:	*Elā sene, Tabe sene*..., etc. *Elā sene bujhim re tor banduār mon.* *Tabe sene mok māinṣe cinibe.*
6. Casuals:	*Jei bāde, Je gone*, etc. *Jei bāde or je gone kākā mok hāṭ dhari geil.*
7. Finals:	*Jhon* or *Jhone* to mean 'lest' in English. *Mok jhon or jhone amon tyāngā kathā nā kais'.*

The most important conjuctions in this dialect are, however, used to express the sense of expletives. *Āji, Āro, Āeketo/Āekheto, Oi, Oki, Kibā, Ge, To, Nā, Nikin, Bā, Re, Śālār, Se*, He, Hay hay, etc.

Āji kaile duska furāy nā piritir ek augdā bhābonā.
Āste dhire maner kathā neo āro śuniyā.
Āekheto bāns bāriyā masā kāmrāile pare phonsā.
Oi āeke kathā hail.
Oki gāriyāl bhāi hākāo gāri tui chilmārir bandare re.
Ei bachar bhoṭot kibā haibe kahāy bara dāy.
Kairlā gārinu sāri ge sāri.
Bandhur bāde dehāṭā jāche to jaliā.
Ghughu nā pankhi hayyā oi ḍālot āchis basiyā.
Tui dekhek nikin jāyyā oṭā kāy bā āsiche.
Pāye bā ghungurā bāje re.
Dui jaivan mor bāndhā re āche santarār matan.
Tabu śālār pāji maśā berāy ṭāri ṭāri.
Bhāt rāndhilu bhāle karilu tui se pāner pati.
Tui more sundara he māmā, mui tore bhāgini.
Hāy hāy nāi jāon mui Gadādharer ghāṭot.

Interjections: Indeclinables are used to convey the sense of assertion, negation, appreciation, disgust, fear, pain, suffering, surprise, pity, clicks, etc. Such indeclinables are – *Hāy, Āccha, Nāi, Bā, Beś, Sābās, Chiko, Oki māo re māo, Āio, Āi ge, Mannu re bābā, Ki bā, Kunbā, Āhāre, Hāy re, Hui*, etc....

Some vocatives are used as indeclinables in this dialect. **Examples:** *Āeo bāhe, O bāhe, Her, Hyār, Hor*, etc.

Onomatopoetics:

Calṭung → Caltung mor dotorā re. Cikkit → Cikkit hāsi; Heiso → Heiso bārār bhuki.
Ghukkut → Ghukkut kariyā nāgil cāler bātā.
Khukkut → Khukkut kariyā bhāsur gharot kāśe.
Cuttut → Cuttut pākerā maidhyot bhyākerā.
Bhyār bhyār bhyāṭṭes → Bhyār bhyār bhyāṭṭes kari pail.
Ḍoloḍong → ḍoloḍong dolodong dotorā bāje.
Ḍyam ḍyama ḍyam → Masā, Pyāṭ konā tor ḍyām ḍyāma ḍyām kare.
Ṭorot ṭārāt → Hukā kare ṭorot ṭārāt.
Ghyāccor → Māch koṭe hyār ghyācchor ki ghyāccor kariyā.
Ghokkor → Ghokkor ghokkor khāl khuriche.

Articles:

Articles, the enclitic definitives commonly found in the dialect are *konā, kuni, kinā, kenā, kāni, khān, gachi, guṭik, ṭā, ṭi,* etc.

Konā – (To indicate small in size) *Mānsikonā, Garukonā, Chāgalkonā, Beṭikonā.*

Ta—Mānsiṭā, Garuṭā, Chāgalṭā, Beṭāṭā, Beṭiṭā, Bauṭā, Kaināṭā

Kunik— (To indicate smallness) *Kunik dhān* (little amount of paddy), *Kunik cāul* (little rice)

Kenā— (To indicate number) Ek + kenā=Ekenā/Eknā (one), *Duknā* (two), *Tin kenā* (three).

Khān— (In case of any objects) *Hātkhān, Piṭhikhān, Pirākhān Bārikhān, Kodālkhān, Kāncikhān.*

Gachi— (Found rarely in poems) *Bāro gachi guā re tor tero gachi pān.*

Syntax

This dialect has followed more or less the same principles as Standard Colloquial Bengali (SCB). There are, however, some special characteristics in this regard.

(*i*) Here the enclitic definitives when used with pronominal adjectives are placed after such adjectives but before the noun. For example:

SCB	Kamrupi
Ei kalamṭā kār? (Whose pen is this?)	*Eṭā kār kalam*?
Ei jinisgulā bhālo nay. (These things are not good)	*Eiglā jinis bhāl noāy or nāhay.*

(*ii*) In SCB indeclinables bearing negative sense are used after the finite verbs, but in Kamrupi they are used before the verbs. For example:

SCB	Kamrupi
Tumi bāri jeo nā (Don't go home)	*Tui bāri nā jāis*
Āpni e bhāve kathā balben nā (Don't speak in this manner)	*Tomrā eman kari kathā nā kan.*

(*iii*) Passive voice takes predominance in this dialect. Even in active voice, sometimes the verbs look like causative verbs. There is also a tendency to use quasi-passive voice even when the sense can be expressed normally in active voice. For example:

Cital base āri mok karāil bidhātāy (God made me widow in young age).
Kāṭhol khuṭār dotorā mok karālu janmer bāudiyā (The Dotara made of jack wood made me a born vagabond). *Bābri urāy bātāse*·(Long curly hair flies in the breeze)
Jaiban urāy mor pubāl bātāse (My youth flourishes)

(*iv*) In SCB the verb 'hay' (is) not used to convey the positive sense in the present indefinite tense. But this dialect follows the rule of English in this regard.

SCB	Kamrupi
Eiṭāi āmār bāri (This is my house)	*Eiṭāy hay mor bāri*
Dekhā dis nā re bandhu (Don't meet, my friend)	*Dekhā nā hais re bandhu*
Āmār jāoā habe nā (I cannot go)	*Mor jāoā habāṛ nā hay.*

Idioms:

From the viewpoint of idioms this dialect has got some distinctive characteristics. The speciality, variety and beauty of this dialect in this regard lie in its characteristic use of verbs. For example:

Ān: *Sukāru ekṭā āri āniche* (Sukaru has begotten a widow).
Eiṭā kaināk poshāni ānichong (I have adopted this girl)

Uṭh: *Ei kathāṭā śuniyā uyār āg uṭhil* (On hearing this he got angry)
Aman kari berāile kalanka uṭhibe (That kind of roaming around will lead to bad name)
Māthār biś uṭhil (Got a headache)
Torsā nadit bān uṭhiche (River Torsa is flooded)
Farki uṭhis kyāne? (Why do you get agitated)

Kar - *Mor khabar-e karen nā*? (You are not bothered about me)
Jadi karen sādhu parabās (Sadhu, if you go abroad)
Ebār pāṭā kariyā lābh nāi (Jute cultivation is not profitable this year)
Khār karite kainyā jāy nadir ghāṭe (The girl goes to the river ghat for soap bath)
Eilā niyā bhābā gunā karo (Think about these)
Uṭho uṭho prāner pati cyātan karo gāo (Please wake up, my dear husband)
Eman āengāpyāngā karen kyāne ? (Why do you resort to such pleas)
Bandhur bāri śobhā kare ām nārikal guā (My friend's house is beautified with mango, coconut, betelnut tree)
Māyer kām kairte melā ṭākā kharac haiche (Huge amount has been spent for the sradh ceremony of mother)

Dekhā haileo āo kare nā (He does not talk even on meeting)
Kirā kāriyā kayā geil (He told this on (oath) promise)

Kāt - *Burāṭā bāṭi kāṭir dhairche* (The old man is making ropes)
Āto āl kāṭis nā to (Don't give so many pleas)

Khand: *Kat dine khandibe maner dukh?* (How long will it take to get relief of unhappiness?)

Kha: *Kathāṭā suniyā uāy hātās khāiche* (On hearing this he got perplexed)
Ei kām karā khāibe (This work will have to be done)
Oi bāudiyā tor ghar khāibe (That vagabond will ruin your family life)
Bihār soāmi more manate nā khāy (The husband is not after my mind)
Dhyānāṭā khāli sodar khāyyā berāy (The widowed/aged unmarried one keeps on visiting his relatives)
Jadi jaiban khāite cāo, hāter khāru kiniyā deo (If you want to have sensual pleasure sex buy me the bangles)
Chengrāṭā mor pasan khāiche (I like the boy)
Ato saram khāis kyāne? (Why are you so shy?)
Dui bhāi āekeṭe khāy (Both the brothers live in joint family).

Khel - *Khel* is used to mean song and dance performance in connection with rituals.
Bhedoikhelā – performance in connection with *Tistāburir gān*
Hudumcuka khelā – performance in connection with Hudum rituals
Bāns khelā– Ei bāns khelāite jāy Kāmākhyā śahar.

Gar- *Ḍhyānāṭār bays gareyā burā hayyā geiche* (The dhyana *i.e.*, aged bachelor has become quite old)
Tānti bhāi śārikhān gareyā de (Weave the saree, O weaver)

Ghat - *Bandhui ghaṭāiche eto jwālā* (The boyfriend has caused such suffering)
Kātire, kon bidhi ghaṭāiche tor tanu? (O Kati, which god has made your body)

Ghur - *Ghur ghur ghur ghur ghurāni kaitor uriyā pare jāle* (Flying around the net, the pigeon gets into the trap)
Ghuriyā/Ghuri āsilen bāri (You came back home)

Car - *Maish carān maishāl bandhu* (Buffalo keeper, my friend grazes the Buffaloes)

cāp - *Je ghāṭe cāpāilen naukā oiṭe āmār dyāś re* (The ghat where you have anchored your boat is my native place). *Kāinṭāt cāpiyā baiso* (Sit on the corner)

Chār - *Bāghāy dhunduli chāre* (The tiger roars)

Chyāk - *Bhijā gāmchā māthāt diā maishāl chyāke dudh* (The maisal, with a wet towel on head, milks the buffaloes)

Jur - *Dui kuruāy juriche hāl* (The two *kuruya* birds have started ploughing)
Kainā juriche (The bride has been settled)
Sei nā jhāre bagulā jorāy bhāsā (The crane makes its nest in that bush)

Ṭān - *Goru bāri jāis re bāpoi gān ṭāniyā* (The boy sings while going to the grazing land)

Ṭuṭ - *Ṭuṭil piriti* (The love-affair is broken)

	Ṭuṭil Rādhār nām (The name of Radha got washed away)
Ṭhek -	*Bhagabāne hāmāk ṭhekāiche* (God has put us in adversity)
	Ghyāgir ghāṭot ṭhekāilen nāo (The boat touched Ghegir ghat)
Tul -	*Gāo tolo mor maishāl bandhu* (Maisal, my friend, get up).
Thak -	*Āmrā āekeṭe thāki* (We live in joint family).
	Elā āmrā thākir jāmo (We will go to bed now).
Tho -	*Bariṭāt māi tui kalong thubu* (You will give bad name to this house, my girl).
	Dhān cāirṭā tho. (Keep this quantity of paddy).
De -	*Ājār deoā hāṭ* (The market established by the King).
	Jamidārer deoā dighi (The tank dug by the zamindar).
	Tiner ghar deoā, Bhaiser dhurā deoā, etc. in the sense of making/building.
Bhakti deoā -	*Ṭhākurak bhakti deo* (Big pronam to the God).
Hāl deoā -	*Kono giri ok hāl nā dyāy* (No housemaster gives him tenancy).
Ḍākāti deoā -	*Kāy umār bārit ḍākāti diche*? (Who has committed dacoity in his house?)
Cheo deoā -	*Māklā bānś dilen cheo* (The makla bamboo is cut into pieces).
Jal deoā -	*Bāp māk jal deoā* (Offerings to deceased parents).
Dekh -	*Tok dekhong mui piritir bairāgi* (I treat you as the love-lord).
Dhar -	*Tor baini bhātār dharir geiche* (Your sister has gone to look for a husband).
	Mitar dharā – (To make friends). *Khoka mor biāt mitar dhariche.*
	Mok bhog dhariche (I am hungry).
	Tor buddhi dhariā ṭhāki genu (I got deceived by your advice).
	Chengriṭā ṭhasak dhariche (The girl shows the hottiness).
	Buriṭa cāul dharia hāṭ jāy (The old woman goes to the market for selling rice).
	Tor kalamṭā manat dhariche (Your pen is after my choice).
	Baiṭhāy nā dhare bhāon (The boat is not under control).
	Chaoāṭā kāndir dhairche (The baby is weeping).
Ni (Neoā) -	*Mor kathā ne* (Listen to me)
	Burāṭā bidhuā nibār cāy (The old man wants to marry an widow).
Par -	*Gāot pari kathā kay* (Shows closeness in behaviour).
	Mānṣiṭā nidānat pariche (The man is in trouble).
	Caukher konāt kāli pariche (Eyes show the grief). *Eibār uāy mor pāitot pariche* (Now he is in my trap). *Nindat parā* (Asleep)
	Bāij/Bāijon parā: (Instrumental orchestration).
	Mailān parā: (Getting stained/dirty or very old).
Dehā parā -	*Nā khāyyā dehā mor pariche* (I have become weak for want of food)
Pār -	*Sintā pārā* > *Kaināṭā sintā pāre* (The girl combs her hair)
	Māthā pāriyā hāṭey (Walks with the head down)
	Kāpor dhubār bādey nāri chekā pāriche (The woman has prepared *alkali* water for wash)
	Chiṭul bidhuār bāri ḍhyānā sodāy pāk pārey (*Dhyana*, the aged bachelor makes daily visit to the house of the young widow).

Bas - *Kāti pujā basāiche* (Has organised *kati puja*).
Ucā dātot nisi basāiche (He has used ink powder as dentifrice on the crooked teeth).

Bāndh- *Bhurā bāndhā* (To build the raft). *Duor bandha* (To close the door).
Mon bāndhā (To control the mind).

Mār - *Bhulki māri dekhā* (To peep into, to indicate).
Umār bārit khāsi māriche— (A goat has been slaughtered in their house).
Hāl māriyā dhān phelāo (Sow paddy after ploughing).
Sagāy nadi bāho (*māch*) *mārir geiche* (All have gone for community fishing).
Phākote mārilek majā (Got the benefit without any effort).
Jhakan kālā bānsit māre ṭān (When Kala starts playing the flute).

Nag - *Biāo nāgā* (To settle the marriage). *Hāṭ nāgā* (To organise the market).
Māyā nāga (To make love). *Galpa nāgā* (To start and continue conversation).
Bāo nāgā (To come in contact with).

Ha - *Gosā byājār nā han bandhure* (Don't be angry, my friend).

Haka - *Gāriyāl bhāi, hākāo gāri tui chilmāriṛ bandare* (O the bullock cart driver, move your cart towards chimari bandar).
Kāy hākāibe mor gāo? (Who will fan my body)

Simile

Use of simile in the day-to-day conversation is a special characteristic of this dialect.

Example: *Mukh āndhāri* – twilight.; *Khāṭāu Khāṭāu kathā* – Bitter words. *Byāng Sosāri Kāndan* – Weeping like croaking of frogs.

Kāchuā chaoā — Small baby (The baby crawling like turtle)
Dhai Dhai — Absolutely white (Sandy)
Nadi hail ekākul — In great adversity
Hāliyā pail sonār jaivan — The youth is going to be over (becoming old).
Dehār bāti nebhā — To die.
Pāror nākhān jorā — Lovers like a pair of pigeons.
Sāgarer kuṭā — In adversity (Floating like a piece of wood on the sea)
Chobā khuṭā — Useless life, as it is devoid of love (burnt wood)

Some words implying the meaning of adjectives, nominal verbs, and adverbs are often used as idioms.

Example:

Hāuriyā kapāl — Bad luck. *Āng sāng kathā* — Nonsense, Useless words
Hāuser din — Luxurious days. *Gulgulā* or *Thurthurā bura* — Extremely old.
Odorbhusi kāmāi — Unsystematic work. *Chanchanā gāvur* — Fully young (Full youth)
Kāl nind — Sleep leading to extreme adversity. Sun dufār — Noon, Midday.

Bidhir Bidhān — Destiny. *Byāceyā khāoā*-To give to marriage. *Guā kāṭā*—To negotiate the marriage.

It has already been mentioned that use of good many indeclinables is a special feature of this dialect. Certain semantic changes are noticed quite often in this dialect. They are:

(*i*) Elevation of meaning: *Hāluā* > the literal meaning of the word is one who ploughs. But this word is often used to mean 'husband' in this dialect. For example—*Mor hāluā bārit nāi*. (My husband is not at home).

(*ii*) Deterioration of meaning: *Akumāri* > literal meaning is not unmarried but this is used to mean unmarried girl.

Bhātārsuāti—Should mean one who is loved by her husband but the word is usually utilised to denounce a lady.

(*iii*) Restriction and expansion of meaning

Basantakāl—Youth (spring). *Cikan*—Beautiful. *Dui jaivan*—Breasts

Bhakti—Should mean devotion but the word is used to mean 'pranam'.

Nāri—means woman but this is used to mean wife or ladylove in some cases.

Nidhuā Pāthār—Solitary open place (ground)

Jaivan—Should mean youth but this is used to mean breasts.

Nāior—Should mean any relation but this is used to mean setting off for the parent's house of a bride.

Devi—Should mean any goddess but here it means Durga only.

Ghar—means room but here it means house as in Hindi

Śāk—means leafy vegetable but here it means any vegetable (Cooked or uncooked)

Naodāri: Should mean newly wed girl but here it means wife.

Apart from the phonological and morphological characteristics, large-scale use of indeclinables, characteristics of syntax, idioms and semantic changes, this dialect has a huge stock of vocabulary, which is to a large extent distinct from the literary Bengali. The vocabulary consists of Tatsama (sanskritised) words, semi-tatsama, derived words, some foreign words and large stock of indigenous (*deśi*) words including Boro and Koch-Rabha. A list of vocabulary is given in the Appendix.

So long we have dealt with the characteristics of this dialect so far as they relate to the day –to- day conversation. Since our purpose is to analyse the musical form of this language *i.e.* its lyrics, we must have some idea about the literary form of this dialect. The history of literature in this dialect centres round the history of literary words developed and nourished in the ancient Kamrup or Kamta Bihar and mainly the palace of Cooch Behar kingdom.

It has been admitted by the scholars that literary works in this region started with the translation works by the poets like Hem Saraswati, Kaviratna Saraswati, Harihar Bipra under the patronage of Durlav Narayan and Indra Narayan in the 14th or 15th century. The literary venture here got amply nourished in the 16th century under the patronage of the so-called Koch dynasty. The literary pursuit started in the 16th century was mainly related to translation of Sanskrit mythology and epics till the 19th century. The direction of this literary pursuit changed towards the end of the 19th century. Study of history, composition of ballads, lyrics, etc. replaced the earlier trend of translation. The most important development-taking place in this sphere was the active patronage and participation of the Cooch Behar palace—the participation of the princes and the princess' and other royal personalities.

"*Lekhanang Kārjancha. Ethā āmār Kuśal. Tomār Kuśal Nirantara Bānchā Karī*". etc. This letter written by the king Naranarayan to Ahom Raj has been given the recognition as the oldest instance of Bengali prose. The language of the letter written by the most powerful king of the Koch dynasty of Kamrup should naturally be considered as the example of Kamrupi or Rajbansi speech form or dialect. The usual expectation could, therefore, be that the growth and nourishment of this dialect would be intimately related to the development of literature in this region. Unfortunately this has not happened, so far as the first phase of literary development is concerned.

There is a controversy amongst the scholars as to whether the language of that literature is Bengali or Assamese. Dr. Sashibhusan Dasgupta in, 'A Descriptive Catalogue of Bengali Manuscripts preserved in the State Library of Cooch Behar' has included one of the two books of Ananta Kadali (*Mahabharat Rajsuya*) in the list of Bengali literature and the other (Bhagavat, Canto 10) in the list of Assamese. Mankar, Durgabar and Pitambar are known as Assamese poets but the language of the poetry in the introduction of Pitambar's 'Markandeya Purana' can hardly be considered anything other than Bengali. For example:

Mahārāj Biswa Singha Kāmtā nagare
Tār putra bhoge tulya nahe purandare

Ekdin sabhāmājhe basi Yuvarāj
Mane ālochiā hena kahilanta kāj
Śuno savāsad jan āmār manat
ākul haiche upasthit jena mat

Or

Tumi Iswari Gosāni, Trijagat janani
Jagat Pālan Samhārini
Habiddān Dever, Habiddān Pitarer
Dui Mantra Tumi Se Gosāni

The compositions and writings of Sankardev, the famous preacher of Neo-Vaishnavism in Kamrup have played vital role in the growth and development of Assamese literature. The comment of Prof. Kshetra Gupta in the discussion whether Sankar Dev's works are part of Bengali or Assames literature is worth mentioning in this connection. He comments— "Assamese literature has claimed on Sankardev. The claim of the Bengalees is much more on him" (*Puratan Bangla Sahityer Itihas*).

The reason for this controversy can be explained taking clue from the observation of Dr. Sukumar Sen, according to whom, no substantial difference has been noticed between the languages Bengali and Assamese till the middle of seventeenth century and Neo Indo-Aryan in Assam Kamrup was not different from the North-eastern dialect of Bengali in the sixteenth century. As such, there was no difference between the language of literature in Bengali and Assamese during that period.

During the latter years, this literary development took place in two streams—one in the form of Bengali literature and the other as Assamese literature. The observation of Dr. Nirmal Das is worth-examination in this context. The literature that developed in Kamta during the fifteenth-sixteenth century has been neglected by the Banglaees, while the Assamese have adopted them with love and care in their literary stock. This literature was the wealth of both Bengali and Assamese in actuality.

Two main courses of literary development of Kamta during the reign of the Koch dynasty were (i) translation and (ii) original compositions. First part included the translation of some poems including *Bhagavat, Ramayan* and *Mahabharat.* Original compositions contained *Mangalkavya, Panchali, Puran*, episodes from the epics, *Lila, Bhajan, Geet*, Drama, etc. The most widely translated subject was *Bhagavat Puran*. Incomparable genius and devotion of Sankardev was the main driving force in this regard. The "Eksaran Namdharma" preached by him was based on the doctrine of Srimad Bhagvat. His followers also aimed at the same. Madhab Kandali, Ananta Kandali, Durgabar and Mankar played a vital role in the translation works of *Ramayan*.

From the mention of various *ragas* and *raginis* in the 'Durgabar Geeti', 'Ramayan' composed in the harmonious (*payar*) and tripod metres during the regime of Biswa Singha, they appear to have been sung as Ojapali. The observation of Dr. Maheswar Neog in "Asamiya Sahityer Ruprekha" is also worthmentioning here.

> Durgabar, Pitambar and Mankar have composed their major portion of works in harmonious verse/metre. This metre used by them has the characteristic of music. Although rhyming has been used in their songs, the cadence and arrangement are irregular in places; the number of words are also irregular as they have to be guided by the necessity of metrical measure.

After the sixteenth century, study of Ramayan was postponed for long two hundred years for various reasons. At long last *Ramayan* became the subject matter of study under the direct patronage of King Harendra Narayan during the nineteenth century. The language of literature and mental make up of the people has undergone substantial changes by this time. This change has had its effect on the mode of translation. The observation of Dr. Asit Kumar Bandhopadhyay is quite relevant in this connection. According to him, the translation works on Ramayan here have not expounded the sense of complete self-sacrifice and devotion in its lyrical expression as in Ramcharitmanas of Tulsidas or Krittibas' *Ramayana*. And this is probably the reason why *Ramayana* has not become an all pervading popular subject in this region.

Translation works on *Mahabharata* commenced much later in the middle Bengali literature. During the same period, four cantos of *Mahabharata* (Sabha, Udyog, Bhisma and Drona) have been translated in Kamta under the patronage of the Koch dynasty. Six cantos—Kirat, Drona, Adi, Udyog, Bhisma and Gada have been translated in the seventeenth century, while the canto Birat translated in the eighteenth century.

Again, wide-scale translation of *Mahabharata* took place in the nineteenth century during the regime of Harendra Narayan. Among the poets of the sixteenth century important ones were Ram-Saraswati, Aniruddha, Gopinath and Kansari. Many have mentioned Kansari's distinction. In canto 'Kirat' of his work one gets the depiction of natural, social and environmental aspects of the then Kamta. Given below the manner of expressing the anger of Urvashi who has been rejected by Arjun in the episode Arjun-Urvashi as an example of his work.

In Vyasdev's description:

> "Ebamuktā Tu Pārthena Urvashi krodhamurchitā
> Bepanti Bhrikuting Kṛtwā Sasapātha Dhananjayam."

But Kansari's Urvashi has expressed her anger in quite indigenous manner:

> "Tuinre pāpiṣṭha āgam purān dekhās dharma āmāt
> Bicāri cāhile tiniyo jagate doṣ bā nāhike kāt.
> Tohār māok sati bākhānas jānon sabe jāti pāti
> Kanyākāle tāk sujjye harilek putra upajālye Kunti
> Pāche Dharmarāj Indra Devarāj tini bhaila upapati
> Bibāhitā chāri goṭā cāri panca Māo tor bara Sati"?

Such an Urvashi is not the apsara of heaven but a garrulous or foulmouthed village woman of Kamrup. This gives an idea about the language of Bengali literature, which has lots of similarities with Kamrupi or Rajbanshi dialect. In the seventeenth century, Srinath Brahman and Dwija Kaviraj were most famous among the translators of *Mahabharat* under the patronage of the Koch kings. Koch kingdom was in severe political turmoil in the eighteenth century and as such all the literary works got disturbed and suspended. As mentioned earlier, thirteen cantos of *Mahabharata* were translated in the nineteenth century under the patronage of Maharaj Harendra Narayan.

Poets more than one, have been engaged for translation of a particular canto and similarly one particular poet engaged for translation of more than one canto. The literary works during the period from the sixteenth to the mid-nineteenth century were mainly translation based but not mere imitation. The translation had its own characteristic and variety, having true allegiance to the original as well. The most important characteristic of this translation was that the poets were not moved and engrossed deeply by the Bhakti-cult (Ram or Krishna devotion). The original literary works of this phase consisted of Manasākāvya of Mankar-Durgabar, Bargeet and Nāṭ of Sankardev, Badh kavya (poems of killings and murders) of Ram-Saraswati and stories and eipsodes of Pitambar, etc.

Cooch Behar palace played a vital role in the literary development of Kamrup-Kamta. They not only played the part of patrons but also took active role in the literary works. We have had an idea about their patronage. We will now discuss about their active participation. The letter written by Maharaj Naranarayan has been recognised as the oldest example of Bengali prose. His grandson Raja Prannarayan was a scholarly person in Sanskrit literature and grammar. He was a poet, singer and lyricist. Literary pursuit of the dynasty took a new dimension from the regime of Maharaj Harendranarayan (1783-1839). Harendranarayan himself translated canto Sundar of *Ramayana*, cantos *Aishik, Sabha*, *Satya* and Santi of *Mahabharata, Skandapuran, Bṛhaddharma puran, Kriyajogsar* and composed original stories on princes, ghosts, etc. His achievement was particularly in the composition of Shyama Sangeet, Umasangeet and Agamoni sangeet. The songs composed by him are considered to be of high quality in terms of their music, rhythm and lyrics.

Two instances of his works:

"Purbe ati apurba jagat je prokār
Sṛshṭi kariyācha sṛshṭikar gunadhar
Sehimata trijagata sṛshṭi karo bidhi
Brahmāk emata bali prabhu kṛpānidhi
Se parameswar Gadādhar sehikshan
Haila antadhyān jnān gamya sanātan. (Kriyajogsar)

Shyama Sangeet:

Hāy tār ki śamaner bhay, mā jār Śhyāmā hay
Atul aprāpya caran tār, ki upamā hay
Kibā dibā bibhāvari, oi nām śaran kari
Antare birāje āmār, Śhyāmā gunadhāmā hay

Sri Harendra Bhupe kay, bhave kibā āche bhay
Ante jābo tārā dhāme, bājāiyā dāmā.
(Geetavali published by Cooch Behar Sahitya Sabha).

Harendra Narayan's son Maharaja Sibendranarayan also was a poet. One of his Agamoni songs:

Giripure ki ānanda haila, āmār umānidhi gṛhe āila,
Āmi ciradiner dukhi he rāj,
O cānd badan heriyā prān jurāila
Kahe Sri Sibendra Bhupe,
Āmār maner āndhār dure gela.

Maharani Bindeswari, the second wife of Sibendranarayan was a learned lady. She wrote the history of the then Cooch Behar (Behar) in poetry by the Title 'Beharodanta', which was printed in Kakina of Rangpur in 1266 A.D. A few examples:

In rhyming metre:

"Sarbakshan ei cintā hateche āmār
Behār bṛttānta kichu karite pracār.
Kharba kalebar mane candramā dhāran
Jena pangu icche giri karite langhan".

In tripod:

Nayan nirete andhā, dhariya sakhār skandha
Rāni jān kunjar gāmini
Bigalita ange bās, ghana ghana bahe swās
Dhulāy dhusar pāgalini.

In one of them she has given the analysis of the conditions of the kingdom:

Sacib jāhārā, dwande matta tārā
Rājya dike nāhi cāy
Prajār sarbaswa hare sab dasyu
Bicār ke kare tāy.

Although no Bengali work worth-literary values of Maharaj Nripendranarayan was noticed, his work in English "Thirty seven years of Big Game shooting in Cooch Behar, the Duars and Assam—A Rough Diary" was worth-mentioning. Maharani Suniti Devi, the queen of Nripendranarayan and daughter of Keshab Chandra Sen, one of the protagonists of the Brahma movement, was a famous literateur. She was writer of a number of books in Bengali and English. They are—Amritabindu, Sahana, Kathakatar Gan, Sisu Keshav, Sati, etc. in Bengali, and the Rajput princes, Nine ideal Indian Women, the Autobiography of an Indian princess, Indian Fairy Tales, etc. in English.

Maharaja Jitendranarayan, the worthy son of Nripendranarayan and Suniti Devi was a poet but he used to write in English. He had two books of poem to his credit—28th of February and 4th of May. An example from his Floods in Cooch Behar:

> "No need to bathe in 'Pukurs' too
> At 'Ghatals' gaily joking;
> Just walk outside your house, and you
> Will get a thorough soaking.

Prince Victor Nityendranarayan, the third son of Nripendranarayan himself was not a poet or literateur but he was deeply devoted to educative works. His library was a storehouse of large stock of valuable books, which included foreign books too. Cooch Behar Sahitya Sabha, an organisation devoted to the literary pursuits was established under his Chairmanship in 1915. His learned wife Nirupama Devi used to edit and publish a monthly literary journal under the title 'Paricharika', which used to publish writings and articles by Rabindra Nath Tagore, Kalidas Ray, Kumud Ranjan Mallik, Priyambada Devi and Nagendra Nath Basu, Akshay Kumar Maitreya, etc. She herself wrote three books of poem – Vasantamalika, Dhup and Godhuli. An example from her composition:

> *"Bauddha ār Jain tār rekhe geche padānker dāg*
> *Hindu rekhe geche tār silpajnān dharma anurāg*
> *Mārāṭhā khodiā geche āpanār birjabān jay*
> *Ḳutab Minār hethā Pāṭhāner kirti paricay".*
> (Indraprastha/Paricharika, 1st yr. 3rd number)

The Cooch Behar dynasty thus contributed a lot to the growth and development of Bengali literature, both by way of patronage as well as direct participation in the literary pursuits. Their contribution has been aptly described by Dr. Sasibhusan Dasgupta in his observation:

> "We get here valuable information about many hitherto unknown important texts and authors of Mediaeval Bengali literature and we have no hesitation in saying that no history of Bengali language and literature is complete without a thorough study of them".

He has further stated emphatically:

> "The Ruling House of Cooch Behar deserves respectful mention in the history of Bengali literature for the valuable contribution both as authors themselves and patrons to a large number of great and small poets. This effort of the ruling House of Cooch Behar for centuries was therefore not inspired merely by a literary motive; it was also something like a cultural mission of which Cooch Behar may well feel proud and for which all Bengal should remain grateful to the Ruling House".

From the aforesaid discussion, we get an idea about the evolution of literature in Kamrup-Kamta. The form and type of language, which was found in the translation works of this area in the sixteenth century, had some similarity with present day Rajbanshi or Kamrupi dialect. That language had gradually evolved into the literary/elegant Bengali in the nineteenth century. Of course, the second stream of this evolution has helped development of Assamese literature. But Kamrupi has not grown as a language of literature in Bengali. The probable reasons are that people engaged in the literary works after the sixteenth century had little connection with the common people speaking this dialect.

Biswas Singha leaned towards Brahminism immediately after ascending the throne of Cooch Behar and brought Brahmin pundits from outside the State to run his administration. This tendency towards Brahminism was intensified during the reign of Naranarayan. It is the outsiders who played vital role in the State administration and the development of education and culture. There was no system and arrangement for spread of education for the common people and as such there was hardly any scope for them to play any part in the growth and nourishment of literature and culture in their own dialect. This gives rise to quite obvious an issue—what is the reason fór such lack of relation between the kings and their subject, when both are supposed to belong to the same community- Koch-Rajbanshi?

We have had an indirect indication of this reason while dwelling upon the history of the Rajbanshis. We stepped into the doubt as to whether the kings and their relatives (who are usually called Rajgan) on one hand and the common people on the other belong to the same stock of people. This doubt gets further strengthened when it is noticed that the folk song form Bhāwāiyā-Caṭkā, the principal item of the cultural trait of this area has not found place in literary pursuits of the kings and their courtiers.

From the qualitative features of its lyrical sentiment, its language, rhythmic pattern, metre, cadence, etc., Bhāwāiyā is considered quite an old form of song, a sixteenth century material. Such a powerful form had, however, no place in the minds of Royalty, which was otherwise keenly interested in literature and music. The patronage of the kings and zamindars of other areas of Bengal in the growth and development of art and culture of that area is quite well known. The patronage of the kings of Burdwan in the growth and nourishment of 'Bhadugan' of Burdwan; similarly the contribution of the kings of Bishnupur in the nourishment of 'Jhumur'; role of the zamindars of Purulia in the progressive development of 'Chho' are establishmed facts.

But the indifferent attitude of the Royalty of Cooch Behar in the development and nourishment of Bhāwāiyā-Caṭkā, the highly powerful form of folk songs of this area is noteworthy. Cooch Behar kings had patronised and encouraged Indian classical music, composed Shyama sangeet, Uma sangeet but remained quite indifferent to a form of music, which is supposed to be their own, in terms of the anthropoligical principles. Respected Krishnadhan Bandopadhyay, the noted musicologist of that period was reportedly engaged in the study of music in Cooch Behar palace. Krishnadhan Bandopadhyay was one of those few who analysed Indian classical music in scientific manner in those days. 'Geeta Sutrasar' written by him is a testimony to this.[6] He had stayed in Cooch Behar for quite sometime but showed hardly any interest in this powerful form of song of the common people there. The lack of interest of the Royalty had its effect on the attitude of the scholars of the kingdom towards the art and culture of the common subjects.

It is, therefore, noticed that there has hardly been any use of Kamrupi or Rajbanshi dialect in the literature and poetry. The language has not developed to that extent. Good many features of ancient and middle Bengali are, therefore, still notably present in this language. It is, however, true that the language has not remained unmixed. Lot many outsiders have come to this region from the sixteenth century itself. They were superior to the local people in education, intellect, and economic standard and naturally the language spoken by them had influenced this dialect at least to an extent.

Moreover, with the development and improvement of communication with other parts of Bengal, the contact between the people of the two areas gradually increased and the influence of Bengali and Rāḍhi on the Kamrupi increased thereby. Particularly with the introduction of tea garden, spreading of tobacco and jute cultivation and trading in the eighteenth and nineteenth centuries, lots of people speaking Bengali and Radhi came to North Bengal for their livelihood and as such Kamrupi language got mixed up with their languages. These outsiders coming from other parts of Bengal are called Bhāṭia by the local people.

Mixing of language got faster as a result of partition of Bengal in 1947 with the independence of India. Lots of Hindu refugees from East Bengal (Bangladesh) started living in different districts of North Bengal. The difference between the people who came to North Bengal in the past and those coming after 1947 was that the latter have been compelled to come as victims of political game and not on their own accord. Moreover, they are huge in number and have had to settle not only in commercial hubs or economic centers, but also at various corners of the countryside. The mixture of language in Kamrupi has therefore been quite widespred since then.

There has been no proper development of prose, poetry, literature, belleslettres, essays and other literary compositions in this language and no proper advancement of the language itself, but its dialectal form has found place in its songs and ballads. The ballads of the then Kamrup have taken the form of various folk dramas based on Bhāwāiyā-

Caṭkā, as the main regional song of the area. This song being orally transmitted for years together with its intense music, rhythm and cadence has had all pervading effect on the folk life of the entire community. It will, therefore, be quite relevant to have discussion on the lyrical form of Kamrupi language used in Bhāwāiyā-Caṭkā.

As it happens everywhere, the form of language used in lyric, here Bhāwāiyā-Caṭkā, is a bit different from that used in everyday conversations. These distinctive features of language in its lyrical form deserve discussions at length. In 'Pranta-Uttarbanger Upabhasa', Nirmalendu Bhowmick has pointed out a few characteristics of the poetic (lyrical) form of this language. Nirmal Das too has mentioned a few of them in "Uttarbanger Bhasa Prasanga" and some other articles in 'Madhuparni', a little journal published from Balurghat, the district headquarter of South Dinajpur. The main features in brief are discussed below:[7]

(*i*) To adjust to the tonal (musical) need, 'O' is inserted in the end of the word. Example: *Bāp>Bāpo, Mā>Māo, Māch>Mācho, Hāt>Hāto, Dhik>Dhiko, Pānch>Pāncho, Chay>Chayo*, etc.

(*ii*) Some words most of which are akin to Sanskrit (Tatsama) undergo poetic transformation (distortions), leading to phonetic changes in vowel and consonants. Example: *Mṛttikā>Mittingā, Basumati Māo>Basomati Māo, Pāglā>pāgelā, Jauvan>Jaivan, Bideś>Baidyāś, Bhānu Bhāskar>Bhānu Bhāsankar, Ciradin>Ciraydin, Abhāgini nāri>Abāgoni nāri, Pākhā>Pānkhā, Māyā>Mayā or Mayhā, Malin>Mailān, Duksha>Duska, Mājā ghasā>Mānjā ghasā, Jena>Jone, Gaurav>Gairav, Seo>Syāo, Mayur>Maior, Raud>Raid, maric>maruc*, etc.

(*iii*) There is a tendency towards subsidiary determinative compounds and attributive compounds. Example: *Upapad-Tatpurush* (determinative):

Bābri chāṭā—Bābrir mato chāṭā cul; Gāburāri—Gābur (young) *je rāri* (widow)
Ḍāngdharā/Ḍangḍhārā—Ḍāng dhare je; Dasā parā—Dasāy (*Duhhe*) pareche je
Deuniā bhātār—Deuniā je bhātār; Ḍhyāngpari—Ḍhyāng (*Ḍhang*) *dekhāy je*
Ḍhongācāṭā—Ḍhongā ceṭe berāy je; Mayhā chārā—Mayhā/Mayā chāre je
Mon bholā—Mon bholāy je; Sitāpārā—Sitā pāṭ kare je.
Bahubrihi (attributive): Example-
Ādhā baysi—Ādhā or *Ardhek bayas jār; Do bhātāri—Dui bhātār jār*
Khalāi peṭi— Khalāir mato peṭ jār; Khopā culi— Khopā bāndhā cul jār
Māthā dāngrā—Ḍāngar (*Bara*) *māthā jār; Maishāl bhātāri—Maishāl bhātār jār*
Māiyā marā—Māiyā mareche jār; Nār pāniyā—Nārite pāni jār (sick)
Peṭ ḍāngrā—Ḍāngar (*Bara*) *peṭ jār; Sāngnā bhātāri—Sāngnā bhātār jār*
Uchal dānti—Uchal (*Uchu*) *dāt jār.*

(*iv*) Reduplication of words and their use in various ways is one of the characteristics of this language both in poetry and conversation. To indicate plural sense:

Barer gharer bairātir dhumā dhumā koṭi; Dhai dhai bālā.
Gadādharer pāre pāre kalā sāri sāri; Hāfā hāfā nāfā re tor ḍhāpā ḍhāpā pāt.

To indicate sense of repetition—

Bānśer ārāy ārāy; Ṭhamake ṭhamake hāṭong
Sadāy sadāy jāng nadir ghāṭe

Some compounds available with the reduplication of supplementary synonymous accompanying, deteriorated, onomatopoetic, etc. words are frequently used in poetry and lyrics:

Supplementary words: *Sāud Sadāgar; Ang tāmesā; sāk pātā; Naijjā saram; Bān bāisyā; Ṭhyāng pāo; Deo devtā; Ghaṭ gachā; Hāl girasthi; Urāng bairāng*

Synonymous words: *Gosā byājār; Bhay hāttās; Ghāṭā path; Bāij bājan; Dhārā cāṭi; Jhāṭā bārun; Sāgāi sodar; Jami jāgā; Jān parān; Aron jangol; Syābā pujā.*

Accompanying/Companion Words: *Myāgh myāghāli; Say sampathi; Pajjā pāli; Paki payāl; Kāmāi kāj; Pāt pāṭuya; Bhār bhārāṭi; Āś paraśi; Mānā cinā; Uddis khabar; Cenā jānā; Chaoā choṭo*, etc.

Counter words: *Dine āite; Michāy sacāy.*

Transformed words: *Cikan cākan; Khāṭo khuṭo; Khyāre kharite; Tyāle tule*, etc.

Onomatopoetic words: *Pāk sāk karā; Jhole jhose; Atāri pātāri; Jai jokār; Dhoi dhāmāli; Ghar girasthi; Gappo sappo.*

Words indicating resemblance: *Nul nulā; Sin sinā; Khāṭāu khāṭāu; Nyāret byāret* or *Norot borot; Sir sirāy; Gal galā* (*bhat*).

Words conveying reciprocity: *Mocrā mucri; Fāsār fusur; Rāoā rāoyi; Kushṭā kushṭi; Kyālṭā kyālṭi.*

Reduplication of participles as supplement: *Jhāriā jhuriā* (*bandha*); *Nukiā ghusiā; Hāliā huliā; Echiā bechiā; Iniā biniā; Nijiri nijiri*, etc.

Infinite verb used as denominative verb: *Hyār hyāreyā; Gyār gyāreyā; Dyāl dyāleyā; Harhari gargari.*

Particularly important among them are the words used as adjectives, adverbs, nominal verbs, verbal nouns, etc. by way of reduplication of imitative/mimic/ onomatopoetic words.

Adjective: *Jhakar-jhakar; Chan-chanā; Chil-chilā; Ṭing-ṭingā; Syām-syāmā; Cak-cakā; Ṭil-tilā; Ṭang-ṭangā; Fal-falā; Cal-calā; Gor-gorā; Jhyāng-jhyāngā; Kum-kumā; Chyāng-chyāngā; Ḍong-ḍongā; Hyādel-dyāl; Uni-jhuni; Hyāṭeng-ṭyāngrā.*

Adverbs: *Korot-korot; Kin-kinā; Pāṭāu-pāṭāu; Ṭāpus-ṭupus; Nāṭāu-nāṭāu; Ghokor-ghokor; Ṭong-ṭongā; Hirhir-girgir; Ṭas-ṭasā/Ṭhas-ṭhasā; Ṭorot-ṭorot; Holok-solok; Uluk-bhuluk; Cilāng-jhāṭāng; Āengā-pyāngā; Nāṭār-pāṭār; Horon-phoron; Ḍum-ḍumā-ḍum; Urāng-bāirāng*; etc.

Verb: *Jhanjhanāy; Phanphanāy; Dharpharāy; Ṭik-ṭikāy*

Imitative Nouns: *Thāng-nā-thāng; Dogdogāy/Ḍogḍogāy; Hākās pākās.*

(*v*) Another important feature noticed in lyrics is introduction of some indeclinables like *ki, re, ār, ge*, etc. in between the reduplicated word: *Bhyāṭṭes-ki-bhuṭṭus; Hirrim-ki-hārrām; Dirrim-ki-dārrām; Ṭippis-ki-ṭappās; Khari-re-khuṭā; Nātāri-re-pātāri; Sāri-ge-sāri; May-ār-maśalā*

(*vi*) The other important feature is the characteristic use of numerical adjectives in lyrics: *Ek-Āeko; Dui-Duio/Dono; Tin-Tino; Cāir-Cāiro; Pāc-Pānco; Chay-Chayo; Sāt-Sāto; Āṭ-Ashṭo; Nay-Nao; Daś-Daśo; Panero-Pondoro; Satero-Sotoro; Ekus-Ekais; Tris-Tiris; Eksa-Sa/Sao; Laksha-Laikhyo; Ādhā-Addek; Der-Ḍyār; Paune-Pone; Paylā-Pailā; Alpo-Alop; Beśi-Faik...*, etc.

In poetry and lyrics:

(*i*) There is frequent use of inflexion 'e' in nominative. Example – *Rojāy Jhāre Baidye jhāre dhekiār āgāl diyā; Bhātāre māriche dhari.*

(*ii*) In objective—accusative case, 'k' is added to both noun and pronoun simultaneously.
Mok nārik chāriyā kyāne holu dyāśāntari.
Tok sundarik pār karite khasāim kāner sonā.

(*iii*) Also there are uses of inflexion 'e' in instrumental case,
Khopote nāire kaitar ki kare tār khope.
Jhari nā haile ki karibe cāshe.

(*iv*) Use of inflexion 'k' in place of 'r' of possessive case.
Nā nāge mok jalṭopā nath. Nā nāge mok ṭisyā-bhok.
Hāt dharong tok pāo bā dharong.

(*v*) Unnecessary but quite spontaneous use of inflexion 'r'/'er'-
Āche to mor ḍālimer phal; Sundar nārir jaibaner miṭhā;
Tok pindāim mui rangcanger pāṭāni.
Dine dine khasiyā paribe angiyā dālāner māṭi

(*vi*) Sometimes 'e' is added after 'r' of possessive case.
Sonāre nāngal, upāre phāl; Eluyā kāśiyāre phul;

Mariyā kolāre soāmi, cital bayse hanu āri.
Kāṭol khuṭāre dotora, tui karlu mok janamer bāudiyā.

(*vii*) In possessive case, the same inflexion 'r' is added to both noun and pronoun to convey some special relation: *Mor nārir ṭyāriyā sitā; Mor ḍhyānāṭār kapāl porā; Bujhunu bujhunu tor bandhuār monṭā re.*

(*viii*) In locative case sometimes the use of 'e' is noticed in place of usual 't' or 'ot'. Guār gore gore nāgeyā diche pāno re.

(*ix*) Some adjectives of quality and condition conveying specific meanings are often found in the lyrics.

Relating to place: *Nidhuyā pātār* (Solitary open place); *Phul bindāban* (Beautiful brindaban); *Nālbājārer cyāngrā bandhu* (Highly evocative lover);

Relating to river: *Ujān nadi, Khirol nadi; Ciral nadi;Tufān dariyā; Agaim dariyā.*

Relating to trees, etc: *Khyāil kadam; Helāni kadam; Hekerā ḍālim; Śālmali-śimilā; Akhuṭā-śimilā; Jor-śimilā; Tarlā-bānś; Biru bānś.*

Relating to cloth, etc: *Kāuyā-rangi śāree; Lakshmi bilāsi śāri; Saru śākhā; Ḍhāluyā/Teriya/Hyadeldyāl/Nāser/Unijhuni/Gunjaribhomrā khopā; Hirāmon banśi; Chiri āngṭi; Naser kākai; Śyāmlāi dhuti; Manirāj pāgri; Hyāmtāḷer naṭhi...*, etc.

Relating to nature: *Maleyāy talāy bāo; Pachiyā bāo; Pubāl bātās/bāo; Śun duphor; Niśi pahar; Nadir basantakāḷ; Kālā/dhaolā myāghā; Dhai dhai bālā; Imi jhimi jhari...*, etc.

Relating to creatures: *Swet kāuyā; Kājal bhomrā; Jal śuyā; Candan kurusā; Gunjari bhomrā.*

Relating to human body and mind: *Cital bas; Kaṭur hiyā; Cikkit hāsi; Aser/Raser gālā; Maṭuk cul; Cyāngrā kāl; Nidān kāl; Cikan kālā; Nautan cyāngri; Naodāri; Dāruno bidhi; Dhāgerā; Dhāgiri; Sonār jaivan; Gālār kāṭi.........*, etc.

Miscellaneous: *Nidārun katā; Nabin bāṭār pān; Ancaler sonā.*, etc.

(*x*) As stated earlier, one of the important poetic characteristics of this dialect is the widespread and multi dimensional use of indeclinables such as: *Āji; E; Einā; Ainā; Oi;O; Oki/Aki; Mari; O Mari; Nā; Re; Bhāla; Ge; Ki Ore; Kibā; Oho; Kintuk; Nāten ki...*, etc.

(*xi*) In poetry and lyrics, there are some characteristic uses of vocative nouns particularly—addressing the lovers one-another: *Aser ḍhyānā; Kavirāj; Kālā; Gāburā; Bandhuyā; Guner bandhuyā; Cikan kālā; Cyāngrā bandhu; Pati dhan; Prān kālā; Prāna pati; Baido; Bāudiyā; Bāpoicyāngrā; Bhāberbandhuā; Sonār bandhu*...., etc.

(*xii*) In poetry and lyrics, certain specific terms are used for abusing or calling bad names: *Kambaktā; Khalāi peti; Gābur marā; Chāi parā; Jhālā pari; Do bhātāri; Sāt bhātāri; Dasā parā; Pāniyā marā; Bhātār suyāti; Bhātār jākāli; Bhātār-khāki; Hābāng-mukhā*..., etc.

As in other forms of folk songs of Bengal, in Bhāwāiyā also there is an intimate relation between the music (tune) and the lyric. This is the reason why lyrical emotions take completely different linguistic dimension through sound waves. The music instils or imbricates the intrinsic feelings and emotions of lyrics in the minds of the listeners and sometimes they act as the agents of making the minds free from emotions. In the words of Dr. Nirmal Das:

> In such cases music makes the factors of sound, particularly those of musical sounds that are intrinsic in the lyrics, audible through the process of adoption/suspension/delaying. That creates an emotional melodic environment. Creation of such melodic environment is the lyrical study of Bhāwāiyā, which can be identified as the musicological sub-dialect. Therefore, from the angle of linguistic identity, Bhāwāiyā is the musicological sub-dialect of Kamrupi dialect.

Viewed from this standpoint some of the distinctive features are:

1. Judged from the standpoint of musical and poetic qualities, it is noticed that in Bhāwāiyā, although there are sufficient musical qualities, the poetic qualities have not always been observed. In many cases, the principles of metre have not been fulfilled. The famous song of Abbasuddin on the bullock cart driver can be quoted in this connection:

Oki gāriāl bhāi katay raba āmi panther dike cāyā re
Jidin gāriāl ujān jāy nārir man mor jhuriyā ray re
Oki gāriāl bhāi, hākāo gāri tui cilmārir bandare re

In the matter of musicological expression of Bhāwāiyā, it is the melody, which takes the precedence and the nature of the tune ultimately regulates its lexicosphere. The lexicosphere of Bhāwāiyā consists predominantly of those words, which are more suited to tune/music in Bhāwāiyā.

Some degree of difference in the word stock used in Bhāwāiyā and Caṭkā is worthmentioning in this connection. The lighter and brisk form of Bhāwāiyā is known as

Caṭkā. Caṭkā is effusive with light joyous emotions from the viewpoints of both lyrics and music. Usually the words with greater sonic elasticity are used in Bhāwāiyā. The words which are amenable to change from the original roots and which can better adjust to the necessity of total arrangments are used in Bhāwāiyā. Generally the remnance of antiquity and torpidity (sluggishness) is noticed in the sound arrangements of Kamrupi dialect. In the articulation of Bhāwāiyā this torpidity and tonal adjustments are noticed frequently. All these imply that the lyrics of Bhāwāiyā are regulated by its music, its tune and the tonal arrangements.

2. It has been mentioned in the discussion that there are a good number of onomatopoetic words in this dialect. The same is true in the case of Bhāwāiyā, the folk song composed in this dialect. It is, however, noticed that the use of such sonorous words are much more common in Caṭkā than in Bhāwāiyā. Onomatopoetic words cannot express the desired phonosomantic reactions if adjusted/changed to suit the tonal arrangements and as such they are rarely used in Bhāwāiyā. Caṭkā does not demand that kind of adjustment, as it is embedded with brisk kind of emotions and movement with quick cadence. The use of sonorous words with consonantal syllables helps this briskness. For example:

Gāo hākāil hay kyārrot ki korrot kariyā.
Māch kuṭil hay ghyāccor ki ghyāccor kariyā.

3. Again on many occasions, certain hackneyed literary phrases (cliches) are used to intensify the pathos in the syntax of Bhāwāiyā. For example, to express the mournful condition of the deserted heroine:

Tolā māṭir kalā jeman re halpal halpal kare.

4. Sometimes the cases of gemination of consonants and glides to cater to the needs of the smooth flow of music are also noticed

Jubbā nāri gharat thuiyā; Bukkote helāni diyā bājāiben dotorā.

5. Many a pleonastic indeclinables are used in the lyrical syntax to meet the tonal needs. For example:

Maish carān mor maishāl bandhu kon bā carer mājhe.
Bhāto nā careyā bhāto nā āndiyā bhāto nā bārinu re.
Hāṭ bā jāiben bājār jāiben.

The above discussions on the linguistics of Kamrupi dialect and some of its characteristic use in the lyrical and poetic forms of the dialect are absolutely necessary to understand the lyrical features of Bhāwāiyā. It should be borne in mind that there is a tradition bound emotional environment, characterised by the bounty of nature and traditional rural ways of life intimately and deeply associated with Bhāwāiyā and this association is the regulatory force of the music, sound environment and lyrical syntax of Bhāwāiyā. Needless to mention, the nature of tune and music has ultimately taken the precedence in regulating the lexicosphere of Bhāwāiyā.

Kamrupi Lexicon:

Words in Kamrupi dialect can be classified in 5 broad categories: (i) *Tatsama* (ii) *Semi-tatsama* (iii) *Tadvaba* (iv) *Deśi* and (v) *Videśi* (foreign)

(*i*) Tatsama words though with a little distorted pronounciation are:

anko, amso, antor, abotār, abosthā, kātor, kāron, tusṭo, dhyān, dān, bairāgi, bhanḍo, minoti, etc.

(*ii*) Semi-Tatsama: Almost no word directly from Sanskrit has been adopted in Kamrupi. There are few such words as Semi-tatsama with again little distorted pronounciation.

akto, aggyān, ākkoros, kainā, kāndon, cait, gāirastho, gondo, thān, niṭhur, nindālu, naijjā, nimantan, parabās, parbhāt, parān, pasan, baisṭom, kesṭo, maiddo, mantor, syābā, sot........., etc.

(*iii*) Tadvaba: Large number of words in this dialect fall in this category. Since the words are largely unknown, their meanings are given in *brackets- āi* (mother), *eṭā* (this), *eiṭe, eṭe* (here), *oiṭe, oṭe* (there), *gach* (tree), *akumāri* (kumari in literary Bengali, maiden), *āo* (speech), *etti* (this side, here), *ilsā* (hilsa fish), *akām* (misdeed), *āṭiā* (banana with lots of seeds), *āeknā* (a small thing), *gyāderā* (dirty), *akhuṭā* (inferior quality wood), *āginā* (court-yard), *gāvin* (pregnant), *ghyāgā* (goitrous), *āṭo* (narrow), *oros* (bug), *kāsulā* (patient of hooping cough), *ānduni* (kitchen-mate), *bain* (sister), *āi* (sister), *bukāni* (piece of cloth for covering breasts), *bhoicāl* (earthquake), *bhāuj* (sister-in-law/wife of elder brother), *bhok* (hunger), *dāo* (axe), *dātuā* (having pointed teeth), *dāduā* (having the skin disease of ring worm), *dhaolā* (white), *dhumā* (smoke), *mailā* (dirty), *māiyā* (wife), *osār* (broad, wide), *khalāi* (bamboo jar to keep caught fishes), *ghongor* (veil put on by women), *cāilon* (bamboo made tray decorated with reception materials like lamp, paddy, dubba grass, banana used for reception of gods/goddesses, bride groom, etc.), *cakoyā* (a bird), *cuā* (well of water), *syāp* (spit), *chorāni* (key), *jedu* (if), *jui* (fire), *jhari* (rain), *ṭāri* (ward, locality), *ṭyāngā* (sour), *ḍhyāl* (stone-throwing), *ḍhongā* (slough or skin of banana tree used for making tray-like pot), *nāuyā* (barber), *nāl* (red), *neṭu* (tail), *pangor* (swimming), *pichilā* (slippery), *fārā* (torn), *mānsi* (man), *hāṭuā* (market-man), *bāudiā* (vagabond type)

Desi words: Good many words adopted by the Aryans from the language of various people belonging to the Dravidian and Austric groups have entered into this dialect. There are lots of sonorous words amongst them. *aghā* (weak, worthless), *acodā* (meaningless), *ācā* (caterpillar), *ācābhuā* (peculiar), *āung bāung* (irrelevant), *ājāri* (empty), *uḍḍā* (vagabond), *kosṭiā* (close-fisted), *kacuā* (full of arams), *kāurhāṭi* (disturbances), *kācāl* (quarrel), *kham khamā* (well-built), *khirkhirā* (condensed), *khong khongā* (hollow), *gissi* (forcefully), *gyālgyālā* (soft and nearly melted, over-ripe), *gyālles* (the way liquid is poured), *gulgulā* (very soft owing to over-ripeness), *juljulā* (idiotic look), *jyāljyālā* (thin), *jyāng jyāngā* (with tiny wholes), *jhamjhamā* (with force or abundance), *ṭāruā* (bone), *ṭas* (puzzled), *ṭika* (buttock), *ṭhyāng* (legs), *ḍhāngā* (tall), *tyātelā* (immatured ripe), *tyānā/ nyācrā* (pieces of torn clothes), *thyār thyārā* (not orderly, disarranged), *thyātlā* (pounded, smashed), *nāriā* (shaven, bald-headed), *neruā* (left handed), *nerā hāt* (left hand), *pārā* (male buffalo), *pāri* (female buffalo) *pukṭi/puṭki* (extreme point of buttock/posterior), *pyātol* (liver), *falfalā* (starch white), *fyādili* (talkative woman), *boyā* (bad), *bārun* (broom) *bhuki* (striking with the first), *bhodāi* (fool), *buci* (woman with flat nose), *māng* (vagina), *mādi* (female elephant), *māroyā* (plaintain trees planted for decoration), *māreyā* (house-owner hosting any festival), *śidol* (food item prepared from dry fish), *sāngnā* (paramour), hudum (naked) hol (testicles), *fyārfyārā* (full of moistrous matter), *bhyārbhyārā* (muddy soft), *byārbyārā* (talking irrelevantly/unceasingly), *honhonā* (walking swiftly), *girgirā* (condensed), *culbulā* (beautiful), *bhyādbhyādā* (talking irrelevent), *myālmyālā* (bleat of goat, sheep).

There are number of words taken from foreign language too- Persian, Arabic, Portuguese, English, etc. Moreover, because of long association with the Koch-Rabha and Bodo people lots of words have come from these languages. Of cours, they are used with little distorted pronounciation.

Persian words: *andor, ānāj, āin, āskārā, ārām, kambaktā, kākā, kāji, kāmāi, jami, tosok, niśān, pāikār, pāji, pasom, śānāi, bandor...*, etc.

Arabic words: *ākkel, āhāmmok, jorul, najor, jabāi, khayrāt, duniyā, sailtā, fājil, fouzdār*, etc.

Portuguese words: *āpil, inci, dabol, ḍāiriyā, gilās, pyāsendār, iskul, āelgāri, tail, peleṭ* (plate), *chiloṭ* (slate), *pencul* (pencil), *kyāpṭin* (captain), *ipoṭ* (report), *eḍio* (raḍio), *eḍi* (ready), *seketāri* (secretary), *pesiḍen* (president), *miṭin* (meeting), *bālli* (barley), *pāspoṭ* (passport), *ḍāiver* (driver), etc.

Bodo words: *āu āu* (no, no) *āylā jhāylā /āul jhāul* (not in order, disorderly), *byāngā* (lock), *bokāli* (baby-sitter), *bādā* (bunch of betel nut/coconut), *bokonā* (bag and baggage), *pāṭā* (male goat), *pāṭi/bakri* (female goat), *bhondā* (male cat), *bhundi* (female cat), *dalong* (bridge), *dāfnā* (wings of bird, portion of human hand close to the shoulder), *ḍābri* (open crop field), *gyādrā* (dirty), *hāngrā* (bomboo hedge), *hāfā* (wild cat), *nāfā* (a kind of green leafy vegetable), *kusiār/kusāri* (sugar-cane), *pākrā-cikrā/citiā-pākerā* (colourful), thuri (hollow bamboo), *uyā/ ruyā* (bamboo pieces used for setting roof thatches), *ukundi* (barren goat/cat), *jāmpoi* (in plenty), *giri* (house hold)...., etc.

Koch-Rabha words: *āng sāng* (irrelevant), *kāmi* (thin piece of bamboo), *gāb* (colour), *gābār* (border, bank), *chām* (wooden husking machine), *gāin* (pestle), *dāghilā/ khyātā* (quilt made of piecemeal cloths), *byādā* (wooden agricultural equipment with bamboo teeth used for separation of grasses, shrubs from the soil), *hāccini* (same as byada but smaller in size), burung (bamboo made fishing equipment), *dhorkā* (long bamboo made fishing equipment), ḍeru (same as burung but bigger in size) – all the three equipments are kept placed in ankle deep or half knee deep water and fishes get caught there; *caru* (thigh), *cāngrā* (bamboo made high altar for sitting and sleeping), *chil chilā* (smooth), *jāklā* and *jāburā* (garbage), *ṭuṭi* (throat), *ṭākoyā* (small sized snails), *byādleng* (water leech), *bhuti* (about 2/3 feet long euipment made of paddy straw properly arranged and tightened to keep fire lit but latent), *hāuriyā* (landless), *ṭoplā* (bag and baggage), *chyāng chyāngā* (very cold), *syāo* (low, sloping), *banu* (brother-in-law, husband of elder sister), *sāgāi* (relatives)...., etc.

Indeclinables: Use of some expressive indeclinables is a speciality of this dialect as well as Bhāwāiyā songs–*hay, hor, āre, o, ei, aki, ge, hyāge, ainā, sābās, āio, ācchā, beiś beiś, hāy hāy, dheit, hyā hyā, āhā, ore, ohore, oho...*, etc.

REFERENCES

1. G.A. Grierson (ed.), "*Linguistic Survey of India*", Vol. V, Motilal Banarsidas, New Delhi, 1904.
2. Dharmanarayan Barma, *A Step to Kamta Bihari Language*, published by Minati Barma Adhikari, Mokhada Pustakalaya, Tufanganj, 1991.
3. Asit Kr. Bandopadhyay, *Anchalik Bangla Bhasar Abhidhan*, Vol. I, Calcutta University, Kolkata, 1991.
4. BanikantaKakati, *Assamese-its Formation and Development*, 3rd edn., Lawyer's Book Stall, Guwahati, Assam, 1972.
5. Mohammad Abu Talib, *Uttarbanga Sahitya Sadhana*, published from Rajshahi, Bangladesh, n.d.
6. Krishnadhan Bandopadhyay, *Geeta-Sutrasar*, A. Mukherjee & Co., Kolkata, 4th edn. 1382 B.S.
7. Nirmal Das, *Uttarbanga Bhasa Prasanga*, Sahitya Bihar, Kolkata, 2nd edn., 1997.

6

Musicology of Bhāwāiyā

It is within the environment bound by the conditionalities characterised by the agricultural folk-belonging to the Rajbanshi community, lands-alluvial and diluvial, rivers-restless and unpredictable, and the topography-picturous and rhythmic, that a specific melody and rhythm developed in ancient Kamrup which with the passage of time has given rise to the regional tradition of musical form and style by the name Bhāwāiyā. This has been intertwined with the regional intonation and mode of articulation of Kamrupi or Rajbanshi dialect. In other words, based on the life, philosophy, culture, natural and topographical environment of ancient Kamrup *i.e.,* present North Bengal and Western Assam, has developed the particular regional music form 'Bhāwāiyā' or 'Bhāoiyā'. Like any folk music, Bhāwāiyā is characterised by simplicity of melody, monotony or rhythm, exaggerated tone colour and a spirit of improvisation. The factors, which do play important role in determining the regional characteristics of any folk melody, are:

(*i*) Tonal structure and style-tonality well established with modal characteristics,

(*ii*) Specific natural, environmental and work-related factors,

(*iii*) Topographical conditions,

(*iv*) Ethnic and phonetic characteristics of the region and modulation of voice characterised thereby.

In case of Bhāwāiyā melody, we have since discussed the nature and work/labour related characteristics, topographical characteristics and ethnic and phonetic characteristics related to Rajbanshi/Kamrupi dialect. Voice-modulation, however, is a matter of practical performance and demonstration and cannot be expressed properly in letters. It is because of the speciality of voice-modulation, tonality and tone colour ingrained in regional folk songs that even an expert Bhāwāiyā singer cannot usually be an expert performer in *Jhumur* and vice versa. The main reason of variety in voice modulation of folk music is the use of microtones with the tone, the main pitch. An individual tone is actually a combination of sound consisting of the main pitch and a certain number of additional tones called microtones. The latter are heard faintly but nevertheless their presence contributes to the characteristic tone colour of any particular instrument or voice. This is particularly relevant in case of folk music. Regional dialect and its articulatory modes too play important role in this respect.

Musicology

Musicology is the scientific study of music. It must include every conceivable discussion of musical topics, being the whole body of systematised knowledge about music which results from the application of a scientific method of investigation or research or of philosophical speculation and rational systematisation to the facts, the processes and the development of musical art, and to the relation of man in general..........to that art (Harvard Dictionary of Music). It is, however, true that the bundle of methods, assumptions, and ideologies, which constitute the mainstream musicology renders it a less than useful resource in many ways. There are problems associated with it—particularly in case of folk songs with different kinds of parameters – melody, rhythm, pitch gradation, timbre and performance articulation techniques.

The other aspect of problem is a methodology slanted by the characteristics of notation. The musicological methods tend to foreground those musical parameters which can be easily notated but have difficulty with parameters which are not easily notated, *i.e.* non-standard pitch and non-discrete pitch movement (slides, slurs, microtones, etc.), irregular, irrational rhythms, polyrhythms and rhythmic nuance (off-beat phrasing, slight delays, etc.), nuances of ornamentation, accent, articulation and performer dialect, specificities of timbre, etc.

It has got indirect effect also. Notation centric training induces particular forms of listening, which tends to be applied to all sorts of music, appropriately or not. Notation centric methods when applied to folk music become problematical. Notation-derived thinking, while by no means irrelevant, is at best partial and at worst likely to distort actual musical practice affecting understanding and valuation.

The third aspect of the musicological problem is an ideology slanted by the origin and development of musicology itself. Musicology is not historically neutral. It arose in a specific context in close association with that movement in the musical practice of the period, which was codifying the very repertory then taken by musicology as the centre of its attention. That movement produced the idea of a body of music, a tradition, which can be called classical. This took place in intimate relationship with the development of a particular body of music and its aesthetic. Such an approach is likely to be not suitable for songs other than classical, particularly folk song, with such factors as ephemerality (that is, contemporaneity), socially significant form and technique, performance rather than fixed text, the experiential rather abstract, etc.

In spite of various problems involved in musicological analysis of folk songs the same is however, not totally irrelevant. Musicological analysis gives some idea at least about the structure of the melody and the characteristics of the tune and tone colour engrained in the particular melodic structure. Here I will try the musicological analysis of Bhāwāiyā with this limited objective.

Melodic Structure and Mode of Bhāwāiyā

The tonal structures usually followed in Bhāwāiyā are:

S R M P D n...
S R G M P n....
M P D n D n D P M.............
M G R S R M G R S.............
n n S R G G M G R S ....
P D n D n D P M

(S = *Sharaja*, R= *Risava*, G = *Gandhara*, M=*Madhyama*, P= *Pancama*, D=*Dhaivata*, and n= flattened (soft) *nishada*. It is worth-noting that in the tonal structure of Bhāwāiyā there is no use of flattened 'R' *i.e.,* 'r', flattened 'G' *i.e.* 'g', flattened 'D' *i.e.* 'd' and sharpened 'M' *i.e.* 'm'. Also there is no use of 'N' (*Nishada*). The use of flattened 'N' *i.e.* n, on the other hand, is a special characteristic of Bhāwāiyā. Dn Dn — modulation in the tonal texture of Bhāwāiyā is like its 'Pakar'. The use of S and M is also comparatively more, but there is nothing like a 'Pakar' centring M.

The other important characteristic of Bhāwāiyā melody is that it does not usually go beyond *madhya* (middle) octave; in other words it does not ascent to 'tara' (upper) octave. The tune rises to flattened (soft) N *i.e.,* n, creates a beautiful resonance with Dn Dn and then comes back to S or R. Of course, there are a few exceptions to this general rule. In a few relatively modern Bhāwāiyā songs, particularly in *Caṭkā* this tendency can be noticed. Also in Bishahara palagan, the tune sometimes ascends to 'tara' octave and goes upto 'R'. On the other hand the tune quite often descends to soft N or n and sometimes to P of mandra (lower) octave. Normally all folksongs are sung in high pitch. Bhāwāiyā is, however, sung in still higher pitch. Since the tune does not go beyond n of the middle octave and sometimes descends to P of the lower octave, it becomes quite convenient for the singers to sing in very high pitch in F or F sharp. The voice quality required for this song is basically with the *Madhyama* (M) characteristics. A resonance centring round the note *Madhyama* (M) is voiced when Bhāwāiyā is sung in the scale above M. The resonance of R and S however, becomes prominent when the tune descends from M to S and this adds to the gravity and depth in the expression. The tune reveals its extra-ordinary beauty in the manner it glides from M to P with the voice modulation expressed in this glide. *Sharaja* (S) and *Madhyama* (M) are predominant notes in most of the songs.

Some scholars have mentioned the use of flattened (soft) G *i.e.* g in Bhāwāiyā. This is not true. The movement from M to R through glide demands the use of microtones (shruties), which sometimes sounds like the use of 'g'. Some others have shown use of N in Bhāwāiyā notation. As mentioned earlier, use of 'N' is strictly forbidden in Bhāwāiyā; with the use of N, the tune tends to become Bhatiali. Some scholars have shown the tendency of analysing folk songs in terms of classical songs. For instance, Late Suresh Chakraborty, one of the great musicologists of Bengal has analysed the major forms of Bengali folk songs in the context of their similarities with the ragas and raginis. In doing so, he has claimed that Bhatiali, the septatonic folk melody of the then East Bengal, now Bangladesh is based on the Jhinjhit ragini of Khambaj. Ṭhāṭ (mode) of Bhāwāiyā of North Bengal and Baul of Middle Bengal (Baul tune that was accepted and adopted by Rabindra Nath) also belong to the Khambaj mode. In other words, according to Chakraborty, the thread of the tonal compositions based on Khambaj mode weaves the basic character of East Bengal, Middle Bengal and North Bengal.

In the Appendix of 'Pranta UttarBanger Lok Sangeet' of Dr. Nirmalendu Bhowmik, Shri Banikantha Bhattacharya has opined that Bhāwāiyā is influenced principally by the raga Bhimpalsree.[1] According to him, the influence of Bhimpalsree on the songs of North Bengal is quite substantial and it is the lifeforce of the songs. The tune evolves around the Madhyama and develops with the words based on g and n; Bhimpalsree does not only have its presence, it rather has its standing effect. This is to be humbly submitted that the above observation of Shri Bhattacharya is not based on musicological characteritics of Bhāwāiyā and hence not true perhaps. As explained earlier, 'g' has no place in pure Bhāwāiyā tune, whereas 'g' is a dominant note in Bhimpalsree.

In this connection, it is quite relevant to question the justifiability of imposing any raga name on any folk form just on the basis of some similarities in tonal compositions. The observations of Hemanga Biswas are worthmentioning in this context. According to Biswas, folk tune cannot be classified on the basis of musical compositions of ragas. The vitality of a folk form is characterised by regional manner of rendition, timbre, regional mode of presentation, metre, phonetics of the regional dialect and the intonation. According to Sri Khaled Choudhuri, various folk songs by way of transformation and reforms restructuring with the passage of time have reached the stage of classical music. This is the reason why so many classical ragas are called after the names of these folk communities or folk music. If there is any similarity between Jhinjhit and Bhatiali, that happens by sheer chance and accident only. The name remains Bhatiali itself-it has its relation with rowing with the stream or downward current (Bhati), its geography.

Coming back to the melodic characteristics of Bhāwāiyā, regarding its high resonance centring 'n' and the tune not going beyond the note 'n', one can deduct some inferences based on practical experiences of performance. Bhāwāiyā performers like Kumar Nidhi Narayan have imputed certain reasons for this. According to him, this characteristic of Bhāwāiyā tune has its relation with the mode of playing of the string instrument Dotora of this region. Dotora playing is done by both hands. On one side of the instrument it is kept pressed by the wrist of the hand and sound is produced by striking the strings with a stroker held by three fingers of this hand. At the other end (top side) the instrument is kept placed on the palm and then various notes S,R,G, etc. are produced by pressing the finger-tips on the strings out of the sounds produced by the strokes.

Dotora has four strings. Two middle strings are set at the note S, the upper one set at M and the lower one at P of lower octave. Dotora usually pronounced as Dotara means two-stringed. Some experts think that the instrument is called Dotara because the middle two strings are tuned in the same note (S). Interestingly, the middle strings of Dotora are called 'Sur' (Tonal) in this region; upper string is called 'Jin' and the lower one 'Bom'. Because two ('dui / doe') strings tuned in 'S' play significant role in this instrument, it is called Dotara *i.e.* two stringed.

The instrument at the top end is placed on the palm, keeping the thumb below it and four fingers on the other (upper) side. Thus stroke on the middle two strings at other end produces the note S, the stroke produces R when these two strings are pressed by the tip of the forefinger of the other hand with which the instrument is held at the top end; stroke on them followed by the pressure with the ring finger produces G; stroke on the uppermost string produces M, while stroke on this string with pressure by fore-finger tip produces P; pressure by ring-finger produces D and pressure by the little finger produces n and not N (as the gap between two pressure points is narrower because of the little finger's shorter length). Thus, without changing the original placement position of the instrument on the palm, the highest note it can reach is 'n'. To produce any note beyond n, the placement will have to be changed and probably the composers of Bhāwāiyā did not want to take that trouble.

The simple-minded self-satisfied composers were happy with whatever they could produce without making much of efforts and without much of trouble. It may be noted that we have not mentioned the use of the middle finger for the pressure on the instrument for producing the notes. The reason is quite obvious. Use of middle finger on the middle strings would have produced flattened notes *i.e.*'r' and 'g'. Similarly on the upper string its use would have produced sharp M *i.e.*'m'and flattened D *i.e.*'d'. Use of flattened and sharp notes would have made the melody complicated, and as such the simple composers did not attempt this. This is why the use of middle finger on Dotora playing in Bhāwāiyā is not recommended. The finger pressure used on the lower string, which is set at P, produces the notes D and n.

Bhāwāiyā has an intimate relation with Dotora and as such these limitation features have been reflected on the musical composition of Bhāwāiyā *i.e.* the evolution of Bhāwāiyā tune. We get a firm conviction about the intimate relation between Dotora and Bhāwāiyā when we see that the songs belonging to the sub-forms of the Bhāwāiyā such as *Bishahara* and *Jag Gan*, where they go beyond n, do not have Dotora as their accompanying instrument. The main accompanying instrument in Bisahara is flat-mouthed flute (*Mukha-banshi*). The main accompanying instruments of *Dehatattwa* or *Manasiksha* type of Bhāwāiyā songs where the tune goes beyond n and ascends upto R of Tara octave are Sarinda and Khanjani.

It may be clarified in this connection that Dotara (not Dotora as called in North Bengal) is used as accompanying instrument for Bhatiali and Baul songs also. There is however, substantial difference in phyɔical structure, mode of playing and sound resonance between East Bengal Dotara and North Bengal Dotora. North Bengal Dotora is inseparably connected with Bhāwāiyā. The argument of Kumar Nidhi Narayan on the reasons for the tune being restricted in the *Madhya* and *Mandra* does not appear to be baseless. I tend to subscribe to this viewpoint.

All twelve notes *S r R g G M m P d D n N* have different characters in the sense that individually and independently they emit different kinds of feelings and emotions. The characteristics of notes present in any melodic structure and their mode of moving thus show the abstruseness, sagacity and penetration, (depth of passion, depth of thought) by that melody. There is a tonal relationship between different notes of the scale. Deryek Cooke has mentioned about these tonal tensions in "The Language of Music". Musical works are built out of the tensions between such notes. These tensions can be set up in three dimensions– pitch, tune and volume; and the setting up of such tensions, and the colouring of them by the vitalising agents of tone colour and texture, constitute the whole apparatus of musical expression. The heart of the problem of musical language is to elucidate the emotional context of music analysing the expressive qualities inherent in the tonal relationships between different notes of the scale-exactly what the notes of the scale are and what tensions exist betwen them. Cooke has mentioned the tensions obtaining between the notes as below.

Note C is fixed, the fundamental note known as the tonic. G is the fifth note in the scale, known as the dominant, a tension pulling it back to C. E is the major third of the scale, though again there is a tension pulling it back to C. Other notes have tensions pulling them back to these three. D-flat and D (the major and minor seconds) are pulled towards C; F (the fourth) is pulled towards E; F-sharp (the sharp fourth), A-flat and A (the minor and major sixth) are pulled towards G ; B-flat (the minor seventh) is pulled down to A and thence down to G ; B-natural (the major seventh) is pulled towards the upper-C. The note E-flat (the minor third) is an unusual case; it has a tension pulling it towards E. There is, of course, a tension pulling every note back to the fundamental C.

He has dealt with the basic expressive functions of all twelve notes of the scale with further details. Usually the major notes express positive emotions-joy, confidence, love, serenity, triumph, etc. and the minor notes express the negative emotions-sorrow, fear, hate, despair, etc. Expressive emotions and functions of individual notes:

Tonic: The fundamental note – emotionally neutral; context of finality.

Minor Second: Semitonal, tension down to the tonic in a minor context; spiritless anguish, context of finality

Major Second: As a passing note emotionally neutral but as a whole note tension down to the tonic in a major context-pleasurable longing, context of finality.

Minor Third: Concord but a depression of natural third; stoic (controlled) acceptance, tragedy.

Major third: Concord, natural third; joy.

Normal fourth: As a passing note emotionally neutral. As a semitonal, tension down to the major third, pathos.

Sharp fourth: As a modulating note to the dominant key, active aspiration. As 'augmented fourth' pure and simple, devilish and inimical forces.

Dominant: Emotionally neutral; context of flux, intermediary

Minor sixth: Semitonal, tension down to the dominant in a minor context; active anguish in a context of flux

Major sixth: As a passing note, it is emotionally neutral. As a whole note tension down to the dominant in a major context; pleasurable longing in a context of flux.

Minor seventh: Semitonal, tension down to major sixth or as whole tone, tension down to minor sixth, both unsatisfactory resolving again down to the dominant; 'loss' note and mournfulness.

Major seventh: As a passing note, it is emotionally neutral. As a semitonal tension upto the tonic; violent longing, aspiration in a context of finality.

The degree and exact nature of the joy, tragedy, pleasurable longing or anguish which is conveyed in various uses of the major and minor notes is, of course, dependent on the vitalizing agents of time, volume and intervallic tensions. As mentioned earlier, the major sixth and minor seventh create special vitalising effect on the Bhāwāiyā tonal structure. Unlike the minor sixth, the major sixth is not an acute dissonance but a mild one, its relationship to the dominant being that of a tone and not semitone. Nevertheless when it is expressed against the major triad unresolved, it produces a pleasurable feeling of being unsatisfied *i.e.* the feeling of a continuous pleasurable longing or longing for pleasure. The minor seventh, like the minor third and sixth, is expressive of painful feelings. It can function in two different ways with the major triad and with the minor. When it is exposed in relation to the major triad and left unresolved, it has a sad empty sound. In relation to the minor triad, it cannot rise to the upper tonic, but is drawn towards the dominant. Being only a mild dissonance, it is not expressive of violent anguish but of a gentle mournful feeling, which is made more woeful by it's undermining of the normal joyful feeling of the major triad supporting it. The minor seventh introduces the mournful element. The major seventh (the note which is usually absent in Bhāwāiyā tune) provides an anti-thesis to this melancholy note, turning upwards optimistically to the tonic.

Emotions: In Indian literature, emotions are divided into nine classes– '*Sringara Hasya Karuna Raudra Vira Bhayanaka Bhibhatsa Adbhuta Santascha Rasah Purvairudahritah*', which correspond to love, ludicrousness, tenderness, anger, heroism, fear, disgust, wonder and peacefulness.

Natural environment has its effect on all forms of folk music. We have seen in our discussions that the naturo-physical conditions of North Bengal are not same as those of South Bengal and East Bengal (Bangladesh). Rivers here are not as wide and deep as of Bangladesh (the Bhatiali region). The rivers here flow and overflow with very strong current during the rains but get almost dry in the winter and summer. Here the rivers do not contribute much to the livelihood of common people; rather they have on occasions become the causes of misery and devastation in the region. Since the rivers do not leave much of silt, lands are not fertile and not much suitable for good agriculture. The water retention capacity of the soil is very low. Uneven lands, hills, hillocks have given rise to the incidence of echoes. It is conjectured that the environmental conditions characterized by the echoes have played some role in the melodic structure of Bhāwāiyā.

In this structural framework of Bhāwāiyā, the tune ascends from S or M in the modes *S R M P D n D n or M P D n D n DP* and following its usual manner of moving descends back to S, the tonic. But this mode of ascending and descending is not that simple. The special characteristic of Bhāwāiyā tune is the specific mode of yodelling. It is conjectured that Bhāwāiyā has adopted in its structure the characteristic features of echoes of the surroundings being staggered on, implying that the echoes have played vital role in shaping the tune of Bhāwāiyā and this has been reflected in the specific mode of yodelling. Doing the yodelling in perfect form and acquiring mastery over it is a difficult task, but Bhāwāiyā cannot be performed without this quality of yodelling. Even a highly accomplished singer cannot properly perform a Bhāwāiyā if he or she cannot acquire proficiency in yodelling. Yodelling applied in Bhāwāiyā should therefore, deserve special attention.

The observations of Hemanga Biswas, the great folk musicologist are worth remembering in this context. The geneses of the musicological expression of folk songs are voice modulation (rurality in voice), figure of speech, folk timbre and style. The folk style evolves out of regional life. This regionality has evolved based on a specific composition of notes or mode (*Ṭhāṭ*), to which has come the contribution from regional manner of speech, voice modulation, and manner of articulation of the dialect. The tone, tune and composition of any folk song are the expression of the communal life engrossed by different modes of labour-intensive production process. The folk singers and composers get their education from the nature as the teacher-the soil, water, sun, rainfall, mountain, rivers and the working life around. The voice tension in open wide plains has to be different from that which comes out in the process of walking and working in mountainous tracks. The pitch at which one sings in open wide field connot be same as that in closed room or courtyard. This is applicable everywhere.

Besides, all, even the maestros, cannot acquire the specific type of yodelling, kink and folk ornamentation engrained in the voice throwing/voice modulation of the specific regions. Good many city based sweet-voiced welltrained singers can acquire proficiency and expertise in the melodic structure and tonal structure of folk songs but they cannot acquire the regional voice throwing and modulation for which the songs performed lack in the intimate relation to the regional life. This is particularly true for Bhāwāiyā. Yodelling engrained in Bhāwāiyā and articulation characteristics of Rajbanshi dialect is very difficult to be acquired by the singers not belonging to the Rajbanshi culture. Even S.D. Barman, the famous folk singer is reported to have stated that he wanted to learn Bhāwāiyā but could not, as the yodelling could not be acquired.

The observation of Dr. Nirmalendu Bhowmick about yodelling of Bhāwāiyā is worth explaining in this context. Two main characteristics of the regional mode of pronounciation of Bhāwāiyā are aspiration and voice breaking (Yodelling). The yodelling is very difficult to acquire. It is a process of moving from high pitch (note) to lower ones overtaking an octave (descending to Mandra octave from Madhya octave all on a sudden), but without discord. There will be no 'mix' or glide in the process. Yodelling in Bhāwāiyā is not 'mix' and not limited to the same octave. This yodelling cannot be eventuated by any one and everyone even with utmost efforts. Those who can do can do it easily, without much effort. This is the regionality involved in it. According to Dr. Bhowmick, this yodelling is thus directly related to the natural and geographical characteristics of North Bengal on the margin. Geographical configurations of land in the marginal North Bengal have made the rivers narrow and shallow but very speedy at the same time. That is the reason why the rivers take bends quite frequently and that abruptness is exhibited through the voice throwing or yodelling. This has, of course, intimate relation with the Bodo culture. In his opinion, aspiration in the pronounciation and yodelling in tune is bounded by the same law of nature. He further mentions about the dance form of marginal North Bengal in this connection. In this form of group dance which is akin to 'khemṭā' performed at the beginning of the folk dramas (*Pālāṭiyā gān*) by the boys dressed as girls dancing around on the stage, the performers do the sudden sitting poses with the accent (shom) of the percussion instrument 'khol'. This sudden pose of sitting is comparable with the yodelling in a sense.

The observation of Dr. Bimal Chattopadhyaya in "Uttarbanger Lok Sangeet Bhāwāiyā and Caṭkā" is a bit different.[2] Agriculture is the main occupation in this area. Simultaneously with the agriculture, the other occupations in this area are driving the bullock cart *i.e.* the work of cart driver (*Gāriāl*), grazing the cattle, particularly buffaloes, *i.e.*, the work of buffalo-keeper (*Maishāl*), the work of catching and driving elephants, *i.e.*, elephant driver (*Māhut*), the work of Ayurvedic treatment, *i.e.*, Ayurved doctor (*Kavirāj*), the habit of theft by some inactive work-reluctant, *i.e.*, thief (*Cor*), etc. According to Dr. Chattopadhyay, the characteristic of the yodelling in Bhāwāiyā and Caṭkā is the creation of the work processes involved in these professions. When the boat man is busy controlling his boat on the torrential river, his body gets jerks and naturally the tune of his song, if he sings in such situations, gets vibrated and trembled.

Similarly, the voice of the bullock cart driver (*Gāriāl*), while taking the cart along the uneven muddy roads and crop fields gets trembled, and the same kind of trembling and voice breaks take place in the song of the buffalo-keeper (*Maishāl*), when he sings with Dotora on hand riding the buffalo, grazing on the uneven lands. The songs sung by the men folk engaged in such subsidiary professions express the actual melodic structure of Bhāwāiyā.

One can very well question the observations of Dr. Bhowmick and Dr. Chattopadhyay. The observations and arguments can at best be partially correct. It is not correct, Dr. Bhowmick argued that the yodelling of Bhāwāiyā is not restricted within the same octave. The yodelling can be within the octave, in between two, three or four notes of the octave and with the notes overtaking the octave. From the angle of lyrics, this yodelling can be effected within a word or between the words. Also it is not true that movement from a note in *Madhya* (middle) octave to a note like 'P' of Mandra (lower) octave takes place without any glide.

It has been stated earlier that yodelling in Bhāwāiyā is intimately related to the mode of pronounciation of the Rajbanshi dialect. One of the main characteristics of pronounciation in Bhāwāiyā is the subtle ornamental use of 'h' in between the letters of the word, in between the words, at the end of the words and also with the much used indeclinables in Bhāwāiyā. 'H' should, however, be used very very efficiently and this is possible only by the natural performers of the region. An example of a song will make the observation clear.

Aki o bandhu mor kājol bhomorā re
Kun din āsiben bandhu kayyā jān kayyā jān re.

In the song, the pronounciation will be somewhat as below:

Ahki Ohh-h-h bandhu mohrh kāhjohl bhohmorāh rehh
Kuhn din āhsibehn bandhuh kayyāh jāhn kayyāh jāhn rehhh

Also to be considered how far the observation and argument of Dr. Chattopadhyay is reasonable and acceptable. First of all, no boatman can be expected to sing while controlling the boat in such torrential rivers. Moreover, if the yodelling came out of the jerks caused by the boat, then Bhatiali also would have had the same kind of yodelling. The kinky yodelling in Bhatiali is quite different from that in Bhāwāiyā. The vibration caused by jerks may therefore be the partial reason. It cannot fully explain the yodelling.

The observation made by Dr. Nirmal Das[3] is rather more important and reasonable in this regard. In the lyrical form of Dariya Bhāwāiyā there is no jerk due to metrically composed 'tāla' (t178ime measure); here it is the tune, which glides from one scale to the other. Yodelling is emitted in the melodic composition of the lyric in the process of this glide. Dr. Das rejects as a generalised cause the conception of jerks, created in the work process involved in the profession of buffalo-keeping and riding, boating in the torrential rivers, driving the bullock-carts etc, as claimed by some. To him, yodelling is a part and parcel of the musical composition. Here a micronote enters into the musical tune as a glide and creates vibration in the continuous flow of the tune which brings forth some variety in the musical tune on the one hand and facilitates stress and emotional expression in the lyric on the other.

Here lies the deep understanding and association between the lyric and its tune. In the cases where the jerks of movement create any effect on the tempo of music, the same has its reflection on the lyric. The tempo tends to go faster and the lyric gets specified time, speed, rhythm and metrical measure. 'Khirol' type of Bhāwāiyā (songs related to

Maishāl, Gāriāl, etc.) is the best example for this. It is however, the subject matter of the song, rather than the jerk of movement, which causes the variation in tempo. In Dariyā type of Bhāwāiyā, sorrows and mournfulness take the prime position and so pathos rather than joy and grandeur predominates and yodelling makes the melancholy situation still graver. The 'Khirol' type of Bhāwāiyā on the other hand, is dominated by joy and enthusiasm and hence briskness and thrill with pathos are intertwined by rhythmic time, speed and tempo. Specific mode of stroke in Dotora adds vitality to it. Here the lyrical structure is controlled by the nature of musical compositions. The lyrical form and linguistic style of Bhāwāiyā is, therefore, controlled by its tune, its music. But music here does not suppress the lyric like Hindustani Sangeet; rather it transcends lyrical sentiment into tone.[4]

From the above discussion, it transpires that the characteristic feature of the yodelling is the outcome of partly the configuration of land, partly the stage of social development and partly ethnic factor. A particular melodic mode has evolved centring round a particular ethnic community. Evolution and development of social condition, production conditions and relations in economic structure, class conflicts and struggle-all these have played vital role in shaping the melodic structure. This has happened in case of Bhāwāiyā too.

But the most important factor influencing the yodelling in Bhāwāiyā has been the ethnic characteristics. My experience in this regard is that performers of Bhāwāiyā belonging to the Rajbanshi community, culture and environment, and also performers belonging to the people somehow anthropologically close to them and nourished for hundreds of years by the Rajbanshi culture, can easily and perfectly apply the yodelling; but to any other singer, howsoever good he or she is, yodelling application becomes a very difficult task. They cannot do it perfectly even after long years of practice.

It, therefore, appears that the physical structure of the Rajbanshi-their nose, cavity of mouth, lips, jaw, vocal chord, etc. contribute much to this. The voice arising out of the throat enters into the cavity of mouth and through the various limbs-teeth, tongue, lips, palate and nostrils transforms into new form. It is, therefore, guessed that the physical features of the Rajbanshis act as helping factors in applying the yodelling engrained in Bhāwāiyā.

Moreover, yedelling is not applied in equal measure in all types of Bhāwāiyā. As suggested by Dr. Das, while following the main melodic structure of Bhāwāiyā, some pieces go at very slow speed, some others go in swing and still others go brisk. Bhāwāiyā is divided into *Dariyā, Khirol*, *Soāri*, etc. Dariyā is again subdivided into *Citān*, *Garān*, *Dighal-nāsā*, etc. The variation in the degree of yodelling depending on the speed and style of Bhāwāiyā is worthnoting. Also there are variations, although not significant in the degree of yodelling, singing style and briskness, in different parts of the then Kamrup, *i.e.* Goalpara, Cooch Behar, Jalpaiguri, Rangpur, etc.

The use of yodelling in Cooch Behar and Rangpur areas is much more than its use in the Bhāwāiyā songs of Jalpaiguri and Goalpara. There is some difference in their singing style too. These variations in the use of yodelling and singing style have given rise to the misconception in the minds of some that the melodic structure in the entire region of the then Kamrup is not same. This is not correct. An analysis of the melodic structure will make it clear that they belong to the same structure. Sometimes the melody appears to be different because of variation in tonal stress and also use of micro-notes by some individual expert performers.

The reason behind such misconception is the ignorance about the sub-division of regionality. This is perhaps the reason why even Satyen Ray, the great performer of Jalpaiguri has stated that Jalpaiguri has its own melodic structure on which there is hardly any influence of Bhāwāiyā and Caṭkā, and the folk song of Jalpaiguri is characterised by its own features. Although it is true that the melodic style of Jalpaiguri particularly Teesta Burir gan, has a leaning towards tribal tune because of the proximity of Jalpaiguri Rajbanshis to the tribal people—like Mech, Rabha, Santhal, Munda, Oraon, etc., the melodic structure is basically same as Bhāwāiyā.

Exactly for the same reason, Pratima Barua of Gouripur, Assam, one of the greatest exponents of Bhāwāiyā, did take fancy in calling her songs 'Goalparia', that is, one that belongs to Goalpara district. Borrowing from Hemanga Biswas again in this connection, one can discuss and examine whether this kind of conception and argument establish the point on stronger grounds. The variation in the ascend, descend and amplitude of Bhatiali of the areas of Sylhet-Tripura-Mymensingh, Faridpur and Dhaka, etc. have given to the Bhatiali the flavour and colour specific to each of them. This is exactly true for Bhāwāiyā. The flavours of the Bhāwāiyā of Rangpur, Cooch Behar and Jalpaiguri are different; again I get a different tinge of the same Bhāwāiyā once I enter Goalpara, Gouripur, and the border areas of Assam. One needs to have some idea about the sub-divisions of the melodic structure, if one desires to have clear idea about the Bhāwāiyā. As stated earlier main Bhāwāiyā has three sub-divisions Dariya, Khirol and Maishali or Soari, on the basis of style, rhythm and tempo.

1. Dariyā: Late Haris Chandra Pal of Cooch Behar, a renowned folklorist and collector of Bhāwāiyā, has described Dariya as follows—It is a tune with long extended breathing, a melody to be smeared along the flow. If the feelings of mournfulness, separation, pangs of separation, sadness, etc. are the central theme of Bhāwāiyā, Dariya is then the form of genuine Bhāwāiyā. Dariya is, therefore, called the embodiment of Bhāwāiyā. In this type of songs, some particular words of the lyric and the last words of every line are sung with lengthened mild but touching resonances. It requires aplication of long breathing and so it is called *Dighal-nasa*.

Two other subdivisions of *Dariyā* are *Citān* and *Garān.* Citān is the song of heart breaking in the pangs of long separation. Usually these songs commence from the high pitch and come down to lower ones very slowly. The word Citan has come from 'Cit' which means lying flat on the back. A kind of emotions and feeling which is emitted by the song sung by someone lying flat on his back in loud voice is expected to be forthcoming in this tune. In Garan Bhāwāiyā one gets the mournful feeling of the ladylove in the pangs of separation. The tune ascends as if the ladylove is rolling on the dust. Tragedy is the main theme of this tune.

2. Khirol: This also falls under tragedy. Commencing from the low pitch it ascends to the high ones. The songs refer to Khirol River or any other river usually. The name has come from the term Khirol, a particular mode of rhythmic stroke on the strings of Dotora by the Dotora player.

3. Soāri Cāl: Generally, the type of songs sung by the buffalo keepers (*Maishal*) are bracketed under this category. Time and tempo of this tune is bound by a particular rhythmic pattern. From the frequentation of this tune, it so apears as if the singer were riding on some moving object and the rhythm of that motion gets transformed into the rhythm of the song. The swinging rhythmic music of the Dotora and the style of song rendered by the Maishal while riding on the buffalo-back and playing Dotora is the characteristic of this tune. This is thus called Maishali tune too. The mela held on the occasion of the festival 'Doljatra' which is characterised by the congregation of the swinging cots of Krishna and Radha placed on them, is called Soāri Mela in North Bengal. The term Soāri might have been derived from the swinging movement of the tune.

4. Caṭkā: Side by side with the grave emotional Bhāwāiyā, some light rhythmic songs are also performed by the name Caṭkā. Getting rid of grief and sorrows, mourning, pangs of separation, etc. one wants to be joyful, enthusiastic, active and lively, even if for a purely temporary period and performs light Caṭkā songs along with the Bhāwāiyā. The songs with musical time and cadence have brisk rhythms and light expression. Bhāwāiyā and Caṭkā are complementary to each other – a perfect and full feeling with the grave and light.

The meaning of the word 'Caṭak', according to the dictionary of Acharya Harisadhan Bandhopadhyay, is beauty, gracefulness and symmetry. The Caṭkā expresses this meaning of Caṭak. There is not much variety in the subject matter of Bhāwāiyā, the song with exuberance of emotions. But Caṭkā is full of variety from the standpoint of subject matter. Generally, Caṭkā deals with light type of subjects- social evils, contemporary incidents, socio-political scandals, etc., although there are Caṭkā songs dealing with grief and sorrows, tragedy of love-lorn separated couple or lovers, courtship, etc. It is easier to sing Caṭkā than Bhāwāiyā as they are in lighter rhythm and subjects. Moreover, giving enjoyment and pleasure to the audience is also easier by singing Caṭkā. Caṭkā, being rhythmic, timespecific, is suitable for dance also. The 'Khemta' dance prevalent in Bhāwāiyā region is generally performed with the Caṭkā. This is the reason why Caṭkā has got more popularity than Bhāwāiyā, particularly to the performers outside North Bengal, and not belonging to Rajbanshi community.

Rhythm and Metre

A succession of musical sounds depends for its meaning and effect on what is called Rhythm. The primary feature of rhythm is the regular occurrence of accent. A rhythm is concerned with regulating and ordering the time relationship of tones, either by accents or by patterns of long and short notes and it is responsible for the flow of music. Rhythm is also identical with metre. The space between accent and accent is called foot. A measure is said to be in double, triple or quadruple time, according to the number of beats into which it may be divided. A rhythmic pattern in longs and shorts is called a time pattern. Although the pitch of any note is fixed at a certain level, the duration of note value can change from one tune to the next.

As discussed, melody implies a separate impetus for each tone with accuracy of rhythm, and intonation is the prime element of melodic vitality. Melody denotes a succession of single notes in conjunction with rhythm. Rhythm of a melody including its basic metre, rhythmic accents and phrasing contributes to its character. Duration and pitch are two musical dimensions essential to melody. The general shape or contour of a melody is determined by the order, direction and rhythmic pattern of the successive intervals. These factors combine to give a melody its distinct colour.

Tāla (time pattern) is the media through which the rhythm takes shape. The concepts correlated to *Tāla* are-*Mātrā* (measure), *Ang* (Division), *Laya* (tempo, cadence), *Tāli-Khāli-sam* (foot-accent), *Ṭhekā* (keeping time with song), *Jāti* (Class), *Ābṛtti* (Recurrence), *Nām* (name), and *Bhāv* (sentiment, emotion):

Mātrā: Equidistant small division of *Tāla* is related to the name and sentiment of *Tāla*. For example, *Tin Tāla*-16 *mātrās*, *Ek Tāla*-12 *mātrās, Dādrā*- 6 *mātrās*, *Kārfā*-8 *mātrās*, etc.

Ang: Denotes sub-division of *Mātrās*; for example, 16 *mātrās* of *Tin Tāla* has got four sub-divisions of 4 *mātrās* each. 10 *mātrās* of *Jhāp Tāla* has got four sub-divisions- 2 of 2 *mātrās* and 2 of 3 *mātrās*, etc.

Laya: It is the indicator of the speed (tempo) of *Tālas-Bilambita* (slow), *Madhya* (middle range speed), *Druta* (fast), etc.

Tāli-Khāli-Sam: In rhythmic clapping, the accent place is *Tāli*, vacuum place is khāli and important accent place is sam.

Ābṛtti: Recurrence of *Tāla* is related to *Tāli-Khāli-Sam*. *Sam* is the point of beginning and ending of the *Tāla* circuit. *Sam* point is usually shown by + sign and vacuum point *i.e.* the space between accent and accent is shown by O sign.

Ṭhekā: Some well accepted words (calls) of *Tāla* are *Dhere, Keṭe Keṭe Tāk, Dhā Dhi Nā Nā Thu Nā*, etc.

Jāti: 5 classes of *Tāla*, namely *Catusra, Tisra, Khand, Misra, Sankirna*. For example: *Tin Tāla* of 16 mātrās:

1	2	3	4	5	6	7	8	9	10	11	12	13	14	15	16
Dhā	*Dhin*	*Dhin*	*Dhā*	*Dhā*	*Dhin*	*Dhin*	*Dhā*	*Dhā*	*Tin*	*Tin*	*Tā*	*Tā*	*Dhin*	*Dhin*	*Dhā*

Discussion on Tāla, rhythm automatically refers to the instruments, which are the means of expression and keeping of the rhythm. *Nātya Shāstra* of Bharata has mentioned four classes of instruments- *Tāra* (string), *Suṣira* (wind), *Ghana* (solid instrument) and *Anaddha* or *Abanaddha* (percussion). In Western music too instruments are classified into four kinds-chordophone, aerophone, idiophone and membranophone. The folk instruments *i.e.* the instruments which are usually used with the folk music are also classified into 4 categories. The instruments are:

Chordophonic: *Dotorā/Dotrā/Dotārā, Gābgubā/Gupi-yantra, Ektārā, Lāuyā, Behālā* (Violin), *Byānā, Sārindā*, etc.

Aerophonic: Flute (*ār. Bānśi, Mukh Bānśi/Mukhā Bānśi*), *Sehnai* (*Sānāi*), *Śingā* (Horn).

Idiophonic: *Manjirā/ Kartāl/ Khāpi, Jhāil i.e.* all types of *cymbals, Gong, Kasi, Nupur* (Nepur).

Membranophonic: *Ḍhol, Ḍholok, Ḍhāk, Ḍhulki, Khol, Khanjani, Mādal, Dhāmsā, Karkā, Tāsā*, etc.

Musical Instruments

Musical instruments developed slowly and comparatively much later than singing. They developed from rhythmically moving limbs, from stamping feet and slapping hands; the hands and feet were replaced by more effectual devices- wooden clapper-sticks or pounding bamboos; or the ground to be stamped upon, yielded to some covered pit in the earth or to a felled and dug out tree. Such simple contrivances and the rattles that shook from the dancers' ankles or in women's hands were the beginning of the first large class of instruments called idiophones or instruments of materials sonorous by the nature without needing any artificial tension such as strings or drum skins. Most of them are struck; but a good many are pounded, shaken, scrapped, plucked or even rubbed.

As second-class, primitive tribes created the aerophones from the air, which constitutes their main vibrating agent- mainly flutes of different types. The third class of instruments was the membranophones or drums where a bladder or skin to be struck or to be rubbed, is tightly stressed across an opening. Two principal sources from which they have been derived are- the carved and hollowed tree and lather, earthen store pot. The fourth class, chordophones or stringed instruments reached in the primitive world only preparatory stages. Most of them share their forms with the hunter's bow and few with swinging traps for big game.

The stringed instruments in the primitive stage had many strings. The player produced notes by stopping one single string at different places. The earliest of the stringed instruments were the harp and the lyre. Around 2000 B.C. some country in or near Asia Minor produced the lute, consisting of a resonance body with a neck on which various notes of the melody were 'stopped' by pressing the fingers on the proper places of one string or two. Almost all the instruments were plucked either with bare fingers or with plectrum of some kind. Bowing became known much later.

Discussion on musical instruments implies descriptions of their structure, the materials of which they are manufactured, the mode of playing, how the pitch of the sound is emitted, etc. Here we will discuss about the main musical instruments of North Begal, which are used as accompaniments of Bhāwāiyā-Caṭkā. The main string instruments used are Dotorā, Sārindā, Byānā and Violin.

Dotorā: It is about 2 to 2.5 feet long log usually of Sāitan wood/Jackfruit wood/ Neemwood with the circuference of about 13/14 inches at one (bottom) end and about 4/5 inches close to the top end. The bottom portion (about 6 inches length) is made hollow and crescent shaped with the help of chisel and covered with the animal skin (usually goat skin or iguana skin). A few holes (usually 6/8) are made on the skin in order to make the sound resonating. From the upper end of the hollow (bottom) starts the middle portion of the instrument.

From here the instrument is made thinner and vertically flat; upper surface of this portion made hollow facilitating the skin cover to continue for a stretch of about 6 inches. The rest of the middle portion gradually becomes thinner and takes the shape of half round with the upper surface slightly flat for a stretch of about 6 inches. After this the shape is like a small chignon (*topknot*) where a hollow is made to facilitate the fixation of the ears made of small pieces of wood for rolling the strings at this end of the instrument. Four ears-two from each side are fixed through the holes made to roll four strings.

After this protion comes the top end portion of the instrument which is horizontally flat for a length of about 5 inches. At the extreme bottom end a very small chignon is carved out from the log to facilitate tying of a rope/thread to support a 1.5 inches long stick in which are tied the strings. Four strings of the instrument are thus tied with a stick placed over the skin cover at the bottom end rolled on the ears at the top end. For tension, the strings are placed on a bridge made of bamboo, wood or buffalo horn over the skin cover. Strings are tightened or loosened by twisting the ears. Strings are usually of muga spin or nylon.

We have already discussed about the mode of playing Dotorā, and use of the notes of Dotorā in making the Bhāwāiyā tune lively and resonating. The primary words (Bol) of Dotorā lesson are-Ḍoloḍong Ḍoloḍong.

Sārindā: *Sārindā* is crude form of the classical instrument *Sārengi*. It is made of a wooden log about 2 feet in length (usually Neem wood). The shape of the instrument is almost like the animal iguana. It is pot-bellied; both ends are thin, while the middle portion is extended and flattened. A stretch of about 8-9 inches from the bottom end is made hollow with the help of chisel. There is thus a big hollow at the mid-portion. This portion is left open while the portion below this is covered with animal skin, preferably iguana skin. At the top end, a 3-4 inch long stretch is made horizontally flat and then a chignon type portion made hollow for fixing the ears for rolling and operating the strings in the same manner as in Dotorā.

Sārindā has three strings. The strings are rolled on the ears at the top and then taken along the length over a bridge fixed over the skin cover and then tied on a little stick, which is again tied back on a very small chignon carved out at the extreme bottom end. Strings are tuned by twisting the ears as in Dotorā. Three strings of Sārindā are tuned in the following manner- middle string at tonic 'S', upper string at 'P' or 'M' and lower string in 'P' *i.e.* pancam of the lower octave. The instrument is played with the help of bow and not stroke. The bow is made of thin bamboo piece with the horsetail hair fixed with it. Strings of the instrument are made of spun thread or tufted horsetail hair. Some Sārindā players also use steel strings.

For playing, the instrument is kept erect usually held by the palm of the left hand at the upper end just on the portion below the upper hollow used for setting the ears. The bottom end rests on the lap or thigh of the player. Naturally the upper portion of the instrument is set near the shoulder. It is played by operating the bow on the strings just near the bridge over the skin cover at the bottom portion. One hand thus operates the bow while the other hand holds the instrument and creates various tunes by pressing the strings appropriately with the fingers.

Byānā: It is a 1.5 feet long string instrument. This instrument, however, is not made of one piece of wooden log like Dotorā or Sārindā. Three parts of Byānā are made of three different materials. The bottom portion is a very small coconut shell cut halfway and covered by animal skin (goat skin or iguana skin). Middle portion is a thin hollow bamboo piece of about 4 inch circumference and about 8-9 inches length. This piece of bamboo is fixed with the coconut shell. At the top end is 4-5 inches long wooden log of almost equal circumference (about 4 inches), which is fixed with the hollow bamboo. An ear made of bamboo or wooden piece is fixed horizontally through a hole made at the joint of the bamboo and wood. Byānā has only one string made of a small tuft of horsetail hair. The string is rolled over the ear and taken along the length of the instrument over a bridge placed on the skin cover and tied at the extreme bottom end on a nail set with the coconut shell. In case of non-availability of horsetail hair, the string is made of thick spun thread or rolled steel wires.

Byānā is a bowstring instrument. The bow is same as the bow for Sārindā. The string is tuned at the tonic 'S', by twisting the ear. For playing, the bottom portion of the instrument is kept placed on the shoulder, while the palm holds the top portion in the same pose as violin (upside down but sloped). Notes S, R, G, M, etc. are thus produced by pressing the fingers of this hand on the string while the bow is operated by the other. As it has one string, only very simple tunes can be played on it. Instruments similar to Byānā are found in Manipur, Assam, Rajasthan and Southern India. In Bhāwāiyā, this is used as an accompanying instrument only in the folk drama named 'Kuśān'. Primary words (Bol) for Byānā lesson are- Kāorāu Māorāo, Kāorāu Māorāo.

Amongst the wind instruments, the main ones are Ār Bānsi and Mukhā Bānsi.

Ār Bānsi : Flute made of thin hollow piece of bamboo (about 1.5 feet long) is commonly used in Bhāwāiyā Caṭkā. The buffalo-keeper (Maiṛāl) used to play the flute in addition to Dotorā to get rid of loneliness and melancholy feelings and also to attract his ladylove who was expected to come to the river-ghat for bath or water. The structure of the commonly used flute is as follows. A small hole is made at a point about 2 inches below the top end and sound is produced with the blow from the mouth on this hole. Another 6 holes, sometimes 7 holes are made on a straight line with gap of about 1.2 inches in between two holes, starting from a point about 4/5 inches below the upper- most hole. For playing, the instrument is held by the palms of both hands, each of the fingers of the hands being placed just above one of the six or seven holes. While the sound is produced with blow of mouth, notes S, R, G, M, P, etc. are produced by following the process of pressure on the holes by the finger tips or withdrawal of tips.

Mukhā Bānsi : The main characteristic of this flute is its big mouth. The flute is made of a comparatively fat hollow bamboo (about 6-7 inches circumference) with the joint intact at one end (top end). A piece of 1.5inch length of a fatter hollow bamboo, whose inner circumference just fits the outer circumference of the main bamboo piece, is fixed on the top end. An aperture like a cap is made just below the joint of the two pieces and immediately above the hole, a thin flat hole is made through the cap to allow the wind to pass through. As in *Ār Bānsi,* 6-7 apertures are made on a straight line starting from a place about 3 inches below the top aperture at equal interval of about 1.2 inches.

For playing the flute, the player sets his mouth on the flat mouth of the flute and blows wind from the mouth by which sound is produced. Pressure from the fingertips on the holes or withdrawal of fingers produces S R G M P D N notes. The speciality of the mode of playing of this flute is that the player does not remove his mouth from the mouth of the flute to take breath and plays without interruption by maintaining regulated continuous breathing into the flute; a technique similar to the Been or the Punjab folk instrument (flute) *ālgogā*. The tune is somewhat like snake charmer's tune. An accomplished *Mukhā Bānsi* player can play up to an hour or more continuously. The flute is mainly used for the folk drama 'Bisaharā' or 'Padmapurān', dealing with the subject matter of the glorious charms and activities of Manasā Devi. The dance 'chokrānāc' performed with the *Bisaharā* takes the style of snake dance following the snake charmer's tune in *Mukhā Bānsi*. This flute is found in use in no place other than the Bhāwāiyā region.

Mukh Bānsi *(End flute or vertical flute)*: It is a beak flute with seven apertures. The tongue or *jivā* is made of bamboo or sugarcane bark. This type of flute, however, is used on rare occasions.

The main instruments under idiophone class are *Kartāl/Juri/Khāpi, Jhāil* and *Kānsi.*

Kartāl: Two bell metal pieces of approximately ½ inch thickness and 8 inch circumference are given the shape of two plates. About an inch around the central point of both the pieces is made deeper so that the portion gets protruded to the exterior. A hole in each is made to put a rope through it. Striking the pieces produces sound. The instrument player holds each of the pieces by tying its rope on his fingers and strikes each against the other by both hands. *Kartāl* can be of different sizes. Smaller ones have mild shrill sound, while the bigger ones have graver sounds. *Kartāl* is called *Manjirā, Juri* or *Khāpi*. This is mainly an accompanying instrument.

Jhāil: Physical structure, materials and mode of playing are same as *Kartāl*. Only difference is that the metal sheets are thinner and bigger-say, 5 inch thick and 1ft. circumference. The sound is louder and high-pitched. This is usually used with very old kirtan type devotional songs whose main rhythm instrument is Dhol.

Kānsi: 3/4 inch bell metal sheet with a hole made on one side through which a rope is fixed. The player ties the rope with fingers and holds it, while he strikes it with a bamboo stick by the other hand. This instrument is usually used as an accompaniment to the instrumental group music of *Dhol, Karkā, Jagajhampa, Sānāi,* etc. in connection with marriage ceremony or other ceremonial functions. All the three instruments described above are with fixed pitch.

The main instruments of membranophone group are *Ḍhol, Karkā, Ḍhāk, Jagajhampa* or *Ḍampha, Ḍhulki* and *Khol.*

Ḍhol: A 2 feet long wooden log of about 3 feet circumference is used for making a *Ḍhol* (Drum). The log is chiselled out from inside and made cylindrical. About 0.5-inch thick wooden hollow has its central portion fat-bodied and both sides gradually and slightly sloped, the circumferences of both sides thus reduced. Circumference of one side is still smaller than the other. Both the mouths of the cylinder are then covered with goatskin. The skins are fixed with the help of gum and bamboo rings around. The bamboo rings are then tightened with the help of ropes or leather strips (hawser) horizontally arranged along the length.

There are some small iron rings fixed with the ropes on the body of *Ḍhol*. Slight variation in the pitch of sound can be possible tightening or loosening the ropes by operating the iron rings. The skin of the narrower mouth of the instrument is a bit thicker than that of the other mouth and naturally the sound of the thicker skin is graver (low pitch). Generally, the instrument is kept at waist level with the help of rope placed over the neck and hung on the front side of the body. A bamboo stick plays the side with the graver sound while the other side played by the palm of the other hand. Sometimes, a thin stick also plays the other side. *Ḍhol* was the most common percussion with Bhāwāiyā in the past. Its place has, however, been taken by Tablā and *Khol* at present.

Ḍhāk: The physical structure and material by which the *Ḍhāk* is made is same as *Ḍhol* except for the fact that it is longer and fatter-almost 3 ft. long with almost 5 ft. circumference. The instrument is played on one side (the side of higher pitch) with the help of two cane or bamboo sticks operated by two hands. The side of graver sound is not played; it helps in producing the resonance. *Ḍhāk* is generally played with the dance tune and at worship of deities. In the Bhāwāiyā region the use of *Ḍhāk* is essential for the songs and dances like *Kātipujār gān, ṣāiṭoler gān, Ghaṭ pujār gān,* etc. While playing, the instrument is kept by the side of the body of the player to facilitate playing by two hands- placing one of them above the instrument for operating the stick by the hand accordingly, the other hand strikes the skin with stick horizontally. This is tuned more or less at a fixed pitch (scale) and there is very little scope to bring the variation by tightening or loosening the ropes by operating the rings.

Ḍhulki: About 6 inches long 0.5 inches thick wooden hollow with 1 foot circumference, both the mouths being covered with goat skin makes the instrument. Skins on both the mouths are tightened and fixed by ropes or leather strips as in case of *Ḍhol.* The instrument is held by the palm of one hand and played by the palm of the other hand. It is usually used for the devotional types of songs with the *Sārindā*.

Khol: (Mridanga): *Astādhyayi* of Panini first mentions the name Mṛdanga. Sangeet Dāmodar of Hariballav says,

> " Mṛttikā nirmitascaiva mṛdangah prakirtitah
> Ebang Mardalakah proktah Sarbabādyanca sobhate"

Sangeet Pārijat of Ahobal says,

> *Madhyadeśe mṛdangasya Brahmā basati sarbadā*
> *Yathā tirthanti talloke deba atrāpi sansthitah*
> *Sarbadebamayo yasman mṛdangah sarbamangalah*

Compilation of Bishnuprasad Rabha compositions mentions a sloka collected from Nabadwip Ch. Brajabasi about *mṛdanga*:

"Mṛdanga brahmarupāya lābanyāng rasamādhuri
Sahasra guna samjuktang mṛdangāya namo namah
Namaste Sri-Jagannatha namaste Sri-Gauda bigrahah,
Namah khola karatālaya namah kirtanamandali."

There is a story in connection with the creation of *mṛdanga.*

> Once delighted by the killing of *Tripurāsura*, the gods rejoiced in dance and Brahma created mṛdanga to keep rhythm of that dance. The *khol* was made by the soil swollen by the spirit of *Tripurāsura*, skin of the demon was used as the covers, his bone dust (tumour), veins and subsidiary veins used as the ropes or leather strips for the instrument. Thus was made this instrument mṛdanga.

The popular common episode about mṛdanga in Assam is:

Iṭo khol bādya āchil Baikunṭha Nagare
Pṛthibit ānilanta Śrimanta Śankare.

Srimanta Sankardev, the preacher of Neo-Vaishnavism in the then Kamrup was the person who introduced *khol*.

Mṛdanga has an intimate relation with kirtan. *Mṛdanga* is intimately related to the rise of Sri Caitanya and the concept "Harirnāmaiva Kevalam" preached by him in Bengal. That is why all the informations about Mṛdanga are mostly available in the Vaisnava Litrature. Bhakti Ratnākar of Narahari Ṭhākur says that Mṛdanga is the best of four classes of membranophonic instruments.

Anaddha prabheda jāno mardalākhya ār
Śriraja ḍhakkā paṭaha ādi e pracār.

In North Bengal, that is, the then Kamrup, the introduction of *khol* and mṛdanga is closely connected with the Vaishnavism of Sankardeva, as stated earlier. Sankardeva preached the Vaishnavism in the entire Kamrup area, that is North Bengal and Assam area with the patronisation of the king Naranarayan of Cooch Behar. While doing so, he made *khol* or mṛdanga the essential instrument to accompany the Harinam Samkirtana.

Khol became the main percussion instrument of North Bengal from that time. *Khol* gradually became the life force of the three main folk dramas *Dotorā, Kuśān* and *Biṣaharā* of Cooch Behar and entire North Bengal and Western Assam, and with the passage of time it became the most essential rhythm instrument of all types of songs in this area. The greatest advantage of the instrument is that it does not have to be tuned in any particular scale or pitch. It can be played with songs of any scale. In fact, this is why the instrument is jocularly called a 'rascal' instrument.

Khol is about 2.35 feet long 0.5inch thick earthen hollow with circumference of about 2 feet near the mid-point. From this point of highest circumference, it gets sloped on both sides, gradient being very little along one side but quite substantial along the other. The circumference at the end-point (mouth) of the side with the less gradient

(*Bāyā*) is reduced by about 5-6 inches, while the circumference of the other side (*Dāinā*) with the higher slope is reduced to only 5-6 inches. Both the mouths are covered by goatskin, on which coloring is done by a pest of iron-dust, etc. The *bāyā* side (usually played by left hand) is engrained partly; middle portion is colored leaving about an inch round the mouth. Coloring is quite deep so that it emits grave sound. The *Dāinā* mouth (usually played by the right hand) is however, fully engrained with color. It produces sharp sound because of the small size of the mouth. Both the mouths are connected and tightened with the help of leather strips fixed horizontally in the same way as in *Ḍhol*. The number of leather strips, however, is much more as the entire body of the instrument has to be thoroughly covered to get proper sound from both mouths heavily engrained. There are no rings fixed with the strips and so the scale (pitch) of the sound on both sides is completely fixed. There is no scope for causing it vary even a little.

Khol is played being held by both hands at waist height like Ḍhol. On standing position, the instrument is held by placing a strap with its ends tied on both sides of the *khol*, placed over the neck of the player and the instrument thus hung in front. On sitting position, it is set on the ground or on the lap.

In *Kirtan*, there are very difficult *tālās* (rhythmic time measures) with complicated *mātrā* arrangements and layas. The *khol* player therefore, has to learn the playing from regular teacher (*guru*). The *tālas* like *Ḍāspāhāri, Jhinjhiṭ, Choṭo daśkuśi, Bara daśkuśi,* etc. are to be learnt under regular guru. Naturally, *khol* has some prescribed words (bol) for primary learning. Moreover, the *khol* player has to utter those words (*bol*) in the midst of *Kirtan* to show his proficiency, to give the singer some relief and also to bring some variety in the whole performance of kirtan.

However, in case of Bhāwāiyā, there is no such system of regular lesson under the guru. Here the tālās are simple with 4,6,7 or 8 mātrās. The players learn it just practising the simple beats while accompanying the songs and following the expert player. There are no regular words (bol) for primary lesson, although very crude types of words are sometimes kept in mind for producing such sounds with the beats. They are:

Khe tāke do-māng
Tumāng, tumāng,
Khe tāke do-māng.

Or,

Jhā gher gher, jhā gher gher jhā
Nā gher gher nā gher gher nā............, etc.

Swarlipi (Notations):

Notations of a few songs may be helpful in understanding the musicological form of the folk song Bhāwāiyā. Although it is almost impossible to translate the essence and emotions of any folk song in terms of notations, one can get an idea about the form with the help of notations. And this attempt is being made with that view in mind.

Notes are indicated as below:

Tonic i.e Saraja> S, Major second i.e Ṛsava> R, Major third i.e Gāndhāra> G, Normal fourth i.e Madhyama> M, Dominant i.e Pancama> P, Major sixth i.e Dhaivata> D, Minor seventh i.e soft Nishāda>n, Major seventh i.e Nishāda> N; notes of lower Octave are shown by underline such as, P̲, N̲ and of upper Octave by the mark(/) upon the note such as, Ś, Ṙ.

(1)   Hastikanyā, Hastikanyā Bāmoner Nāri—
         Mathāy Niyā Tāmkalsi O Hastē Sonār Jhāri.
         Sokhi O, O Mōr Hāy Hastir Kanyā Re—
         Khāniko Doyā Nāi Māhūtok Lāgiyā Re, --(the refrain).

O elephant girl, O elephant girl, O Brahmin woman, / with your copper pitcher on your head and the golden jhāri in your hand./ O Sokhi, O my elephant girl, won't you have a little pity for the māhūt ?

         Pāttirā Kariyā Kainyā Bādeyā Dilen Pāo
         Māthār Upor Kāl-jiṭi O Sakhi Kare Panca Rāo
         Bālu Ṭilṭil Pankhi Kānde Bālutey Padiyā
         Gouripuriyā Māhut Kānde O Sakhi Ghar Bādi Chādiyā.

You left your house on an auspicious day. But it was the ominous lizard, O Sakhi, that croaked above your head. The sandpiper cries in the sands. The Mahout from Gouripur, O Sakhi, cries for his home.

         Āi Chādilong Bhāi Chādilong Chādilong Sonār Puri
         Biāo Kareyā Chādiyā Āsilong O Sakhi Alpo Bayser Nāri.

I left my mother, I left my brother, I left my golden house. I married and then left behind, O sakhi, my young wife.

```
S    S  S  RG | SR   RS  S   S   | RM  M   P   Dn | pD   P   --  --
Has-ti Kan-nyā | Has -ti  Kan-nyā | Bā- mo- ne- ro | Nā - ri  --  --

--   -- -- -- |  --  --  --  --  | MP  P   P   PD | MP   -P  Dn  DP
--   -- -- -- |  --  --  --  --  | Mā-thāy Ni- yā | Tā-mka    -la - si

M    -- -- -- |  --  --  M   D   | P   P   S   S  | D̲S   S   R   G²
O    -- -- -- |  --  --  So- khi | Has-tē So- nār | jhā-  ri  Sa  khi

R    -- -- -- |  --  --  G   RG  | S   S   R   GR | S    n̲   P̲   --
O    -- -- -- |  --  --  O   Mōr | Hā - y Has - tir | Kan- nyā  Re  --

P̲n   n̲  n̲  n̲ |  S   S   RG  SR | SP  P   M   GM | RG   GS  R   G²
Khā - ni- ko |  Do- yā  Nā - i  | Mā  --  hu  -- | --   -- tok la

R    Rn̲ S  -- |  --  --  --  --  |
gi- yā  Re -- |  --  --  --  --  |
```

(Same tune for other couplets also.)

(2) Āji Āulāilen Mor Bāndhā Moyāl Re—
Hātir Piṭit Thākiyā Re Māhūt, Thor Kolā Bhāngo,
Nārir Maner Kathā Tomrā Kibā Jāno Re.
Rāstā Chādo Rāstā Chādo Re Joler Kalas Kānkhe,
Nārir Mon Bhāngiyā Re Māhūt Chādiyā Jāiben Moke.

You have set in confusion my settled home, Sitting on the back of your elephant,
O Māhut, you can breakdown the banana stalks. But what do you know of a woman's heart?
Leave my way, leave my way, O Māhut, I have my pitcher at my waist,
You will break my heart, O Māhut, and leave me alone.

M - PD P | M M G RS | RG RS R GM | GM GG R S

Ā u la i | le n Mo r | Bā - n dhā | Mo - yā l

S - - - | - - - - | - - - -

Re - - - | - - - - | - - - -

S S R R | G -- GMG RS | RS^2 G^{2}RS RG GM | GM GMG RS S

Ā -ji Au- lai | le -- -n Mor | Bā -- n dhā | Mo -- yā - l

S - - - |

Re - - - |

M M -M G | M M P P | Dn P D -- | n -- -- --

Hā - ti - -r Pi | ṭi t Thā ki | yā Re Mā -- | hu -- -- --

-- -- -- -- | Dn DnD P -- | P Dn PD M | P -- Pn Dn

-- -- -- -- | -- -- t | Tho -- r Ko | lā -- Bhā --

P -- -- -- | -- -- P D | n -- -- -- | Dn DnD P --

ngo -- -- -- | -- -- Mā- hut | Re -- -- -- | -- -- (he) --

P Dn PD M | P -- PD PD | P -- -- -- | -- -- P M

Thō -- -r Ko | -Lā -- Bhā -- | -- ngo-- -- | Ā r

pn n -- n | DnD PM P Dn | DnD PM M -- | M -- -- --

Nā ri -- ra | Mo -- ne -- | ro -- Ka -- | thā -- -- --

-- -- MP PM | G M GMG R | S -- S R | RM GM R --

-- -- -- -- | Tom- rā -- Ki- | bā -- Jā -- | no -- Re --

-- -- -- -- | -- -- R RS | RM M MP PD | MP M GMG RS

-- -- -- -- | -- -- Ā -ji | Ā -u lā -i | -le -n Mo -r

RG^{2}G^{2}RS RG GM | GM GMG RS S | S -- -- -- | -- -- -- --

Bā -- -n- dhā | Mo -- ya- l | Re -- -- -- | -- -- -- --

S S R R | G -- GMG RS | RG^2 G^{2}RS RG GM | GM GMG RS S
Ā -ji Au- lāi- | le- -- -n Mōr | Bā -- -n dhā | Mo -- yā - l
S -- -- -- |
Re -- -- -- |
(Same tune for other stanzas too).

(3) Āji Geile ki Āsiben Mor Māhut Bondhu Re, --
Hasti Norān Hasti Chorān 'Kekoā Bāsher Tole,
Ki Śāpē Dongśhilek Māhutok Koyā Jāo Bā More Re.
Rojāy Jhāre Gūnine Jhāre Dhekiār Āgāl Diyā,
Mūin Nāri Jhārim Māhutok Kyāśer Āgāl Diyā Re.

If you go away today, O my Mahut friend, will you come back again? You graze your elephant, you make it go round and round, under wild bamboo tree./ But what snake has bit you, O Māhūt, do tell me. The 'Rojā' and the 'gunin' use the 'dhekiā' to purge the venom./ I shall use the tail of my hair on you, O Māhut.

Khāṭo Khuṭo Māhut Re Tor Mukhe Cāp Dāri
Satya Kariyā Kan Re Māhut Kon Bā Dyāse Bāri
Hasti Narāng Hasti Carāng Hastir Pāye Beri
Satya Kariyā Kailām Kainyā Gouripurey Bāri Re
Hasti Narān Hasti Carān Hastir Galāy Dari
Satya Kariyā Kan Re Māhut Ghare Kayjan Nāri Re
Hasti Narāng Hasti Carāng Hastir Galāy Dari
Satya Kariyā Kailām Kainyā Biāo Nāhi Kari Re

O my short-statured Mahout, with your thick beard, will you tell me the truth, O Mahout, where do you have your home? I move the elephant, I graze the elephant, I chain the elephant's feet. I tell you the truth, O girl, I have my home in Gouripur. You move the elephant; you graze the elephant; you chain the elephant's neck. But tell me the truth, O Mahout, how many women have you at your home? I move the elephant, I graze the elephant; I put the cord on the elephant's neck. I tell you the truth, O girl, I have not married as yet.

P | PD DP M M | GM GR SR GM |
Āj | Gei- le Ki Ā | si- be- -n Mor |

| RG^2 G^{2}R S S | S S -- -- |
| Mā - hut Bon- dhu | Re -- -- -- |

| S S S RG | SR RS S S |
| Has- ti No - rān, | Has - ti Ca - rān, |

| RM M P Dn | PD P -- -- |
| Keko- ā Bā sher | To - le -- -- |

| -- -- -- P | P -- n Dn |
| -- -- -- (ki) | O -- Re --) |

| Pn n DnD PM | M M M GM |
| Ki Sā - pē Dong- | shi - lek Māhu - tok |

| RM MR R -- | RM M M GR |
| Ko - yā -- -- | -- -- Jāo Bā |

| RS -- RG RS | n̲ -- -- RG |
| Mō -- rē -- | Re, Āji |

| SR R R GM | RG GR SR GM |
| Gei - lē Ki Ā - | si - be - -n Mor |

| RG² G²R S S | S -- -- -- |
| Mā - hut Bon - dhu | Re, -- -- -- |

(Same tune for other couplets too).

(4) Godādhorer Pārē Pārē Re—
O Mōr Māute Chorāy Hāti,
Ki Māyā Nāgāilen Māhut Re—
O Tor Gālāi Roser Kāṭi,
Ki Māyā Nāgāilen Māhut Re.

On the banks of the Godadhor, my Māhūt grazes his elephant./ What a spell you have cast on me, O Māhūt, / With your love beads on your neck./ What a spell.....

Ucā Kari Bāndhen Chāpar Re
O Muin Jal Bharite Dekhim
Ki Māyā Nāgāilen Māhut Re.
Ucā Kari Bāndhen Mācā Re
O Muin Āiste Jāite Dekhim
Ki Māyā Nāgāilen Māhut Re.
Doi Khoāilen Dudh Khoāilen Re
Māhut Nā Khoāilen Māṭā
Ebār Hyāte Ṭuṭiyā Gelo Re
Oi Nā Āisā Jāoār Ghāṭā
Ki Māyā Nāgāilen Māhut Re.

Do build your hut on a high place, so that I can see it when I go to bring water. What a spell... Do build your resting seat on a high place, so that I can see it when I move up and down. What a spell.... You fed me on curd, you gave me milk; but O Mahout, you never gave me the dregs of the liquid curd. Do I expect that you are going to give up your journeys along this road from now on?

Nā Kānden Nā Kānden Kainyā He
Nā Bhāngen Raser Gālā
Eibār Jadi Ghuriyā Āisong He
Kainyā Sonāy Bāndhim Gālā
Eibār Jadi…………………

Do not weep, do not weep, O girl. Do not waist your sweet voice with weeping. I shall bind your neck, O girl, with gold, if I come back this time.

P P -- | D D P | Ś Ś n | P n n |
Go - dā -- | dho - re - r | Pā - rē -- | Pā rē -- |

D P -- | P P P | P P P | D P P |
Re -- -- | - - | - | - - - | O Mō - r |

P P P | n D P | M - - | G R - |
Mā u te | Ca rā y | Hā - - | ti - - |

R R - | G G M | R G G | G R S |
Ki Mā - | yā Nā - | gāi le n | Mā hu t |

S - - | - - - | - - - | S - - |
Re - - | - - - | - - - | O to r |

S R R | R R R | M -- -- | G R -- |
Gā - lā - y | Ro - se - r | Kā -- -- | ṭi (hi) |

R R -- | G G M | R G G | G R S |
Ki Mā -- | yā Nā -- | gāi - le - n | Mā - hu - t |
S -- -- | -- -- -- |
Re -- -- | |

(Same tune for all the stanzas, and hence same notations).

(5) Oki Gāriāl Bhāi,
Katay Raba Āmi Panther Dikey Cāyyā Re
Jedin Gāriāl Ujān JāyNārir Mon Mor Jhuriyā Roy Re
Oki Gāriāl Bhāi,
Hākāo Gāri Tui Cilmārir Bandarey Re
Ki Kaba Duskera Jālā
Gāriāl Bhāi Gāthiyā Cikana Mālā Re
Oki Gāriāl Bhāi,
Kata Kāndim Mui Nidhuyā Pāthārey Re

(O Gāriāl (Bullock cart Driver)! How long shall I look to your ways? This woman's heart laments when move towards the up-country and O Gāriāl, you drive your cart to the Cilmari market. How do I express my grief? How long shall I weep with this fine garland on hand?)

S S | SR R RM G | R -- M M | M M M M |
O Ki | Gāri āl Bh ā | i - Ka ta | Ra ba Ā mi |

P -- PM GM | GMG RG R - | - - - - | RM GM - - |
Pa n the r | Di - ke - | - - - - | Cā - - - |

RM G RS -- | S -- -- -- | - - - - | - - - - |
yā - - - | Re - - - | - - - - | - - - - |

M M G G | M -- P -- | P Dn n - | - - - - - |
Je din Ga ri | ā l U - | jā n Jā - | - - - - - |

-- -- -- -- |-- -- Dn D | P -- P P | P D Dn D |
-- -- -- -- |-- -- -- -- | y - Na rir | Ma n Mo r |

PD P M M | P DP P -- |-- -- -- -- | -- -- S S |
Jhu - ri yā | Ra y R e |-- -- -- -- | -- - O Ki |

SR R RM G | R -- M M | M M M -- | P P MPM GM |
Gāri āl Bhā -- | i - Hā Kāo | Gā ri Tu i | Ci l mā - |

GMG RG R -- | -- -- R GM | RM G RS -- | S -- -- -- |
ri r Ba -- | -- n da -- | -- -- re -- |Re -- -- -- |

-- -- G G | -- RG S -- | R S RM -- |M M -- -- |
-- -- Ki Ka | -- ba Du s | ke -- ra -- |Jā lā -- -- |

-- -- -- -- | GG M RG MG |GR G SR R| - G G R |
-- -- -- -- | Gāri āl Bhā -- | -- I Gā thi | -- yā Ci -- |

G S RM G | RS S S -- | -- -- P P | PD Dn n -- |
ka -- -- na | Mā lā re -- | -- -- O Ki | Gāri āl Bhā -- |

-- -- -- -- | -- -- -- -- | -- -- Dn D |P -- P P |
-- -- -- -- | -- -- -- -- | -- -- -- -- | - i Ka ta |
D D nD P |PD PDn D P | M G R -- |- - RM GM |
Kān dim Mu i |Ni -- dhu -- | yā - Pā -- | - - thā - |

RM G RS -- | S -- -- -- |
-- -- re -- | Re -- -- -- |

(6) Āmār Bāri Jān O Mor Prāner Maishāl Re
O Maishāl Boistey Diba Morā
Bukkotey Helāni Diyā Re,
O Maishāl Bājāiben Dotorā.
Āmār Bāri Jān O Mor Prāner Maishāl Re
O Maishāl Boistey Diba Pirā
Jalpān Kariyā Diba Re,
O Maishāl Saru Dhāner Cirā.

[O my dear Maishal! Please come to my house. I will give you a Mora (a seat made of bamboo) to sit on and you can play your Dotora leaning against my breasts. O Maishal my dear! Please come to my house. I will give you a Pira (an wooden seat) to sit on and fine flattened rice for your tiffin.]

| P P -- | PD n D P | P P n | D P P |
| Ā mā r | Bā ri - | Jā - n | O Mo r |

| M G R | R G M | G R -- | -- -- -- |
| Prā ne r | Ma i shā | Re -- -- | -- -- -- |

| -- -- -- | -- -- -- | -- -- R | G S -- |
| -- -- -- | -- -- -- | -- -- O | Mai shā l |

| R R -- | M G M | RG R -- | S RG R |
| Ba -- is | tey -- -- | Di -- -- | -- ba -- |

| S S -- | -- -- -- | -- -- -- | -- -- -- |
| Mo rā -- | -- -- -- | -- -- -- | -- -- -- |

| S R -- | R R RM | M M -- | -- -- -- |
| Bu kko -- | tey - He | lā ni -- | -- -- -- |

| G R R | R M GR | R -- -- | -- -- -- |
| -- -- -- | Di yā -- | Re -- -- | -- -- -- |

| -- -- R | R G S | R R -- | M GM -- |
| -- -- O | Mai shā l | Bā -- -- | jā i -- |

| RG R -- | S M G | S S -- | -- -- -- |
| be - n | -- Do -- | to rā -- | -- -- -- |

(Same tune for other stanzas)

(7) Ki O Bandhu Kājal Bhomorā Re
Kondin āsiben Bandhu Kayyā Jāo Kayyā Jāo Re
Jadi bandhu Jābār Cān
Ghārer Gāmchā Thuiyā Jān Re
Bandhu……………………Re.
Baṭa Bṛksher Chāyā Jeman Re
Mor Bandhur Māyā Teman Re
Bandhu Kājal Bhomorā Re
Kondin .... Re.

M -- | M -- -- | -- -- | -- -- | -- -- -- | M -- | G R |
Ki -- | O -- -- | -- -- | -- -- | -- -- -- | Ba n | dhu -- |

RG S - | R M | M G | R S - | n D P |
Kā - - | ja l | Bho - | mo rā - | Re - | - - |

n -- -- | n -- | n -- | S S -- | G -- | G -- |
Ko - n | di n | Ā - | si be n | Ba n | dhu - |

M P -- | M -- | M P | GM G --| S -- | S -- |
Ka yā - | Jā - | - o | Ka yā - | Jā - | - o |

S -- --| -- -- | -- -- |
Re - - | - - | - - |

M M -- | G -- | M -- | P P -- | P -- | -- M |
Ja di - | Ba n | dhu - | Jā bā r | Cā - | - n |

D -- | n -- | D -- | D P -- | Pn D | P M |
Ghā re r | Gā m | chā - | Thui yā - | Jā - | - n |

M -- -- | -- -- | -- -- | -- -- -- | -- -- | -- -- |
Re - - | - - | - - | - - - | - - | - - |

-- -- -- | M -- | -- -- |
- - - | Ba n | dhu - |

M M -- | G M | R G | SR R S | M -- | P M |
Ba ṭa - | Bṛ kshe | r - | Chā yā - | Je - | ma n |

M -- -- | -- -- | -- -- | -- -- -- | -- -- | -- -- |
Re - - | - - | - - | - - - | - - | - - |

M P -- | P n | D P | M G R | R G | G M |
Mo - r | Ba n | dhu r | Mā yā - | Te - | ma n |

MG R -- | -- -- | -- -- | -- -- -- | -- -- | -- -- |
Re he - | - - | - - | - - - | - - | - - |

-- -- -- | M -- | G M |
- - - | Ba n | dhu - |

REFERENCES

Bhowmik, Nirmalendu, Pranta *Uttarbanger Lok Sangeet*, Chirayata Prakashan, 2nd edn., Kolkata, 1997.

Chattopadhyay, Bimal Chandra, *Uttarbanger Lok Sangeet*, Granthamandir Prakashan, Kolkata, 1992.

Das, Nirmal, *Uttarbanger Bhasa Prasarya,* Sahitya Bihar, Kolkata, 2nd edn. 1997.

Ibid.

THREE REPRESENTATIVES OF 'BHAWAIYA' REGION

The Author with Ferdausi Rahman (Bangladesh) and Pratima Barua (Assam)

Interview of Pratima Barua by the Author

The Author Performing Bhâwâịyâ on Ṛiver Erosion

Massive Erosion Caused by the Kaljani Ṛiver

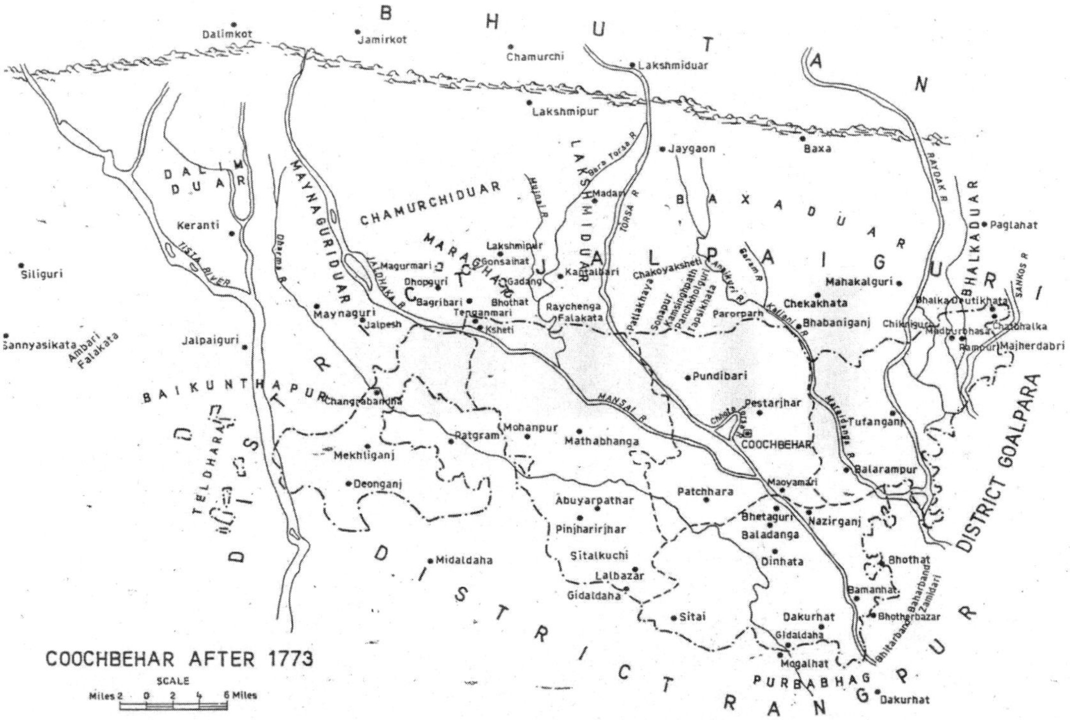

Coochbehar Palace

TWO LEGENDARY BHAWAIYA SINGERS

Abbasuddin (1901-1959)

Pyarimohan Das (Lalan Awardee)

7

Ritual-based Songs of Bhāwāiyā

Vrata-based Religious Observances and Bhāwāiyā

While dealing with the theoretical base of folk music and music at length, it has been established that music in every society and culture, commenced with rituals to propitiate the gods and goddesses, revered by the particular social and cultural group. From the very dawn of the creation, women have devoted themselves to the altar of the welfare of the family. They have used the magic power of mantra, tantra, and tantric titbits for the benefit of the family. In addition, they have made the voluntary religious observances (vows) their life-long companion. Women in traditional societies are closely related to the vows (*Vrata*). They have tried to derive pleasure and happiness in the midst of all kinds of odds by the performances of songs and dances associated with different vows (*Vrata*).

The most important vratas (vows) of North Bengal are *Shāiṭol, Kāti, Subacani, Hudum*, and *Shāiṭ Māo,* etc. Each of such vratas has songs associated with the ritual. Again longest of them is the *Shāiṭol pujār gān*. Shaital is the deity (goddess) of fertility (*Shasṭhi*).

1. **Shāiṭol:** The theme of the *Shāiṭol pujār gān* covers the reception of the deity, ghaṭ (earthen jar) *sijjan, sindur* (vermilion) *sijjan, dhup* (incense) *sijjan*, arrival of the gods and goddesses from heaven, creation of flowers and flower-basket, Nilavati (Lilavati) giving birth to two sons Dhanai and Manai by the blessings of Shāiṭol, etc. The theme centres round the singing of glory of the Shāiṭol Devi. They reflect some aspects of the social life of the Rajbanshis. The songs are sung in simple tunes and rhythms. Some of the songs are tetratonic.

Example: Being invited by the house owner (house-wife), the female singer of Shāitol takes the full responsibility of performing the Puja. Songs and dances are part and parcel of the Puja. The main instrument is *Dhāk* (long cylindrical drum).

Kāngāl māreyā garib māreyā, Tomār bāri kiser nimantan,
Nay korā kari dyāo, bāirār kholān āmāk chāri dyāo
Āmrā karomo e nā ronger pujā re.
Kāngāl māreyā garib māreyā, Panca devatā tomār bāyrā āche khārā re.
Āno māreyā gangār jal re, āno māreyā tulsir jal re,
Dhoāy māreyā panca devatār caran re.

Oh poor house-owner! You have invited us. Give us nine kadis (money) and leave the outer courtyard for us. Five gods are standing outside. Bring Ganga water and Tulsi water for washing their feet. Various parts of the song are:

Sendur Sijjan: *Sendur re tor jaram hail kār ghare*
Jaram haice mor bākālir ghare.

O vermillion! In whose house you were born? I was born in the house of Bakalia.

Dhup Sijjan: *Dhup re tui jaram nilu kār ghare*
Jaram haice mor dhupamatir ghare re.

Dhoop (incense)! Where were you born? I was born in the house of Dhupamati.

Swarga haite nāmil Basumati mance dilen pāo
Kon khāne āsan haibe māo cinha kari nyāo.
Swarga haite āsil Dharm Gosāin mance dilen pāo
Kon khāne āsan haibe Dharma Gosāin cinha kari nyāo .....

Came from heaven the Basumati, Dharma and other gods. They are prayed to take their respective places (seats) for accepting the Puja.

The singers then start singing the life history of Nilā. There is a beautiful piece of song regarding Nila's hair put up in a bun (chignon). Depending on the style, the names of the bun differ.

(1) *Ānil ṭokrāi Nilā ghucāil ḍhākini, Ṭān diyā bāir kari nil raser kākai khāni.*
Māthā konā kākeyā culir chārāil jāṭā, Raser kākai diyā Nilā cul karil goṭā.
Khopā konā bāndiyā Nilā āge pāche cāy, Manote nā khāy khopā khaseyā phyālāy.
Tār pāche bānde khopā nāme unijhuni, Tār talot bhāsā bānde bāngā bāriyā ṭuni.....

Nila opened the dressing box, brought out the nice comb with which she untied the matted hair and made a bun. She looked at the mirror, did not like the style of the bun and untied it. Then she made a style called unijhuni, which resembles the nest of cotton bird. Finding it not after her liking, she untied it again and tried different styles one after another.

Eko nā cāndote eko nā māsote, hayyā geilek mor sāto byāṭār biāo re
Kāon hailek byāṭār māo, kāon hailek byāṭir māo

Tui Nilā janomer bānji re, jā Nilā tui bāpo māoyer ghare re
Āji sasur nā balong mui, bāpo nā balong mui, āji samay dyāo bābā ārāi diner nāiyor re.
Āji chi chi re Nilā re bānji naijjā nāi re tor, jā Nilā tui sasuri māoyer kāche re.

All the seven sons of mine were married in the same month. All the daughters-in-law except Nila gave birth to a son or a daughter. Nila is barren for life. So, Nila, you go back to your parents. Nila prays for only two and a half days' leave for going to her parents from the father-in-law. He asks Nila to go to her mother-in-law for the permission. She asks Nila to go to somebody else of the house, etc.

Nila is barren and so she is despised by all the members of the family and that is the reason why every one except the younger brother-in-law of Nila, turns his or her face when Nila asks for permission for going to her parents only for two and half days.

Āji bhāio nā balong mui dyāorāo nā balong mui,
Samay dyāo dyāora ārāi dinkār nāiyor re.
Chi chi re ādarer baudi kathā sonek more re,
Dyāng hukum mui caliā jāo bol bāri re.

You are my brother; you are my brother-in-law and give me permission to go to my parents. Younger brother-in-law says, 'Listen my dear bhabhi; go to your parents without hesitation. Her brother-in-law tells her not to put up with this kind of mal-treatment and allows her to leave the house on being approached by Nila.

Nila then sets off and stops on the riverbank, spends the night there weeping through out. Seeing her in such conditions of grief, Shāiṭol Devi took pity on her and asked about the reasons. Nila tells her the experiences of daily life. Shāiṭol blesses her that she will give birth to two sons-Dhanai and Manai in due course but Nila will have to arrange for the worship of Shāiṭol afterwards.

Nila goes back home and asks for permission to live with her husband but every body in the house except her brother-in-law seems to be averse to her prayer. On the insistence of the younger brother-in-law, Nila enters the room of her husband Charan Sadhu, spends the night with her and conceives. She gives birth to two sons in due course and arranges Shāiṭol Puja, as advised by Shāiṭol Devi. As stated earlier, songs and dances are part and parcel of this Puja. The song starts with the prayer to Sasthi (Shāaiṭol). For example:

(i) *Sasṭhi māoyer janma re hailo Nandi goāler ghare*
Ki Sasṭhi māo mandise ghore.
Āiso āiso Sasṭhi māo rathote cariā
Ki Sasṭhi mā mandise ghore.

Āiso āiso Sasṭhi māo hastite cariā, Ki Sasṭhi.....
Tomāro nā pujā āche cātāl bhareyā, Ki Sasṭhi.....
Tomāro nā pujā neo māo hāsiyā khiliyā, Ki Sasṭhi.....
Jadi māreyāk māo rākhen bhāle bhāle
Tomāke māo dibe pujā bachare bachare, Ki Sasṭhi māo mandise ghore.

Sasthi Ma (Mother Saitol) was born in the house of Nandi goala. O mother, please do come on your chariot, on your elephant. Here we have arranged your Puja. Do accept the same with pleasure. If you keep the Mareya (household) in good conditions, he will workship you every year.

(ii) Āji deba bandong Ganapati he, āre o Gaonāi tui baro sundar re
Āji Mao hailek Candikā Devi, āre o Gaonāi pitā Maheswara re
Āre eko māso hailo Ganāi he, āre o Gaonāi garbhe nilo bās
Āji deba.....
Ār duio māso hailo Ganāi he, āre o Gaonāi hailo rakter golā
Āji deb... he.....

Let us now offer prayer to Ganapati, the pretty god. His mother is Chandika Devi and father Maheswar. In the first month the pregnancy starts; it turns into blood clot in the second month and so on. The singer describes the position of pregnancy in ten months and Ganapati is born in the tenth month. From here the singer goes to describe the pregnancy position of Nila in the same way and in the tenth month of her pregnancy Nila gives birth to two sons – Dhanāi and Manāi. After this, she arranges the Puja of Shāitol and the ballad ends.

2. Kāti Pujār gān: *Kāti pujār gān* is a part of female rituals of Kamroop. The puja was usually held in the month of Kartik (November). The puja is named 'Namla Kati' if it is held some other time of the year. Four plaintain plants are planted at a distance of about a metre in between two such plants under a big tent open on all sides (*Samiana*). The deity Kartik with his carrier peacock is placed in the middle for the worship. An earthen pot full of water mith a mango twig emersed in it is placed at the foot of each of the plants. Mango twigs and arrow and bow are tied on the plants. A pair of green betel nuts and leaves is also placed at the root of each such plant. The women devotees fast through the day and attend the puja in the evening with a pair of green betel nuts and leaves for offering the same to Kartik.

Behind the image of the deity Kartik is planted a twig of Moyna tree (a thorny bushy plant). Just in front of the altar is planted a brunch of paddy plants with the green or semi-ripe paddy on them. Kartik puja is also a manifestation of fertility cult. The barren women do pray for son. The puja is usually organised by any well off households who also suffer from the same problem of not having any issue. Songs and dances are inseparable parts of the Kartik puja. The song starts usually with a prayer song to Kartik. Marriage of Siva and Parvati, birth of Kartik, description of the image of the deity, prayer for the blessing of son, etc. form parts of the song.

The women move round the image with songs and dances. Sometimes a few of them participate being dressed as men. Women, desirous of being blessed with son, do participate with calun-bati (prayer tray with puja articles and lighted mustard oil lamp on it). It is believed that Kartik will give the blessings of sons if satisfied with the songs and dances. *Ḍhāk* (long drum) is the main instrument for the songs and dances. Singers are women but the *Ḍhāk* (drum) player is man.

Examples of Songs:

Dhupa dilām dhunāo dilām māreyā sāri sāri, ki Kāti dheyāne baise re.
Dhupa dilām dhunāo dilām ghaṭ basāilam sāri sāri, ki Kāti dheyāne baise re.
Dhup dilong dhunāo dilong nabud sāri sāri, ki Kāti dheyāne baise re.
Āji dhupa dilām dhunāo dilām thāit basāilām sāri sāri, ki Kāti dheyāne baise re.
Āji Kāti Ṭhākurer mukher āge purna ghaṭa baise, ki Kāti dheyāne baise re.

We arranged in rows the plaintain trees, the sacred water pots, and offerings with the incense-pots in resin and Kati has taken his seat for meditation. The full sacred water pot has been placed in front of Kāti Ṭhākur. After the prayer song the singer goes to describe Siva-Parbati's marriage-Chandi's marriage.

Chaoā kāl geil Siber khelā nā khelite, ki pāgal burā Sib re.
Ār gābur kāl geil Siber śmasāne masāne, ki pāgal burā Sib re.
Elā briddha kāle burā Sib biyār āṭus kare,.....
Āji jāy jāy burā Sib māoyer āge,.....
Tomāko nā balong janamer janani māo, ...
Kathā suniyā Siber māo bhābe mane mane.....
Eo nā bayase Bābāk kāy bā dibe kainā,.....
Jā jā re Bābā tui Nārad bhāginār bāri
Āji jāy jāy re Nārad bhāginā Panditero bāri,

The old mad Siva spent his childhood in games, sports and amusements. His youth was spent wandering in the funeral places and burials. Now at this old age he desires to marry and discloses it to his mother. His mother naturally thinks twice – who will give their daughter to this old groom? She however, advises his son to go to Narada and ask him to look for a suitable bride, ..., etc.

Jāy jāy Nārad bhāgina Panditera bāri, ki namo Nārāyan
Kibā karen Pandit Ṭhākur niscinte basiyā,.....
Nutan Panijikā dekho purāno chāriyā,.....

Kibā karis māmā tui niscinte basiyā,
Tomāro biyār din jāy se chuṭiyā, ki namo Nārāyan.

Narada goes to the house of the Pandit, asks him to bring out the new almanac and foretell who will be the suitable bride for Siva. On getting the clue he comes back and requests Siva to get ready for the marriage..., etc. The songs and dances continue.

Kātire tor munḍa bānāiche kon jane, Chay mās bharmiyā re tapaisyā kariyā re
Munḍa banaiche Basudebe,
Kātire tor coukh bānāiche kon jane, Chay mās bharmiyā re tapaisyā kariyā re
Choukh bānāiche Basudebe,
Kātire tor pyāṭ bānāiche kon jane, ānu janame re nārkol bilāichong re
Pyāṭ bānāiche Basudebe.
Kātire tor nāk bānāiche kon jane, ānu janame re bānsi bilāichong re
Nāk bānāiche Basudebe.....

O Kati! Who has made your head? I have wandered and prayed for six months and Basudeva has given me the head and ears too. Who has given you the belly and the nose? I made gifts of coconut in earlier life and the belly I got as reward of that piety; nose I got as reward of making gifts of banshi (flute) in earlier life. Similarly, different limbs are supposed to have been gifted as reward of piety out of gifts made in earlier life.

With the progress of puja, songs and dances, at a certain point of time the presence of males is prohibited at the puja place. Even the drum player (ḍhāki) has to leave the place. The reasons are that the women folk now enact the sexual union; the songs are full of indescent words and the dance movements also resemble sex actions. The belief is that this will make Kati happy and he will bestow blessings of sons on the devotee barren women.

Dur hyāte āsil re bādur kalā khābār āśe,
Gacher kalā gache raila bādur geil mor dyāśere
Gacher āre thākiyā bādur kamorer sāri jācere
Tir pare jhāke re jhāke, bāṭul pare rayyāre
Kutti gelu re māreyār māiyā tir kurāo āsiyā re, Dur hyāte
.....aśe.

The bat came from a distant place to eat the banana but keeping the banana untouched on the tree left for its own place. From the treetop he wants the Sarees. (Here the bat is considered as the male lover.) Arrows (of kati) fall in swarms. Where are you, the houselady? Come and collect the arrows. (Arrows are considered as the blessings of Kati). The drum player and other men folk enter after this and the songs and dances continue.

3. Suvacani Puja: Su (good) vacan (words/speech) or subha sucana (good beginning), that is, prayer for welfare or wishing good is the inner meaning of Suvacani. This is a part of female rituals. It is believed that for anything, which relates to the welfare of an individual or a family, one should have the blessings and good wishes of family goddesses. Therefore, to have success in good things of life like marriage, safe delivery of pregnant woman, success in a court case, in other words, to have success in any affair of the family one should have the blessings of the supernatural powers. The main articles of the puja are betel nuts, betel leaves and lime. "Subacanir bāri jāmo, guā pān tyāl sendur sagāy pāmo."

We will go to the house of Suvacani where all of us will get betel nuts and leaves, oil and vermilion.

Example of Song:

Swarga hyāte nāmiyā āsuk nāmore Kāli
Mui sundari pujāre basāicung najor karo āsi :
Kalāo dicong sāri re sāri dimāo dicang sāri
Swarga hyāte nāmiyā āsuk nāmore Māo Bisahari,
Mui subdari..... āsi
Tyāl o dicang sāri re sāri, senduro sāri sāri
Swarga hyāte nāmiyā āsuk nāmore Māo Śitali
Mui sundari..... āsi
Doi o dicang sāri re sāri, dudho sāri sāri
Swarga hyāte nāmiyā aāsuk, nāmore Māo Candi
Mui sundari..... āsi
Dhup-o dicang sāri re sāri, dhunāo re dicang sāri
Swarga hyāte nāniyā āsuk nāmore Māo Suvacani
Mui sundari..... āsi
Phul o dicang sāri re sāri, puspa dicang sāri
Swarga hyāte nāmiyā āsuk nāmore Dharam Ṭhākur
Mui sundari..... karo āsi.

This is a song praying for the presence of the deities to accept the offerings. We have arranged in rows as offerings for the Puja, eggs, oil, vermilion, milk, curd, incense pot in resin and flowers. Let the deities Kali, Bishahari, Sitali, Candi, Suvacani and Dharma Thakur descend from the heaven and accept our Puja.

4. Hudumer gan: The Kamrupi word 'Hudum' means 'udom' in literary Bengali, which means naked. Hudum dyao is the deity worshipped by the female folks with songs and dances. Hudum dyao is supposed to be the god of rains. Hudum is worshipped at the prevalence and continued sustenance of acute drought conditions to cause rains by propitiating this rain-god. The psychophysical background behind the performance is the belief in fertility cult, vegetation cult and sympathetic magic.

For the performance, a plaintain plant is planted in a spot in open field quite distant from the residential areas of the village. The women folks congregate at the point at about 8/9 p.m at night, do simple worshipping and then start singing and dancing. The lyrics of songs often are full of so called indescent words and the movements of dance also are indescent in the light of average middle class aesthetic standard. The dance movements do imitate sexual lovemaking. The participating women with the plaintain tree, the symbol of the deity, enact sometimes copulation.

At some point of time, when the Hudum is considered to be propitiated, some water is poured and three women enact the tilling of land-two of them do the acting of cows while the third one enacts the farmer. The performance thus refers to fertility of both the land and the women. Because of the nature of the performance, men folk are not permitted to witness the performance. Rhythm of dances is usually maintained by playing any broken tin by one of the women or a little boy expert on keeping the beats. Here there is no audience for the performance and all present in the place of performance are the participants.

Examples of songs:

Jāgore jāgore hudum ājikār rāti
Gāirasthay kare pujā diyā dhup cāilon bāti
Ākāsete kare pujā ākās kāmini
Pātālote kare pujā ek kāl nāgini.
Kālā myāghe dhaolā myāghe ḍyākeyā āno jhari
Āndhār kariyā dyāoyā āise dābāri
Kālā myāghe dyāoār jhari āy re.

Awake, o Hudum! Awake for this night, the house-owner worships with incense and light. He worships Akash Kamini in the sky and Kal Nagini in the nether world. You black and white clouds! Bring the rain, you together.

Hilhilyāche kamorṭā mor sirsiryāche gāo
Konṭe konā geile āelā mui hudumār nāgāl pāon.
Pāṭāni khān pareche khasiā āisek re hudumā dyāoā.
Tor bāde mui āchong basiyā.

My waist is eager to be clasped in arms; my body is love sick to meet Hudum. My dress is deshevelled. O Hudum, I am waiting for you. Do come and embrace me.

Āmi kacuri latār maton helibo nā, alpa bayaser Hudum dyāo.
Āre āy āy re kālā myāgh āy parbat dhāyyā
O mui māthā konā ghasiyā re āchung nā cāyyā re.
Ār sendur niyā kyāne āsilen nā ālpā bayaser Hudum dyāo.
O mui gāo konā ghasiyā re āchung nā cāyyā,
Tyāl niyā kyāne āsilen nā, alpa bayaser Hudum dyāo.

I am not to be shaken like esculent creeper, o young Hudum! I am ready after washing my head. Why didn't you come? Come with vermilion and oil.

Bāro bachari Hudum dyāo tor tyāroy nāio pare re, Ki bāro bachari Hudum dyāo re.
Ki ei nā Hudum āre biyār āṭus kare, Ki bāro bachari Hudum dyāo re.
Eo cānde eo māse nāi deong Hudumer biāo.

Hudum is just twelve years old and is yet to reach thirteen; but he wants to marry at this age.

Humdumer ghar hail panca bhāi, cal dādā biyāt jāi
Biāo jāy mor bāmon ṭāri diyā nā re.
Bāmaner gharer gālāt nagun umār kainā burā śagun
Eo cānde eo māse nāi deong Hudumer biāo re.
Hudumer ghar panca bhāi, cal dādā biyāt jāi
Biāo jāy mor ḍhuli ṭāri diyā re.
Ḍhulir ghar bājāy ḍhol umār kainār ganḍagol
Eo cānde nā hail Hudumer biāo re.

These are some jokes about the would be bride. Hudums are five brothers and let us join their marriage. The marriage procession goes via the wards or residential areas of the Brahmins and the wards of the drum players. But their daughters are not good brides.

Āyre hāriyā myāgh āy parbat dhāyyā, Hāriyā myāghok bariyā nilong dhoā māng diā.
Kāla myāghe dhaolā myāghe duiṭi sodar bhāi, Ek cilkā jal dyāo goā dhuiyā nei
Goā dhuiyā phyālāilong pāni, cinā bārit hāṭu pāni,
Hāṭu pāni theṭu hail, nāo hayyā geil kāit, Kāner sonā bāndhi thuiyā code cāipor rāit.

O deep black clouds! Come and wave through the mountains with force and vigour; we will welcome you with our clean private organs. Two of you, the black and white clouds, the full brothers! Give us some water for washing the private parts and then we will have love making acts throughout the night.

Dhaolā myāgh kālā myāgh, myāgh sodor bhāi, Ek cilkā pāni deo goā dhuiyā nei
Sāt jan Hudumer bhāi kāray cyāṭot pāni nāi, āiso sagāy nācan nāci māngot bhareyā.

White and black clouds; you are full brothers; give us water to wash our private organs. You are seven brothers and none of your private organs is watery. Let us put their organs into us and dance.

Hudum dyāo Hudum dyāo hāgi āisci pāni deo
Hāmār dyāsot nāi pāni, hāgā ṭikāt bāra bāni.
Hudum dyāoer ghar sāt bhāi karāy cyāṭot pāni nāi
Ek cilkā pāni deo ṭikā dhuiyā bāri jāi.

The song speaks of acute scarcity of water so much so that even the women folk can not get water for washing the anus and private parts after urination. Hudum! Give us water to wash the anus.

5. Biyār geet (Marriage songs) : Marriage songs are the most important of the ritual-based songs of all clan-based communities. The Rajbanshi community of Kamrup has marriage songs on almost all the events of marriage ceremony. The eternal truth is that a daughter as she is grown up, has to be given to marriage.

Bāroso hāri re teroso kodāl re,
Bolo hāy ai kodāle Moynār bāp mālli bāndhere
Māllire kināre re jor campār gachore,
Bolo hāy tāre tale Moynāy juriche khelā re.
Sarok diyā jāy re sadāgarer byāṭā re
Bolo hāy tāy dekhi geil Moynāk khelā khelāite re.
Takhane kaicong re dayār bābāre
Oki bābā sāt dālāne ghiriyā rākho bāri re.
Tomār parān totā re, pare laiyā jāibe re
Aki Māo ancale ḍhākiyā rākho rupo re.

Moyna's father is making ridge of earth to protect water in the field for the corn with spade, and Moyna is playing under the Champa tree just on the bank of the ridge. The son of the merchant saw her playing and found her to be after his liking. O dear parents! I told you to keep your pretty dear daughter in secret place; otherwise the merchant will take her away.

Rubbing turmeric on the body of both the bride and the groom immediately before the day of marriage is a part of the ceremony. Song on that event:

Halodi re holodi tui baro halodi re
Oki bāchāre halodi pāilen kon khānere
Tor māok ki bāndhā thuiyā haldi āincen jāyyā re,
Oki bāchāre sei haldite hailen ḍagomago re.
Kāon dyāy re hāte kāon dyāy pāye re
Oki bāchāre māye dyāy re cāndo badone re.

Where did you get the turmeric? Did you get it by mortgaging your mother? The turmeric then grew up well. Some put the turmeric on hands and some on the feet, but the mother puts it on the face of the daughter.

Even there are songs when the bride and the groom are doing the make-up. This is a song about the make-up of the bride.

Sājan sājere pardip māoyer kole re
Ār dine sājere pardip hāsiyā khiliyā āre

Āij din sājere pardip dui ānkhi ḍhākiyā āre
Tolo tolo re pardip cān mukho tolo āre
Sājan sājāite pardip panca āio āilo re,
Sendur candone āro gondo tyāler bāse āre
Sundar pardipak āio sājān bhālo mate re
Sājiyā kāciyā pardip ṭalomalo kare āre
Sājaner bhārere pardip hāliyā hāliyā pare re.

Pardip (bride) is getting dressed on the lap of the mother. Usually on other days, she used to do the make up with pleasure and smile but today she is doing it with her eyes closed. Do raise your face Pardip. Five wards have come for your make up. Let her be smeared with perfumed oil, prepare her nicely with ornaments. After make up, she looks so bright and she just swings with the weight of the dress materials. At the arrival of the bridegroom, the women folk start singing:

Rām Laksman dui kalā duore gāriyā
Hor āise tomār jāmāi ghorāte cariyā.
Dekho dekho āio gan jāmāir keman rup
Cān suruj dui ānkhi hengul baran mukh
Eketo pandito jāmāi rāj honsa gālā
Gālāt ḍhuliyā pare sonār kanṭha mālā

The groom comes riding the horse through the gate with two banana trees planted on both sides. Marriage maids! Just notice how beautiful he is. His eyes resemble the moon and the sky and his colour is yellow. The neck of the scholarly groom resembles that of the goose, which has been beautified by a necklace.

Here is a song on the cailon, the tray made of bamboo, which is used for reception, the sacred earthen pot..., etc. Some songs are on jokes with the close relations of both the bride and the groom.

Āre kon bā rasiyā ḍomnā ei cāilon bānāilo
Āre cāilone lekhiyā tuliche bālir śisero sendur.
Cāilon dekhiyā barer māo hayyā geil pāgol
Thāuk bol mor byāṭār biāo mui jāong ḍomnār sange....

Who is the witty Dom who has made the tray depicting on it the vermilion put on the bride's hair portions. On seeing the bamboo tray, the groom's mother has become made after that Dom so much so that she wants to go with him.

Sometimes caustic remarks are made about the parents and other relatives of the groom by the singers of appropriate relations belonging to the bride's side and *vice versa.*

Pākṭir pārer kadamre kadam phuṭil ḍhalo ḍhalo,
Āji kāy āsice kainār gonde ai he kodam curi kare

Chiriyā kadam duiṭā kocā nā bharāy re
Barer bhāi jāy tāy baro asiyā re
Bābrir jhaṭkāne āinlek dhāgrik bāri re
Āji tulsi pārer kaillā kaillā baray dhare re.
Kainār bain jāy re tāy baro cunni re
Ei je cunni kaillā curi kare re.
Barer bhagonpait tāy baro naṭkāni re.
Bhyākra nāṭir gutāy kaillā ādāy kare re.

The Kadam tree on the vicinity of the well has bloomed. Who is there to steal the flowers and who has come to steal the bride's kadam (breasts)? He has torn (distored) two Kadam fruits and put them on his lap. The groom's brother is a loving playful person and he has brought a woman of infamous character. The bride's sister is thievish and she has stolen the bittergourd grown by the Tulsi plant. The ingenious brother-in-law of the groom has got back it beating her with a curved stick.

At the solemnisation of the marriage, both the bride and the groom look at each other, signifying the union.

Ghar hyāte birāil gāburāi coudole cariyā
Ār basāil gāburāik Śiber mukhāmukhi nā re
Śibe dāce gālār hār gāburāi kare namaskār
Āji hyāte hailo gāburāi Śiber adhikār
Tuliyā dharo tuliyā dharo gāburāir simhāsan
Cāri coukhe duio mukhe houk daraśan
Rātri prabhāt kāle gāburāi jāy patir sane.

The bride is brought out of the room in palanquin and made to sit face to face with Siva, (The groom is compared to Siva). The bride who offers the garland and the groom greets with bows. From now onwards the bride goes under the control of Siva. Raise the seat of the bride; let four eyes meet. Early in the morning the bride moves for in-lover's house.

Also there are songs on the occasion of formal giving of the hand of the daughter to the groom in front of the people attending the ceremony with due regard to the rituals.

Ek jorā guā ek jorā pān, bābāy kare sampradān
Kānde Nilman māoyer kole
Āge kare dhān dubbā dān, tār pare kare bastra dān
Kānde Nilman māoyer kole
Āge kare thāl-bhāra dān, tār pare kare āngṭi dān
Kānde..... kole.
Āge kare sonā-rupā dān, tār pare kare kanyā dān
Kānde..... kole.

Bāmon ṭhākure kay sampradāner samay jāy
Kande..... kole.
Nāpite āro kay, Gour bacaner samay jāy
Kānde..... kole.

The father of the bride gives away the daughter in marriage. First he gives a pair of betel nut and leaf, then paddy and durva grass followed by utensil, marriage ring, gold and silver and then the daughter. The priest worries about the right moment of the auspicious ceremony. The barber is also worried about the time of reciting the Gaur vacana.

With the completion of the main function of Sampradan (giving the hand of the bride to the groom), the women folk rejoice in joy and enjoy their happiness with songs and dances.

Golāpire sitār sendur golāpire demo nā
Sur helāni diyā nācere Golāpi.
Golāpire gālār mālā golāpire demo nā
Sur..... Golāpi
Golāpire kāner dul Golāpire demo na
Sur..... Golapi
Golāpire gāyer belāuz Golāpire demo nā
Golāpire kamorer sāri Golāpire demo nā
Sur..... Golāpi, Kār helāni diyā nācere Golāpi.

The marriage is over and it is now time for merriment, songs and dances. Golapi dances and others declare jokingly that Golapi will not be given the *sindur* (vermilion), the necklace, the ear ring, the blouse, the saree and so on. Let her dance to the tunes.

After the ceremonial function is over, the newly married couple will be taken to the bridal chamber. But they cannot have so easy an entry. The bridegroom will have to pay some money to the women folk and girls who were managing the ceremonial affairs so long for their feast. Now they stand on the door of the bridal chamber, scoff at the groom calling him a miser and ask him to pay due price for taking their friend/relative away.

Sendur peci tel cakire, caki ālipan diyā re, Kirpin kasṭiyā Bāli re.
Kāro nā hukume bāli re, bāli takotāy carilu re, Kirpin kasṭiyā Bāli re.
Kāy bā tor bābār cākor re, takotā bicāil re, Kirpin..... re.
Phelāo phelāo phelāo Bāli re, āro bā tin ṭākā re, Kirpin..... re.
Māṭi kāṭā ṭākā Bāli re, tor baonāir pakoṭe re, Kirpin..... re.
Garu carā ṭākā Bāli re, Bāli tor bhāiyer pakoṭe re, Kirpin kasṭiyā Bāli re

With whose permission are you standing on the wooden seat duly decorated in oil, vermilion and white rice-paint, o miserly groom? One who placed the seat is not your father's servant. Bring out money, three more rupees – the money earned by your brother-in-law by the labour of cutting earth and the money earned by your brother for his labour as cowboy. In the bridal chamber, the couple is made to participate in various rituals and games. Songs on various subjects are sung on the occasion.

Nautan dighir pāre ḍingā Nākheswar, ḍālo bhānge fulo tole baideisā kumār.
Oiṭe nā pāilo kumār akumāri nāri, Tumi dharo sāji kainyā āmi ful tuli.
Tumi to baideisā kumār āmi akumāri nāri, Kemone dhariba kumār tomār fuler sāji.
Ei kathā baliyā kainyā nukāil pusper tale, Ek ḍāl puspa dui ḍāl kariyā uṭkāy kumāre.
Kothāy geile rajkanyā dekhā deo more, Hājār ṭākār gaynā kainyā parāmo tomāre
Hājār ṭākār sāri kainyā parāmo tomāre.

The unknown outsider prince met the girl in the garden grown on the bank of the newly excavated tank and asked her to handle the flower basket. The girl did not agree to do the job for an unknown person and did hide under flower. The prince looked for her from branch to branch and prayed to her, 'Please come out. I will give you ornaments and saree worth rupees thousand each'.

Ṭiyā māriyā jhilmilre sundari, aṭi kālār cān mor bāndhāre.
O mor kālār cān āise ki nā āise.
Takhane nā kaicong re kālācan nā jān Balarāmpurer hāṭo re,
O mor... āise.
Takhone nā kaicong re kālārcan nā jān Kesṭapurer haṭo re.
O mor... āise.

Our Kalachand has been in bondage with the dazzling beauty and it is not known whether he will come back or not. We told him beforehand not to go to Balarampur or Kestapur *bazar*. Now it is difficult to say when he comes back.

After the marriage ceremony is completely over, it is time for the bride to go to her in-law's house with the husband leaving her parents, brothers, sisters, relatives and friends with whom she had spent so many years of her early life. It is quite natural that she weeps and her parents and relatives too weep. Song of separation—

Uriyā jāy mor ghar bharā ḍābki (ḍāuki) re, Caliyā jāy mor bāsar bharā ḍābki re.
Ḍābki caliyā geile mandir haibe khāli re, Dābki āchil mor māyer mukher dosor re
Ḍābki āchil mor bābār caukher tārā re, Dābki āchil mor bhāiyer khelār sāthi re
Ḍābkir janye mui nāi bānong āi bārā re, Dābkir janye mui nāi sāmtong āginā re.
Ḍābkir janye mui khāicong dudhe bhāte re.

The *Dabki* (bride) is now going away, making the whole house empty and dark. She was everything for her mother, pupil of the eyes for her father, play mate for her brother. It is for her presence that we did not have to husk the paddy, sweep the court yard, fetch water and so on. She used to look after us so well.

Oki hāuser Kānduni ār kāindo nā.
Jābār kālere kānduni bhāi bā jāibe sange re, Hāuser kānduni ār kāindo nā
Bābār dulāli kānduni bābā baliyā kāndere, Māoyer dulāli kānduni māo baliyā kāndere
Jābār kālere kānduni māo bā jāibe sange re, Hāuser..... nā.
Bhāiyer dulāli kānduni, bhāi bā jāibe sange re, Hāuser..... nā

Don't weep so much just for the sake of it. Being so much attached to parents, brothers and sisters, she weeps by taking their names. Don't worry, your parents, your brother and sister will accompany you.

6. Other sub-forms of Bhāwāiyā: In the history of evolution of Bengali music, the next stage to the ritual ceremony based songs was growth and development of devotional *bhajan* type songs based on the doctrine that there is no soul beyond the body and psyche *i.e.* materialism was the main theme for such songs. About 150 years after the Muslim invasion in the 13th century when the administration in Bengal got settled, the liberalism preached by the Sufism had profound influence on the poetry, literature and music of Bengal and the Sufis, Auls, Bauls invaded the rural Bengal with their songs, dances based on materialistic doctrine.

Side by side, the Vaisnavism of Sri Caitanya had tremandous influence on the music scene of Bengal. The influence got manifested through the predominance of Radha Krishna and Gouranga in the folk scenario of Bengal. The material (*loukik*) stream of the Vaisnava thinking got itself manifested through the songs based on physiology. Under this doctrine the human body considered as a temple became central figure for the songs of Baul and Sufi sects of singers, although Radha Krishna came into the picture occasionally in various contexts and episodes.

North Bengal has not been an exception to this history of evolution. Such songs based on the supremacy of human body found place in Bhawiaya form too. At the initial stage, spiritualism and metaphysics was the main theme of such songs. Gradually, the influence of Vaisnavism got reflected through the entry of the love dalliances of Radha, Krishna into the songs and dances. Of course, the influence of Sri Caitanya in Kamrup was very limited and as such the influence of Radha Krishna on Bhāwāiyā was not significant and widespread.

In Kamrup, the philosophy of Sankardeva, the preacher of Neo-Vaisnavism was predominant. In the Vaisnava philosophy of Sankardeva, Radha does not picture as the prime character. Referring to Kamta literature, Rai Saheb Panchanan Barma has observed—we have observed the predominance of Śakta and Vaisnava doctrines. Vaisnavism has been established under the patronage of Maharaja Lakshmi Narayan. But this Vaisnavism is free from the influence of Nadia.

Although the Vaisnavism in Kamta was divided into various sects, Krishna is the main object of devotion for all. Krishna is one and only adorable one in this material world. Radha is not considered important and adorable. Sri Hari form of Krishna and Narayana is, therefore, much worshipped and popular in this region. Complete devotion to Sri Hari is the philosophy of spiritual life of this part of the globe. The popular songs under this category are:

(1) *Mon ekbār Hari baile bhaba pāre man calore jāi, o tor din bayyā jāy.*

(2) *Bhabe keu kāro nay sakale phāki, ghucibe jātanā munjilere dui ānkhi.*

(3) *Hari din to gelo saindhā hailo pār karo āmāre.*

Side by side with the Baul and Sufi in Bengal, there was widespread influence of *Yoga dharma*, especially *Natha Yoga* in Kamrup. Such influence of *Yoga dharma* got manifested in *Moynamatir gan, Monai jatra, Jag gan* or Kamdever gan, etc. Sufism also had its influence in the form of Satyapirer gan but this came much later in this region.

Not that Radha Krishna did not have any influence at all, they did but in limited way. Not only that. Here the lovesick separated heroine (representative of Radha) has accepted his Krishna, the hero in the form of *Kala, Kanai, Naiya*, etc. In course of time, the bullock cart driver, buffalo-keeper, elephant keeper, ordinary farmer etc have occupied the place of the hero. In other words, the day to day pleasure and sorrows, love and separation of human life have become the main theme of these songs with the passage of time.

The relationship between music and religion, between music and magic are so time-honoured that they appear as being inseparable. Religious worship was accompanied with music even when man was savage. Sexual love, however, received the aid of music only in comparatively advanced stage of society. Sexual love has thus appropriated music to such a large extent today. Dalliances of Radha and Krishna lend good support to this.

Natha Yoga was initially an offshoot of tantricism. Tantricism, that is, obedience to *Tantra* had widespread influence in Kamrup. Kamakhya temple now in Gouhati is considered as the seat of *Tantra*. Tan-the body; *yantra*-the vehicle: *Tantra*. The use of the human body as a vehicle in a sensuous mantra to seek and experience divinity became the primary principle of the art and science of *Tantra*. *Tantra*, with all its rituals like yoga, meditation and sexual union is only a roadmap to be followed to reach the destination.

Tantra calls for action—action with total involvement on all fronts physical, mental, sexual and spiritual to seek the highest level of ecstatic pleasure. Ancient Indian heritage and cultural traditions have absorbed the very dynamics of *Tantra* in all its art forms. Erotic temple sculptures, music, dances, poetry and painting seeped with passionate expression, have withstood the ongoing corrosion of time mainly because it appealed to mankind's basic instinct, to make love.

A dormant potential reservoir of energy is symbolised by showing a coiled golden *naga* (serpent), called the *kundalini* where resides peacefully in the first *chakra* (centre or whirlpool of psychic energy) the muladhara. Infinite energies and psychic and spiritual experiences originate from muladhara chakra. The other chakras are Swadhisthana, Manipuraka, Anahata, Ajna and Sahasrana. The blooming of these chakras begins with a 'cosmic sexual embrace' of Siva (the male principle of universal creation-*Purusha*) represented by an erect male organ (*lingam*) with Sakti (the female principle of bearing and sustaining existence-Prakriti) represented by the female generative organ (*yoni*). This is a union of celestial nature; not an ordinary union.

Every ordinary act of making love has in fact shades of cosmic celestial union-the more completely it is carried out, the closer it gets to experiencing the vastness of divinity. Sexual union (*sambhog*) is, however, not the only way to awaken the kundalini. Unlocking the store-house of cosmic conciousness can take place in various manners. But the most spectacular of them is the Tantrik initiation-way involving secret rituals under the guidance of a grand master-paramguru.

It is important to have a structured insight into the Siva and Sakti aspect, the yantras (a sacred geometric enclosure in which the deity resides). The Maha Siva Yantra holds the Beeja (golden fluid) of life itself. The Maha Kali Yantra holds the entire universe in her golden womb. Together in union, the Siva lingam and the Sakti yoni represent the eternal desire to procreate, echoing a state of bliss and ecstasy.

Tantra attributes tremandous importance to the woman—the woman as female gender as well as the woman in every man (feminine values). She is the 'power holder,' the fountainhead of creativity and hence is worthy of worship. A genuine tantrika (one who practices *Tantra*) will look at any woman as his eternal mother goddess only. The whole effort in *Tantra* is to seek and exprience the Absolute Truth (Sublime). It is the exotic pathway of spirituality.

Man, a spiritual traveller ultimately seeks only enlightenment, liberation and moksha. As stated, tantricism described above had wide- spread influence over the vast region called Kamrup. It had widespread impact on social and cultural life of the region. There are Siva temples and Kali temples in almost every village of the region. Famous Siva temples like Jalpeswar, Baneswar, Mahakal in Jayanti, Shandeswar and other temples in Cooch Behar, Jalpaiguri and adjacent areas have been the meeting places of innumerable devotees on various occasions of Siva worship. Saivism and devotion to Sakti cult have remained the spiritual wealth of the people of Kamrup for ages together.

Devotion to the Sakti cult has found its expression amongst the common people of Kamrup in form of Candi, Kali or Bhagawati symbolised and named as 'Māyer Thān', 'Burir Thān', etc., located in the courtyard of the house hold or under any special tree.

For the ruling class and the aristocrats of the society, the concepts of a mother cult has found expression through Kamada, Kamini, Kama, Kanta, etc. various forms of goddes Kamakhya of *Kalikapurana*, so much so that the chieftains and the feudal lords have acquired the title Kamadeswar or Kamateswar and the country under them has been named Kamatapur.

Nilambar, the king of Khen dynasty was the last Kamadeswar or Kamateswar. It is believed that Kamadeswar has subsequently taken the form of Devi Bhagawati during the reign of the Koch-kings and has been worshipped as the Devi Durga with the Brahminisation of the society. This had impact on the folk life as a whole-their songs, dances, rituals, etc. as mentioned earlier. We will now discuss in brief the various types of songs under the above-mentioned category, that is, the songs falling within the ambit of Natha yogic faith based on myth and Sufism.

(i) Maynamatir gan:

One of the important songs under this category is Moynamatir gan. Moynamatir gan was first collected by Sir George A. Grierson in 1898 and published in Asiatic Society Journal by the title Manik Chand Rajar gan. 'Gopichandrer gan' collected by Bisweswar Bhattacharyya in 1922 and compiled by Dr. Dines Ch. Sen was published by the Calcutta University and included in M.A. class syllabus. The main theme of these songs is narrating the glories of the Natha gurus (Preceptors).

It has two parts. The first part deals with the descriptions of proceeding for Sannyasa by Gopi Chandra along with the descriptions of supernatural powers of the guru and the second part contains the story of Gopi Chandra, his mother Moynamati and his wives Aduna and Paduna. According to Dines Ch. Sen, Raja Gopi Chandra reigned during the period 1063 to 1112 and these songs were composed immediately after. It is assumed that his capital was Patikapara village of Nilfamari police station of the district of Rangpur (now in Bangladesh). But according to Dr. Mahmmad Shahidullah, the linguist of Bangladesh, Gupi Chandra was the king of the seventh century.

The story of the first part is that Parvati held the test of yoga power of all the disciples at the instance of Siva and only Gorakshanatha could pass the test. Gorakshanatha saved his guru Minanatha from the state of illusion and attachment.

The second part is sung as Maynamatir gan. The luxurious king Manik Chandra had five queens. The principal queen Moynamati was banished at the instigation of the other queens. Moynamati somehow was present at the time of king's death and tried her best to protect the king from death by dint of supernatural yogic power but could not. She was pregnant at that time and gave birth to a son who was christened Gopi Chandra. Moynamati herself ruled the kingdom after the death of Manik Chandra. Gopi Chandra was married to Aduna and Paduna, two sisters on his attaining the youth. It was expected that Gopi Chandra would be given the responsibility of ruling. But this did not happen.

Maynamati a great ascetic (*mahayogi*) and a very wise woman could know by her supernatural yogic power that Gopi Chandra was destined to die as soon as he completed 16 years of age. She, therefore, decided that Gopi Chandra would go for renunciation (*Sannyasa*) and would acquire yoga power from *guru* Harisiddha to win over the untimely death. Gopi Chandra was therefore asked to go for renunciation by her mother at his full youth when he was supposed to enjoy his life with two fully grown up wives.The wives, naturally put the blame directly on their mother-in-law with the words:

Āner māo bain bale byāṭā bhāle thāuk.
Tomār gharer niyāsi buri kay sadāy bairāgi hauk.
Mariyā jāuk buri śaśuri gharer jāuk śani
Buri śaśuri mairle dim laksa ṭākār bali.

Usually all mothers want that their sons should live well-settled family life. But your mother wants otherwise; she wants you to go for renunciation. Such an old mother-in-law should die. We will offer lakh rupees worth of sacrifice if she dies.

The two beautiful young ladies cannot accept the argument of their mother-in-law; they take the plot organised by their mother-in-law as a conspiracy for separating them from Gopi Chandra at the height of their youth. So they insist on accompanying their husband.

Sange kari ne re swāmidhan lagat cali jāi
Bhāi ār bainer mata pantha bayyā jāi.

Please take us with you; we will travel like brother and sisters.

Gopi Chandra tries to dissuade them by narrating the kinds of problems and dangers they may face on the way-

Śāl ban śimilā ban cālitā mandār
Ki khābu re ruper kainyā tāt dinate āndār.

The route is full of jungles, so much so that it is dark even at the day- time and nothing much is available as food on the way. Moreover, the dangers of going through the forest with two beautiful young women are manifold:

Bhāl bhāl rasiyā cyāngerā milibe āsiyā
Choṭo choṭo lāṭhi nibe bagalat kariyā.
Āmāk māriyā kainyā tomāk laibe sāthe
Takhan hārāim prān mui cikan kainār bāde.

Handsome young boys with bamboo sticks will attack us. They will kill me to take both of you away. I will have to die for you, the young ladies.

The queens, however, are not convinced and they put forward their ultimate argument that their youth will wither away and they will have hardly any scope for the company of their husband. The metaphors used are unique.

Lāu kumāra nā hay bayas cāle jāngi diba
Campā kalā nā hay bayas jale mākhi khāba.
Guyā pān nā hay bayas parāk bilāba
Kāpod khyātā nā hay bayas jhāmpāt bhareyā thuba.
Swaragete nāi candra ki kare tār tārā
Jei nārir soāmi nāi tār gharat andhiārā.
Khopat jadi nāi kaitar ki kare tār khope
Jeinā nārir soāmi nāi ki kare tār rupe.....
Tui soāmi abay haile mui hāṭ kholār bāli
Jāy baliche mok jyāṭāi khurāi seo balibe mok śāli.

Youth of women is not a vegetable like the gourd plant that can be mended to scale the hedge, not a banana for eating, not the betel nut and leaf to be offered to guests, and also not the clothings that can be kept in the box. In other words, youth cannot be retained and used like the ordinary things.

It has also been argued that the life of any woman without the husband is meaningless. People do not give proper respect to the women who have been deserted by the husband. The woman gets reduced to the status of the sandy soil of the local market place (*hatkholar bali*). Even those who used to respect her as aunte will now look down upon and call her the sister-in-law (*sali*). One can notice the influence and tone of Brahminism in the above lines.

Moynamati could know the conversation between Gopi Chandra and his wives through her yogic power and rushed to Gopi and asked him to get ready for renunciation, deserting his wives. She referred to the vices of women (wives):

Badhu badhu kais bāchā badhur antar kālā
Purushak bhāreyā khāy māiyār ḍāngar gālā.

You are speaking so much about your wives. But they are crooked and they just exploit the males and their simplicity and talk big.

She described the qualities (vices) of four categories of women in the world-Hastini, Padumani, Sankhini and Atustani. Thus while trying to poison the mind of her son against his wives, Moynamati attracted the wrath of their daughters-in-law who pointed to the illicit relation between Moynamati and Hadipa.

Hāḍir khāiche guā māo hāḍir khāiche pān
Bhāv kariyā niche māo ei Brahmajnān.

Hāḍir giyāne tor māyer giyāne ekāntar kariyā
Tomār bāpok māriche Mahārāj thapat bish diyā.

Your mother has made love with Hadipa and thus earned the Brahmajnan by illicit love. Your mother and Hadipa have joined together and killed your father by poisoning. In reply, she described how sincerely she performed the post-death rites of her husband and told that she was sending Gopi Chandra for renunciation in the interest and welfare of her son only. She then described the nature of love and affection of mother in this world.

Āg ḍhālā bheje māyer guye ār mute,
Pāch ḍhālā bheje māyer māgh māsiyā śite
Ek kāni cherā nekerā jādur gālāt diyā
Āpane ray māo hāṭu bukat diyā.
Jāduk khoyāy doi dudh māo khāy pāni.
Sansār bharmiyā dekho māo hena janani.

While the excreta of the child water the front side of the mother, the back gets wet with the winter dews. Mother wraps the small piece of cloth on the child's neck, while she herself tries to get heat placing her head between the knees. She feeds her child milk and curd, leaving only water for herself. This is 'Mother' throughout the world.

In this way after lot of altercations the mother ultimately succeeded and Gopi Chandra got ready for *Sannyasa*. Moynamati advised Gopi not to be tempted by anything on the way, particularly by women in the process. She advised—

Phul guṭik dekhiyā bāchā phul nā pāribi
Parār bou dyākhiyā bāchā māo bali ḍākibi.

If you see flowers, do not pluck them. See someone else's wife and address her as mother. Her advice yielded good results subsequently when Hadipa tested his power of restraint. Gopi Chandra could tell on the face of the prostitute—

Ki tui dekhāis naṭi tor pānjāy pānjāy cul,
Dui stan dekhong jena āro dhuturār phul.

Why do you show me your hairy arm pit? I see your breasts as 'dhutura' flower (a flower without fragrance). Not only that. Gopi Chandra devoted himself completely to the Guru and acquired the Brahmajnana and came back to his wives Aduna and Paduna and ascended the throne.

Gopi Chandra Rājā āro pāṭote basilo
Samāj suddhāy prajā sab Hari Hari balo.

The king Gopi Chadra sat on the throne. All the people of the community, now, sing the glory of 'Hari'.

It is quite evident from the lyrics that the language was Kamrupi. Some lines of the lyrics are popular as parts of the present day Bhāwāiyā Caṭkā. So many aspects of the Rajbanshi society have been reflected through this song-the eternal quarrel between mother-in-law and daughter-in-law, the eternal attitude of the mother that the son does not become a henpecked husband, etc. are well exposed in the ballad.

(ii) Nayansari:

The other form of songs in this category was Nayansari *geet*. This is sung in folk-drama style. Here the gidal (main singer) plays the role of *Gosai* (Baistam) or Vaisnava *guru* and the Doari (the main accompanying personae of the gidal) takes the role of *śisya* (disciple). Through them are sung the key features of a branch discipline of Vaisnavism by narration of small episodes. Various spiritual and philosophical truth of Hindusim, Islam and Vaisnavism are sung here.

It starts with a prayer song:

Harinām kṛsna nām baray madhur
Jei jan bhaje nām se jan catur.
Hari balo kṛsna balo kṛsner nām sār
Ihakāl parakāl tinkāl haibā pār.

Harinam and Krishnanam are very sweet chants. Those who chant them are clever ones. One can achieve the essence of life-both this world and the other world by such attachment and chanting.

The Baistam reaches the house of Ghutu a rich disciple. While Nayansari, daughter of Ghutu was to arrange some food for the Baistam, he raises some basic issues about the spiritual learning of the girl:

Kainyār kathā kalu tui e ār keman
Śiksā diksā nā thākile jal nā karim grahan.

The Baistam will not take the food served by Nayansari, as she has not taken diksa *i.e.* has not received initiation. It was however, decided that there will be no problem in taking food if the Baistam is paid a fine of Rs. 15. Ghutu and his wife agree to pay. But Nayansari declines. She wants to know the genesis and the truth from the Baistam and also wants to test his knowledge of Shastras.

Śon pitā callung mui gosāin daraśane
Dekhong mui guru gosāin ki ki śāstra jāne.
Ei je mor hāter jal kene nā kare grahan

Sei janye jāng mui gosāin daraśan.
Tarka kariyā jadi artha kayyā dyāy
Tabe gurur danḍa mui dim niścay.

Listen, my father! I am going to see the Baistam. Let me see how much he knows. Let me know why he has not taken water from me. I will pay the fine, only if he can beat me in debate.

Then begins the debate between the Baistam and Nayan. The argumentative dialogues are full of satire, sarcasm, joke, etc. For example—Guru speaks of the vices of women, while Nayan not only refutes them, but also mentions the vices of men, the gurus.

Guru- (i) Hay jadi tiri jāti param panḍit
Tathāpi nā jāne kono śāstra hitāhit.

A woman, even if learned, does not know the pros and cons of *Shastra-vakya*.

(ii) Māch māmsa nāri, ei tin anācāri

Fish, meat and woman – all these three are to be forsaken.

(iii) Tumi to strilok jemon mākāler phal
Dekhite sundar kintu bhitar halāhal.

You women are 'makal' fruits, outside charming but poisonous inside.

Nayan does not give in. She refutes the charges levelled by the preceptor (*guru*) against women. Not only that. She brings the counter charges.

Nayan– (i) Guru guru sakale bale guru kāk kay
Pānch jagate gurur kathā kon jagote hay.
Kāsyaper putra Indra guru haila Gautam
Śiṣya haiyā Ahalyāk kariche grahan.

Everybody speaks about the *Guru*. What is *Guru* ? Indra, the son of Kasyap takes the hands of Ahalya, the wife of his Guru Gautam.

(ii) Māiyā haite ādya śakti kaiche bidhātā
Māiyā mariyā hay tor pitā mātā
Māiyā haite śun Baisṭam dekhā jāy duniyā
Śāstrat nāi māiyār nindā ore śun Baisṭam bāudiyā.

Woman is the basic source of energy. She gives you your parents. You have seen this world only because of woman. There is no word of despise for woman in the sastras. No one should therefore, speak ill of women.

The arguments and counter arguments continue in this manner during which lots of proverbs, Puranic episodes, loukik episodes, etc. are brought in as proofs in favour or against the arguments. Ultimately the guru gets defeated and gives in. Nayan also accepts him very sportingly and makes rapproachment. They are, in the process, in love now. Nayan says:

Hāt dhariā kang kathā śon Baiṣṭam bāudiya,
Asamaye mor swāmidhan geiche mariā,
Manobānchā purna karo hey Baiṣṭam bāudiyā.

O vagabond Baistom! Let us join hands. My husband died at early age. Please satisfy my desires. The Baistam guru also accepts the gesture- '*Baiṣṭam bale Nayansari sab pheleyā dei*'.

Baistam agrees to desert everything while Nayansari also agrees to leave everything for the Baistam.

The above narration probably points to the pervertion of Vaisnavism *i.e.* corrupt Vaisnavism.

(iii) Jāg gān (Kāmdev Pujār gān):

The other important form of songs in this category is the *Jāg gān* which is known by other names, such as, Madan Kāmer gān, Bānśpujār gān, Kāmdeber gān. The song is based on the episode of Madan burnt to ashes by Śiva because of the couple's (Madan and Rati) audacity to attempt to incite Śiva and disturb his meditation.

Bamboos covered with white or red decorative pieces of cloths, fly-brushes being fixed on the top of the bamboos, are worshipped in connection with the Madan *Kām Pujā* and songs are performed. Bamboos are worshipped as symbols of phallus according to the folklorists. A number of objectives are fulfilled by the worship of bamboos—the eternal tribal instinct of tree-worship, worship of phallus, prevention of supernatural evil forces and prevention of diseases, etc. Madan Kām pujā and the Jāg gān performed in connection with this puja can therefore, be considered as manifestation of the practices of fertility cult. Naturally, the song compositions contain some such lyrics and words, which in the standard of urban educated tastes, may not be accepted as civil. In fact, they are often termed as vulgar.

Examples of songs:

(i) *Rāma re Rāma re Hari Rām se Nārāyan*
Ore eibār more karo dayā hey
Ainā Ṭhākur Madankām.

O Ram, Hari, Narayan! O Madankam Thakur! Please have mercy on me.

(ii) Āilo āilo re khelār gosāin āilo re
Āilo re Madaner māo Madanok bariyā neo.
Āi bairāti sabe mili āilo re.

The playful Gosain has come. Let us receive him.

One of the main items of offerings to this deity is hemp, the favourite drink of Śiva. So the song describes how the hemp is prepared to be offered as '*prasada*'.

> (*iii*) *Ḍhekite pheleyā bhāng hār karil gurā*
> *Ḍhekit kuṭiyā nil bhāṭiā bhānger murā.*
> *Bhāṭi hyāte āil kucuni hāte niyā khāru*
> *Tāy sen garāite pāre Madankāmer nāru.*

The hemp-roots are smashed in the husking pestle to prepare hemp (*bhang* drink). Kucuni coming from the lower region is expert in preparing Naru for Madankam with the extract of *bhang*.

> (*iv*) *Tok balong ore bāchā mālā giri bar*
> *Mor bānś khelāite jāy Kāmākhyā śahar.*
> *Kāmākhyā śaharer nok āgeyā nyāy bari*
> *Bariyā nyāy śaharer nok putra bānchā kari.*

Our worshipped bamboos go to Kamakhya town and the citizens of Kamakhya town receive them with full heart to pray for the boon of having son.

> (*v*) *Jāy dharibe cāilon bāti, tāy pāibe bar pāchā rāti.*
> *Āre, hāpsi āsil Madankām gachā nāgeyā dekho māng.*
> *Madan phiriyā āsil re.*

Those who will receive Madankam with open heart will get good bridegroom. Madan has come back. Be prepared for the sexual union.

(iv) Songs on Pir Phakir (Muslim mendicants):

History says that good number of Muslim mendicants came to Kamrup since the time of the Bakhtiar Khilji's invasion. Some of them have settled in different places of Kamrup. Thus the place has historically been the happy home of both the Hindus and the Muslims. This is the reason why there are various forms of songs based on Pir-phakir in this region. They are *Manāi Jātrā, Satyapir* or *Saitpirer gān*, etc.

(a) Manāi Jātrā : Sultan Badshah the father of Manai became a phakir under the influence of a Darvesh. The pieces of good advice given to Manai by his father are the themes of *Manāi Jātrā*.

> *Māo baro dhan re Manāi māo baro dhan*
> *Jār ghare māo nāi tār nisphal jiban.*
> *Dai miṭhā dudha miṭhā āro miṭhā nani*
> *Tār cāite adhik miṭhā māo hena janani.*

O bāchā Manāi re:

Ek karaṭh bheje māyer guye ār mute
Ār ek karaṭh bheje māyer māgh māsiyā śite.
Māoyer pendoner ācal khān chāilār gāot diyā
Cāirpor rāti poāy māo tuṣer āgun niyā.

Mother is the most precious wealth in one's life. Fruitless is the life of a person who does not have mother. Mother is sweeter than any of the sweet things-curd, milk, butter, etc. While her child's excreta soaks a part of her body, the other parts get wet with the winter dewdrops. Mother protects her child by wrapping the body of the child with her own cloth while spending the night sitting by the side of the fire made of husk dust. This is almost the same song as we find in Moynamatir gan.

(b) Satyapirer gan:

Satyapir is supposed to be combination of Satyanarayan, a Hindu god and Pir, a Muslim saint.

(*i*) *Ekdin Satyapir cān karite jāy*
Nur nadir ghāṭe jāyyā Korān hārā pāy.
Sālāmo kariyā Korān tuli nilo māthe
Ānande caliyā gelo pitār sāksāte.
Korān dekhiyā bāmon karilo sālām
Āmrā Brāhman jāti Korāne ki kām.
Satyapir bale pitā śuno mor kathā
Śunibo basiyā pitā Korāner kathā
Brāhmane Korān pare kon śāstre kay
Jeṭe pāiyācha Korān seṭe thuiyā āy.

Once Satyapir got a Koran on way to bathing place and came home with much joy to his father. The father bowed down to Koran and said what we Brahmins will do with Koran? Satyapir expresses his eagerness to listen to Koran-vani. His father however, asks him to put back the Koran at the place where it was found. There is a beautiful ballad singing the glory of Satyapir.

Satyapir ballad:

Moyadānab nāme Rājā Mālanca nagare
Sandhyābati nāme kanyā āche tār ghare.
Rājāk karite sājā Shāh Satyapir
Janmila āsiyā ai kanyār udar
Tāhār apār lilā ki kaba bujhāiyā
Śiśupāl Rājār deśe upasthit haiyā

Birale basiyā dhir Sanyāsir beś
Gālāt rudrākshar mālā śire pingal keś
Hāte danḍa śire jaṭā geruyā basan
Jhalmal kare anga suryer kiran
Kaṭite kapin sāje ange mākhe dhuli
Ek pāye nupur dila ār ek pāo khāli
Neelā nadir tire ek sriphal taru āche
Satypir base tāte Sanyasir beśe.
Daivajoge sei din Śiśupāl Rājā
Narabali diyā kare asṭakāli pujā
Sundar chāwāl ek dibe balidān
Sei ghāṭe gelo niyā karāite snān.
Satyapir dekhi tāk karay puchāri
Kena bāchā kānda tumi phukāri phukāri
Ṭiki dhari chāilāṭāk sommukhe basāilo
Akshay amar mantra kāne kāne dilo.
Chāilāṭāk niyā gelo karāiyā snān
Satyapir cali gelo Rājā bidyamān.
Rājā bale bara bhāgya karāimo pāran
Sanyāsi bole Rājāk chāilāṭāk de dān.
Nā diba nā diba chāilā Mahārāje bole
Tār par Satyapir ati krodhe cale.
Jal puspa diyā ghāḍe purohit mantra paḍe
Khānrā hāte āsil balidār
Jei mantra diche Pire, sei mantra dhire dhire
Jape chāilā hriday mājhār.
Hena kāle balidāre khānrār prahār kare
Khānrā jemon paḍila pāthare.
Khānrā haila dui khanḍa nāhi kāṭā gelo kanda
Dekhi Rājā hailo camatkār.
Rājā bole ohe chāilā kāṭā nā jāo kyāne
Chāilā bole sei kathā Sannyāsi guru jāne.
Kathā śuni sange kari pātramitra gon
Sannyāsir nikaṭe Rājā dilo daraśan.
Śiśupāl narabar, gālāy dhari kāpaḍ
Karapuṭe kare nivedan
Tumi to manusya nao kalir devatā hao
Nararupe tumi Nārāyan.
Mui bara abhāgiyā kariāchi pānc biyā
Putra kanyā grihe mor nāi
Śuniyā Sanyāsir bāni tabe kay Nṛpamani
Śono guru Sanyāsi Gossāin.

Mānas kairāchi mone laksha bali diba dāne, Narabali diba ābār
Satyapir bale Rājā gandha puspe karo pujā
Narabali deoyā mahāpāp.
Nija punye tare lok nija pāpe mare
Ek śata putra kainyā kichu nāhi kare.
Āchilo Ravon Rājā Lankāpuri nagare
Nija kanda kāṭi Rājā Śiva pujā kare.
Bhumit pariyā munḍa jape Harihar
Punarapi lāge munḍa kāndher upar.
Kathā śuni Śiśupāl kāndite lāgila
Hāhākār kare Rājā cakshu chalachala.
Pir bale āji niśākāle āsiba ekbār
Sangat kari āniba oi balir kumār.
Sei rāitat niśākāle Rājā Śiśupāl
Sange kari nila oi balir chāoāl.
Satyapir bale Rājā śunaha vacan
Kali kāle avatār mui Satyanārāyan.
Hindur devatā mui Musalmāner Pir
Ghare ghare mor nāme bharilo jikir.
Satyanārāyaner sevā bhariyā antare
Pānc Rani tap karbe Nilā nadir tire.
Jadi bhāgye phal mile khāibe pancajan
Abaśya tomār ghare janmibe nandan.
Panca Rāni snāne jāy gandha taila mākhe gāy
Sange jāy pānc jan dāsi
Kāro bā hātat jhāri kāro hātot tyāler khari
Kāro kānkhe suvarna kalasi.
Ek mon hayyā sabe purba mukhe dharma bhāve
Rani sabe dhyānot basilo
Hena kāle Satyapir āsiyā nadir tir
Panca kalā jale bhāsāilo.
Kalā pāilo pancajane harasita mone mone
Sabe pāilo manomata phal
Dharmak pranām diyā dāsibāndi sange niyā
Nija gṛhe calilo sakal.
Diyā dhan bojhe mon kāḍiyā nite katakshan
Satyapir māyār sāgar
Dhariyā kapaṭ māyā kuḍiyā phakir hayyā
Basi railo panther upar
Eke eke Rāni cāir ḍingāil Satyapir
Phakirak kata dilo gāli
Upar diyā deoyeyā geil paril pāyer dhuli

Satyapir kare caturāli
Choṭo Rāni Bindumati āilo henakāle
Kalāṭā bāndhiyā niche nijera ancale.
Phakir vacane Rāni karil bayān
Tapasyā kariyā pāichi ekṭā kalā dān
Ei kalā khāile bole habe bonśadhar
Balinu gopan kathā tomār gocar
Khāile bā nā khāileo banśa habe ghare
Ādhākhān kalā Rāni diyā jāo more.
Rāni bhābe ei kalā srjil darabeśe
Jodi kalā nāhi di kibā hay śeṣe
Kon karma kare pāche anāther nāthe
Satyapir khāilo kalā basiyā oi pathe.
Cocakhān diyā Rānik bale dhuiyā khāo jal
Abaśya khodāy tok dibe banśa phal.
Cārijon ḍyāgeyā geil niyā cāriṭā phal
Kichui nā pāibe jābe rasātal.
Chotorāni Mahārājak dekhāilo cochā
Tāk dekhi Mahārājer haila bara gosā.
Cārijan phal khāy ānanda ullās
Choṭorāni cochā khāy chāriyā nihśwās.
Choṭorānir garbha hail Satyapirer bare
Cāri rāni bānjā railo durbhāgyer phere.
Choṭorāni garbhadhari cāri rāni hailo bairi
Ukun haile jemon nakhe tuli māre
Dine dine garbha bāde cāri rāni jukti kare
Kon mate māribe ihāre.
Choṭo rāni bale tabe sono dāi māo
Jāhā jāno tāhā karo āmāk bācāo
Sāt pardār lechat cakshu kariā bandhan
Prasab hailo rānir janmila nandan.
Hāḍite rākhiyā ḍhākane ḍhākiyā
Cāmrār putuli dilo sanmukhe rākhiyā
Cāri rāni bale ore akhanḍa kapāli
Garbhate rākhis ei cāmer putuli
Ei sab bārtā rājā śunibāre pāilo
Kruddha hayyā Rājā tabe dukhate balilo
Bahu apamān Rānik satin karilo
Raj koṭhā chāḍiyā Rānik ḍhekiśāle thuilo.
Buddhi kari chāilār hāḍi phele Nilā nadir jale
Omni ek nāo hailo ḍheuyer upare
Tājbij kariyā khoāj pir jānilo takhan

Mantronā kariyā māre sat māo gan
Jale dubiyā mare chāilā khoāj jānila
Sevaker sevak buli kole tuli nila
Satyer chāilā laiyā calila khoāj
Āponār sthān nila dariyār mājh
Sahite nā pāri duhkha Choṭorāni māo
Nilā nadir ghāṭe gelo tyājibāre jiu
Chāilā laiyā Khoāj āilo henokāle
Rānik ḍākiyā tabe Satyapir bale
Purbe je phakirak dichis kalā vikshā
Sei to phakir mui putra hailo rakshā
Chāoāl dekhiyā Rāni haila ānandita
Satyer caran tale paḍila twarita
Dui cakshu bhāse Rānir nayaner jale
Cumbite lāgila chāilār badan kamale
Swapan dekheyā Rājāk Pir pṛsṭhe dila car
Cetan pāiyā Rājā kare dharphar
Cali gelo Mahārāj duhkhita haiyā āj
Praveś karilo je ḍhekiśāle
Śuiyā āche ḍhekiśāle dekhi Rājār parān phāṭe
Śiśuputra laiyā Rāni kole
Tabe Rājā bale Rāni putra kuṭe pāilā śuni
Bala tumi sakal kāhini
Jor kari dui hāt bale Rāni sab bāt
Satine karilo atakhāni
Hayyā Rājā krodh bhār nā kichu baliyā ār
Putrake kariyā nila kol
Anāth adhame kay pitā putra dekhā hay
Ehi sab bhāgya phalāphal
Sabhāsad ḍākiyā tabe kahila Rājan
Prān dhan dila more Satyanārāyan
Śuniyā sabār mon ānanda apār
Kata dān karilek khuliyā bhānḍār
Balidāner chāilāk āniyā satwar
Pānc khān grām tāk dila debottar
Pāṭhāiyā dila tāk pitāmātār ghare
Tabe dekho Mahārāj kon karma kare
Bhānḍārik ḍāki ai karilo apamān
Cāri Rānik śāsti dilo kāṭiyā nākkān
Nām kalpa kare Rājā ek mās bāde
Mahā dhumdhām kari Satyer pujā pāte.

English rendering of Satyapir ballad:

The king Mayadanava ruled in Malancha city,
Sandhyavati his daughter graced his home.
To her womb came Shah Satyapir
To punish the king Śiśupal.
Who am I to unravel his infinite Leela?
In Shishupal's kingdom
He bore the appearance of the unruffled *Sannyasi*
With the *rudraksha* garland around his neck, and browned hair,
The staff in his hand, a tangled knot of hair, and saffron *garb*,
His body ablaze like the sun.
He tied a thong to his waist, covered himself with dust,
Put jingling bells to one foot, left the other bare.
Under a Sriphala tree on the bank of the river Neela,
Satyapir sat as a *Sannyasi*.
As chance would have it, that was the day chosen by Shishupal
To offer a human victim in adoration of the eight Kalis.
Satyapir beheld the handsome boy chosen for sacrifice
Brought to the *ghat* for the ritual bath.
Satyapir asked him:
Why do you cry so piteously, my child?
He drew him by the tuft of his hair,
And spoke into his ears the changeless, deathless *mantra*.
The boy was bathed and taken away.
Satyapir went to where the king sat in state.
'What good fortune!' said the King.
The Sannyasi says, 'Give me the boy'.
The king says, 'No, I won't, I won't.'
And Satyapir leaves in a rage.
The priest touches the victim's neck with water and flowers, and reads the mantras.
The executioner stands ready with his axe.
The mantra, spoken by the Pir, slowly spreads and covers the victim within.
Till the executioner strikes,
And his stroke seems to hit a rock
That splits it into two, and the neck remains intact,
Leaving the king amazed.
The king asks: How do you remain uncut, my boy?
The boy says: Ask my *Sannyasi guru*.
The king rushes to the *Sannyasi* at once,
With his ministers and counsellors and all others.
Shishupal the king, his scarf around his neck, pleads with folded hands:
You are not a human being; you're a *kali-time* god, Narayana himself in human guise.

I'm an unfortunate soul, with five wives, and no children.
At the Sannyasi's assurance, the king tells him: listen to me, my *Sannyasi* master,
I have sworn to make a hundred thousand sacrifices,
And sacrifice five human beings.
Satyapir says: O king, offer only fragrant flowers to the deities,
It's a grave sin to offer men in sacrifice.
Men reach salvation by their own virtues, and die by their own sins.
A hundred sons and daughters are of no avail.
Ravana the king ruled in Lanka.
He cut off his head in adoration of Shiva.
The head fell to the ground and called out to Harihara.
Then it fitted back to the shoulders.
Shishupal broke into tears at the words.
He wept aloud with streaming eyes.
The Pir says, come tonight to me.
Bring the boy you chose to sacrifice.
That night the king Shishupal
Took along with him the boy he had chosen for sacrifice.
Satyapir says: Listen to me, king,
I'm Satyanarayana, the *avatara* of the *Kali*
A god to the Hindus, a Pir to the Muslims,
They pray aloud to me in every home.
Let your five queens pray on the bank of the Neela,
Holding to Satyanarayana in their hearts.
If their fortune brings them the fruits,
The five will have taste of them,
And you're sure to get a child.
The five queens go for their bath,
Anointed in fragrant oils,
With their five maids,
One holding the sprayer, another the oil bowl,
Yet another carrying the golden pitcher at her waist.
As they all sat, facing the east, their minds set on
Devout meditation,
Satyapir appeared at the bank of the river,
And set afloat five bananas.
The five of them got their bananas, and delighted
With their gifts,
They paid obeisance to the deities, and left for home
With their maids and slaves.
Satyapir, an ocean of enchantments,
Gives treasures, tests the takers' minds, and snatches

Away in a trice.
He puts on the false guise of a Fakeer
And sits in their way on the road.
One by one, the four queens cross Satyapir,
Berating the Fakeer in annoyance.
As they pass him by, their dust fall on
Satyapir who provokes them by his magic.
Then comes Bindumati the youngest queen,
The banana tied to the edge of her sari.
At the Fakeer's beseeching, the queen tells him:
"I've prayed to get this gift of a banana,
I've been told I'll get an heir if I taste of this banana.
And that's my secret, you know.'
'Whether you eat it or no, you'll get your heir anyway.
Why do not you give me half of it, o queen?"
The queen tells herself: The holy man asks for the banana.
He may do me harm if he's refused.
The lord of the wretched may punish me, she fears,
And lets Satyapir have the banana to eat on the road.
He gives the peeled-off skin to the queen, and asks her
Wash it and drink the water,
And the Almightly will surely give you an heir.
The four who overstepped me with the four fruits
Will have nothing from them, and fall to their ruin.
The youngest queen showed the King the banana-skin,
To his utter annoyance
The other four eat their fruits in great glee,
The youngest queen eats the skin with a sigh.
It was the youngest who became pregnant with Satyapir's blessings,
The four queens remain barren by the twist of fate.
With the youngest queen pregnant, the four turn foes,
Dying to crush the child the way they crush the lice in the hair.
As the womb grows, the four queens conspire
How to kill the child?
The youngest queen pleads with the midwife:
Do all that you know to keep me safe.
The queen gives birth to a darling son,
Her eyes tied fast with seven layers of cloth.
The queen hides the child in a bowl under a lid
And lay before her a leather doll.
The four queens berate her: 'Ill-fated you are,
To hold a leather doll in your womb!'

The King hears the news
And breaks into rage and grief.
The co-wives pour humiliation on the queen,
Banish her from the palace to the husking cell.
They plot it out together, and throw the bowl
With the child into the Neela river
That throws up a boat at once on the waves.
The holy Pir in his meditation learns
How the stepmothers conspire to kill the newborn.
The holy man sees the child thrown into the water
And as servant of those who serve, he draws it up to its lap
He carries the child along to take his place
In the stream itself.
The youngest queen shattered with grief
Comes to the bank of the river to give up her life.
The holy man appears there with the son
And Satyapir addresses the queen:
It is the Fakeer whom you gave the banana
That has saved your son.
In ecstasy over the child restored
The queen falls at once at the feet of Satya.
Her eyes, with tears rolling down,
She goes on kissing the child's face, as charming as a flower.
The Pir shows the King the entire in a dream,
And slaps him on the back,
To arouse him in confusion.
In utter grief, the King makes his way
To the husking cell,
Where his heart breaks at the sight of the queen
Asleep on the floor with the child.
Then the King asks: Tell me, my queen,
Where did you find your son?
Tell me the whole story.
The queen tells him the co-wives' entire plot,
All with folded palms
The King, in a rage, didn't say a word,
He took the child in his arms
And regretted his fate
That had to bring father and son together in this way.
The King called his courtiers together,
And told them how Satyanarayan had given him both life and wealth,
To endless joy for everyone,

He opened wide the doors of his treasury, and gave gifts in profusion,
He brought back at once the boy chosen for sacrifice,
And gave him five villages to be enjoyed through posterity.
He sent him back to his parents' home
As a royal act to be cherished.
He cast humiliation on the Treasury keeper,
And punished the four queens by severing their noses and ears
A month later the King offered a grand puja to Satyanarayana.

(c) Car juger gan:

Car juger gan falls under the same category. This however, refers to the Islamic religious norms-Koran and Shariyat. The master (*guru*) gives lessons on various *Sastra-vani* to the disciple (*sishya*) in the form of song. Here the performer (*gidal*) carries a *Veena*-like instrument. The song starts with a *Vandana* and then a *Dhua gan,* after which the question answer session starts. Of course, dhua gan is introduced at intervals to break the monotony and to add variety in the performance. The main singer (*gidal*) usually belongs to Muslim community, but there are instances of Hindu singers too.

Vandanā:

Ekbār āsorete eso niranjan; Eso he Hari, eso Golok-behari
Ei āsare ese Hari; Karo ai nāmer bitaran
Ekbār............................Niranjan

O Niranjan, Hari, O Golok Behari! Please do appear in this assembly of audience.

Eso mosalmāner Sāin o hendur Sri Hari gossāin,
Ei āsore ese Hari; Karo ai nāmer bitaran.
Ekbār............................Niranjan
Eso dayāl bhagawān; Prabhu nailām tomār nām
Ei āsare..........................bitaran
Ekbār............................Niranjan

You are the saint of the Muslims and Shri Hari god of the Hindus. Just appear before us to bestow your blessings.

Dhuā- *Dhua is the connecting rhyme between the parts of the story/episode /*
O cānder bāzār, āre hāt bhāngiyā gelo bhāire.

Or

Bhāsilām golāper phul re, agaim dariyār jale.

After this starts the question-answer session.

Question*: O mor dayel Prabhu go-*
Kon harafe āśmān paydā guru kon harafe jamin,
Kon harafe hendu paydā ār kon harafe momin,
Cānder bājār.... bhāire

O kind prabhu! Tell me, which letters have created sky, land, the Hindu and the Muslim.

Āśmān jakhan nā chilo guru kothāy chilo tārā
Indra Rājā nā chilo guru kothāy chilo dharā,
Cander bazar.... bhaire

Where the stars were when there was no sky and where was the earth with no Indra king?

Āśmān jakhan nā chilo guru kothāy chilo cān
Mānab dehā nā chilo guru kothāy chilo mon.
Gach bṛksha nā chilo guru kothāy chilo phal
Nadi nālā nāi chilo guru kothāy chilo jal
Cānder bāzār.... bhāire

Where was the moon when there was no sky and the mind when there was no body? Where were the fruits without trees and water without river and streams?

Gābhi goṭā nāi chilo guru kothāy chilo ghiu
Mānush jib nā chilo guru kār haste chilo jiu
Cānder bāzār.... bhāire

Where was ghee without cows and life without animal world?

Kon phakirer byāṭā guru-dhan kon phakirer nāti
Āśmān hailo kay tabak jamin kay rati
Cānder bāzār.... bhāire

Which Fakir is your father and which Fakir the grand father? How many layers have the sky and how many *ratis* (weight) the land is?

Jadyapi kahite pāro mor śaoāler uttar
Tomār sāthe caliā jābo Sri Jagannāth khettar
Cānder bāzār.... bhāire

If you can satisfy with the replies of these questions, I will accompany you to Jagannath.

Replies: *Dhuā:*

Ore, din gelo duniyār kāje rātri gelo ninde
Nā bhajilām Rādhā Krshna caranārabinde,
O man guru bhajare.
Jakhano nā chilo Sāmdes nitya nairākār
Takhano je khodār duniyā jalomay sansār
Ore din.... bhajare.

In the amorphous stage the whole world created by Khoda (god) was full of water.

Āleph harafe āśmān paydā be harafe jamin
Te harafe hendu paydā se harafe momin.
Ore din.... bhajare.

Sky has come out of the letter Aleph, land out of Be, the Hindus out of Te and the Muslims out of Se.

Āśmān jakhan nā chilo Sāmdes gopte chilo tārā,
Indra Rājā nāi chilo Sāmdes niore chilo dharā,
Ore din.... bhajare.

O Samdesh! Stars twinkled in the mysterious world when there was no sky; earth was in nior when there was no Indra King.

Gach bṛksha nāi chilo Sāmdes gopte chilo phal
Nadi nālā nāi chilo Sāmdes niore chilo jal
Ore din.... bhajare.

With no trees the fruits were in secret region and with no rivers and streams, water was in nior.

Gābhi goṭā nāi chilo Sāmdes gopte chilo ghiu
Mānush jib nāi chilo khodār haste chilo jiu
Bhāsilām.... jale

With no cows, ghee was in secrecy. With no animal world, life existed in the hands of *khoda* (god).

Mon phakirer byāṭā Sāmdes tan phakirer nāti
āśmān hailo sāt tabak jamin sāt rati
Bhāsilām.... jale

We are the sons of the *Fakir* 'mind' and grand sons of the *Fakir* 'body'. Sky has seven layers and land measures seven ratis.

Āśmān porā geil jamin porā geil uriyā paril chāi
Nānir udare māo porā geil chilām gurur ṭhāi
Bhāsilām.... jale

When sky, land everything burnt into ashes and the mother took her place in the womb of grandmother, we were with the *guru* at that moment.

Kahilām kahilām Sāmdes saoāler uttar
Āmār sāthe calo ekhan Sri Jagannāth Khettar
Ore din.... bhajare.

I have thus replied to your queries and now come with me to Jagannath.

An interesting point to be noticed here is that the Muslim mendicant is desirous of going to Jagannath, the Hindu pilgrimage.

Question:

Kon jagate āche guru mor binā dudhe doi
Kon jagate āche guru binā dhāne khoi
Bhāsilām.... jale

Where do we get curd without milk and khoi (parched paddy) without paddy?

The question and reply session goes on in this way where all kinds of issues contained in the Muslim sastras are dealt with.

(v) Gorakshanāther gān:

We have discussed the importance of 'Natha' dharma in North Bengal in connection with Moynāmatir gān. According to 'Natha yogi' belief, Gorakshanath was the disciple of Minanath.

Some scholars associate the name of Natha guru Gorakshanath with the song of Gorakshanath. Folklorists like Ramani Mohan Barma of Cooch Behar, on the other hand, differ. According to them, the themes of this song, the ritual and worship associated with it suggest that it has no relation with the 'Natha' yogic system. Here Gorakshanath is the eldest of the three brothers-Gorakshanāth, Sonā Rāi, and Rupā Rāi. One song of Sona Rai goes like this:

Sonā Rāi bale Rupā Rāi bhāi,
Tinojane mili āmrā narer pujā khāi.

Sona Rai tells Rupa Rai, let three of our brothers go to the human world to get adored.

The prevalent myth is that Sona Rai and Rupa Rai are the deities of tiger. Kamrup was full of jungles infested with wild animals of which tiger was the most dangerous and harmful, particularly in the matter of the safety of cattle, the most valuable wealth for the agricultural economy and human beings.

Worshipping Sona Rai- Rupa Rai, the deities of tiger associated with songs was therefore, quite significant in North Bengal. Gorakshanath, on the other hand, is the deity for the domesticated animals, particularly cows, the most important animal for a farmer household. It is actually Sri Krishna, acting as a cowherd tending cows who is worshipped in the form of Gorakshanath. This is called Rakhoāli song *i.e.* pastoral song also. Gorakshanath song is known as Gorokhnath song also. In the gāvi sijjan part of Gorokhnath (sometimes called Gonnath in short form) song, we get:

"Uttar hyāte āsil Pir mukhe cāmp dāri,
Doi dudh māgite geil Nan-goāler bāri.

The Pir came from the north side and went to the house of Nanda milkman to ask for milk and curd.

In the song, we get the reference of Pir, Nanda *goālā*, etc. The Rajbanshi cow-boys, about 8 to 10 number go from house to house singing the songs and ask for alms during the period from December to February, the harvesting time of aman (*kharif*) paddy.

After collecting reasonable amount of paddy in the form of alms they organise the Rakhoali (Gorakhnath) puja where a herd of cows are kept in front of the place of Puja. Sometimes some well-to-do households perform the Gonnath Puja to propitiate the deity to prevent cattle diseases and cattle epidemic. This puja is performed on the door of the cow shed with usual puja materials. Songs are used as the mantras for the Puja. The most important part of the song is called Gāvi sijjan, that is revitalisation (curing) of diseased cows. Some parts are called 'Hāicāo'. The word 'Hāicāo' is probably the changed form of 'Hāucāu', which means 'wailing in chorus'. Might be, they are called 'Hāicāo' because these are sung in chorus in heart-rending voice asking for the life and well being of the cattle, the most valued possession of a farmer household. Also to chase away the tiger *i.e.* wolf or chitah, they have to raise hue and cry – alarm, which convey the sense of 'Hāicāo'. Examples of songs:

(*i*) 'Subhe'

'Etakonā pakire mor goṭāl guā khāy
Khāite khāite jāite jāite narāi kairbār jāy.
Narāi kairte kairte pyāṭot nāgil bhok
Āekke coṭe kāṭi phelāil nay hājār lok.
Nay hājār lok re mor citor pātor
Gangā śālā bhāsā kairce ṭuiyer bhitor.
Gangāre gangi ebār bara bān
Uca kari ḍhipi pāto kālāḍhyāpā dhān.
Kālāḍhyāpā dhān re mor Gorakhnāthe khāy
Tāk dekhiyā bāgh bhāluk chāriyā pālāy.
Nā pālāio bāgh bhāluk nā pālāio tumi
Khānik jāgā chāri dyāo āsan kari āmi.
"Subhe!

A little bird eats a full betel nut, grows strong and goes for the fight, kills nine thousand people by a stroke. The Ganga bird has built its nest on the top of the house in the apprehension of the impending flood. Paddy (crops) has to be stored in highly placed bins. Gorakhnath will eat the paddy (*i.e.*Gorakhnath will be offered puja with that paddy) and the tiger will run away in fear of Gorakhnath, who asks them not to run away but to leave a place for his seat to be able to take the puja.

(*ii*) 'Subhe'

"Korā bale kurire bhāi ebār bara bān
Ucā kari bāndo ḍhipi kālāḍhyāpā dhān
Kālāḍhyāpā dhān re mor tulsi sāri sāri
Tāhār nice darbār kare Gaurman Chaudhuri.
Rām balo bhāi Hari balo Mukunda murāri
Gorakhnāther nāme ebār balo Hari Hari
Subhe!"

Kora, a water bird tells his wife that there is likely to be extensive flood and so the paddy has to be stored in a high place. The song refers to the court of Gaurman Chaudhuri *i.e.* the British rule. Let us take shelter of Gorakhath.

(*iii*) *Uttar hyāte āsil Pir mukhe cāmp dāri*
Doi dudh māgite geil Non-goāler bāri.
Goāl bale āchere goālni bale nāi
Goṭot pariyā mail sāt soā gāi.
Sāt soā gāire bhāi nay soā tār bāchā
Gāvir badale kyāne nā mail mor byāṭā.
Kāndere goālnani hāte niyā bāṭā
Gāvir badale kyāne nā mail mor byāṭā
Kāndere goālnani hāte niyā māṭi
Gāvir badale kyāne nā mail mor byāṭi.

Coming from the North, the Pir with the long beard, begged milk and curd from the milkman. While he was ready to give it, the milkmaid his wife negated. The moment she did it, all the cattle in her shed fell and died. She then started wailing, being repentant for her lying to the Pir. She places her hands on different houseold articles and wails that her son or daughter, brother, sister, mother or father, for that matter, any person dear to the family could and should have died in place of the cattle, which are so valuable to the farmer household.

Some milk was therefore, asked for the puja of the Pir but the milkmaid (the wife of milk man) told a lie that no milk was available. Her lying resulted into the instant death of all the cows owned by them. The wailing goes on:

'Kāndere goālani hāte niyā dudh
Gāier badale kyāne nā mail mor put.
Kāndere goāloni hāte laiyā doi
Go-dhaner badale kyāne nā maril mor bhāi.

Thus goes the description of her wailing for the life of cattle.

Realising the fault, the milkman arranged for Gorakhnath puja and prayed to Gorakhnath for the life of the cows. Goraknath being pleased with the puja granted the prayer and the cows got back their life. The other version of the story is that the son-in-law of the milk-man (goala) arranged the sacrifice of a goat to please the Pir and the cows regained life.

"Goālanir jāmāi re sāccāi kāmelā,
Ṭān diyā bāhir karil khāsir cāmerā.
Khāsi nā māriyā goāl karile hyār ādusi
Tāk pāyyā Pir sāheb baro hailo khuśi
Choṭo Pir uṭhiyā dhāmāilat dil khāṭi
Jatare goāler gābhi kare neoṭā-neuṭi
Baro Pir uṭhiyā dhāmāilot dil kop
Jatare goāler gābhi jiyāil goṭāgoṭ
Sāt soā gāi jiyāil nay soā tār bāchur.
Burā māṭā jata jiyāil bahut bistar".

Son-in-law of the milkman is a very clever and active person. He sacrificed a goat and offered Puja to the Pir with that meat. Being pleased with the Puja, both the elder and younger Pirs activated their magic and charms, and all the cattle regained their life.

"Hāsere goālnani hāte niyā bāṭā
Tār pare jiyā uṭhil goālnanir byāṭā.
Hāsere goālnani hāte niyā dāo
Tār pare jiyā uṭhil goālnanir māo.
Sāt soā gāi jiyāil nay soā tār bāchur
Hāṭu pānit jiyā uṭhil goālanir bhāsur
Hāsere goālnani hāte niyā māṭā
Sāt soā gāvi bācil nay soā tār bāchā."

The milkmaid now smiles in joy that all the cattle now got back their life. Not only this. The near relations, who died at the wrath of Gorakhnath, regained their life too. The Puja is now offered to the cattle. The contributions of cattle are now sung and different Puja articles offered to them at the door of the cowshed. Example of Haicao:

"Hāicālo re hāicālo,
Hāicālo re kālā balad Tor pasāde dhān gharot,
Hāicālo re hāicālo
Hāicālo re dhauli gāi Tor pasāde dudh bhāt khāi,
Hāicālo re nāl balad Khai phyāle dyāng goāil gharot.
Hāicālo re myāni gāi Hācle hācle khai chiṭāi.
Khai nā pāyyā doi chiṭāi".

(vi) Sonā Rāi gān:

As stated, Sona Rai is considered as the deity of tiger. People, particularly the cowboys perform the Sona Rai puja to have proper safeguard against the attack of tigers on the cowherds. Groups of 8/9 boys go from house to house for alms singing the glory of Sona Rai and the harming powers of Sona Rai, if defied and neglected.

Sonarai ballad

Ṭhākur Sonārāi Rupārāyer bhāi,
Bāger pṛsṭhe cariyā maisher dugdha khāi
Je hāṭe goāler māiyā dodhi niyā jāy
Āṭkurā baliyā dadhi kiniyā nā khāy
Je gacher talete Nanda basiyā dārāy
Āṭkurā baliyā pankhi bhāsā nā karay.
Ek pakhi ḍākeya ar pākhire bale
Āṭkurā Nanda āji basil gacher tale.
Ek pakhi ḍākeyā bale ār pakhi bhāi
Chārare gacher mayā anya deśe jāi.
Pakhir mukhete Nanda etek śunila
Bishad bhābiyā Nanda kāndite lāgila.
Nandarāni bale prabhu kānda ki kāran
Dharmer sevā karite lāge katakshan.
Mui Jadi goāler meye e nām dharong
Dharamer sevā kari putrabaṛ neong.
Kubuddhi goāler meye subuddhi karilo
Dharomer sevā karite citta sthir hailo.
Rajani prabhāt hailo pratyusha biyān
Puber ānginãy kanyā dilo Chaṛāchān
Khailā khār laiyā nāri snān karite gela
Jāhnabi Jamunār jale snān ārombhila,
Hāṭu pānit nāmi kanyā dilo panca ḍub
Kughāṭe nāmiyā kanyā sughaṭe uṭhila
Bhijā bastra thuiyā bastra sukān parilo
Bhijā bastra pheleyā sukān pariyā
Akhanḍa kalār pāt ānila kāṭiyā.
Ālo cāul gur cini tār upar diyā
Ekatra māthār keś dui ardha kariyā.
Dharamer sevā kare dui hāṭu pāriyā.
De de Dharam Ṭhākur de dharma bar
Jadi tui Dharam Ṭhākur nā dis putrabar
Stribadh haim mui kāṭāri kari bhar.
Nava puspa diyā puje nāhi lekhā jokhā
Goālinir sevāte Dharma dilen dekhā,
Ego ego goālini toke dei bar
Toke bar diyā jāon mui kailās śikhar.
Urdhamukh hayyā kanyā nihswās chārilo
Swet māchi hayyā Kṛshṇa garbhe prabeśilo.
Ek mās hailo garbha jāni bā nā jāni

Dwitiya māser samay ānāgonā śuni
Tritiya māser samay rakte chānde golā
Caturtha māser samay hāḍe māmse jorā.
Pancam māser samay panca puspa phuṭe
Shasṭha māser samay ulṭiyā baise.
Saptam māser samay sādher bhoj khāy
Ashṭam māser samay mon pavan jiyāy.
Navam māser samay nava gun sthiti
Daś mās daś dine kātar prasuti,
Daś mās daś din purna haila
Sonārāi Rupārāi ubhay upjila.
Sonārāi Rupārāi āmrā duiṭi bhāi
Dui bhāiyer parāmarśe grāmer pujā khāi
Hari Hari bandiyā gāo Hari se ādya mul
Janmiyā Nander ghare rākhila gokul
Gokulete thāka tumi gokuler Kānāi
Tumi bine Rāmkṛṣṇa tribhuvane nāi.
Keha bale calo calo keha gāy bhāl
Sahite nā pāri āmi bāgher janjāl
Ājikār rātri śunichi dhur dhur
Berā bhāngi niyā geiche gṛhasther kukur.
Kukurer śoke giri juriche korohāl
Jukti chiri garu pālāy bhāngiyā jongāl.
Bhāngā jongāl dhari giri bāri cali jāy
Madhya pathe nāgāl pāyyā bāghe āpcāy.
Bāgher thāpare girir ange basil nakh
Kher kāṭite niyā gela ek gṛhasther bauk.
Sāt pāc gṛhasther beṭā jukti kariyā
Sonārāyer nimitte berāy māgiyā
Jangaler jib jata charāil bhitābhiti
Āponi dharil prabhu Sannyās murati
Sanyāsir beśe Ṭhākur phere ghare ghare
Ardhapathe nāgāl pāil durjay mogale.
Mogaler senā se Sanyāsik poche kathā
Uttar nā dila Ṭhākur nārā dila māthā
Dhākkāite dhākkāite nila agelā kariyā
Sādhu nay asādhu cor durjoy bhābiyā
Katak dur haite sādhu katak dur jāy
Katak dur jāite se magaler bāri pāy.
Dibā abāsān hayyā niśā bhāg hailo
Madhyarātre sādhur pāye jorā kundā dilo.
Kundāte thākiya Ṭhākur chārilo hunkār
Triś koṭi bāgh āsi hailo āgusār
Uṭha uṭha ohe prabhu sthir karo mon
Bāgh jati āmadiyā ḍākechen ki kāran.

Āiso āiso bāghgan āmār hukum lao
Magaler Senāpatik māriyā je jāo.
Bara magalok mārek tui dhari hāto hāt
Choṭo magalok mārek tui āchāri parvat
Hāti śāler hāti mārek ghorā śāler ghuri
Bāchiyā bāchiyā mārek pālita prahari.
Magal sainya mārite rātri prabhāt hailo
Jor kundā bhāngi prabhu palāiya gelā.
Jamunā pār hayyā Ṭhākur bāgher nila lekhā
Sakal bāgh ache mor nāi berāḍhipā.
Berāḍhipā bāgh āsi jor kar kari
Ṭhākurak pranām kare jor hāṭu pāri.
Sanyāsi balen bāgh oi khānete bais
Māthār chāl kemone geiche swarup kaire kais.
Bāgh bale sandhyā kāle āiler ot dhari
E kāl pyāner jwālā sahite nā pāri
Bahu kashṭe bahu srame jib hatyā kari
Ek jibke dhariyā kairāchi bara bal
Cāler ruyā lāgiyā māthār geiche chāl
Sanyāsi kay baner bāghā oi khānete bais
Dāt bhāngiche ki rakame swarup kaire kais.
Bāghā bale prabhu āmi peṭer dāye mari
Kāl sama peṭer jwālā sahite nā pāri.
Mānusher hāḍ jeman teman gorur hāḍ ḍāt
Garu khāite bhāngiyāche kāmer chay dāt.
Ei mate Sonārāi prakāśita haila
Bālake jāni sabe pāncāli gāila,
Dhanya Ṭhākur Sonārāi gṛhasthak de tui bar
Dhane bonśe bāruk giri puruk bhānḍār.
Goilete bāruk girir bhānḍāre bāruk dhan
Deoyāni darbāre giri pāuk phul pān.
Sonārāyer dakshinā lāge bharā kulā dhān
Sonār nay bhari kaḍi guā panca khān.
Sonārāyer dakshinā dite jāy karibe helā
Tār bhāṭārer nāgāl pāmo garu carebār belā.

English rendering: The Sonarai Ballad

Thakur Sonarai, brother of Ruparai
Rides the tiger and drinks buffaloes' milk.
When the milkman's wife goes to the market with her bowl of milk,
They won't buy her milk because she's barren.
The cattle won't drink the water from the river
Where the milkman's wife goes to bathe because she's barren.
The birds won't make their nest in the tree
Under which Nanda stands because he's childless.

A bird calls out to another:
The childless Nanda sits under our tree.
Let's leave the tree and fly to another land.
Nanda hears what the birds say
And begins to cry in grief.
Nandarani pleads: Why do you cry, my lord?
It's not hard to serve *Dharma* (the good deeds, also religion)
If I am known as a milkman's wife.
I'll serve *Dharma* and win the boon of a son.
The foolish milkman's wife flushed with wisdom
Pledges to serve *Dharma*.
As the morning beams at the end of night
The young maiden cleanses the courtyard with drops of cowdung,
She goes to bathe with oilcakes,
And begins her bath in the Jahnavi Yamuna,
She dips to her knees and cleanses her knees.
She dips to her chest, and dips five times,
She enters the water at the unholy *ghat* and rises at the holy one.
She casts aside her drenched clothes, and puts on a dry set
Dressed in dry clothes
She cuts for herself a seamless plantain leaf.
On which she places rice and sugar and the red sweet molasses,
She ties her hair in two braids,
And falls to her knees in adoration of *Dharma.*
She pleads: O god of *Dharma*, give me a boon.
O god of *Dharma*, if you refuse me the boon of a son,
I swear I'll die on a knife.
She offers flowers of innumerable variety
Till the God appears, moved by the milkmaid's devotion.
Come to me, milkmaid, he says, I'll give you a boon
And then return to the peak of Kailash
The maiden raises her face upwards, and draws a deep breath,
Krishna enters her womb as a white fly.
A month passes, with no intimation,
There's stirring in the second month,
In the third month, blood passes into the lump,
In the fourth, the bones and the flesh come together.
In the fifth, the five flowers bloom,
In the sixth, the foetus turns,
In the seventh month, she has her *sadh* feast,
In the eighth, the heart fans it with life,
In the ninth, the nine virtues are in their place,
On the tenth day of the tenth month, the maiden is in pain,
At the end of the day,
Sonarai and Ruparai, the twins, are born.

We're two brothers, Sonarai and Ruparai,
The village adores the twins,
Praising Hari, the source of all things,
You've saved Gokula, they say, born to Nanda,
Live in Gokula, they plead, as Gokula's Kanai,
There's no Ramakrishna beyond you in the three worlds.
Some of them are in a hurry, 'let's go', they say, others are relaxed,
I can't bear the stink of the tiger's shit, one says,
It'll be a perilous night, one says,
They've snatched away the householder's pet dog,
Giri sits mending his plough, sorrowing for his dog,
The Ox tugs at the string, and breaks loose, snapping the yoke.
Giri goes home carrying his broken yoke.
The tiger stops him in the way,
And mauls him with his claws.
It snatches away a householder's wife
Who was cutting straw for her home.
Five or seven young men go round in a band,
Begging for Sonarai.
The animals in the forest spread out here and there.
The lord assumes the appearance of a Sannyasi.
As a Sannyasi he goes from home to home,
Till he is accasted by the invincible Mughals,
Who interrogate him.
The god does't say a word, he only shakes his head.
The Mughals push him ahead,
Convinced it's not a holy man, but a thief or a villain for sure.
They take him to the Mughals' den,
Where the day ends, and the night's share begins,
At midnight, they put the holy man in the stocks.
From his bind in the stocks, the god roars.
Drawing to him at once three hundred million tigers,
Pleading: Arise, O lord, and tell us your desire,
Tell us, why you called us up, the tribe of tigers.
Come to me, O tigers, he says, carry out my orders.
Kill off the Mughal general for me.
The big Mughals you kill fighting hand to hand.
The small Mughals you kill hurling hills at them.
Kill the elephants in their camp, and the horses in their stable
Pick out and kill all their trusted sentries.
It takes them till the dawn to kill the Mughal army.
The lord snaps his stocks and makes his escape.
The god crosses the Yamuna and calls the rolls
To find all his tigers except Beradhipa.
Beradhipa approaches him with folded palms,

Bends his knees to pay obeisance to the god.
The Sannyasi tells him: Sit there, tiger,
And tell me how you lost the skin of your head.
The tiger says: I sat in the evening behind the raise between the plots.
Suffering the pangs of hunger,
Killing creatures with great effort,
And lost the skin of my head at the beam of his hut.
The Sannyasi says: Sit there and wait, tiger.
How did you break your teeth? He asks now.
The tiger says: I suffer the pangs of hunger, my lord.
I can tackle human bones somehow, but the cattle's bones are harder,
I lost six of my teeth trying to eat a cow.
Thus Sonarai revealed himself,
And the boys sang his ballad.
Glory to Sonarai, who blesses the householders:
Let Giri grow richer and fruitful, let his Treasury be full,
Let there be more cattle in his farm, and more wealth in his store.
Let Giri be hounoured in the court with *paan*
For Sonarai's kindness offer him a basket of grain,
Nine gold coins for him, five paan leaves with betel nuts will do.
One who neglects to give alms for the worship of Sonarai
Will be duly treated at the time of grazing the cattle.

The description with the same monotonous tune becomes boring. The performers therefore, with a view to breaking the monotony and boredom and bringing in some variety in the process, introduce the 'dhuā gān' in between. 'Dhua' is an isolated couplet sung in between and the performers quite often use them for passing on the messages about various socio-economic-problems to the audience.

Dhua- *Jangal porā geil re ore uriyā pare chāi*
E-hena sundari kainyār nāi bāpo-bhāi
Jangal porā geil re.

The jungle (forest) got burnt and the ash spread away. Such a pretty girl does not have parents and after relations. Or

Bāne dhān khāilo re,
Are sarishā khāilo bhure, Ki diyā khājnā demo girhasther ghare
Bāne dhān....

The flood has destroyed paddy and mustard crops. How to pay the rent to the landlord?

He Rām, āus gelo pāni abhābe śāli khāilo bāne
Nāgil dyāśat hāhākār dām bārilo kyāne
Bāne dhān....

Aus paddy has been destroyed for want of water, while the kharif by floods, resulting into price rise and cries of distress all around.

He Rām, mahājane dhān kiniyā gudām bharti kare
Pyāṭer dāyat garib loke garu bikri kare
Tabuto nā bāce prān mahācintāt pare
Upāy nā dekhiyā śyāṣat jami bikri kare.

The *Mahajan* (money lender) purchases the paddy and hoards it, while the poor peasants starve and sell the cattle. Finding no other means to live they sell their lands at last.

Bhālore Sonā Rāyer daksinā dite jāy karibe helā
Tār bhātārer nāgāl pāmo garu carebār belā.
Sonā Rāyer daksinā nāge purna kulā dhān
Tāhār upurā nāge jor guā pān.
Satya Ṭhākur Sonā Rāi gāirasthak de tui bar
Dhane banśe baruk giri candra dibānkar.
Gaile bāruk gāi garu golāt bāruk dhān
Dewāni darbāre bāruk bāṭā bhorā pān.
Gaile bāruk gāi bāchur jāngāle bāruk lāu
Girir gharer śatru duśman baner bāghe khāuk.

Those, who neglect to offer the alms for the Puja of Sona Rai, will have to face the tiger while grazing the cattle. The gift to be given consists of a full yanow of paddy, betel nut and leaves. Glory to Sona Rai, who blesses the houseowners; let him (giri) be richer and fruitful, let his treasury be full; let there be more cattle in his farm (shed) and more wealth in his store. Let him be honoured in the court with pan (betel nut and leaf). Let there be more cows in his farm, more gourds (vegetables) on the sheds. Let the enemy of the giri be killed by tiger.

O Saiṣyā bārit feisyā kānde
Tānku bārit bāgh
Gharer pāchilā burār byāṭā
Kare bāpre bāp.
Balare balare Hari Hari Nārāyan.
Rām chārā gati nāi balo Rām Nārāyan.
Sab dosh khanḍibe
Balo Rām Nārāyan.
Bhālore, Satya Ṭhākur Sonā Rāi
Gāirasthak dile bar
Dhane banśe bāruk giri
Candra dibānkar hey.
Sonā Rāyer dakshinā dite jāy karibe helā
Tār bhātārer nāgāl pāmo garu carebār belā.

The jackal barks on the mustard field indicating thereby that the tiger is somewhere nearby, may be on the tobacco field, just behind the house. So, chant the name of Ram, Narayan and Sona Rai. The family will prosper and live in peace, if Sona Rai does have mercy on you. There will be danger from the side of Sona Rai to be faced by the households, if they neglect the deity.

A particular way of howling of the jackal indicates the presence of tiger somewhere nearby. Hearing that kind of howling, human beings and animals get scared and cautious too. Howling of *feisya* (jackal) in the mastard field tells the presence of tiger in the tobacco field and so the old man gets terribly scared. However, there is no problem or fear if the houseowner gives sufficient alms for the Puja of Sona Rai, and denying the alms will give vent to the wrath of the deity and his immediate adversary and grief.

Sometimes the glory of Sona Rai is sung in brief description. The name Sona Rai is believed to have been derived from the golden (Sonali) colour of the tiger. In the formal rituals of Sona Rai, the puja starts with the song describing the birth of Sona Rai.

Rajani prabhāt hailo hailo bihān,
Gobarer jale kanyā dilo charā chān.
Charā-chān diyā kanyā bharāilo thuri,
Bām haste khailā khār dān haste khuri
Khailā khār gangār jal ek-lage (ek-sāthe) kariyā
Hari Hari baliyā dilo mastake ḍhaliyā.
Hāṭu pānit nāmiyā kainyā hāṭu kare jor
Kamor pānit nāmiyā kainyā kamor kare jur.
Kughāṭe nāmiyā kainyā sughāṭe uṭhilo
Bhijā bastra chāri kainyā śukān parilo.
Til tulsi phul āro nila bel pāt
Dhup cini gur nila naibedyer pāṭ.
Jadi he Dharam Ṭhākur nā dis putrabar
Stree badhya haim mui kāṭārik karim bhar.
Dekhā dil Dharam Ṭhākur nārir gocar,
Stree badhya nā kariyā dila tāke bar.
Bar pāyyā goāler nāri ghare bāurilo
Amrita kadali phal bhakshan karilo.
Ucā gachat thāki Ṭhākur chārilo nihśwās,
Swet māchi hayyā Ṭhākur garbhe nilo bās.

Then the song describes the development of the pregnancy for ten months.

Ei rupe daśmās daśdin purna hailo
Samay haite Ṭhākur bhumite parilo.

■■■

8

Sensual Love in Bhāwāiyā

From the analysis so far done, it has come out that the themes covered by Bhāwāiyā relate to every aspect of the Rajbanshi life. As in other forms of folk song, there are lots of the songs centring round the belief in magic and rites and customs connected with the worship of various gods and goddesses. They are sung to meet the day-to-day requirements of the social life; to win over the nature's power by propitiating the deities and/or to ensure protection from the wrath of various supernatural forces. The songs commonly used are—*Kātipujār gān, Sāiṭol Pujār, Sonārāyer gān, Gorakhnāther gān, Madan kāmer gān*, etc. The second categories of songs relate to devotional songs, songs based on Sufism and Neo-Vaisnavism. The influence of Sankar Deva, the preacher of Vaisnavism was much more predominant than that of Sri Caitanya in this part of the country. Hari form of Krishna without much association of Radha was much adored in North Bengal and the songs also related to Hari.

Side by side with the Baul and Sufi in Bengal, there was wide-spread influence of *Yoga dharma/Natha dharma* manifested in *Maynāmatir gān, Nayansari gān, Manāi Jātrā*, etc. These were performed in the drama form popularly known as *pālā gan* (folk drama). The influence of Tantricism in this part of the country got manifested in *Moynāmatir gān* and *Nayansari gān*, etc. Mangal dharma also had some influence in both Bengal. Particularly important was Manasā Mangal based on which developed the much popular folk drama *Bishaharā* or *Padmapurān*, the story of Behula and Lakshmindar for preaching the glory of *Padmā* or *Bishahai*, that is, *Manasā*. Other popular folk dramas developed in this area are *Dotorā, Kuṣān, Rang Pāncāli, Khās pāncāli, Khan*, etc. The songs of all such folk dramas are Bhāwāiyā and its brisk form Caṭkā.

The relationship between music and religion with its associated customs and rituals is so time honoured that the two appear as being inseparable. It is however, not true that music was born of religion only. It is a fact that religious worship was accompanied with music even when man was savage, while sexual love which, of late, has appropriated the major share of the domain of music received the aid of music only in comparatively advanced stage of society.

As stated earlier, love had not attained in primieval days that degree of refinement, which the etiquette of modern civilisation has called into existence. Primitive man was nude and only a few leaves of trees served, if at all, as his clothing. Love was based upon instinct. As time went on, barks of trees, cotton goods, silk and muslin came into use; social rules were framed for regulating the conduct of sexes towards each other.

With the passage of time, with change in socio-economic-political and educational structure, sexual love attained importance in the ethnic society. Taste in speech, gait and dress attained a high degree of perfection so much so that each of these adjuncts of life came to be looked upon as accomplishments. Under these circumstances, courting became an art and sexual love a mystery. Its pains and pleasures became themes of poetic effusion and music soon lent its helping hand to its achievements. Music fanned the flame of love better than it did religion. Religion and music, at the same time, formed a healthy combination of production and eternal bliss.

The above rule of evolution applied in case of the Bhāwāiyā too. The songs on the customs, rituals and worship of folk gods and goddesses as also the repertoir of dhuā gān (refrain songs) gradually evolved into solo Bhāwāiyā-Caṭkā. Bhāwāiyā songs became the solo songs portraying the pains and pleasures, union and separation of the heroes and heroines of rural North Bengal.

The songs now relate to the pains and pleasures of the Gāriāls, that is, the bullock cart drivers and their lady loves. Bhāwāiyā songs now reflect the sorrows and pains of the young widows, the sāngānis (concubines), the wives deserted by their husbands, or even the young ladies who have fallen in love of the sweet voice and melodious music of Dotorā, the string instrument played by the Māhout, Maishāl or Gāriāl. Gradually Dotorā became the major instrument of Bhāwāiyā. The musical structure of Bhāwāiyā can be shown in the following paradigm:

Magico-religious songs: *Kātipujār gān, Shāiṭol Pujār gān, Goraknāther gān, Sonārāyer gān*, etc.

Religious and ritual based songs: *Maynāmatir gān, Satyapirer gān*, devotional songs based on Vaisnavism, *Bānspujār gān* or *Madankāmer gān* or *Jāg gān, Hudumer gān* and marriage songs.

Folk drama-based songs: *Dhuā, Khosā and Payār gān*,

Songs in *Dotorā, Kuśān, Bishaharā*, etc. folk drama

Bhāwāiyā [Bhāoiā-Caṭkā (Solo)]:[1]

Songs on all subjects covering the entire life of the Rajbanshis of the then Kamrup

The traditional form of music evolved and developed by the interactions of the characteristic voice, timbre and style of the speech form spoken by the Rajbanshis, the geophysical environment and specific production relations of the ancient Kamrup, which has been in use in this vast area of Kamrup for centuries is called Bhāwāiyā. This area of Kamrup lying at the foothills of the Himalayas is full of jungles and just below the area lie the plains partially used as agricultural fields. Here the rivers are torrential as they flow through the hilly tracts and the river-ways are fraught with dangers. Frequent floods of the rivers Teestā, Jaldhaka, Raidak, Sankosh, Torsha, and Kaljani etc disturb the rural life.

The regional background of the form of Bhāwāiyā is thus different from that of other forms of Bengal folk. The physical, mental and emotional life of the people here has been largely influenced by the bounty of nature. The singer and the composer intoxicated by the feasts of nature have sought inspiration from woman, the like figure of nature. Judged from the angles of natural cultural traditions, socio-economic psychological background, Bhāwāiyā has an extra ordinary situation completely different from the usual world of Bengal's folk songs. Women assume an all prevading right and predominance in such musical environment.

Side by side the nature, the cultural tradition of this area also points to the woman-centric features. From the point of view of the population, this area was mainly inhabitated by the Koch-Mech-Rabha-Rajbanshi groups. One of the important features of this society was the proximity to the matriarchal society. The cultural base of a matriarchal society has not faded away from the minds of this people at grass root level in spite of their close association with patriarchal Hindu religion, influence of 'Natha' cult, Islam and Vaishnavism.

Woman has played predominant role in the 'lokayata' (folk-based) religion that has evolved out of the effects of interaction of various religious groups and speech groups. The role of woman in the society has been well recognised particularly because here woman is the companion of man in his economic pursuits of labour intensive agriculture and related activities.

Woman plays important role in socio-religious activities too. Woman is accepted as the priest of the rituals to agriculture. Agri-based folk (*loukik*) society is controlled by the mother figure who is the source and abode of fertility and reproduction. This is why there is tremendous influence of folk goddesses (*loukik devis*) on Kamrup's social life and lots of songs have evolved based on the glory and greatness of these deities.

All the three forms of woman-mother, daughter and lover are reflected in Bhāwāiyā, although it is true that the lover (lady love) predominates as in other forms of folk in

Bengal. Love has placed women to the realm of dream distant from the hard realities. Union, seperation, grief and sorrows, and happiness on the other hand accompany love for either of both the sides.

In Bhāwāiyā, the mother form of woman we get mainly in the songs relating to the worship of deities and rituals—*Shāiṭol gān, Bishaharā gān, Tistāburir gān, Subacanir gān, Biyār geet* (marriage songs), etc. These loukik devis (folk deities) are adored as mother goddess. Besides, the folk dramas start with the *Vandana* (prayer songs) to the mother goddesses like Saraswati, Kali, Candi, etc. There are, of course, a few songs reflecting the eternal love between mother and son or mother and daughter. For example:

> *O mor kāgā re kāgā;*
> *Jakhan māo mor rānde bāre patra nā dyān kāgā māyer haste*
> *Mairbe māo mor āgunot pariyā re.*
> *O mor kāgā re kāgā,*
> *Jokhan māo mor ānjā (tarkari) koṭe, patra nā dyān māyer haste,*
> *Mairbe māo mor gālāt kāṭāri diyā re ....*
> *Jakhan māo mor bichināt śote patra dyān kāgā māyer haste.*
> *Mairbe māo mor bichināt śutiyā re.*

Here the woman (daughter) in distress and grief is communicating her tales of sorrow through a letter to be carried to her mother by the crow. She is in such abject poverty and distress that the mother will commit suicide as soon as she knows the content of the letter. The daughter is asking the crow to deliver the letter in an appropriate time so that she can die in peace. The most appropriate time will be when she goes to bed after completing her day's works.

In spite of all such examples, the moot point remains that the women as ladylove and the stories of their eternal love have occupied the major portion of the domain of Bhāwāiyā. Woman is principally a ladylove in Bhāwāiyā. In the language of Dr. Haripada Chakrabarti, former Professor of North Bengal University and a scholar on folklore:

> "Bhāwāiyā is a song of love. Viewed minutely, it is the song of the grass widow or it is the expression of erotic sentiment of a deceived and disappointed. Suspense and anxiety of separation of a destitute woman is the vital issue. The hero, somewhere it is Sadhu; elsewhere the Boatman, Maishal, Mahout, Cowboy or Baidya (Ayurvedic kaviraj). The expression of the painful youth is straight and simple."

The deep pangs of the heart of a woman is so touching in Bhāwāiyā that it overtakes the boundary of land, time and environment and creates an ever-lasting appeal. The expression of her feelings is very straight and simple without any hesitation and fear. The depth of man-woman relationship gives an extra-ordinary glory and prestige to this form of song. The spokesman, that is, the singer is the man although he tells the feelings and emotions of woman.

In this connection, one should bear in mind that in Bhāwāiyā love is not something which is unworldly, supernatural and heavenly wonder; rather it is the central figure of hard-working real life situation. The hero and the heroine meet in the extensive bounty and boundless solitude of nature for a moment only. Love through mutual understanding between them acts like touch stone in the midst of the fatigue of hard labour. And this immediately relieves the pains and stress of every day life.

The woman absorbs the feeling that she can move forward through any kind of difficult path if she gets the man as her comrade and companion. In other words, despite its nature as emotional love songs, Bhāwāiyā has become a real life-oriented music with the segments of hard realities; at the same time, it is full of exquisite beauty beyond the earthly life.

In this connection, we have mentioned the comment and observations of some eminent folklorists and folk performers. Khaled Coudhury's observation is that the close relation between nature and people is greatly available in the folk songs of North Bengal, while the same is found lacking in East Bengal (Bangladesh) folk songs because of the overwhelming influence of Radha Krishna; because of the influence of Vaisnavism and Sufism.

Similarly, Hemanga Biswas observed that the songs of North Bengal are much more life-orinted than those of East Bengal. Here Torsha has not become Yamuna (Radha-Krishna's), Cilmarir bandar has not become Vrindavana; here the composers and singers have not yielded so much to the feudalism. According to Kali Dasgupta, the North Bengal songs are much more 'down to earth'; here Kala does the works of tilling lands, rowing boat and grazing cows and does not behave like Krishna with the banshi (flute) in hands. There is no kind of hypocrisy in Bhāwāiyā.[2]

The exquisite qualities of Bhāwāiyā coming out of the observations of the exponents and experts deserve to be discussed with appropriate examples from the popular numbers of Bhāwāiyā-Caṭkā. We will make an attempt in this regard by way of analysis of a few Bhāwāiyā-Caṭkā songs.

It is clear that Radha-Krishna of Vaishnava cult could not have much influence in North Bengal because of the predominance of Saivism in ancient Kamrup. The psychological factor is inherent in the name of Kamrup itself. According to the mythologists the name is derived from Kamdev, that is, Madan burnt into ashes by the anger of Siva. After the dissolution of body (demise) by Sati, the wife, Siva goes for deep meditation.

Madan irritates him while trying to rouse desire in the mind of Siva in meditation and in the result gets burnt into ashes by the wrath of Siva. After long last, Siva being satisfied with the prayer of Rati, the wife of Madan, gives the former life to Madan. Thus Madan-Kamdev gets back the former life, that is, Kam-roop. The region has been named Kamrup in this way.

That is the reason why the real life sex-oriented love, and not the unworldly heavenly love, has been deep-rooted in the songs of this area. Moreover, even the Vaishnava influence that worked in this region was of Sankardeva variety, not the Caitanyadeva variety. Sankardeva was patronised by the Kamrup king Naranarayan and he preached his Vaishnavism in the whole region of Kamrup from the central place Madhupur, near Cooch Behar, the capital town. In the Vaisnava sect of Sankardeva, there is no place of Radha. Krishna alone in the form of Hari and Madanmohan is adored. That is why Cooch Behar area of Kamrup is full of Madan Mohan temples.

Woman senses the feeling of love in mind right from the beginning of her budding youth. She feels the necessity in her life of a man who will meet her mental and physical needs and make her life fulfilling. If however, the hard realities of life do not make this possible and she does not get anybody after her mind she feels frustrated, dejected and all her hopes and aspirations of womanhood remain unfulfilled. The simple illiterate young girl at that moment has nothing to rely upon, except for putting the blame on God. We get the expression of feelings and emotions of such a young girl in some of the old songs of North Bengal. One of such songs is given below:

Parthama Jauvaner kāle nā hail mor biyā,
Ār katakāl rahim ghare ekākini hayyā re Bidhi nidayā.
Hāilā pail mor sonār jauvan maleyār jhare
Māo bāpe mor hail bādi nā dil parer ghare re Bidhi nidayā
Bāpok nā kao sarame mui māok nā kao lāze,
Dhiki dhiki tushir aghun jaleche dehār maje re Re bidhi nidayā....
Emon man mor karere bidhi emon man mor kare,
Moner matan cyāngrā pāile dhariyā pālāo dure Re bidhi nidayā.

The woman in the bloom of youth has not been given to marriage in her prime of youth, which is gradually being withered away. Her parents are not in a position to arrange the marriage. The youthful woman cannot even express her mental feelings to anybody out of shame and fear. She feels like running away with a man of her choice marrying him and spending the conjugal life in peace and happiness. She won't mind even if people speak ill of her and despise her for this act.

It is interesting to note that this song on *partham* (first) jauvan was the first known Bhāwāiyā song available in printed form. This song found place in the Linguistic Survey of India edited by George A. Grierson in 1904 collected through one Babu Muralidhar Ray Choudhury of Jalpaiguri in 1898.[3] There is no Bhāwāiyā song available in printed from before 1904.

A few words regarding the problems involved in the collection of folklore, folk songs may not be irrelevant in this connection. In the field of collection of folk songs besides the knowledge on the characteristics of folk song the basic knowledge of the dialect in which the songs are composed—its grammar, pronounciation, intonation, throwing of words, etc. is an essential quality of the collector. In absence of such qualities, there is every possibility of mistakes being committed at every step. For instance, in the above quoted song, the words in the lyric—hāilā, jauvan, kao, tushir, pālāo should have been *hāliyā, jaivan, kaong, tusher*, and *pālāong* respectively in Kamrupi or Rajbanshi dialect.

Since the collector of the song Babu Muralidhar Raychoudhury did not belong to the Rajbanshi community, his knowledge about the dialect was imperfect as usual, and as such he could not distinguish between *hāilā* and *hāliyā*, kao and kaong. The mistakes could also be the result of ignorance of the composer and proof readers of the printing press about the characteristic features of the dialect.

We face this kind of problem even today. While getting the songs in this dialect printed it has been experienced that proof reading requires intense kind of attention, because the employees of the printing press do not have proper knowledge about the dialect. They can not distinguish between *kao* and *Kaong* or *pālāo̩* and *pālāong*—kao means you tell and kaong means I tell, the verb roots of second person and first person respectively.

Coming back to the main discussion, there are lots of Bhāwāiyā songs on the grief and sorrows and lamentations of woman. For instance:

Aki dādāre jaivan dekhiyā chāti mor phāṭe.
Tolā māṭir kalā jeman re halphal halphal kare.
Ai matan nāriro jaivan dine dine bāre re.
Māye bale choṭo choṭore bāpe nā dyāy biyā
Ār katakāl rākhim jaivan ancale bāndhiyā re
Dādāre jaivan dekhiyā chāti mor phāṭe.

The worries and anguish of the youth in bloom have been beautifully expressed in the song with the help of a natural truth—a case of metaphor. The growth of banana trees planted on the newly raised soil is very rapid and so is the growth of youth of young girl. Her grief and distress however, knows no bound if her parents still consider her a baby and do not give her to marriage. The woman at this stage needs one appropriate companion who can meet her physiological, emotional and mental demands. How long can she suppress the youth?

The second song in the collection of George Grierson also relates to the love of husband and wife.,

Prān Sādhu re,
Jadi jān sādhu parabās, nā karen sādhu parār āś,
Āpan hāte sādhu āndhiyā khān bhātore.
Prān sādhure,
Kocer kari sādhu nā karen bay
Parār nāri sādhu āpan nay
Par nāri sādhu badhibe parāno re.
Prān sādhure,
Pube nā pacciyā bāo
Ghopā cāyyā sādhu nāgān nāo
Dāri mājhi sādhu āken sābodhāne re,

In this song, the woman is giving her merchant husband some advice on the eve of his setting off for trading by boat. She is advising how he should behave with the boatmen and other assistants, where to anchor the boat, etc. She is also giving him proper caution that he should not get attracted to any other woman because such women could be dangerous and could cause his death. An apprehension that her husband might be attracted to any woman on the route in her long absence from the proximity of her husband has been beautifully revealed in this song.

There are lots of such songs in Bhāwāiyā. We can now deal with the types of songs where nature and human love have come quite intimately related. These songs give intimate descriptions of nature and unobstructed love between man and woman, whether they are legally married husband and wife or not, that is, irrespective of the legitimacy of their relationship.

We have discussed that the surroundings and socio-economic environment have tremandous influence on Bhāwāiyā. The man has to travel from village to village on economic reasons, that is, to earn the livelihood. The helpless woman has to spend her days with the agony and pains of separation. Bhāwāiyā is full of lamentations on account of such separation—sometimes temporary, but often permanent.

The woman may be one with the youth in full bloom and afflicted with love or a grass widow or a married one in deep love with the paramour (strange man) or any young man. When the Garial (cart-driver) travels from hat (weekly market) to hat with various types of agricultural commodities on the bullock cart owned by his master, a rich person of the village, his young wife spends her sleepless nights alone in their small thatch in fear of various kinds of danger and in pains of separation.

Similarly, when the Maishal has to spend months after months in the bathan (char-land used for keeping and grazing the buffaloes) to graze and look after the buffaloes in danger stricken shrubs and jungles or when the Mahout has to go for participitating in the trapping operation of elephants either as trapper or a member of the chasing party owned and organised by a zemindar engaged in elephant trapping and trade, their wives or lady loves have to spend sleepless nights in fear of unknown dangers with the pangs of separation. Their men that is, the Garial, Mahout or Maishal too suffer the same feelings and pains of separation and fear of dangers.

But there is no way out. Their profession compels them to undergo this plight. Moreover they get addicted to the life in course of time and cannot give up the profession. So they give expression to their own feelings and the feelings of their ladyloves and wives in the Bhāwāiyā songs:

1. *Aki gāriāl bhāi, katay raba āmi panther dike cāyyā re.*
Jedin gārial ujān jāy nārir man mor jhuriyā ray re
Ạki gāriāl bhāi hākāo gāri tui cil mārir bandare re.
Ki kaba duskera jwālā gāriāl bhāi gāthiā cikana mālā
Aki gāriāl bhāi katay kāndim mui nidhuā pātāre re
Aki gāriāl bhāi katay raba āmi panther dike cāyyā re.

O Garial (cartman)! How long shall I await your come back? When my garial sets off for the up-country, my mind gets afflicted. O garial! Drive your cart towards the Chilmari market.

Or the Maishal sings:

2. *Bātān bātān karen maishāl o,*
Maishāl bātān karilen bāri
Jubbā nāri gharat thuiyā kāy kare cākiri maishāl o,
Choṭo kāle haice biāo re, maishāl bayas bhāṭi geil
Nā hailong chāoār māo mane duska rail maishāl o.

O Maishal (buffalo-keeper)! You always think about the buffalo herds and sheds, which have become your home, leaving behind this young woman at home. Such is your service. I was married at very early age and I am almost old now and yet I have not achieved motherhood. This is so sad. Similarly the Mahout sings—

3. *Hastir kainyā hastir kainyā bāmanera nāri,*
Māthāy niyā tām kalasi O, sakhi haste sonār jhāri sakhi O,
O mor hāy hastir kainyā re, khāneko dayā nāi tor māhutok nāgiyā re.
Bālu ṭil-ṭil pankhire kānde bālute pariyā,
Gouri puriyā mahut kānde O, sakhi ghar bāri chāriyā sakhi O,

O mor hāy hastir kainyā re, khāneko dayā nāi tor māhutok nāgiyā re.
Āi chārilong bhāi chārilong chārilong sonār puri,
Biāo kareyā chāriyā āsilong O, sakhi alpa bayaser nāri sokhi O,
O mor hāy....re
Phānd lādilong phāndā lādilong āro lādilong ḍori
Māhut phāndi jukti kari O, Sakhi cholilong sikār bāri
O mor hāy....re, etc.

O elephant girl! O Brahmin woman! With the copper pitcher on your head and the golden *jhari* (water sprinkler) in your hand, O my friend, my elephant girl, won't you have a little pity for the Mahout (elephant keeper)? The sandpiper cries in the sands; the Mahout from Gouripur cries for his home, O my friend; won't you have a little pity on the Mahout? I left my mother; I left my brother; I left my golden house; I married and then left behind my young wife; O my friend, won't you have a little pity on the Mahout? We took the lasso; we took the cards and ropes along. Us, the Mahout and the *phandi* (trapper) planned together before we set out for the hunting ground. We bound the elephant all over.

The first song speaks of the pains of a woman whose husband, a Garial goes to *Cilmari hat* (market) and the poor woman suffers the pains of separation. The second song tells the tale of pains of a budding young lady whose husband has been away from her for long and she has as a result been deprived of becoming a mother by this time; in other words her youth has been deprived of the enjoyment of consumation. In the third one the Mahout sings that he has left behind in his thatched house the newly married young wife and prays for early catch so that they can go home early.

It is therefore, noted that the songs, apart from describing the pains and afflictions of the lovers, speak of the oppression and exploitation inherent in the feudal society. The socio-economic scenario of the ancient Kamrup was characterised by the dominance of the land-owning class—*Jotedars, Zemindars, Chukanidars*, etc. A wealthy man used to be owner of vast areas of land. Animal energy, that is, cattle population was essentially required for farming and other activities relating to agriculture.

Moreover, the vast amounts of alluvial and diluvial land (*char* lands), fallow lands and jungles have paved the way for animal husbandry in the area. The landowning class like *jotedars* has kept good number of buffaloes as additional source of income by selling buffalo milk, curd, ghee, etc. and by selling the animal for use in agriculture. So they had 'bathans' for the buffaloes. Each bathan would have arrangement for keeping about 100-150 buffaloes.

Bathan used to be made on an alluvial land full of clump of reeds, quills and common reeds, the kind of land, which does get usually water logged. Buffaloes were kept after some cleaning of the shrubs, and the buffaloes themselves would clear rest of the shrubs. A few huts would be constructed with the grass and reeds and bomboos available nearby for using them as living huts of the Maishals (Buffalo Keepers). Usually there were 5-6 Maishal in one average sized bathan of 100-120 buffaloes.

The jungle areas of North Bengal used to be infested with the tigers, cheetahs, wolves, boars, hayenas, etc. in those days. The keepers of buffaloes (Maishals) therefore had to protect the pets from the attack of those wild animals—particular attention had to be given to the young little kids of buffaloes. Maishals were young strong able-bodied men. Early in the morning, the Maishal would have meals of flattened rice with curd and set for grazing the buffaloes in the pastures around. The moving herd of buffaloes would be controlled and given protection from either side as well as from behind by the Maishals with bamboo sticks and cudgels on their hands. They would shout and call quite often—*hei nālo, hai baramāin, hei choṭo māin, hai kājli, hei dhauli—kutthi Jāis, sojā hāṭek....*

The mode of addressing the buffaloes with affectionate voice is worthnoting. They would be addressed according to their colour of body—a white female buffalo addressed as *dhauli* from the word *dhaolā* (White), a black male buffalo addressed as *kālo* or *kājlā* (black), etc. and would be commanded to go straight and follow the leader. The buffaloes would also respond to their commands. Every herd will have a leader usually a black strong built male buffalo. He would be in front of the herd leading others while grazing in the jungles and shrubs. He would have medium sized metallic long cylindrical bell tied on his neck, so that others can follow the sound of the bell. The Maishals also would have the advantage of controlling the leader to control others too, by following the sound of the bell.

With the apprehension of attack from any wild animal, the leader would bend his horns to keep his herd ready for the counter-attack and would take deep quick breath with hissing sound to make others alert and ready for the fight. The animals would follow him. While grazing in the jungles, the Maishals would have to take precaution so that no one gets out of the herd and does not become prey to wild animals, particularly tiger and wolf. In course of grazing the herd, the Maishals would do practise the Bhāwāiyā song whenever they find some time. They would come back to the bathan before the evening sets in. The buffaloes have moved on and on for filling up their stomach with grass. In the evening they would take rest and chew the cud; on some rare occasions the Maishals would have to face the attack of tiger or hayena on the herd and they would face the attack with stick on one hand and torch on the other. This is why the Maishals would have to be very storng and courageous young men with real muscle powers. They would shout with sufficient courage "Aei kutta (He dog)! Go way".

In case of any fight, the buffaloes with long horns would come forward to help the Maishals. The Maishals had to acquire other qualities too. Some of them must have had basic knowledge on veterinary science, since they had to deal with and keep in healthy conditions so many animals. Sometimes they had to take the herd for grazing across the rivulets and rivers and as such they should be good swimmers too. He was on the other hand a good dotorā player, singer and composer of Bhāwāiyā songs.

In other words a young strong built Maishal with so many qualities could easily be a hero to any young lady, whether she is his wife or not. The Maishal would milk the milch cow-buffaloes, prepare curd, ghee, etc. and sell the same in hats (weekly markets) nearby. He would have to deposit the sale proceeds to the owner on return home.

Thus was spent the bathan life of a Maishal. At the advent of the rains the Maishal would come back with the herd to his master in the village who is known as 'giri', a term probably derived from 'gṛhi' or 'gṛhastha' meaning household owner, usually a jotedar owning huge amounts of land and so a rich person in the village. There will be joy and entertainment in house of the giri with the coming back of the Maishals with the herd. The Maishals would again set for the bathan at the close of the rainy season.

A Maishal would thus spend the major part of the year in the bathan as well as in the house of the 'giri' for looking after the buffaloes and for protecting them from various adversaries in exchange of a paltry sum as salary. He could spend hardly 2/3 months with his family. A young strong built Maishal might have to leave her newly married young wife immediately after the marriage and set for the bathan. He could spend hardly a few days with her and as such their conjugal life did not have the full consumation. The young wife therefore, expresses her pangs in Bhāwāiyā that she did not have the opportunity of becoming mother because of the forced absence of her husband. She sings:

Bātān bātān karen Maishāl o!

Or,

Āji kat dine bāuriben o mor cyāngrā Maishāl re
Bhaiser (maisher) piṭhit cariyā re Maishāl, cheren kāsiār phul
Āshāro śāvan māse nadi hulāsthul re.
Dudh khoāilen syāre syāre re doi khoāilen bhāre
Tui Maishāl chāriyā geile gābur bayser āri re.
Āji kat dine bāuriben mor Maishāl bandhu re.
O my young buffalo-keeper! When will you come back?

You tear away the reed flowers while riding the buffalo, and the same implies that the river is in spate in the month of *Ashar* and *Sravana*. You fed us milk by seers and curd by yokes; if you now desert me, I will cosider myself widow in this young age.

We see the same history in case of Garial (bullock cart – driver) and Mahout (elephant – driver) also. A giri, that is, landower would need carts drawn by bulls or buffaloes to carry agricultural crops from the fields to his house or storehouse and further from the storehouse to the weekly markets. Here also the owner of the cart is the landowner but the cart-diver is a poor salaried land-less farmer. He would take the agricultural commodities like paddy, jute, tobacco, etc. to the markets on various *hat*-days. Naturally he would move from *hat* to *hat*.

The road conditions were not good-mostly muddy and water logged during the rainy season, and such roads through the jungles and shrubs. There was therefore, every possibility of being attacked by wild animals like tiger, wolf, wild boar, etc. The Garials would usually start for the *hat* from a village in group-say, about 8/10 carts in row. They would start in the afternoon; drive the cart throughout the night so that they could reach the hat at a distance of, say15/20 kms early in the morning.

After completion of transaction during the day, they would set for return journey and reach home at night. After again one or two day's rest, they would set for another weekly hat at a distance of say, 12 kms from the village. Thus most of the days of the week they would spend the time on the move and their wives get very little time to spend with them. Such a wife therefore expresses her agony and pains through the Bhāwāiyā song:

Jidin Gāriāl ujān jāy, nārir man mor jhuriyā ray re.
Oki gāriāl bhāi katay raba āmi panther dike cāyyā re.
Oki gāriāl bhāi hākāo gāri tui cilmārir bandare re.

Cilmarir bandar in the song is the symbol of the hat. The life cycle of a garial, moving from hat to hat has been depicted beautifully in a song:

Bāo kumṭā bātās jeman ghuriyā ghuriyā mare
Ki ore ai matan mor gārir cākā panthe panthe ghore re
Oki gāriāl mui calong rāja panthe.
Biyāne uṭhiyā garu gārit diā juri
Ki ore sonā mālār sonār bāde cānder deśe ghuri
Deś videśe ghorong re mui sonāmanir bade
Ki ore seo sonā abaśeshe gharot basi kānde re
Gārir cākā ghore āro maidhye kare rāo
Ki ore sei matan kāndiyā uṭhe āmār sarba gāo re
Oki gārial....panthe.

The wheels of the cart move from road to road like the cyclonic wind moving round and round. Myself, the Garial (cart driver) move along the royal path. I set the cows to the cart early in the morning and set out for the country of the moon in search of the golden girl. I move from country to country in search of my Sonamani; but I find her weeping in my own house at last. The wheels make cracking sound while moving round and round; my body does react in the same way.

The life cycle of the Garial has been compared with baokumta batas, that is, whirl wind. It is usually noticed during the season of North-Wester, that is, in the months of April-May that the dried leaves, sweepings and rubbish materials would move in round shape—would go up and come down with the wind. The cartwheels move on the roads like the whirlwind and the Garial also moves from hat to hat like the whirlwind and his wife spends the sleepless nights at home.

The thick forest areas in the foothills of the Himalayas on the western border of Kamrup are abounded by the elephant population. Man has found the devise of catching the elephants from the forest, training and using them for various purposes. The kings and zemindars would organise such operations of catching the elephants with the help of trappers, Mahouts and their associates from jungles infested with wild animals.

In autumn on the eve of the winter the catchers and Mahouts would set for the jungle, prepare camp with tents just on the border of the forest. Two main jobs in the operations are (*i*) ensnaring the wild elephant by setting the nooses on its neck and legs with the help of the tamed elephants and (*ii*) chasing the wild elephants towards the trappers again with the assistance of domesticated trained elephants.

The characteristic of the elephant herd is that each of the herds will have a conductor, a female elephant who is considered as the queen of the herd. The herd is led by a male big elephant who does the job of keeping his 'hārrem' (group of females) away from the other grown-up male elephants; and naturally the leader will drive away from the herd any male elephant as soon as it attains the adulthood.

The Mahouts and catchers would participate in the catching operation during the day and would come back to the camp before the advent of the evening. In the evenings, they would assemble around the fireplace for warming up as well as for protection from wild animals. They would rejoice in case of success of operation. Otherwise also they will take part in gossip, Bhāwāiyā songs and dances. The songs would relate to the griefs and sorrows of the lover and the beloved, or the devotional ones. The other job done at this hour is to tame and train the wild elephants which have been caught.

While imparting training, they would sing songs on elephants and other subjects. The songs performed by a group of Mahouts and catchers regularly every evening would have tremandous effect on the wild animals. Their initial reaction would be irritation and violent movements. The same kind of songs with same tune and rhythm day by day would however, gradually make the wild animal used to it and after some days it would react favourably to such songs. The Mahouts would thus spend the camp days for the operation of catching, training and taming the elephants.

At home the wives, relatives and near ones of the Mahouts and catchers would spend their anxious days. The wives will have the pangs of separation along with the apprehension of danger. The Mahout who has gone for the catching operation might not come back from the forest. Their feelings and emotions are expressed in the song:

O mor dāntāl hātir māut re
Jedin māut śikār jāy, nārir man mor jhuriā ray re.
O mor sārin hātir Māut re
Jedin māut ujān jāy nārir man mor puriyā ray re
Ākāsete nāi re candra ki kare tar tārā
Jebā nārir purush nāi re O tār dine andhihārā.
Pukurite nāi re pāni naukā kyāmane cale
Jebā narir purush nāi re O tār rupe ki kām kare.
O mor mākhnā hātir Māut re
Jedin Māut Āssām jāy nārir man mor jhuriyā ray re.
O mor ḍhuin hātir Māut re
Jedin Māut jangal jāy nārir man mor kāndiyā ray re.

O my Mahout of the tusker! When he goes on his hunt, my woman's heart languishes. What use are stars in a sky without a moon? A woman without a husband is darkness in daylight. How can a boat move in a pool with no water? What use is beauty to a woman without her man? O my Mahout of the 'Makhna' elephant! When he goes to Assam my woman's heart languishes. O my Mahout of the 'Dhuin' elephant! My woman's heart gets sorrowful when he leaves for the jungle.

Elephants are called by different names according to their nature and physical characteristics. For example, an elephant with long tusk is called *Dāntāl*, one without tusk is *Mākhnā*, one with short tusk is *Cākhnā* and a female is called Dhuin. Sometimes, beautiful episodes are associated with the songs. For instance, in the song on elephant mentioned earlier the elephant has been described as Bāmaner nāri *i.e.* Brahmin woman. This refers to a popular folklore. Smt. Nihar Barua of Gouripur, Assam, has mentioned this folklore in one of her articles. The floklore is like this—

In a small cottage on the bank of the river 'Dyāoā Siā' flowing from the Bhutan hills lived a happy family of Jainath, a Brahmin and his beautiful wife Jaimala. The Brahmin Jainath had the second marriage with the ugly daughter of a rich man. They built a palacial building for living, while Jaimala was left to a corner of the cottage. She was given the duty of bringing water from the river to fill up the drinking water jar of her husband. She was given the food of uncleaned rice in exchange. Everyday Jaimala would give the rice to the birds and would go to the river *ghat* (bank) with the golden porous waterpot in her hand and a pitcher made of copper on the head.

While taking water from the river she would weep in grief, her tears rolled down on river water. One day the King of the elephants, while taking bath and playing with his companions down the ghat from which Jaimala was taking water, felt that the river water tasted saline and tasteless. They wanted to know the reason and following the salinity could find out the reasons. They could know the cause of Jaimala's grief. The king of elephants then took Jaimala on his trunk to their kingdom and placed her on the throne.

Immediately, thousands of elephants came forward to pay their respect to Jaimala as their queen. The elephant King then took Jaimala on the trunk to a beautiful fountain and poured the fountain water on the head of Jaimala. As soon as it was done, Jaimala's human body turned into a beautiful elephant maid. The copper made water jar on her head took shape of a jar on the forehead and the golden pourous water-pot in hand turned into the trunk. Jaimala thus became the queen of the elephant herd. Young female elephant has thus been described as 'Bamaner nari'. In this folklore based song, the composer has conveyed the influence of money in the divine love of a man and his wife; the bad effect of second marriage and greed, etc.

We have so long discussed the love between the husband and wife, love between two legitimate lovers in Bhāwāiyā. A considerable part of Bhāwāiyā, however, has remained occupied by illicit love, the extra-marital love.

In the song on the Gāriāl 'Jedin Gāriāl ujān jāy, nārir man mor jhuriyā ray re' mentioned earlier, the woman whom the song has referred to, could be the illicit lover of the Garial. While going to and coming back from the market every week, the young sweet-voiced dotora player Garial must have met an young woman of the village and they had love in the process. But their love did not get fulfilled. The Garial has to go back to his place with the cart; he cannot stay for long with his beloved. The next day he would have to go to some other market. So he expresses the feelings of his grief and sorrows and also the pains of the beloved through the song, 'Jedin gārial ujān jāy'.

The extra-marital love has occupied considerable portion of the Bhaiwaiya songs relating to the Maishal. The Maishal has his bathan (cow-pasture/buffalo-pasture) mostly on the riverbank not far from the locality. The young women of the village would come to the bathing place of the river for bath and fetching water. The strong-built young Maishal expert on dotora playing and Bhāwāiyā songs might have attracted the heart of one of such young ladies. The Maishal also had seen her quite a number of times looking at him in gaze and wonder. The result is love between the two. The environment itself is such as to favour the growth of love and affection between them. But the love of Maishal is short-lived, because he would have to go back to the giri with the buffalo-herd as soon as the rains set in and his beloved will be left in grief and distress with the pangs of separation. Their love will not get the desired fulfilment.

We will now mention and analyse a few such songs. In the song given below the introducer describes the situation that the young girl is cleaning her body and breasts in the chest-high water and a strange Maishal plays the stroke on the string of the dotora just at that moment. Introducer:

Hāy re, bukka pānit nāmiyā kainyā bukka mānjan kare
Kon ṭhākār baideiśā Maishāl dotorāt ṭhokar māre.

The feelings and emotions of the two youths get transformed into a Bhāwāiyā song in the form of conversation between the two.

Maishāl: *Jal bharo sundari kainyā kāchārat nāge ḍheu*
Ekelāy āisāchen ghāṭe songe nāi ki keu kainyā hey.

O beautiful girl! You are filling your pitcher with water and the waves strike the banks of the river. Have you come all alone to the bathing ghat and nobody with you?

Kainyā: *Ekelāy pāṭhāiche bidhi ekelāy ghare thāki.*
E bharā jaivaner bhar ekelāy dhari rāki Maishāl o.

God has sent to this world all alone and I live all alone in my house. And I put up with my youthfulness all alone.

Maishāl: *Keman tomār bāp māo kainyā keman tomār hiyā*
Ekelāy āisāchen ghāṭe bukke pāshān diyā kainyā hey.

How are your parents and how is your heart? You have come alone to the ghat with rock stone on your heart (cruel heart).

Kainya: *Bhāle āmār bāp-māo Maishāl, bhāle āmār hiyā,*
Ekelāy āisāchi ghāṭe bukke śirphal niyā, Maishāl o.

Quite well meaning are my parents and pretty is my heart. I have come to the ghat alone with marmelos fruits on the bosom.

Maishāl: *Bāpo-māo chāriyā kainyā jangale bane ghuri*
Ai śirphaler nāigya pāile chāri maishāl giri, kainyā hey.

Leaving the parents, O girl! I roam in the jungles and bushes. I can leave the job of Maishal, if I get reach of those marmelos fruits.

Kainya: *Kāṭār gachat śirphal Maishāl tāte bhyāngruler hāri,*
Keman kari ai nā śirphal khāiben tomrā pāri.

The marmelos fruits are on the thorny trees with horents' nest there on. How can you reach those fruits to snatch them?

Maishal: *Nal khāgrā kāṭā bārit āser byāpar kari.*
Tomrā jadi sahāy thāken śirphal khāmo pāri.

My job is to deal with juicy things in the midst of reeds and thorny bushes. I can reach and snatch the fruits if you accord your consent.

The Maishal asks the girl indirectly whether she has come to the bathing place alone and the girl in a sarcastic manner replies that she has to bear the burden of her youth all alone. The Maishal also does not miss the opportunity and comments in satire that her parents are unkind and so she also has a heart as hard as stone. The girl replies that her heart is not unkind; rather it is with two grown-up breasts, which are like two marmelo fruits. The Maishal avails the opportunity and proposes that he would like to eat those fruits. The girl now cautions him that the fruits are in a thorny tree with hornet's nest there on and as such he cannot have those so easily. The Maishal now shows his bravery that his business is to deal with juicy things in the midst of jungles of reeds and as such he can have those if the girl helps with due concurrence and approval.

I have explained the song in between the lines just to show the poetic quality, the satire, comparison, etc. used in this song. The expression is so simple and straightforward. There is no hypocrisy in the language of proposing. The youth of woman vindicated by the grown-up breasts has been identified with marmelos fruits.

There are quite a number of very popular 'Maishal' songs, which deserve brief analysis in this connection. They are based on extra-marital relations between the Maishal and his ladylove. For example:

Āmār bāri jān o mor prāner Maishāl re, Maishāl baiste diba morā
Bukkote helāni diyā Maishāl re, Maishāl bājāiben dotorā
Āmār bāri jān o mor prāner Maishāl re, Maishāl baiste diba pirā
Jalpān karite diba Maishāl re, Maishāl śāli dhāner cirā
Śāli dhāner cirā re Maishāl, Banni dhāner khoi
Gharat āche cāmpā kalā Maishāl re, Maishāl gāmchā bāndhā doi.

O Maishal! Please come to my house. I will offer you cane stool. Sitting on it, you can play your 'dotora' leaning your body on my bosom. Do come to my house. I will offer you the small plank to sit and tiffin of flattened rice from 'Sali'paddy (very good quality paddy). The tiffin will be of flattened rice from 'Sali'paddy, sweetened rice from 'Banni'paddy, banana called 'campa'and thick condensed curd.

The heroine, who has met the Maishal quite often on her way to the bathing place of the river, while going for bath and water and has been attracted by his dotora playing and melodious songs, invites the Maishal to her cottage where the Maishal would be in a position to play the dotora sitting very close to her and leaning against her breasts. Not only this, she will give him good food too. This is a direct invitation to Maishal to enjoy the pleasure of extramarital sexual love. We get almost same feelings of the heroine on hearing Maishal's dotora from this song:

Aki Maishāl re, ghāṭer upurā kiser bātān, Maishāli ḍange dotorā bājān,
Man kānde mor bhāoiā gāner sure re.
Oki Maishāl re, āl nacholāy āisong ghāṭe, Buk phāṭe tabu mukh nā phoṭe.
Mukh phoṭeyā kyāmone kaong muin śaram nāge.

O Maishal! While you play the dotora in 'Maishali' stroke in the buffalo sheds on the bathing ghat, my heart wails on the Bhāwāiyā tune. O Maishal! Then I come to the ghat on some plea or other. My heart is painful but my lips do not express so. How can I express the feelings so openly? I feel shy. The heroine is so impressed and overwhelmed by the dotora and melodious voice of the Maishal that she cannot resist the flame of her youth kindled by him and cannot but come to him on some plea or other.

The Maishal, however, cannot give due honour to the love of the village lady who has been so much in love with him because of the compelling circumstances that he has to go back with the buffalo herd as soon as the rains set in. The heroine thinks that some other girl might have attracted the Maishal and so he is indifferent to her and he is going elsewhere. In a tone of complaint the song expresses—

Maish carān mor Maishāl bandhure, Maishāl kon bā carer mājhe,
Elāo kyāne ghantir bājan nā śonong mui kāne Maishāl re,
Adiyā adiyā jān mor Maishāl re, Maishāl nā bājān dotọrā,
Kon bā kathāy haicen gosā, nā dyākhen phiriyā Maishāl re.
Takhane nā kaicong Maishāl re, Maishāl nā jān Goālpārā,
Goāl pārār cyāngri gulā jāne dhulā parā Maishāl re.

Maishal my friend is grazing the buffaloes on a char (silted and little raised land with reeds and grasses), but I can't hear the sound of the bells tied on the neck of the buffaloes now. Maishal! You are restricting your movements by the other side of the char, even not playing on the dotora. Why have you been angry with me that you do not even turn your eyes this side? I told you just then not to go to Goalpara because the girls of Goalpara are expert in the magic of attracting the young lads. The heroine therefore, makes her intense pitiful appeal to the Maishal not to leave her and go away.

Āji chāriyā nā jān cyāngrā Maishāl re.
Maisher piṭit thākiyā Maishāl cheren kāśiār phul
Āṣāro ār śāon māse Maishāl, nadi hulāsthul re.
Dudh khoāilen syāre re syāre, dai khoāilen bhāre,
Āji tui Maishāl chāriyā geile gābur bayser āri re.
Maisher pāl carān re Maishāl tolen sairṣār phul
Tor piritit pariyā Maishāl bhāngil jāti kul re.

O young Maishal! Do not leave me behind. That you are collecting the flowers of reed from the buffalo back implies the advent of *Asadh* and *Sravana* months when the rivers are in spate. You have fed me milk in seers and curd in yokes and if you leave me now, I will become widow in this young age. While grazing the buffalo herds, you collect the mustard flowers and for you I have been outcaste.

The story of extramarital love can be seen in songs on the elephant driver also. The elephant driver takes the elephant for grazing on the bank of the river and also for bath in the river. While grazing the elephant, he sings Bhāwāiyā with the dotora on hands or he plays flute. The girl with the youth in bloom sees him everyday and gradually gets attracted and falls in love. She wants in life as companion such a healthy young man with so melodious voice and sound of dotora. Her feelings are expressed in the song—

> *Gangādharer pāre pāre re, O mor Māute carāy hāti,*
> *Ki māyā nāgāilen Māut re, O tor gālār raser kāṭi.*
> *Ucā kari bāndho chāpor re, O mui āiste jāite dekhim,*
> *Ki māyā nāgāilen Māut re,*
> *Dai khoāilen dudh khoāilen re, Māut nā khoāilen māṭā,*
> *Ebār hyāte ṭuṭiyā gelo re, ainā āisā jāoār ghāṭā.*

On the banks of the Gangadhar, my Mahout! You are grazing the elephant. What a spell you have cast on me O Mahout, with the love beads on your neck! What a spell ! Do build your hut on a high place so that I can see it when I go by. What a spell! You gave me milk, you fed me on curd but you never gave me the dregs of the liquid curd. Your journeys along this road are now meaningless.

Bhāwāiyā song sung by the Mahout, while grazing the elephant, has caused great stir in the mind of the young girl. She is not in a position to control her passions, which have so long been restrained in some way or other. This feeling has been revealed in a very popular song:

> *Āji āulāilen mor bāndhā mayāl re,*
> *Hātir piṭit cariyā re Māhut kiser bāṭul māro,*
> *Parāro kāminik dekhiyā jaliyā kyāne māro re.*
> *Hātir piṭit thākiyā re Māhut thor kalā bhāngo*
> *Ṇāriro manera kathā tomorā kibā jāno re.*

You have thoroughly disturbed my settled house. Sitting on the back of your elephant, o Mahaut, why do you shoot with the arrow of love and go into blaze at the sight of some other's woman? From the elephant back, you can breakdown the banana stalks, but what do you know of a woman's heart?

It is worth-noting in this connection that songs conveying marital or extra-marital love in Bhāwāiyā are there not only relating to the Garial, Maishal or Mahut but on other professions also. There are songs where the hero is a professional gold smith or a weaver or an ayurvedic doctor (*Kaviraj*). By nature women are fond of ornaments. The goldsmiths are therefore, liked by them.

In earlier days, the gold smith of the village would go from house to house-particularly the well-off houholds and get orders. A young woman having no financial capacity, might be fascinated by the gold smith and might ask him to make a pair of bangles or a nose-ring. In this song, the heroine asks the gold smith to make a nose-ring for her. She will wear the nose-ring and go to her boy friend. She promises that she will pay the making charges in instalments.

Bāniyā bandhure ekṭā nolo gareyā de
Bānir pāisā dim dim re bāniyā dhire dhire

O goldsmith, my friend! Make a nose-ring for me. I will slowly pay back your charges.

Similarly, the weaver is quite important for woman, who, by nature, is fond of sarees of various designs. In this song, the young woman (heroine) is asking the weaver to weave a saree for her. She is telling her the design of the saree too.

Tānti bhāi, sāree khān bāneyā de, Tānti bhāi sāree khān bāneyā de mok
Ki chānde bānābu sāree tāko suniyā ne, Tānti bhāi tāko nā kayyā dyāng tok.
Dui pāke dui nadir dhār madhye calkā bālur car,
Carer māthāt jor cakoyā baise, urāy khelāy re.

O Weaver! Make a saree for me; I will tell you the design in which you should make it. River banks on both the sides and a bright sand char in the middle and a pair of cakoya bird sitting on the top of the char–all these should be woven on the saree.

The heroine is in need of the help and service of a doctor, usually a *Kaviraj* (ayurvedic doctor) in the village in times of sickness of the members of her family. The popular songs addressed to the *Kaviraj* or *Vaidya* are:

Oki Kavirāj! Bhāl kariyā dekho chāoār nāri re.

O *Kaviraj*! Please see the pulse of my child carefully. There is a very famous popular song on *Vaidya*.

Nadi nā jāio re baido, nadi nā jāio re
Baido nadiro gholā re gholā pāni.
Nadiro badalere baido bārite dhon gāo re
Baido āmi nāri tuliyā re diba pāni.

O Baido, do not go to river for bath; it is full of muddy water. Rather you take bath at home; I will fetch water for you.

So far we have discussed about the love of a girl or woman with youth in bloom, whether married or unmarried. Bhāwāiyā deals with the love affairs of young widow too. There are young widows who lost their husbands at their tender age. The system of dowry for the bride was prevalent in Kamrup as in any traditional society. A poor man had to earn some money to be paid as dowry before he could think of marrying. This resulted into overage of the groom. The obvious result was large number of widows.

The poor person might have been otherwise sick because of poverty and hard labour. Such a person, marrying a young girl of another poor father, never cared to think what would come out in near future. Such young girl married to a sick old person is easily fascinated by a Garial, Maishal or Mahut or any such able-bodied young man. The sick old man dies within a few years and the young girl becomes widow. In Bhāwāiyā there are lots of songs conveying the grief, sorrows and depression of young widows. For example:

Nadir pārer kuruyā re mor jāmer gacher suā
Kyāne kānden aman kari coukher jal phyāleyā re
korāre muio kāndong ciṭal biduā hayyā.
Ḍhāl kāuyāṭār kāndon śuni citer āgun jwale
Pati je mor mariyā geice ādar nāi mor ghare re.
Korāre muio kāndong ciṭal biduā hayyā.

The Kuruya bird of the riverbank and the sua bird of the Jam tree! Why do you lament so sadly on tears? I also weep as a grass widow. The heart laments in grief hearing the wailing of the big crow. There is none at home to love me as my husband has died. *O Kora* (bird)! I also weep, as being a grass widow.

Again, this phenomenon of large number of young widows in the society has led to the system of widow marriage in such societies. The widows in poor families having no means of livelihood remarried such a poor young man or aged man.

Sometimes, some rich people of the village would keep such widows as *sangani* or *pachua* (second or third wife) mainly for the reason that she can be a good labour for everyday works like boiling paddy, keeping the house clean, making rice out of paddy, cooking food, etc. However, in most of the cases of re-marriage the widow got frustrated and she became the victim to misbehabour, physical assault and oppression from the husband. She has to give hard labour but she cannot get two meals a day in exchange, although she agreed to such re-marriage mainly with the expectation of getting two meals for herself and her children. Naturally, such widows could be easily attracted and allured by the young strong singer. The *sangna* (husband) and the *sangani* (widow) live together as a couple but there is hardly any feeling of love between them. The husband quite often beats the wife on some plea or other. Here is a famous song on this:

Aki ore sāngnā mārilu kyāne.
Bhāter duhkhe ore sāngnā kāinat basinu mui
Kon doshote duor bāndhi mārlu āji tui, re sāngnā mārilu kyāne.
Mok mārilu bhāle karlu chaoāk mārilu kyāne
Chuā bārun nāgāim āji tor sāngnār kapāle, re sāngnā mārilu kyāne.

O Sangna (husband), why did you beat me? I have come to you in such informal marriage for want of food; and you beat me without any fault of mine. Why? You have beaten me alright. Why did you beat my child? I will treat you with the broom, which is used for cleaning the unholy impure place.

The matter of oppression, physical beating, mental torture, want of food and shelter, etc. signifying the distress and grief, which the women have to pass through in male dominated society has been revealed in so many songs. Although woman here is a participant in the production process, and she has some degree of dignity of labour in the society, the usual practices of a male-dominated society make her subjected to such oppression and torture. There is considerable number of songs on this:

Oki bhābere dyāorā thuiyā āisek mok bāpore bhāiyār dyāśe.
Bāpo bhāiyār dyāśe jābo, bārāni bhukiyā khābo.
Oki bhābere.... ghare
Bāpo bhāi mor durācār byāceyā khāice mok durāntar re,
Byāceyā khāice mok madaśiyār ghare re.
Madaśiyā mad re khāy, pāni dite mor rāti pohāy
Naler dānge śaril hail mor kālā re.

The young girl has been married to an aged man who has not been in position to give her mental and physical satisfaction leading to strained relation between the two. The others in the family are also not happy with her. Physical beating, mental torture has made her life intolerable. The only silver lining in such an oasis is the presence of younger brother-in-law of almost same age of the young girl. Naturally some sort of friendship develops between the two. May be, she is in love with the brother-in-law. This is particularly relevant when we see so many instances of marrying the brother-in-law, the younger brother of the husband in our *shastras* (scriptures). The girl therefore, makes appeals to the brother-in-law to take her to her parents. There she will prefer to lead the life of a labour even.

The songs mentioned and described above speak of the love, marital or extra-marital, love of the deserted lady-love, love of widow, etc; in addition they speak of various social systems, practices prevalent in the society of the Rajbanshis. The songs have given references to dowry for the bride, widow marriage system, active particapation of women in the production process, that is, agricultural activities, etc.

There are songs on various other socio-economic relations too. In a song, beauty of a young girl working in the paddy field, engaged in making provision for irrigation water by preparing low mud-walls and at the sametime, weeping in grief for her husband who has been away for some time, has been discribed in extremely befitting manner. It gives a beautiful depiction of a fair young lady working in muddy water with her hands busy in managing the flowing water but eyes full of tears in grief.

Āilo bāndho kainyā jalore chyāko, sundor gāye kainyā kādo mākho,
Coukh tuli kainyā dyākho āmār āge hey.
Haldi gāye kainyā kādo re hāthe, āilo bāndho kainyā kiser āśe
Āji kao kathā kainyā baideśiār āge he.
Coukher jal bandhu jalere pail, bāndhā jal bāndhu besi hail
Bāndhong āil jal ātok karibār āśe hey.

You are making the mud walls and irrigating your crops but your beautiful body is rubbed with mud. Raise your eyes and see me; with mud in your hands of such a brown body, on what kind of desire you are making the mudwalls? Just disclose it to this stranger. The field water has increased because of my tears falling on it and I am making the mud-walls to control that water.

Bandhur bāde kāndi āmi seo bandhu āmār hṛdyer swāmi
Āji bharā jaiban bandhu dyākhe ainya loke hey

I am weeping for my friend who is none else but my husband. He is away and others are lying at my full youth.

We have described earlier the nature of the rivers of Kamrup. They having originated from the mountains are usually narrow but torrential. During the rains they overflow and cause devastations on both the banks. Miles of paddy fields, houses, thatched cottages are devastated by the floods of almost all the rivers—*Teestā, Torshā, Gadādhar, Kālijani, Dharlā*, etc. But the same rivers become almost dry, narrow rivulets during the winter and early summer. There are songs, which describe the devastating activities of rivers:

Man mor kānde re Gangādharer bhāngni re dyākhiyā
Bāri ghar mor bhāngiyā re nilu dyākheyā dyākheyā
Man mor kāndere.
Āji ghar girasthi mor bhāngiyā nilu re,
O nadi tui bhāngiyā nilu car,
Bhāt nāi kāpor nāi mor thākong parār ghar
Man mor kāndere.

My heart laments on seeing the erosion of Gangadhar river which has destructed my household, my house just before my eyes. O River, you have destroyed my family and destroyed the char (lands), I do not have food and clothing now. I have to live in someother's house.

The river gets almost dry and narrow with little water towards the close of the winter and the lovers, residing on either side of the river, can easily meet by crossing the river walking on foot.

Prem jānenā asik kālācan,
Kālā jhuriyā thāke man, katay dine bandhur sange
Habo dariśan bandhure
O bandhure, nadi opare tomār bāri, jāoā āisā anek dyāri
Jābo ki rabo ki sadāy kari manā,
Hāṭiyā geite nadir jal khāklāng ki khuklung ki khālāu khālāu kare re
Hāy hāy parāner bandhu re.

My humorous Kalachan does not know what love is, and my mind laments over it. I do not know after how long shall we meet, o my friend. O my friend, you live on the other side of the river, coming and going naturally takes much time for which I hesitate whether to go or stay back every now and then. River water makes bubbling sound while I walk on it, o my heart's friend.

There are good many songs in which various aspects of nature have been beautifully depicted while speaking about the love.

Diner śobhā suruj re mor rāiter śobhā cān,
Ore hāluār śobhā hāl kirshi jaminer śobhā dhān.
Saraker śobhā sabuj re māṭh māṭher śobha ghās
Kāśiār śobhā dhaolāre phul āsile bhādar mās.
Phanir śobhā mani re bhāi gajer gajamati
Mor āginār śobhā re hailen tomrā rupabati.

Beauty of the day is sun and that of the night is moon. A farmer's beauty is farming and field's beauty is paddy (crops). Road is beautiful with green fields and field's beauty is its grass, while the beauty of the reeds are its white flowers in the month of *Bhadra* (August-September). Serpent's beauty is the gem on its head and the elephant's beauty is its pearl. The beauty of the courtyard of my house is you the beautiful girl.

To the lover his beautiful lady love is like the sun to the day, moon to the night, green-field to the road, grass to the field, white flower to the reed in the month of *Bhādra* (August), jewel to the serpent, and fabled pearl to the elephant. Their match is so beautiful, inseparable and eternally true.

There are songs describing even the small creatures of nature like mosquito, frog, etc. For example:

Ore maśā pyāṭ konā tor ḍyām-ḍyāma-ḍyām kare,
Bāns' bāriyā maśā re tor lambā lambā ṭhot,
Eman kari kāmor kāmrāy ḍyām kurāler coṭ re.
Maśā pyāṭ.... kare.
Maśār kāmore āi mui gāye dinu khyātā
Tabu sālār pāji maśā kay piritir kathā re
Maśā pyāṭ.... kare.

Maśār kāmore āi mui gharot dinu dhumā
Tabu śālār pāji maśa gāler khāilek cumā re
Maśā pyāṭ.... kare.

O Mosquito! Your belly sounds 'dyam-dyam'. You live in bamboo bushes having long bills and your bite is like the blow of an axe. I put the patched quilt over my body in fear of the mosquit bite, yet the mosquito sings love songs to my ears. To dispel the mosquitoes I fumigated the room but it just kissed on my cheeks. By nature, the mosquito is nagging. You cannot protect yourself from the attack of mosquito in spite of your best efforts. The mosquito will sing to your ears even if you cover your whole body; it will kiss on your cheeks even when you fumigate the room, etc. A song describes the nature of various kinds of frogs at different seasons.

O myāgher ḍāke re, āsārh māse byānger melā hay.
Dolā bāriyā ḍholā byāng sogul byānger guru re sogul byānger guru,
Pāil bāyin joṭeyā sabe gāner kare śuru re.
Myāgher ḍākere.... hay.
Bānś bāriyā gachuā byāng thāke bānśer gore re thāke bānśer gore,
Dyākho, saindhā haile gachuā byāng ṭyāros ṭyāros kare re.
O myāgher.... hay.

With the clouds roaring in the month of Asadh, the frogs, assemble. The large sized frogs of the low lying fields are the gurus of all the frogs, and they start singing in chorus. The tree-frogs of the bamboo bushes live under the trees and at the advent of evening, they start crocking 'tyaros ṭyaros'. At the first shower of rains, the frogs assemble together and start croacking in joy.

There are songs on various types of diseases, which were very common in Kamrup, such as *malaria*, *kala-azar*, *diahrrea*, etc. Two very common but not fatal diseases of Kamrup were goitre and skin disease, particularly ring-worm. There are very popular songs on goitre and ring-worm.

Baro dādāre, choṭo dādāre, ehān boyse nā hail biyāo ghyāger doshote.
Baro ghyāgi uṭhiyā kay choṭo ghyāgi bhāi,
Caṭ kariyā dono jane hāspātāl jāi,
Hāspātāl jāyyā ghyāgi ṭākā dilek dui
Vijiṭ pāyyā ḍaktār bābu ghyāgot nāge dil sui.
Baro dādāre.... doshote.

O elder brothers, it is because of the goitre that I am not married even at this age. The elder goitrous lady tells the younger one, let both of us go to the hospital. Reaching the hospital, they paid Rs. 2/- as fees and the doctor gave injection for the goitre. It may be mentioned in this connection that goitre was very common in Kamrup because of the deficiency of iodine in the water of this area. Law prohibits even today eating of non- iodised salt in North Bengal.

There are very interesting songs on ringworm. Itching of ringworm-affected parts of the body is done with the help of various things like knife, blunt axe, oyster-shell, blunt chisel, etc. Virulent type of ringworm has to be itched by the wife with those kinds of things.

> *Māior māo āsiyā de dādu culkiyā,*
> *Muriyā kāṭāi diyā, muriyā beki diyā ki bhotrā jhināi diyā.*
> *O Māior māo, culkāo ki culkāo ki culkāo,*
> *Muriyā pāsun diyā, bhotorā kāci diyā ki muriyā bāṭāl diyā,*

The mother of my child! Come and scratch the ringworm with the blunt small axe, blunt sickle and blunt shell. Scratch on and on, with the blunt weeding spade, blunt axe or blunt chisel.

There are songs on various kinds of fishes, which were available in this region and various methods of fishing too. I would particularly mention about a special method of group fishing called 'bāoyāit' as this group fishing is organised on the eve of the new year on the belief that any body able to have good catch in *bāoyāit* will have good fortune in the coming year. The song is about the method of group fishing but while discribing it, the love-sick heroine speaks of her distress she has to bear when her lover is away.

Under this method of fishing, a few people select a river or a beel for fishing and the leader plays the buffalo horn (*singa*) on the evening previous to the day fixed for fishing or even the previous evening indicating that there will be *bāoyāit* somewhere. On the scheduled day as soon as the horn player starts playing, the villagers with fishing implements assemble in a particular place following the singa sound and they go for fishing after a sufficient number of people have assembled there to match the water area chosen for fishing on that day. For example:

> *Bāoyāite māch māre re,*
> *Āji bāoyāite māch māre jor singā diyā,*
> *Ore dinmaner kām āuljhāul singār bāij śuniyā re.*
> *Jeman re tor ḍāk ai matan sonā bandhur gālā*
> *Singār bājan re bandhu bukat dharāy jālā re.*

The group fishing (*Bāoyait*) has been organised by giving signals to the fish catchers with the help of a pair of horns. While pair of horns are played, hearing their sounds, all the day's works are set in confusion. Call of the horns is like the voice of my golden friend and this call causes passionate sensation in my heart.

> *Bāccāte karāicen biāo gāmchā māthāt diyā*
> *Elā je chāriyā jānre kibā dosho pāyyā re*
> *Bāoyāite māch māre re.*

You have married me at very young age putting a gamcha on the head. Why are you leaving me now throwing such a dart on my heart?

We have stated in so many places that dotorā and Bhāwāiyā are inseparable. Bhāwāiyā songs cannot be performed in its real qualities—feelings, emotions, passions involved in it, without the melodious sounds of the 4-stringed instrument dotorā. There are songs eulogising the melody created by the dotora and its madding effect on the minds of young boys and girls.

Oki hāyre dotorār ḍānge, bāndhā man mor āulāil re
Bāndhā man mor āulāil dotorār ḍānge.
Gān pāgol dotorār jainye, dotorā pāgol gāner jainye
Mui pāgol oi nā dotorār ḍānge.

The dotora stroke upset my controlled mind. Music is mad after dotora and dotora is made after music and I am mad after the tune of that dotora.

Or,

Ore kāṭol khuṭār dotorā,
Mok karlu tui janamer bāudiyā.

You, the dotora, made of jackfruit tree you have made me a crazy men.

Dotorā and Bhāwāiyā have an intoxicating effect. Some people, who are the real connoiseurs have gone mad after the song. They do not bother about the family and wander like crazy vagabonds performing the songs, particularly the folk-dramas *Dotorā, Kusān* and *Bishaharā*. This mental condition of a *gidāl* (singer) is depicted nicely in this song.

Gān gān kariyā sarbanāś tabu nā meṭe gāner hāus
Kon kulote janma niyā hailong gāoiyā.
Ki hāyre āmār abodh man chāribar nā pāong ei gāner māyā.
Gāner neśāt man pāgelā, sei neśāte berāng ghuriyā
Sonār sansār geilek bhāsiyā
Ki hāyre āmār abodh mon chāribār nā pāong ei gāner māyā.

Music has ruined me and yet I cannot give up the longing for music. I do not know how I became such a born musician. I am engrossed by the stupor of intoxication of music for which I wander about and my family life is ruined completely. O stupid mind! Yet I cannot give up the love for music.

Bhāwāiyā thus covers all aspects of life of the Rajbanshi society of Kamrup. One can go on describing and explaining various aspects with suitable examples of songs. The songs cover and touch the all-pervading life of the Rajbanshis. We would however, desist from such efforts due to shortage of space and complete our analysis of songs with that of a very popular song pregnant with significant ideas and implications.

The song depicts a simple natural picture happening quitely in the village. A crane, while looking for food, gets caught in the trap set by the trapper with the bait of a tiny fish 'puntiac'. The more he tries to free himself the more he is entangled. The message of his being caught is passed on to his wife, the she-crane by a partridge, who happened to see him caught. The she-crane sets off for the river Dharlā and meets her husband. With the re-union they weep and weep on. This simple picture of the sad plight of a couple of insignificant birds rendered in Bhāwāiyā is so touching that the audience gets thoroughly involved in and moved by tragic union and the song leaves a long-standing effect on their mind:

Āji phānde pariyā bagā kāndere.
Phān basāice phāndire bhāiyā puṭi mācho diyā,
Mācher lobhe bokā bagā pare urāo diyā re
Āji phānde.... kānde re.
Phāndote pariyā bagā kare ṭānā ṭunā
Āhāre kunkurār sutā hailek lohār gunā re,
Āji phānde.... kānde re,
Uriyā jāy re cakoyā pankhi kayyā jāy re ṭhāre
Tomār bagā bandi haice Dhallā nadir pāre re
Āji phānde.... kānde re.
Ei kathā śuniyā re bagi pānkhā meliyā dilo
Dhallā nadir pāre jāyyā daraśana dilo re
Bagāk dekhiyā bagi kāndere, bagik dekhiyā bagā kānde re.
Āji phānde.... kānde re.

Being entrapped unknowingly the crane starts crying. The trapper has set the snare with punti fish as the bait and being lured by the fish, the foolish crane sat on it. Being caught in this way, the crane started pulling in all directions, which resulted into tightening of the snare (as if the thread became iron wire). While flying by, the chakoya bird told indirectly that the crane has been caught on the bank of Dharla river.

The first few lines of the composition are pregnant with significant inner meanings. They can be interpreted in terms of spiritual implications. Man in this world is caught in the midst of so many allurements that he gets entangled in the worldly affairs and is not in a position to free himself for achieving the ultimate goal.

The profound importance of the song however, lies in its implicit meaning of 'phānde pariyā bagā kānde re' the crane weeps and weeps on being caught in the trap. Man is the prisoner of circumstances. Whether it is politically, economically or socially he cannot escape the complexities of life. The more he tries to obtain freedom, the more he is entangled. The circumstances sometimes compel even an honest straightforward highly dignified leader to accept the conditionalities of crooked dishonest ones and compromise with them.

Similarly, highly unfavourable unacceptable economic conditions are compromised under compelling circumstances. Some socio-religious practices otherwise not acceptable are revered and respected by us under compelling circumstances. This universal truth of 'Prisoner of circumstances' has been beautifully depicted in this song. There are good many songs of such nature, which imply highly significant inner meaning, although these have been composed by illiterate village lyricists. This is the beauty and strength of folk-folklore, folk songs, folk dance, and folk drama.

REFERENCES

1. Sukhbilas Barma, *Bhawaiya*, Lok Sanskriti and Adivasi Sanskriti Kendra, I & C.A. Dept., Govt. of West Bengal, 1990.
2. Kali Dasgupta, *Ethnic Songs,* Rabindra Sadan, Kolkata, 1977.
3. G.A. Grierson (ed.), "*Linguistic Survey of India*", Vol. V, Motilal Banarsidas, New Delhi, 1904.

■■■

9

Bhāwāiyā-Based Folk Drama

The faith in magic or any sort of supernatural element in the psyche has given birth to a variety of songs of religious and ritualistic nature. Among many types of *voodoo*, an important genre is replicative and imitative magic. The major feature of 'nai jadoo' is mime. In times of prolonged drought many *voodoo* practices are carried which essentially imitate rainfall or they are its symbolic enactment. A few people go from door to door and collect water from every home. One person climbs a tall tree and while sitting on the tree begins playing the *ḍhol* (drum) from the tree; another person pours the water that had been collected and put in a container. Those who were expectantly standing under the tree absorb the thrown water into their bodies. The whole practice is an exercise in mime. The tall tree symbolises the sky; the beating of 'dhol' mimics thunder. Thus to show actual rainfall the water, collected in a container, is sprinkled from the tree on to the waiting people below. It is this imitative mime in voodoo that has given rise to folk theatre all over the world. Therefore authorities and experts on folk theatre hold imitative voodoo practices as the primary cause of the birth of folk theatre.

However, these voodoo practices contain only certain salient features of theatre. There are some other features too. Folk theatre often does not fulfil the conventional theatre framework. The plot of a folk theatre is seldom very compact or organised. Very often there is no clear planning and characters lack lucid step-by-step development.

Another aspect of replicative magic deserves mention. Each and every clan in folk culture has its own particular totem. This totem could be an animal, a tree or some sort of root like substance, etc. The totem is considered responsible for the well being of its particular clan. Hence the annual festival dedicated to the totem, by which the respect of the clan is paid to it for its satisfaction, is especially important among other rituals. The means of satisfying a totem is generally a song and dance programme enacted by the clan members themselves where the totem is shown to bless its dedicated followers. Sometime this is shown with masks or costumes and at times without. Obviously the theatrical angle present in this ritual is important.

An important part of folk life is communication. Over the period of an year many political, moral, economic and nature-related happenings occur. On the last day of the year all such happenings need to be told to every clan member. This is done at an open community centre, or in the shades of large trees like the banyan tree among others, where all members of the clan may congregate, or by means of a procession, which goes to every house and informs the family of the year's occurrences. Often these incidents are told to the clan by a clown.

The crude acting in children's games, like dolls, cooking with toy vessels, hopscotch for girls and the traditional stick and marble game for boys also bring to light various experiences of folk existence. In this manner at varying times of the year, at the festivals of certain gods and goddesses, songs, dances and drama were chosen to be the ideal medium for the presentation of religious legends concerning those deities whose festival was underway, or for the presentation of contemporary happenings that were laudable or otherwise or some imaginary happenings to the entire clan. Late Shanti Deb Ghosh, the respected expert on Tagore has beautifully explained the reason for the usage of this medium:

> "Heartfelt emotions may be expressed all the more beautifully in verse rather than ordinary dialogue; when blended with a 'ragini', to take on musical forms, it becomes more touching. Ordinary dialogues in theatre have certain appeal but when communicated through music it becomes more appealing. It becomes most attractive when rhythmic dance movements are added to it".

It was for this reason that ancient clan members expressed themselves through the media of song, dance and mime, and the places where these would be staged gradually came to be known as 'Mandap'. These theatrics were not always performed by humans; often puppets were used. In this way, with time, folk theatre was born.

Of course, what was once a ceremonial event has today, to a great extent, become mere object of entertainment. This progression from ceremony to entertainment has divided folk theatre into two genres-the ceremonial folk theatre which is staged on a particular day by a particular clan and the non-ceremonial or entertaining folk theatre which may be performed at any time, by any one.

Folk theatre was created with many rural festivals as the root. At rural festivals or fairs common people congregate leading to social union and interaction. In the words of Rabindranath Tagore:

> 'Every day man when alone is small, poor, but on a day of festivity man towers. On that day he towers, being at one with all other men; on that day he is great, having experienced the power of humanity'.

The spontaneous dialogue and rhythmic chatters with music and dance in various rural festivals have gradually evolved into folk theatre; the expression of the thrill, the overflowing happiness in dialogue on festival days has gradually taken the form of folk theatre. To present various dialogues through song, dance and theatre, it was naturally necessary to compose folk music and suitable dance movements to complement the music. It was to meet this necessity that the tradition of folk songs began. The introduction of dance movements and simplistic acting followed it.

In later times 'Bhāwāiyā-Caṭkā' was created to meet the need for presenting the 'dhuā gān' in between the analysis of the central happening of the folk theatre. Consequently, a certain amount of discussions regarding the folk theatre traditions of North Bengal must have to be entered into.

Folk theatre (or Opera)

Acharya Sukumar Sen was the first person to give his expert opinion regarding the root of these words 'Naṭ' (actor), 'Nāṭya-Nāṭak' (theatre), when he said that the word 'Naṭ' of pre-modern and modern Bengali rose from the Sanskrit work 'Nāṭya'. 'Naṭ' means wild dance, strange amusements, acting, puppetry, simple magic etc. Before this opinion of Acharya Sen became known, it was believed that the word 'Naṭ' came from the root 'Nrit'.

However, that 'Nṛtyati' (dancing) and 'naṭati' (acting) do not convey the same meaning in Sanskrit, had not been seriously considered by any one. In Acharya Sen's opinion, the nominal verb (denominative root) from the noun 'Nāṭya' (causative verb of Naṭ) is Nāṭaya to convey acting, mime with colourful dress, etc. The word 'Nāṭak' has developed from this nominal verb. This opinion of Acharya Sen has gained popular acceptance now.

Regional playwrights for local rural audiences have created folk theatre. It may lack urban theatre's celebrity actors but it has its own artistry of presentation. According to Dr. Ashutosh Bhattacharjee:

> The theatrical compositions as reflection of day-to-day rural life transmitted and popularised orally are those which make up folk theatre.[1]

Folk theatre's uniqueness lies in its songs, music, dance and acting. Indian pundits believe 'Sangeet' or music has 3 equally important constituents: song, instrumental music and dance. In this sense 'Sangeet' is presented in its perfect form in folk theatre. Here a narrator along with his supporting singers, dancers and actors presents to the audience the play's happenings and themes through song, dance and dialogue. Certain episodes of events are acted.

As music and dance are most important, folk theatre therefore, like folk music, contains regional specialties. The dialogues in folk theatre are generally in the local dialect. Similarly, the languages in the songs, the melody and the dance mudras have the same regional flavour. The same is applicable with regard to the musical instruments.

Generally only those instruments, which are used for song and dance in a particular region, are used in the folk theatre of that area. Folk dance is for the most part 'nritta' *i.e.* rhythmic, but non-emotive body movements despite the fact that on some rare occasions 'nritta' are transformed into 'nritya' (dance) with the gain of the requisite emotional and expressive quality.

Folk theatre exists in every region as a medium of expressing the every day joys and sorrows of local life. The erstwhile region of 'Kamroop', that is present Northern Bengal and the neighbouring regions that is, Kochbihar, Jalpaiguri, the Terai area of Darjeeling, Goalpara (Assam), Rangpur (Bangladesh) and other areas have their own particular folk theatre which reflect the local lives in the region.

On the basis of subject matter and form there are 3 major names of folk theatre – 'Dotora', 'Kuśān' and 'Vishahara' or 'Padmapuran' in North Bengal. In terms of subject matter, 'Dotora' has mainly fairy-tale-esque, legendary or religious stories. Therefore, innumerable folk plays may be found in the Dotora tradition; 'Roopdhan Kainya', 'Bishwaketu Chandraboli', 'Maroochmati', 'Karim Badshah', 'Harish Chandrer Dan', 'Dhanpati Sadagar', 'Shrimanta Sadagar', etc.

The 'Kuśān' tradition of folk theatre is based on the stories of the Ramayana, although plays with legends or the Mahabharata as their bases may also be found. These are known as 'Kuśān Gan' among the populace of this region. No one refers to the plays as Kuśān or Dotora folk theatre; they are simply Kuśān gan or dotora gan. "Lalit Dewānir bārit kuśān gān/dotorā gān haibe (Kuśān/Dotora gan will be held at Lalit dewani's house). These folk theatres are known as gān, or song, probably because the songs are the most important part of the folk theatre. Dialogue and acting exist but in comparison they are small parts of the whole.

Speaking about the folk theatre of Goalpara, Dr. Birendra Nath Dutta has commented, "In spite of the fact that the word 'gān' is used in the sense of song, in the local dialect a theatrical programme is also called gān." It is assumed that the name 'Kuśān' has come from the names- Lav and Kush, the sons of Ram. One can mention the observation of Dr. Ashutosh Bhattacharyya in this connection:[2]

Here instead of one lead singer, two boys, dressed and acting as Lav and Kush, are the medium through whom the entire story of the Ramayana is performed.

This is however, to be clarified that in reality no such thing happens in Kuśān gan, and as such his observation is not correct.

The subject matter of 'Vishaharā' or 'Padmapurān' is the 'Mangalkāvya' only and specifically the 'Manasāmangal Kāvya'. The basic subjects of the expression in 'Vishaharā' are singing the glories of the snake goddess 'Manasā'.

The narrator in all forms of North Bengal folk theatre is called 'Gidāl' or principal singer as he is the lead singer and conductor. Along with Gidāl, the second most important singer is the 'Doyāri or Bairāgi' or 'Bāze lok'. In addition there are 6 or 7 supporting artistes who alternate as chorus, instrumentalists and actors. 4 to 6 young boys are the dancers. These boys are known as 'Chokrā' and they crossdress as girls. The dance is known as 'Chokrā' dance.

In all three types of folk theatre plays, the language is used within a specified format. First, there is the 'vandana' (prayer); then the singing with dancing and finally the dialogue. The prayer section (*vandana*) is ceremonial and therefore extraneous to the main play. The most outstanding feature of the vandana in folk theatre is its attempt to accord to all faiths an equal respect. The play is begun after the Gidal and his supporting cast pay their respects to the major gods and goddesses, Mecca and Medina, and all the members of the audience, Hindu and Muslim.

After the vandana, comes the basic play, which in a sense is the dialogue section as the songs are in actuality dialogues in a different form. What the characters sing, after having spoken in prose for a while, may either be a complement to the opinion introduced in the prose dialogue or an alternative means of presenting the same opinion.

The use of song and dialogue for complementary or/and alternative purposes may be seen in urban plays as well. There the songs, however, generally concentrate on emotions and are not narrative statements like the prose dialogues; aside from this, the lyrics follow poetic metres and thus are very different in form from the viewpoint of the linguistic style of prose dialogues. But in folk theatre prose and poetry are simultaneously present. In this form the highly emotional musical content is expressed through narrative style. There is a loose rhythmic pattern in the lyric, which is an extension of the dialogue, the difference in the language being grammatical and not prosodic. The songs are sung with stylized pronunciations where words are elongated musically. This prosodic difference between song and dialogue is deliberately maintained to emphasize and highlight points of dramatic importance by extending the dialogue into a song in the higher pitch. The narrative style in the lyrics makes it similar to prose at times in terms of form but the prosodic speciality remains.

On the other hand, the poetic elements like end-rhyme, internal rhyme, etc. are much more pronounced. Spontaneity is the basic quality of the folk drama. Folk theatre is, therefore, not compact and systematic; it is quite simplistic. Unlike conventional theatre, folk theatre is not rigid, systematic, complex or sophisticated and does not demand mathematical exactness. There is no specific 'stage' required for performing the folk theatre. The stage is generally constructed in an open field or in front of a temple with a large tent (*shamiana*) raised. The performers and instrumentalists sit on one side and the area facing them is considered to be the stage. It may be mentioned here that the above mode was applied in Sanskrit theatre as well.

In all the folk theatre traditions of North Bengal, the instrumentalists and the accompanying performers sit or stand in the centre. While the Gidal, along with the Doyari, leads the play, others follow them. In between the songs, the Gidal explains the events in normal narrative. Simultaneous with the music the cross-dressed boys (*Chokrās*) dance round and round the associate performers. Surrounding the 'stage' is the audience.

While the *Gidāl* explains and advances the play, soft instrumental music continues to be played and the dancers continue to dance slowly. Certain episodes are also enacted, while the songs and speech go on. The acting is done by the *Gidāl, Doyāri, Chokrās* and other members if necessary without any costumes. Here a king need not have a royal outfit. Dotorā play can be on any subject—social, political, *puranic*, folklore based, episodes from *Ramayana*, *Mahabharata*, etc. Here the principal singer, that is, Gidal carries and plays the instrument Dotorā. The main subject matters of Kuśān gan are taken from *Ramayana* and *Mahabharata*. In Kuśān gan the Gidāl plays an instrument called 'Benā'. This instrument has one string, which may be of steel, a thread or several horsetail hairs and is played with a bow, whose string is also made of several horsetail hairs. Violin is an important supporting instrument, especially in the presentation of tragic episodes from the Ramayana and Mahabharata. The main rhythm instruments are 'khol' and the 'manjirā'.

An example from the play 'Mahirāvan Badh' (killing of Mahiravanas) of Kusān gan is presented here for analysis and discussion.

Ram *Vandana*:

O eso he prabhu nilada barana Rām
Ei āsare eso prabhu Niranjan
O... ho... o... prabhu... go...
Ayodhyār pati bandong Dasaratha Rājā
Tāhāro banitā bandong Candramukhi Sitā
Rāma bandong Laksmana bandong Bharat Satrughan
Tāhāro mitrak bondong Rājā Bibhisan.

Vandana explanation by the Gidāl:

At the very outset, we offer our respect to Ram, the king of Ayodhya, Dasaratha, the father of Ram, Sita, his wife and Laksmana, Bharat, Satrughna, his brothers, Bibhisana, his friend and then we offer deep regard to the members of the audience:

Adham sabhāy uṭhiyā
Bandilām bhāi daser caran śire rākhiyā.
Ati dinahin Bilās Gidāl kichui jāne nā
Nām laiyā dārāilām sabhāy Iswar bhābiyā
Tomrā dasjan karo dayā, adham bhābiyā.

Myself, the poor wretched singer prays to the audience considered as the god for their blessings. The main theme of the play starts in continuation of the *Vandana*:

Ādi kānḍe Rāmer janma vivāha Sitār
Ayodhyā kānḍete Rām tyāje rājyabhār.
Aranya kānḍete Sitāk harilo Rāvan
Kiskindhyāy Bāli badh Sugriv milan.
Sundara kānḍete hailo sāgara bandhan
Lankā kānḍete ubhay pakshe ghora ran.

The contents of different cantos are as described. Adi tells the birth of Ram and the marriage of Sita; Ayodhya deals with Ram's desertion of the kingdom; Aranya with the abduction of Sita by Ravana; Kiskindhya with the killing of Bali and union of Sugriva with Rama; Sundara with the construction of bundh over the sea and Lanka with the great war between Ram and Ravana.

Explanation by the Gidal: Look folks! The story of the Ramayana is divided into a few cantos- Adi, Ayodhya, Aranya, Kiskindhya, and Lanka, etc. Today we will describe the plight of Ravana and an episode from the Lanka canto. The great war is being waged. Ravana gets regular reports from the battlefield. Just now he has received the news that Rama and Laksmana have recovered from the attack of the Saktisela and they have killed innumerable number of soldiers of the Ravana's army. Almost all of his male heirs have been killed. Today Laksmana has killed Indrajit too.

Song continued on main theme:

Kolāhala śuni bhābe rājā daśānan
Mariyā mānus byāṭā pāilo jiban
Rāvaner putra ek se Mahirāvan
Māyār sāgar byāṭā ār buddhi bicaksan

Hearing the hue and cry, Dasanana got perplexed as to how they regained the life and pondered the way to teach them a good lesson. He recalled his son Mahiravana, who is an expert on black magic.

Ravana now recalls Mahiravana. Dialogues for acting:

Ravana — *Mariyā nā mare byāṭā biparit bairi*
Jānilām majilo mor kanak Lankāpuri
(My Lanka is ruined).

Bhavna — *Ghar śunya bir śunya hailo taba doshe*
Indrajit pari āche āji Laksmaner bāne
(Your Lanka is ruined at your fault).

Ravana — *Ekhan āmi ki kari*? (What should I do now?)

Nikasha (Mother of Ravana) — *Ore jakhan kahinu bāchā nā śunilu kāne*
Majila rāksaser kul Sri Rāmer bāne
(You did not listen to me and entire tribe is now at its peril).

Ravana — *Māgo, ek laksa putra mor soyā laksa nāti*
Eko jan nā rahilo mor banśe dite bāti
(All my descendants have been killed)

Nikasha — *Ek putra āche taba banśer bhitar*
Ṭāhāre ekhani bapu pāṭhāo samar
(You have still a son left and he may be sent for the war)

Song — *Ek mane cinte e-je Rājā Daśānan*
Tanak parilo ebār Mahir kapāler upar
Pātilek anka Mahi khari laiyā hāte
Eke eke tribhuvan lāgila ganite

Ravana recalled Mahiravana in his mind. And Mahiravana could know it.

Explanation by the Gidal: As soon as Ravana recalled him, Mahiravana could know through yogic and magic power that his father was remembering him. So he announced that he would set for Lanka on Monday.

Acting: Mahiravan: *Som bāre jābo āmi kanak Lankāpuri*
Daraśona haba giyā pitā daśagiri
(I will set for Lanka on Monday.)

Khetua: (Servant) *Sombāre jātrā kari je jan pube jāy*
Dhane banśe prāne tār abaśye hārāy

Anybody setting out for a good deed towards the east on Monday cannot achieve success.

Folk drama is a medium of folk education. Sometimes some moral sayings are quoted for this purpose. Here through Khetua, the performer (composer) wants to communicate that one should not set for any work on Monday if he has to go eastward. Khetua, therefore, suggested that his master Mahiravana should set for Lanka on Wednesday and not on Monday. There is a proverb:

Some śani pube bādhā
Jadi phale to ādhāmādhā
Mangale ushā budhe pā
Jethā khuśi sethā jā.

Journey eastward is not recommended on Monday and Staturday. One can go anywhere at the dawn of Wednesday.

But Mahiravana did not listen to him-rather he was very angry with Khetua for giving such moral instructions. With much anguish Mahiravana says:

Jātrākāle bāran tumi karo ki kāran
Tarbāri diyā munḍa taba āmi kariba chedan.

You are resisting me on the eve of departure. I will behead you with this sword.

Explanation by the Gidal: Look, Mahi is approaching the time of his death-this is destiny and so he does not listen to good advice.

Dhua gan: *Bhabe keu kāro nay sakale phāki*
Ghucibe jātanā munjile re dui ānkhi
Omā Janani go, kothākār Bhāgwati elo
Kibā mantra mā karne dilo
Sei din haite mā pāgol āmār mon
Omā Janani go, āmār janye mā kāndore akāran
Bhabe... ankhi

In this world, nobody is yours. Everything will be over once you close your eyes (die). A learned man came from somewhere, put some mantra on the ears and made my mind so restless. O my mother, do not cry for me unnecessarily.

In rhyme: *Hāyre ei bhābe Mahi upanita hailo āji Lankār mājhāre*
Sinhāsone basiyā āche dyākhe ekbār ai Rājā Lankesware.

Mahi reached Lanka in this manner and found Ravana on the throne. In this manner the play continues with songs, dances, speech and acting. At Ravana's command, Mahiravana kidnaps Ram and Lakshman and tries to give them for sacrifice to mother Kali in Hell. But the devout Hanuman follows him to Hell, threatens mother Kali and ultimately with her help kills Mahiravana. Hanuman and Kali have acting roles. A certain amount of humour is present in Bairagi's portrayal of Hanuman in his dialogue with Kali. As advised by Kali Ma, both Ram and Lakshana ask Mahiravana to show them how to do the pranama (bowing):

"Ami bali sono Rājā pranām nāhi jāni
Kemane pranām kare dekhāo āpani.

O King, we do not know how to bow down. Please show us the way.

Mahiravana bows down and as soon as he does so, the Bairagi, enacting Hanuman snatches the Ma Kali's chopper and beheads Mahiravana, saying:

"Jai Sri Rām Chandra Ki Jai, 'Jai Kāli Mātā Ki Jai'.

The Gidāl immediately gets up and starts the main theme,

"Rām nām niyā je jan pantha bahiyā jāy, dhanurvān niyā Rām piche piche dhāy".

Rama with the bow and arrows on hands follows the devotee who treads with the name Rama in mouth.

Following the Gidāl, the Doyāri here presents humour. The Doyāri makes a double-toned comment:

'Rām nām niyā je jan pantā bāriyā khāy'.

Rama protects the person who takes his name even while eating rice soaked in water.

In a disciplinary tone the Gidāl tells him not to crack jokes keeping in mind the status of certain members of the audience. The Doyāri is dauntless and explains with his own logic that his comment was not at all jocular. He argues that Ram will protect his devotee who even at the time of taking food (*panta*-watered rice) remembers Ram, which signifies that he is a great devotee of Ram. At his logic and the manner of presentation the audience laughs out profusely.

The pala i.e. ballad ends in happy mood with the Dhuā gān.

Dhuā Gān: *Man tor dinā cāri bhaber māyā, ek din pākhi jābere uriyā;*
O abodh manore, jei din prān caliy jābe bhāi bandhu sab pariyā rabe
Smasān ghāṭe sonār dehā puriyā karibe chāi
Man tor... uriyā.

This life is short and it can leave any day. The 'māyā' (all concern) is for a few days only.

Main song: *Pār karo Rām Candra pār karo more*
Tumi bine gati nāi e bhaba sansāre.
Bhaba sindhu pār haite bāndho Rāmer bhelā
Hāyre bāndho Rāmer bhelā.

Lord Ram! Please have pity on us and take us to the other world. There is none else to bless us. Thus ends the play. Everybody says, 'Jay, Shri Rām Candra ki Jay'.

From the 'Mahirāvan badh' described above it is clear that the songs, conversations and speeches of the play are in mixed dialect. As stated, Kusān, Dotorā and *Bishaharā* plays are prevalent in North Bengal and its neighbouring areas where the majority of the people are known as Rajbanshi, which is also the name given to the local dialect spoken by them.

Also known as the Kamrupi dialect it has blended with a certain amount of Bengali, Barendri and Rarhi often to give rise to a mixed language. This has inevitably happened for historic, geographic and social reasons. Because of the social inertia and conservativeness of the speech group, their language has still retained certain characteristics of middle Bengali language.

However, Maharaja Nripendranarayan's attitude towards Brahminism and modernism and the growth and expansion of the tea industry, brought many educated and semi-educated people of eastern and central Bengal who had gradually settled in this region. Besides, a large number of Bengali refugees settled in this region after the partition as neighbours of the Kamrupi speaking people. From the 60s of this century large-scale activities of the defence forces, opening of the Farakka barrage and other developments led to an improvement in road and rail transport in North Bengal and as a result, a large number of people from South Bengal also started moving to this region. Modern Bengali as used in textbooks and newspapers, language spoken on the radio also reached the people of this area. So like other areas of Bengal, modern Bengali (standard) language became the *lingua franca* for both the educated and semi-educated people of North Bengal.

According to the eminent linguist Dr. Nirmal Das, this process of the evolution on a mixed language has three elements: diglossia, code-mixing and code-switching.[3] Diglossia is a result of the social exchange between the two classes and because of the mutual expansion in dialects there has been code mixing in limited fields. Besides, as the use of the colloquial language in education and various other media has become prestigious, it has also increased a tendency towards code switching. Not that this code switching process has been faultless. There have been various aberrations and mixing from the point of view of both phonology and morphology; yet this attraction to colloquial code is still continuing as one of the major features of the language situation in North Bengal.

If we analyse the songs and dialogues from the folk play already quoted, the illustrations of diglossia, code mixing and code switching are quite prominent. Here it must be mentioned that the use of colloquial and mixed language in Kuśān gan is much more than what we find in Dotorā. In Dotorā folk play, the use of Kamrupi is more. Because this opera is based on social themes, the dialect used by the poor and illiterate is quite prevalent there.

On the other hand, Kuśān is based on stories from the two epics and great deeds of the Kings and the Emperors. That is why there is a mixture of literary and colloquial language code, which fits well with the elevated background. Vishaharā based on the Mangal Kavya also has the similar language pattern.

This suggests that the linguistic scenario is entirely dependant on social mobility. Whenever the events or the characters of those folk plays and operas have attained that mobility, its dialogue has been immediately affected. Where the lifestyle of the main characters lacks such mobility the dialogue remains entirely the dialect of the region. That is why the dialect Kamrupi dominates Dotorā gān. However, all these three types—Dotorā, Kuśān and Vishaharā, reflect the socio-political life and the dialect of this region.

It may be noted that *dhuā gān* (refrains) are used in the drama to make the play proceed forward and to make the drama emotive and interesting, and also to remove monotony. These *dhuā* (choral) songs may or may not be related to the sequence of the main play. While the songs and the dialogues of the main play proceed forward, the Gidal or his main supporting voice (daina pali), for that matter anyone of them, suddenly starts a *dhuā* just to bring a little variety in it. It is believed that these refrains and chorus used in the folk ballads became the source of Bhāwāiyā Caṭkā in course of time.

Bishaharā or Padmapurān

As stated, Bishaharā or Padmapuran is one of the greatest wealth of the folk dramas of North Bengal. The stories related to Manasa—the marriage of Behula-Lakshindar, the death of Lakshindar in the bridal chamber, lamentations of Behula, the journey of Behula with the dead body of her husband to Devpuri on the raft and the regaining of life of Lakshindar and his six brothers in Devpuri—all these are the themes of Bishaharā. Behula succeeded on condition that Cand Sadagor, the father of Lakshindar will bow down to Manasa and worship her. After so many incidents, Cand Sadagar ultimately worships Manasa and this incident resulted into the wide spread worship of Manasa on the earth.

It is worth noting that Manasa Mangal is not a popular name in North Bengal. Here Manasa is popularly known as Bishahari, Padmā, etc. She takes away the *bish* (poison) and so she is Bishahari; she is blind of one eye and so *kani*. She was born in Padmā vana *i.e.* lotus grove and so she is known as Padmā. The folk drama is known as Bishaharā from the name Bishahari and Padmapurān from the name of Padmā. The mode of performance of Bishaharā is the same as other folk dramas, that is, Dotorā and Kuśān.

The only difference is that here all the performers, that is, associate performers, instrumentalists, chokras, etc. remain on standing position and move on circular path while performing the songs and dances. Nobody is in sitting position as in Dotorā or

Kuśān. They sit and take rest only when the Gidāl, Doyāri or some others enact or explain any part of the story.

The Gidāl of Bishaharā does not carry any instrument—but a Flywhisk. The most important feature of this play is the wind instrument-' *Mukhā-bānsi* or *Kupā-bānsi*. *Mukhā-bānsi* has a round big mouth. The mode of playing of this flute is such that the player does not remove his mouth from the open round mouth of the flute and alternates his breath in that position so that, the music remains continuous without pause as in the case of snake-charmer's flute. The same modes of snake movements are noticed in dance too. The *mudras* (poses) and hand movements of the *chokrās* (dancers) do resemble the movement of the hoods of snakes.

The drama enacts and tells these stories of the Manasā Mangal and as such it moves towards the finality with slow pace. The tune is lengthened with *vilamvit laya* (speed). The *tala* (rhythm) is also with *vilamvit laya*. It is assumed that the *Bishaharā* play performed in the western part of Assam and North Bengal is based on the Manasā Mangal composed by Sukavi Narayan Dev, who was supposed to be the resident of Goalpara district of Assam, an important area of the then Kamrup. In the olden days, every Rajbanshi household used to maintain Bishaharā altar in his house. *Bishahari puja* was an inseparable part of any social festival like marriage.

In the comparatively well-off households *Bishahari puja* used to be associated with the *Bishaharā gan*. A household patronising any puja or gan is called Māreyā in Rajbanshi or Kamrupi parlance. Bishahari puja is called Mārāi puja also; *Mārāi*, a term derived probably from the term Māreyā.

A few examples of songs of Bishahara are quoted below:

Here is a dialogue between Behula and Lakhindar in their bridal chamber. Lakshindar is vigorously excited and desirous of consummation of the marriage. Behula resists him to ensure that they do not fall asleep. She wants to convince him by citing some examples justifying the wait for the right moment. Moreover, she wants to maintain her chastity till now.

Baro bhay lāge prabhu dekhite sundar
Pāche bā bhāngiyā pare mor mastaker upar.
Kāme kātar haiyā Lakhāi harasita mon
Behulār ṭhāi Lakhindar māge ālingan.
Kāncā kalā khāile prabhu jibāt dhare kas
Pākāiyā khāile kāle seo lāge ras.
Tapta dugdha khāile kāle jibār jāy chāl
Supta kariyā khāile tabe nāge bhāl

Kāncā ḍālimber phal kono kājer nay
Pākāiyā khāile ḍālim baro swād hay.
Kāme kātar Lakhāi bhay laijjā nāi
Bephulā jatak kay nā sone Lakhāi.
Beulā bale śuno prabhu dullabh Lakhāi
Satya nasṭa karo jadi dharmer dohāi.

I am afraid, lest this beautiful roof should fall on our heads. The passionate Lakshindar does not listen to anything and wants to embrace Behula. Behula tries to resist by saying – green banana makes the tongue bitter and one should wait to get it ripe; hot milk burns the tongue, green pomegranate is useless and so we should wait for the right moment. Lakshindar, being thoroughly passionate does not want to listen to any reason.. So, Behula takes refuge to Dharma as the last way out. Here is another example.

Behula, on her way to heaven with the vow of regaining her husband's life reaches the *ghāṭ* (bathing place) of Goda, a person with hunch-back. Goda gets tempted by the beauty of Behula on the raft with the dead body of her husband and he proposes to marry Behula. Here the poet gives an estimate of the expenses of the marriage and how to meet them, as planned by Goda.

Godār bibāher hisāb (Accounts of the marriage expenses of Goda):

"Gudire becile nata habe shāiṭ pon
Karna phul becile pābo ek kāhan.
Bhikshā sikshā kariyā ānibo pon dui
Karaje baraje ār pone pānc thui
Ek kāhan pondro pon kari hailo jamā
Ihā diyā kājer karite cāi simā".

Total receipt of 1 *kāhan* 15 pon will come from the following sources:

60 pon by selling Gudi, the wife
1 kahan by selling her earring
2 pon to be earned by begging
5 pon to be taken on loan.

The whole expenses are to be kept limited to this.

Tanḍul kāran dibo ser das dhān
Pondro guā karā daśeker pān.
Tāmāku gonḍā chayeker dui karār cun
Ek poner tail ganḍā daśeker nun.
Pondro ganḍār dudh ek poner dai
Cirā gure ḃuri chay ganḍā chayeker khai

Der burir cini gur sāt karār kalā
Suci māṭi karā duyeker daś karār molā.
Haridrā marice lāgibe ganḍā dui
Pāṭil bāsane hāri ek pon thui.
Halidrā sendur kinibār chay rage
Kanyār kāporer kari pon daś lāge.
Prācin kāpore habe sājan āmār
Maṭuker ganḍā chayek nibe mālākār.
Ei melā darba jata ānibo kiniyā
Cāir poner cukiyā ānibo rajiniyā
Sāt buri kari joyā rākhiyāche Gudi
Ihāte karibo dhār nāhi āṭe jadi
Nimantan karibār bistar kāj nāi
Kebal Siālu māmā Ṭagru biyāi.

What are the items required and what is the budget for that?

10 seers of paddy to be husked for rice,
15 betel nuts and leaves for 1 kara.
Tobacco 6 ganda and lime 2 kara
Oil 1 pon, salt, 10 ganda
Milk, 15 ganda, curd 1 pon
Flattened rice and molasses 6 buri, parched paddy 6 ganda
Sugar, etc. 1ṡ buri, banana 7 kara
Holy soil 2 kara, Moya (sweetened puffed rice) 10 kara
Turmeric and pepper 2 ganda, utensils 1 pon
Turmeric, vermilion, etc. 6 ganda
Dress for the bride 10 pon
For bridegroom, old clothe only.
Marriage crowns, 6 ganda
With all these articles, earthen pot, 4 pon
Saving of Gudi worth 7 buri will also be spent
In addition to further loans, if necessary.
Not many invitees to be there
Only Sialu, the maternal uncle and Tagru, son's father-in-law.

It is noticeable that the accounts have been placed in terms of kara, ganda, pon, kahan, which implies that, kari was once the medium of exchange in the rural areas of Kamrup. The description also reveals the mentality of the male dominated society and their attitude to life. Goda a lame man with hunch back wants to marry the beautiful Behula on the raft and he is ready to sell his present wife to meet the expenses of marriage. Also to be noticed that there is no *purohit* (priest) to solemnize the marriage. This has been described as a simple affair. There is, however, a list of items required for arranging a community feast. In fact, feast for the *samajiks*, that is, small group of the clan, was a must for the marriage ceremony amongst the Rajbanshis. The recognition of the marriage used to be signified by the acceptance of feast by the *samajiks* (clan men).

Goda is a poor villager and even then he wants to have a second wife. To meet the expenses, he proposes to sell his present wife Gudi to some other household where she will work as a maidservant. He proposes to go through the simple ceremony himself wearing an old cloth since his capacity does not permit purchase of a new one. Above all, he is ready to borrow from anybody on any condition to meet the expenses of the marriage ceremony. This, to some extent, reflects the attitude to life of the Rajbanshi gentry in those days in Kamrup. This gives a picture of the social conditions prevailing in the Rajbanshi society in the olden days.

Like all other folk plays Bishaharā pālā starts with *Bandanā gān*, that is, prayer song. The Gidal and the accompanying performers pray to Saraswati (the goddess of music), *Bhagawati*, that is, Manasa (the goddess of snakes), other gods and goddesses and above all, the assembled members of the audience irrespective of their caste and creed to have their blessings so that they can perform well and entertain them properly.

O Māgo, śarano nailām tomāre
Āre o māgo dayā karo morey
Āre adham bālako bailey dayā karo morey.

(*i*) *Tumi balo chāro chāro mā āmi nā chāribo*
Bājan nepura hayyā carane bājiba
Māgo, śarana... karo more.
Adhama baliyā jadi mā dayā nā karibe
Patita pābani nām mā kon gune dharibe
Māgo, śarana... karo more.
Māli jeman gāthe puspa miliyā paṭer ḍor,
Ai matan jogeyā (śikhiya) dyān māo gāner āgāl gor,
Māgo, śarana... more.

O mother! Please descend on the assemblage where we have to perform your puja with songs and dances. We are taking your shelter. Please have pity on these poor souls. You can't desert us, even if you want. We will play as the jingling anklet at your feet. How can you be regarded as the rescuer of the fallen, if you do not bestow your blessings on us? You have to supply the songs in our mouth seriatim as a gardener does it for garland.

(*ii*) *Aji satate karilām pranām bāmenera pade*
Hāyre bāmanera pade hạy,
Bāmanera ḍom kul bale cāri Ved-e
Ore bāmanera ḍom kul hāy.
Bāmanok dekhiyā jebā pranạm nā kare

Hāy pranām nā kare
Karade kāṭiyā munḍa phelāibe narake
Ore bāmanera ḍom kul hāy.
Jadu banśa dhansa hailo bāmanera śāpe,
Ayhe bāmanera sāpe
Bāli gelo pātālete niyā mano tāpe,
Ore bāmanera ḍom kul hāy.

I always bow to the feet of the Brahmins, whose glory has been described in four Vedas. Those who do not respect the Brahmins will go to hell. The Yadu race was ruined at the curse of the Brahmins and Bali had to go to hell for the same attitude.

The influence of Brahminism because of large scale Sanskritisation of the Rajbanshi community is extensively pronounced in the above 'Vandana' song.

(Note: Baman > Brahman> Brahmin).

Although it is usually believed that the Bishaharā or Padmapurān plays performed in Kamrup were based on the compositions of Sukabi Narayan Dev, the references of some other composers also are available in this region. Sri Sankhanath Roy of village Madhabdanga of Moynaguri, P.S. of Jalpaiguri district, who is one of the performers (*Gidal*) supplied this information mentioned below:

One Malati offered the puja to Manosa first. One of the compositions describing this refers to Narayan Dev.

Sābdhāne pujaha Mālati diyā pancaphul
Ṭap karite gela ṛshi sāgarer kul
Tapo bhanga hailo ṛshi nā pāilo kul.
Parbater kule āche ek jorā ṛshi
Tāhār kāche āche Rām tulasir bici.
Ajnān kāler lok kichu nāhi jāne
Gorer patra thākite āgāl dhariyā ṭāne.
Tulasir patra māreyā kare stare star
Suddha hailo māreyār tulasir jal.
Juriyā jatek cāilon bāti dhup dhunā karo ārati
Aro lāge aguru candan
Campā kalā padmer pāt, til cāul diyā tāt
Padmā pujā karaha sakale.
Asādh srāvan māse sukla paksha pancamite
Jei puje sei siddhi pāy
Nārāyan Dev-e kay Sukabi pallab hay
Rahe Padmā sansār bhariyā.

The lyricist Narayan Deb asks Malati to offer the Puja very carefully, with due respect and Puja materials. After being purified with Tulsi water, the house-owner has to offer the puja articles-incense, resin, scent, sandal, banana, til-seed, rice, etc. on the lotus leaves. One who worships Padma with due respect lives in peace and plenty? The Puja is to be done on the 5th day of the bright fortnight in the months of *Asadh* and *Sravana*. Narayan Dev assures that the person who offers puja to Padma will have all success in life.

Reference of Kavi Ramananda is found in a prayer (*vandanā*) song:

Hey mā, hā-putriyāy putra deo nidhaniyāy dhan deo
Rog sok karo bimocan
Manosāre Sricaran jor kari hey śaran
Tār nāme śatru hay kshay.
Ramākānta Suddhamati Padmār caran gati
Biraciā rāngā pada cāy.

O mother! Give son to the issue-less, wealth to the poor; remove all ills, destroy the enemy. Ramakanta prays to Padma, sings to her glory and takes shelter at her feet.

In another composition, one gets the reference of Jagajjivan and Dwija Bansidas. At the death of Lakshindar, the relatives prepare for the burning of the body but Behula does not agree to hand over the body for burning because she wants to take it to the gods for his life.

Mṛta nā pāiyā sabe ghare ghare jāy
Jagajjivana pada biraciyā gāy.
Dwija Bansidāse kay bhram hailo mon
Dhātār likhan tabe nā hay khanḍan.

Everyone leaves for his/her house when the dead body was not given for burning. Jagajjivan composes the story accordingly. Dwija Chandidas too is bewildered and composes the songs accordingly. Who can escape the destiny?

It, therefore, appears that the plays performed in this area are taken from the compositions of not one particular but different composers and improvised by the performers in course of renditions.

REFERENCES

1. Ashutosh Bhattacharya, *Banglar Loka Sahitya (Folk-literature of Bengal)* Vol. III, Calcutta book House, Kolkata, 1996.
2. *Ibid.*
3. Nirmal Das, *Uttarbanga Bhasa Prasanga,* Sahitya Bihar, Kolkata, 2nd edn., 1997.

■■■

10

Dance used in Bhāwāiyā

Dance basically means and involves structured body movements system. Dance or structured movement systems may be universal, but dance is not a universal language. Structured movement systems can communicate only to those who have 'communicative competence'in this cultural form for a specific society or group. Elaborating on the social aspects of dance makes reference to its most general and comprehensive features, because dance is in essence a social interaction.

Dance is a powerful symbol. The power of dance considered in its artistic features, lies in the ecstatic function, which takes the dancer out of himself, removes him from everyday life and transports him into a virtual world of time and space. Dance has been an important symbolic instrument in ritual contexts, in art events, in social communication and political action. Dancing as a multi-dimensional cultural text integrates all the dimensions that define dance as a coherent and dynamic factor of culture and bring together the anthropological and ethnochoreological perspectives on dance.

A multi-dimensional text does not occur in isolation from other similar and dissimilar texts enacted by a given social group; for example, weddings, ancestor celebrations, family festivities, informal gatherings, sports activities and staged performances. In the process of communication, dance does not function in isolation, but incorporates non-choreographic components, such as pantomime, expressive or codified gestures, facial expressions, music, verbal utterances, text/poetry, props, costumes, staging, proxemies and social rules. Dance movements are not always of primary importance, and may, in certain contexts, function only to support and reinforce other expressive elements that are the principal carriers of meaning.

Dance traditions generally continue on among the peasants as archaic remnants of the olden days. The connection between folk dance and folk music is a subject of investigation for researcher of both dance and music. One can try to have replies to queries like –What is the connection between dance and music? How do they influence each other? Does music regulate dance and does dance transform music?

Musical aspects help us to undersand dance and choreographic aspects help us to understand music. In optimal cases, we could create a complex system in which all the closely connected branches of folklore (music, dance, drama, play, text) were equally taken into consideration. There are broadly three characteristics of folk music used in dance:

(*i*) Rhythm, consisting of an emphasis on rhythmic formulae rather than melody;

(*ii*) Melody, consisting of an emphasis on vocal or instrumental elements rather than rhythm,

(*iii*) Complexity, consisting of both melodic and rhythmic elements.

It is however, revealed that a piece of dance music is a complex structured acoustic composition having melodic and rhythmic components. Melodic factors however, seem to be less important. More important factor is the rhythmic element made with the cooperation of rhythm-producing instruments. Instruments used for creating the rhythm of dance in Bhāwāiyā music are-*Bānśi*, *Benā*, *Ḍhāk*, *Ḍhol, Dotorā, Kānsi*, and *Mukhā-bānśi*, etc.

Dancing is primarily a non-verbal medium of communication which establishes contact between humans or between humans and supernatural world. Movement patterns and style function as symbols for social relationships between individuals, between individuals and groups and between groups (ethnic, religious, social, etc.) with respect to gender, age, kinship, marital status, profession. Both being human and socio-culturally determined, dance may function as identity symbol.

A dance system changes because of changes in world view, need of expression, socio-political and environmental conditions. One can inquire into the future of folk dancing in traditional social contexts, considering the new circumstances when disco-dancing becomes the most important dance event for young people- discotheque being substituted for the village dance taking on pre-marital and entertaining functions and becoming the place where teenagers practise local traditional dances to recorded music. Such changes have occured in the case of Bhāwāiyā based dance too, though to a limited extent.

Traditionally the ritual songs have been accompanied by dances. *Kāti pujār gān, Shāitol pujār gān, Hudumer gān, Biyer gān* (marriage songs) etc., where the female folk are the singers, the dancing is performed by the female folk themselves. In case of Kati and shaitol, they dance to the beats of *Ḍhāk* (long drum). For Hudum and marriage songs there are no instruments used and the performers dance to the hand clapping.

Madan kāmer gān, Sonārāi gan, on the other hand, are accompanied by the dances performed by the male folk. The instruments used for *Madankāmer gān* are *Ḍhol, Karkā, Kānsi, Sānāi*, etc., while for Sonārāi gān *Khol* (*Mridang*), Kartāl are the main instruments. Madankam dance is performed by the youths with long thin and clean decorated bamboos, fitted with yak tails on the tops, on their hands. *Teesta burir gān* is another ritual based song where the dance is performed by the females to the beats of clapping and sometimes Ḍhāk.

A very popular number of dance performed with Bhāwāiyā is Baran *nritya* (reception dance). This dance is performed to the tune of *Ḍhāk, Ḍhol, Kānsi, Kārkā* by the females to receive the deities in case of puja, to receive the bride or bridegroom in case of marriage and to receive the guests and dignitaries in case of any sorts of reception parties.

The other popular dance form used in Bhāwāiyā based song is known as *Chhokrā* dance where a few young lads cross-dressed as girls perform the dancing in the folk dramas. The folk dramas described in the relevant chapter are characterised by the chorus event of song, dance and acting. *Chhokrā* in Rajbanshi dialect means boys. Here the cross-dressed boys dance to the beats of *Khol*, which is the main rhythm instrument of the folk dramas. The dance style and the *mudras* used by the dancers are almost same for all the folk dramas, namely, Bishaharā, Kushān, Dotorā, etc.

Talas used in such dance are of 3-matra, 4-matra, 7-matra. Body movements of the young dancers are special features of this dance. They use *Bhramari* (both inner and outer) quite extensively to move round and round while dancing. The *mudras* used are of both single-handed and joint-handed. Single hand *mudras* like Patak, Tripatak, Alapadma, Mushti, Padmakosh, Shikharam, Mrigshirsha, Tamrachud, etc. and joint hand *mudras* like Swastik, Gajdanta, Kapot, Anjali, Puspaput, Karkat, etc. are commonly used in this Chhokrā dance. The *mudra* Sarpashirsha is frequently used in the folk drama Bishaharā which relates its relevance to the theme of the drama *i.e.*, narrating the glory of Manasa, the deity of Serpent.

With the passage of time, some notable changes are noticed. Now the *Baran nritya* (reception dance) is being performed in any cultural function as the item for beginning the show to the tunes of dotorā and *khol* or dotorā and *tabla*. For the *Chhokrā* dance one can hardly see young lads performing such dance. The dance is being performed by the girls in the folk dramas. It is however, a fact that such folk dramas in traditional form have become rare items now.

■■■

11

The Issue of Today's Concern and its Future

Bhāwāiyā had it's beginning in a distant past out of specific geophysical, natural, socio-economic, linguistic backgrounds of ancient Kamrup to meet certain needs of the people of Kamrup. It is, however, difficult to say exactly when the process of evolution started. But the fact remains that the favourable geographical, natural, socio-economic conditions helped the growth of such a healthy strong tradition of songs and dances and with the passage of time the same has become the media of expression of the total cultural life of the Rajbanshis, the principal group of people of Kamrup.

Our discussions lead to quite natural and obvious query – what is the present position of Bhāwāiyā and what its future is? Replies to such question have to be sought for and evaluated in the context of the changes in the geophysical, socio economic conditionalities under which the tradition had developed and got nurtured over time.

Whatever their disagreements, folklorists almost always take it axiomatic that folk music and folk society are intimately linked. For Cecil Sharp, peasant society produced peasant song. He wrote, folk music

> "is the product of a race, and reflects feelings and tastes that are communal rather than personal.... The racial character of a ballad or song is due, therefore... to communal choice... they reflect the popular taste, express the popular ideal, and are stamped with the popular approval (Sharp 1972)".

Lloyd, subscribing to a broader historical dimension, developed a Marxist version of the theory (Folk Song in England—Lloyd 1967). The nub (gist) is still the same-but reflection now governed primarily by economic factors is explicitly related to class and is mediated by change:

> "songs are born into a tradition that fits a certain society.... folk song is the musical and poetic expression of the fantasy of the lower classes.... as the life of the common people is changed, however slowly, through the movement of society, so their folk music alters too".

Lloyd's historical scheme centres around four 'moments' of change. The transition from 'clan' society to a class of small individual producers and serfs resulted into shift from collectively organised 'variative' singing, often with ritualistic functions, to the symmetrical strophic solo song. (Dating is hazy: sometime between fall of the Roman Empire and the Middle Ages). The rise of the bourgeoise and the influence of its culture on that of the lower classes, resulted in squarer, robust common chord-based kind of tune (Between 1550 and 1750). Then the rise of capitalist agriculture and the resulting pauperisation and disruption of rural lower-class life produced a new sort of tune: longer, tonally unstable, meandering highly ornamented-reflecting uncertainty and crisis (Period between 1750-1850). This period and process is overlapped by the emergence of 'industrial folk song' (1800-1914 with a revival after 1945), reflecting the psyche of industrial revolution and the development of an urban working class.

The industrial songs drew on rural song traditions and on the written music of the towns; but they are harsh, direct, less poetic in expression, the text reflecting industrial reality, poverty, protest and class-consciousness. Folk song for Lloyd cannot be understood except in an awareness of the whole society.

In more recent periods, when 'folk' styles come to exist in much more fluid social situations, when they change more rapidly, and take on new functions and audiences, these problems become even more acute. This happens in spite of the fact that the characteristics of folk practices are thought of as static, conservative and different. Folkloristic sociology is always defensive and it defends an ideology. As Alan Lomax (Folk song style-Lomax, 1959) puts it:[1]

> "musical style may be symbolic of basic human value systems which function at the unconscious level and evolve with glacial slowness because the basic social patterns which produce them also evolve slowly".

Most folklorists now agree that folk music itself is rarely homogeneous but is subject to social and geographical specification, historical change, and cultural layering. Also they agree on the importance of interaction between folk music and other musics. As traditional societies modernise, isolated folk enclaves are assimilated into capitalist cultural relations, old-fashioned rural populations are urbanised and commercially organised practices supersede folk practices, the folk music is found to give way to a form of music, commonly known as *popular* music. This is precisely the way that *popular* music historians visualize the emergence of *popular* music. Many also would like to refer to the influence of folk sources on popular genres. References may also be made to various twentieth-century folk revivals and multiplicity of neo-traditional styles and hybrids developing in 'third-world' countries. This points to the problems that attach to the conceptual distinction of 'folk' and 'popular'.

The scholars now criticise the view of folk music associated with Cecil Sharp. Lloyd (Folk Song in England 1967) devotes a good deal of space to an attack on Sharp's remantically idealised 'folk' – a construct which had been developed simply as an antithesis to the threat of industrialisation. This 'folk' never existed in European culture. The culture of the common people of England had been marked by a myriad of sub-cultures and functional categories, and has been inseparable from the culture of the whole society, contributing to and drawing on the practices of other groups.

Lloyd argues that creators and transmitters of folk songs were not ignorant and cut off from learning but tended to be the most educated of their class; that songs were created not communally or anonymously but by particular individuals, where names are often unknown simply because of historical distance, lack of cultural legitimacy or absence of property rights in their work, and that creation was not 'spontaneous' in some mystical sense but the product of deliberately exercised skill. Similarly, he argues that while oral transmission was central, the roles of manuscripts, printed broadsides and songbooks, and travelling professional performances were important as far back as the Middle Ages. This brought the influence of commercial products together with interchange between country and city, lower classes and bourgeoisie. Folk music, it follows, has changed continuously, but in particularly striking ways at moments of general social upheaval, when interclass contact and intracultural movements were at their greatest. For Lloyd then, the 'authenticity' of folk music should be sought not in a particular social origin but in its 'realism', its reflection of changing, historically determinate social conditions.

While the revisions of Lloyd and others have enabled them to widen the boundaries of 'folk song' and to liberalise its definition, it did not follow that the concept of 'folk' was dead—far from it. Certainly the achievements of these folklorists have been enormous. We know that industrial workers made songs and that they continued and adapted older, rural practices and materials, and took over and folklorised commercial products. We have learnt something about the contexts in which these songs were used. This same impulse has carried work not only into historical areas but also, especially in the United States, into the new field of 'urban folklore' in today's cities or urbanising countryside.

For some scholars, the folk became simply a group of people united permanently or temporarily by shared common experiences, attitudes, interests, skills, ideas, knowledge and aims. Those shared attitudes are elaborated, sanctioned and stabilised by the group over a period of time. Any such group or any communally shaped culture trait might be the subject of folklore study.

This opens the way to studying the communality and continuity of any musical practice—though so far actual work has been largely on examples of transition between rural and urban cultures or of the urbanisation of rural music. This is largely the way the histories of 'ethnic' American music in general have been treated by folklorists. One clear conclusion to emerge is that recordings, far from threatening the existence of these musics, have encouraged their continued vitality; and in the process they have helped to articulate ethnic and subcultural identities. It may be that studies of this process could provide models for the more general investigation of how materials from folk sources entering the orbit of mass cultural production can bring with them, or be conferred with, the capacity to symbolise the cultural values of a folk or subcultural group.

Nevertheless, most urban and industrial folklorists have not relinquished the 'folk' concept itself. The golden age of folk myth is still there, even though it has been moved or extended and it is still seen as under attack from today's corruptions. A 'liberal' such as Alan Lomax 1968 who considered that workers have not, as certain scholars expected, ceased to make and sing folk songs in 'urban' twentieth century America, that living in city slums, working on huge industrial projects, watching T.V. they continue to come forth with fresh song ideas – nevertheless attacks modern urban society and mass media for destroying the variety of cultural 'gene pool' resulting in a cultural grey-out; and all the familiar stereotyped dichotomies – between rural and urban, oral and literate, tradition and innovation reappear in his description book.[2] But in the modern world the characteristics traditionally ascribed to folk music – orality, community of response, continuity, variation of formulae and received material – are all around us.

Similarly, Lloyd having attacked Sharp's concept of folk music, himself sticks with the 1954 International Folk Music Council definition of folk song derived from Sharp's. In order to maintain a folk category, Lloyd is forced to hang on to older criteria – lack of commercial motive, unselfconcious, and amaeture composition – and apply them to the definition even of industrial songs. In the process, he romanticises his 'worker' just as Sharp remanticised his 'peasant'.

Dave Harker in 'Fakesong: the manufacture of British Folksong' (1985), has shown that construction of folk song by bourgeoisie collectors, editors and publishers, as a category operating not within lower class culture at all but within bouergroisie culture, has been a long-standing practice, part of an active ordering and defining of the national culture in the interests of hegemony. C. Keil (1978) argues that the invention of the 'folk' concept serves to protect the ruling class from the threat and suffer of proletariats by first exoticising them and then adsorbing their culture into its own.[3] He says,

> "there never were any 'folk' except in the mind of the bourgeoisie. The field is a grim fairy tale—high art versus folk art represents a dialectic that is almost completely contained within bourgeois ideology. One requires the other. Can not we keep the folk concept and redeem it? No! You can not, because too many volkswagons have been built, too many folk ballets applauded, to many folk songs used, too much aid and comfort given to the enemy".

Evolution of Folk song: The history of evolution of folk music in the capitalist Western countries like U.S.A and U.K. gives a broad idea of the process of evolution of the folk music in India, and in Bengal, specifically in North Bengal. The factors playing their role in the evolution process are almost similar and as such the course to be followed is also likely to be similar. In order to understand the process of evolution of Bhāwāiyā, one should bear in mind the background provided by the nature, geo-physical and socio-economic conditions of Kamrup in which developed the tradition of Bhāwāiyā and the changes they have undergone with the passage of time.

The wide-spread open fields, vast alluvial lands left out by the rivers, massive forest areas, jungles and bushes, pastures of vast magnitude, buffalo *bathan* (pastures), jungles for catching elephants of the then Kamrup are no longer there. Today the cart driver does not have to travel from *hat* (market) to *hat* with the agricultural commodities loaded on the bullock carts passing through the jungles infested with wild fierce animals and muddy roads, leadership role of *Dewani* (Village headman) has now withered and cow-sheds full of cows and buffaloes have been non-existent with the disappearance of pastures on alluvial lands.

The large areas of alluvial lands of the forceful rivers like Dharla, Mansai, Kaljani, Teesta, Torsha have now been inhabitated by the refugees coming from Bangladesh (the then East Pakistan). Gods and goddesses worshipped and the rituals associated with them are now mostly the Hindu gods and goddesses and the worship of local deities like Kati, Shaitol, Kamdeb are almost non-existent with the completion of Hinduisation and Brahminisation of Rajbanshis and the change in their attitude and belief.

Begging of alms with group songs and dance for the collective worship of Sonarai, Kamdev or Teesta-buri is hardly noticed these days. Soari melas during the Holi festival and Ashtami melas during the Annapurna Puja have now changed colours. They are no longer the places of the performance of folk dramas—Dotora, Kuśān, Bishahara, Rang Pacali, Khas Pacali, etc. Jag gan or Madan kamer gan, which used to be held on the occasion of Kamdev *puja* or Bans *puja* during the month of Chaitra in course of group begging or in the assemblage of the worshipped bamboos has now become object of research and preservation.

With the improvement of veterinary infrastructure, Gorakhnath *puja* to appease the Goranath Thakur for the welfare of cattle is not required today. Group hunting of wild animals like deer, hare, boar, wild, hens, porcupine, etc. and group fishing under the system called 'Bawait' or 'Baho' on the day of vernal equinox was a compulsory ritual in Kamrup. This was associated with the belief of good or bad year which is starting from the next day. Suitable jungles for such hunting and suitable water areas for such fishing are non-existent in the villages now. Jungles have disappeared due to large-scale deforestation; water areas have either been filled up or have been settled with cooperative societies or fishery groups for pisciculture as a result of which common villagers have lost fishing rights there.

The rituals on the occasion of vernal equinax are therefore, hardly observed. Use of cowdung as organic manure has been largely substituted by the use of chemical fertilizers, pesticides and insecticides, which have contributed to the dearth of tiny fishes like punti, khalisa, mourala, barbel and other fishes. The interesting scenes of fishes, particularly koi fish swimming upwards against the current at the beginning of the rains are hardly noticed now. So there is hardly any occurence of 'ujāi nāge māch' as described by Rati Ram Das in his Jāg gān.

There were massive amounts of rains in Kamrup because of its geo-physical positions—forest and jungle. It is said that there were only two seasons—rainy season and winter season in Kamrup. Descriptions of rainy season have occupied ample space in Bhāwāiyā. One of the songs very popular in the region is:

"Āṣāro srāvana māse dyāoā jhare Kānāi madhu rase re.
Dhan mor Kānāiyā re,"

O Kanai, it rains incessantly in the month of Asadh and Sravana.

The other popular songs describing the rainy season are:

"Dyāoāy kairce myāgh myāghāli tolāil pubāl bāo
Dhire kyāne baoāo naukā dhire kyāne bāo."

The sky is overclouded and the wind is flowing eastward. Ply the boat in slow speed.

Or

"Torsā nadir utāl pātāl kār bā talāy nāo
Sonā bandhur bāde re mor kyāmon kare gāo?"

No one knows whose boat will capsize in the tumultuous Torsa River. I am worried about my golden friend.

Or

"Nadir bān āsil re Teestā nadir bān
Ghar girasthi māiyā chaoā dhariā pālān bandu re."

Teesta River has got flooded. Move away with the household materials, wife and children.

"Man mor kāndere Kāljani nadir bhāngni re dyākhiyā
Bāri ghar mor bhāngiyā nilek dyākheyā dyākheyā
Man mor kāndere."

My heart is lamenting at the sight of the erosions of the Kaljani River. House broken and family ruined just in front of my eyes. My heart laments.

Or

"Aki banure gāo khān mor khijir bijir kare
Eṭe kado oṭe jal, ghar sondāite hāṭu jal
Khān sakhe nā nin dhare nā, tyāreng byāreng ghare.

O Banu (brother-in-law)! I am just feeling irritated; mud here, water there and knee deep water just on the entrance of the room. One does not feel like eating and sleeping in such a confused tormented house.

Because of the excessive rains the climatic conditions of Kamrup was cool through out. Winter would start from the month of October and continue till April. People would however use rags even during the rains.

"Kato pāshān bāindhācha pati monote.
Jaisṭha māser mishṭa phal āsāḍh māaser nayā jal re
Son mās gelo kainyār hāsite khelite
Pāshān bāindhācha pati monote."

You are so unkind by heart o my husband! The month of Jaistha is characterised by sweet fruits and Asadh by the advent of the monsoon. The girl spent the month of *Sravana* in merriment and sporting spirit.

"Agan māser hyāmti dhān, pous māser śiter bān re,
Māgh mās gelo kainyār uṭhite basite
Pāshān bāindhācha pati manote"

The month of *Agrahayana* is characterised by kharif paddy and *Paus* by severe cold. She spent the month of *Magh* in sheer idleness.

The condition has changed now. Large-scale deforestation, denundation of jungles have made the climate dry and there are not so much of rains in North Bengal now. Sufficient availability of varieties of tiny fishes led to the food habit of eating dry fishes in the area. A delicacy named 'śidal' prepared by dry fishes was very popular in this area. Tiny fishes are hardly available now and as such songs on various equipments for catching fish *i.e. dhorkā, ḍeru, burung, jalangā* and songs on 'śidal' are hardly composed now.

Any auspicious activity of a reasonably well-off household was to be preceded by Manasa Puja (the goddess of serpent) in Kamrup. Manasa Puja before the marriage ceremony—particularly from the side of the bridegroom was must. The poor household would do it in shorter form, while the well-off ones would do it with pomp and grandeur with the full rituals of worship by making an image called 'Mārāi' in this region, followed by the performance of folk drama named Bishaharā or Padmapurān as stated elsewhere. The performance of Bishaharā narrating the glory and greatness of Padmā or Manasā would sometime continue for several nights. This gradually reduced to three nights and then one night. Today there are only a few households who have continued this, and that too in shorter form.

Although most of the village Rajbanshis do follow the practice of worshipping Manasa and making offerings to her by the newly married couple, they do it in brief form without the performance of Bishahara folk-drama. Hindi pop songs in microphones have mostly replaced this. Similarly, in other village festivals various other folk dramas—Dotora, Kuśān, Rang Pacali, Khas pacali, etc. used to be performed regularly. These have also been replaced by microphone borne Hindi, Bengali pop songs.

The reasons for such changes are many. To quote a few, they are lack of patronization by the land-owning class with the implementation of land-reform measures; non-availability of young boys to act as 'chokra' for dance performing in female dress, etc. According to the tradition, the 'chokras' would be taught by the performing gurus on various aspects of the folk drama—someone would gradually become 'gidal', that is, the main singer, some one 'doari', that is, the principal assistant and a jester too and some one the bayen, that is, *khol* player for rhythm. The whole tradition is now under decay and extinction.

We have already mentioned the fury of nature and rivers. Torsha, Teesta, Kaljani, Dhorla, which used to destroy villages after villages on both their banks during the rains have now been largely tamed by the irrigation bundhs. Some good effects of science and technology have reached the remote villages of North Bengal at least to some extent.

The system of preparing rice, flattened rice, etc. from paddy in traditional husking machines with the help of pestles is hardly seen. Husking pedal and husking machines have been replaced by diesel run or electricity run husking mills. The incidence of pretty young maidens husking (pounding) rice or flattened rice with the pestle in exchange of wage (kind or cash) has been reduced to almost non-existence and as such themes of this nature no longer find place in the minds of Bhāwāiyā-Caṭkā composers today.

The incidence of early marriage of girls with quite aged persons was quite rampant in this society. This was the result of the system of money dowry the groom had to pay to the parents of the bride. The poor man had to earn by his physical labour the money required and so had to wait till that time for marriage. This system had the ultimate effect on the fate of the young girls—there were lot of young widows.

Nadir pārer kuruyā re tui jāmer gacher suā
Āji kyāne kāndis amon kari couker jal phyāleyā re,
Korā re mui-o kāndong ciṭal biduyā hayyā.

Ḍhāl kāuāṭār kāndon śuni citer āgun jale
Pati je mor mariyā geice ādar nāi mor ghare re
Korā re mui-o kāndong ciṭal biduyā hayyā.

Not only this. Because of so much of age differences there was hardly any cordial relationship between the two. The young girl rather developed friendship with the younger brother of her husband. Sometime she would be attracted to the young 'maishal' or 'garial' or any other young man of the village. Her husband would naturally inflict various types of physical and mental oppression on her. The young bride would express her sorrows in this manner:

Aki bhābere dyāorā thuiyā āisek mok
Bāpo bhāiyār dyāśe re.
Bāpo bhāiyār dyāse jābo bārāni bhukiyā khābo.
Aki bhābere.... dyāśe re.
Bāpo māo mor durācār byāceyā khāice mok durāntar re
Byāceyā khāice mok gānjāruyār ghare re.
Gānjāruyā gānjā khāy āgun dite mor rāti pohāy
Naler ḍānge saril hail mor kālā re
Aki...... dyāśe re.

O my younger brother-in-law! Please take me to my parents. I will go to the parents and live by the labour of pounding rice from paddy. My ill manoevered parents have given me to marriage at a distant place with a *ganja* (hemp) addict. The hemp addict husband takes *ganja* and I have to spend the night by supplying (providing) fire. The whole body of mine has turned black by the beating with the water pipe.

The position has changed now. The system of dowry for the bride has now changed to the system of dowry for the groom. With the spread of some amount of education and literacy here even in the remote villages, the incidence of early marriage of girls with aged persons has been reduced to negligible few.

One recalls the good old days of bullock carts out of nostalgia when he or she notices the regular plying of rickshaw vans, diesel driven vans, and rickshaws with much more speed. There is hardly any use of bullock cart for transport of commodities. Bullock carts are hardly used as mode of transport for '*naior*' that is, young bride going to her parents and back. Songs on '*naior*' are rarely composed now:

Gāriāl re o mor gāriāl,
Aji āste dhire bolān tomār gāri
Chāriyā geite māyā nāge dayār bāper bāri, gāriāl o.
Byāṭā āpon cira kāler, byāṭi hailek cira par
Bāpo māye āsibe nibār dui diner nāior gāriāl o.

O my garial (cart driver)! Please drive the cart slowly. I feel so sad to leave my kind parents. A son belongs to the father but a daughter belongs to someone else forever. Parents may take the daughter to their house for just a few days to spend with them as Naior.

The alluvial lands created by frequent changes of the course of rivers are no longer fallow open jungles. They have been densely pupulated now. As such the possibility of using them as pastures and setting up 'bathans' for buffalo grazing has been remote. No Maishal is therefore found in the villages with their usual melodious dotorā and Bhāwāiyā. Elephant catching and trade in elephants has been prohibited. Mahouts, *i.e.* elephant drivers have now taken up agriculture as their full time profession. There is no song composed on elephants and Mahouts, as a result.

With these changes Bhāwāiyā-Caṭkā songs also have undergone lot of changes. We have observed from our discussions that the principal heroes of the Bhāwāiyā belong to the poverty-stricken downtrodden people of the society and so are the heroines. Maishal does not have a house of his own to live in. He lives in a thatch placed in a corner of the house of a jotedar or well-off household. His livelihood depends on his physical labour put for keeping the cattle population of the houseowner. Most of the time he is away from his family in the midst of buffaloes and other cattle population in the bathans or in the cattle shed of the jotedar. He is in an environment of open sky above his head, trees and jungles around, sweet breeze, musical flow of the rivers, which make him highly philosophical and romantic. There is no parallel to such a romantic environment of making love or recollecting reminiscences.

The other characters of Bhāwāiyā, that is, Garial and Mahout have the same history. They represent the oppresed, depressed, deprived and exploited. Out of sheer necessity of livelihood, they are away from the near and dear ones. They are so poor that they cannot raise their voice against such deprivation, oppression and exploitation. But their protest gets reflected in terms of sorrows, pains expressed through their songs.

Bātān bātān karen Maishāl bātān kairien bāri
Jubbā nāri gharat thuiyā kāy kare cākiri Maishāl re.

Or

Āi chārilong bhāi chārilong chārilong bāper bāri
Biāo kareyā chāriyā āsilong o
Sakhi alpa bayser nāri sakhi o,
O mor sārin hātir Māut re,
Jedin Māut ujān jāy, nārir man mor jhuriyā ray re.

Or

Jidin Gāriāl ujān jāy, nārir mon mor jhuriyā ray re,
Aki Gāriāl bhāi hākāo gāri tui chilmārir bandare re.

Deprivation and exploitation have sufficiently been expressed in all of them.

Today there are no forest lands, jungles, open green fields for use as pastures, no vacant lands, no fallow lands, no bullock carts to ply as transport vehicles—no geophysical, social environment suitable for the creation of the traditional Bhāwāiyā. The whole of environment has undergone changes and as such Bhāwāiyā melody and themes have also undergone substantial changes.

We have seen that this process of evolution is not unique to Bhāwāiyā-Caṭkā; rather this is universally applicable to all the traditional forms. The folk culture—folk songs, folk dance, folklore of all the countries and regions, its characteristic features face the onslaught whenever the quiet simple folk life comes in contact with the pompous and complicated urban life. The concept of folk gradually gets narrowed with the spread of education and literacy through schools and colleges, media as well as through the improvement and development of transport and communication.

The traditional region-based folk concept gets obliterated. Because of easy and frequent contact with the towns and cities rural people get familiar with polished city language, dresses, and other ways of life; and gradually try to adopt them as their own. The market for the folk creation also changes. He gets gradually detached and out of contact from the geophysical social folk environment in which the culture grew initially. This is how Jhāpān gān, Gombhirā, Bāul, Katipujār gān, Madan kāmer gān, Sonārāyer gān, Sāitol pujār gān, Teestā Burir gān, Bon Bibir gān, etc. gradually lost their basic ritual characteristics and became mere objects of performance.

The audience and spectator of such performances got changed; market got changed. They are now performed in radio, television, and cinema and on the stages. The folk items adapt themselves to the urban situations, improvised and sophisticated to make themselves acceptable to the new class of customers. This adaptation and change comes partly through intervention and partly out of necessity.

Arranging and encouraging the performances of Baul, Bhatiali, Bhāwāiyā, Bhadu, Tusu with the western instruments on the city stages and for recording are instances of intervention. The performer is compelled to accept the imported ways of performance for the new class of customers. Also the performer feels the necessity of evolving new ways, accepting new technology and accompaniments to suit the taste of new class of customers under changed circumstances. He has to keep in mind, while performing on the rectangular stage in place of circular all sides open village stage, the restrictions of the stage, lighting and microphones. The songs like *Teestā Burir gān, Kātir gān* or *Sāitol pujār gān* which used to be performed only on the occasion of those pujas or rituals, are now performed on the stage.

Fulti gidāli of Kāti, Shāitol gān does not have the independence of performing her songs and dances with the same spontaneity, as she has to do it on the fixed stage in front of the microphone. The *dhāk* player also has to play the *dhāk* (long drum) in a way so that the sound over the microphone doesn't surpass the songs.

Moynāmatir gān, which was very popular folk drama at a time has now become Gopichandrer gan included in the syllabi of Calcutta University. Mymansingha Geetika has similarly been reduced to an item of syllabi of the Calcutta University. This is an unavoidable sort of evolution and folk culture has to face such a situation today or tomorrow. This is inescapable; this is a travel from one particular way of performance to the other. Folk culture is bound to assimilate so many things of the urban culture in course of time. This evolution is irresistible. One cannot expect that folk culture will continue to be unblemished and pure when the traditional society itself does not remain as it is.

Following Dr. Pabitra Sarkar, a reputed linguist of Bengal and former Vice Chancellor of Rabindra Bharati University one can enumerate the reasons in the context of the evolutionary changes of folk culture:[4]

(*i*) Change in mental attitude and taste of the artistes (performers) and the audience (customer) due to spread of education and literacy; contact and familiarity with modern urban life, urbanisation in the region, use of urban oriented media (radio, television, etc.) Owing to the growth of a sense of individual freedom, the creator (composer) seeks an independence from the predetermined idealism and principles. Folk creation changes its form as a result; it tends to be the creation of an individual with the characteristic personality of the individual creator. Bhāwāiyā-Caṭkā thus on many occasions has been termed as Abbasuddiner gan, Pyarimohoner gan, Nibaran Panditer Gan, Pratima Baruar gan.

(*ii*) Change in the taste of traditional customers also gives rise to change and in probable cases, decay of the folk creations. Change in taste has led to the largescale demand for cassettes on Caṭkā with light rhythmic tunes and light themes rather than Bhāwāiyā with grave tunes and themes.

(*iii*) Creation and performance of folk items of one particular folk group/region by people belonging to some other group/region, being attracted by its beauty and greatness.

For example, being attracted by the melody of Bhāwāiyā-Caṭkā lot many performers not belonging to the Rajbanshi community, sing Bhāwāiyā in distorted pronounciation, wrong lyrics and tunes. Some of them even try to compose Bhāwāiyā in their own ways.

(*iv*) When the large numbers of customers do not belong to the same society but some other society with different kinds of attitude, taste and social values, their tastes and attitude will have effect on the folk form. Quite often the synthesizers, western drums and equipments are used with the folk songs to satisfy the taste of urban audience, particularly Non-Bengali and young groups.

(*v*) Creation of folk items with new technology adopts new mode of preformance. Performance of Saitol in front of the microphone has already been mentioned.

(*vi*) The economic principle of bad money driving out good money from the market applies in place of folk culture too. The market is full of cassettes of Caṭkā songs with cheap sexy lyrics, while Dariya Bhāwāiyā with serious tunes and themes are very few in the market. Performers singing Bhāwāiyā-Caṭkā with mixed lyrics and mixed rhythmic tunes are high in demand, while those singing in genuine tune and lyric do find hardly any call.

However without going into the details of the vexed question of aesthetics, one can reasonably argue that every step and all the aspects involved in the evolution may not be fully pure and beautiful and unadulterated. Neither, they are essential and utility based. In many cases, unimaginative imitation plays quite active role in folk culture. Incapable destroys real genre. We have elsewhere mentioned the observations of Verrier Elwin in this connection:[5]

> "It is true that a great many of the songs are the possessions of the people as a whole; nobody knows when they are composed; they are repeated again and again, and the only change is often a change for the worse."

In course of evolution of Bhāwāiyā-Caṭkā nothing good has happened; some kind of improvement has been achieved in some cases. But in most of the cases, what has come out is distortion, the result of incapable imitation. In the case of Bhāwāiyā the distortion has been quite significant because of the characteristics of Kamrupi or Rajbanshi dialect and specific ways of pronounciation of the dialect, in which the Bhāwāiyā is composed. It has not been possible for unimaginative imitators to pronounce correctly the nouns, pronouns, verbs and indeclinables of the dialect to apply correctly 'the throwing of words' and manner of rendering and the result is largescale distortions.

Since folk culture is the reflection of the total life of a folk community, socio-economic political changes taking place in Kamrup, that is North Bengal have thus got reflected in Bhāwāiyā Chatka themes, particularly in Caṭkā. Replacement of bullock cart by the motorcar has been described in Bhāwāiyā-Caṭkā.

Śono o nagarbāsi o,
Jalpāiguri śaharat gāri nāmise
Mādārganjer bālur ḍhipot jāyā mārice top
Śono nagarbāsi o.

Listen o city dwellers! Motorcar has come to Jalpaiguri town. The same has dashed against the heap of sands at Madarganj. Similarly, incoming of husking mill, which has replaced the husking pedals and husking pestles, has been described in Caṭkā songs.

Bhoṭ paṭṭite āsice micin cal dekhibāre jāi
Suno mor oho ge bāi
Ingrājer buddhi bhāri ānise dhān bhukā kal
Āek dike uiṭche dhumā āek dike pairche jal
Āek dike pairche bhusi āek dike pairche cāul

Dear sister! Let us go to Bhot Patty to see a husking machine which has been installed there. Englishmen are intelligent; they have brought the machine that emits smoke on one side and water on the other and brings out husk from one side and rice from the other.

Dhāner dar hail āsṭo ānā cāul cāir pāisā
Oi bāde bhukāti gilā hārāice diśā,
Śuno mor oho bāi ge.

While paddy costs 8 annas, rice costs only 4 paise and this is so confusing to the women doing the job of makings rice from husking pestles.

I cannot resist the temptaion of mentioning a song composed by Pyarimohan Das, sung in 1984 in ballad form of Bhāwāiyā tune in this connection. The song describes the situation of crises arising out of the Second World War and in this process also describes the contribution and progress of science.

Dyākho bhāi sārā dyāśe māir mangā juddher āek hai cai
Hāsi khili nāi mānuser mukhat dhān dile hay khoi,
Terośo pancāś sane.
Kāro sukh śānti nāi eibār kār juddher bājāre
Bujhi eman larāi ār hay nāi tin juger bhitare
Śāstre nā jāy pāoyā

Brothers! Just see the conditions of famine and war cries throughout the country. Everybody is unhappy and worried. This was in 1350. Such a war situation did not occur in three 'Yuga' and not even mentioned in the 'Shastra'.

Goṭāy duniyā juri uṭhil sorāo hāy hāy hāhākār
Top kāmāner dhumāy ākāś hail andhakār.
Jāhājer ham-hamite.
Jāhājer ham-hamite dum-dumite kāne nāgi geil tālā,
Juddha jemon haice teman tār kāydā kauśal gulā,

Juddha sābās baṭe
Juddha sābās baṭe māinser pyāṭe eta buddhi chilo
Kata rakamer kal kārkhānā nautan taiyār hailo.
Mānuser śakti baṭe,

There was universal cry of suffering and distress and the sky was full of smoke of guns and canons, and the noise of aeroplanes. The sounds of warplanes grated the ears. War is great. Human intellect worked on it and various kinds of machines and equipments got invented out of war necessity. Man is so powerful.

Mānuser śakti baṭe śunyot uṭhe urojāhāje cari.
Seite juddha kare bomā māre nāme pyārasuṭ dhari.
Kaler kāydā kato
Kaler kāydā kato bailbo kato nāi tār nyākhā jokhā
Kalir loker kal-kārkhānāy devatā hail bokā,
Āśmān jamin kāpe.
Hāyre hir cāite hur cāite jakhan juddha nāmil jore
Takhan pālā urā kariyā mānuṣ bācibār fikir kare
Khāl khandar khuriyā kare bācibār āstānā
Reil iṣṭimāre miliṭāry ār pyāssenjār dhare nā
Śahar bandar hāṭ-bājāre bandha hailo bāti
Man bhayātur hail mānuser ek samān din rāti.

With this power, they fought in the air with the planes, and descended by parachute after bombing from the air. One cannot describe the intricacies of such machine. Even the gods have been befooled. Both the sky and the ground were shaken and when the war reached the peak, people started escaping to survive. They dug out trenches for survival. Trains and steamers were full of civil passengers and military. Lights put off in the cities, towns and markets. People got pannick-stricken, day and night being equal to them.

The composer singer has described the pitiable economic conditions of the common people caused by the scarcity of commodities and price spiral because of the war.

Loker durabasthā roge śoke āro pyāṭer bhoke
Byācāy hāler garu gaynā gāṭi ek ṭukāo nā coke.
Jibanṭā bācuk āge,
Hāyre bhiṭā māṭi bāsan kosan jār jā chilo hātey
Byācāil nagad ṭākāy dhani gulā tāk kinil dui hātey
Gariber prān bāce nā,
Gariber prān bāce nā eman dine nāi Rengooner cāul
Kāon nā pāy eknā bhater māri kāon ṭākār kailye maul.

People's sufferings in disease, distress and hunger knew no bounds. They sold the farming cows, jewelleries without little hesitation. Life saving is the priority. They sold the homestead land, other landed property, utensils- whatever they had and the rich ones had purchased these. The poor had no way to live on. Even Rangoon rice was not available for the poor. So, some could not have even the rice gruel, while a few lived on the heap of money.

Dinkāl eman hailo re bhāi āro kibā hay kāle
Beci kini neoyā deoyā soug hail kanṭole.
Rājāy reṭ karil.
Rājāy reṭ karil bhālok nāgiyā kāro nā hay jhon hāni
Āsole āche jinis nā jāy pāoyā nā hayyā āmdāni.
Kāpod bine dāy hail mān ijjat rākhā
Khāli hurā huri kariyā maran āsol jinis phākā.

The situation became so much tense and nobody knows what will happen in future. All transactions got restricted to control (rationing), rates being fixed by the king. King fixed the prices with good intention not to harm anybody. Goods available but nothing coming to the markets created the crisis. It was even difficult to save the honour and modesty for want of clothes. There was confusion everywhere and nothing fruitful came out.

Kiser dhamma-kamma jāl-juācor ghus khorer hail ṭākā
Juddher ei bājāre beci kini kariyā corā nukā.

Who cares for honesty? People earned money by forgery, cheating, bribery, hoarding and other fraudulent means in this condition of war.

Khāli kāur-hāṭi sār bābu bhāiyār teon kono rakame cale
Pārmit kāḍer māl āise tār mās kābār haile
Mairce cāsā bhusā.
Mairce cāsā bhusā nā pāy diśā ki misṭi ki cukā
Kono din labon chārāo bhāt khāy tāo jaleyā sinnār ukā.

White colour baboos, however, carried on somehow. They got the articles with permit or ration card at the month's end. Only the poor people were in trouble. The poor peasants were confused. They had to live even without salt and cook food with jute-stick only.

The political psyche of the Rajbanshi population during the freedom movement has also been reflected in Bhāwāiyā. The song performed on the occasion of Gandhiji's visit to Jalpaiguri is quoted below:

Mahātmā Gāndhiji āmrā khaddar dhairechi
Bilāti kāpod ār pendomo nā deśi dhaireci.

Mahatmaji, we have started using khadi. We will no more use the English clothes. We have got on the 'deśi' now.

In order to enthuse the Rajbanshi breathren to make themselves aware of their rights, the folk singer has sung—

O bhāi mor gāoāliyā re,
Caturdike jale suraj bāti tomār kyāne dekhong āndhār rāti
Parār bojhā tomrā kaddin baiben bhāi.
Bāluṭiṭi pankhi kānde nijer āhār joṭer bāde
Tomrāo bujhi nyāo nijer adhikār, Bhai mor gāoāliyā re.

O my village brothers! There is light all around. Why are you still in darkness? How long will you carry others' burden? O brothers, the Balutiti bird cries to have its own food. You should also place demand on your own rights.

Election has started playing a vital role in the society after the merger of Cooch Behar estate with West Bengal in 1950. Election of democratic leaders at various levels of the governance is one of the sacred duties of the citizens of India. Lots of songs have been composed by the folk singers on the matter of election.

Tomrā ebār neo ciniyā
Āische kata dyāś daradi bhoṭābhuṭir gondo pāyyā.
Śunibār pāi hāṭ bājāre ebār jata jamidāre
Ṭākā paisā kharchā kari bhoṭ nibe kiniyā.
Khaddar ṭupi dhairce kāon kolābbar chāriyā
Āiste jāite jijnās kare kyāman āchen sālām diyā.

The so called country lovers have now come at the smell of election (voting) and you should know them well. It is rumoured that the jeminders will purchase the votes this year by money power. Some have taken on khadi, leaving the usual clothes. Now, they ask about our wellbeing and wish properly whenever we meet on the way.

Kata dekhim bhāi bhoṭer bhyāk dhāri
Kāngāler bandhu sāji berāche bāri bāri
Nyātā-lā bhoṭer bāde haiche bāhir
Nijer bahar kairche jāhir
Burā nyātā-lā kahechen nayā nayā buli
Bārāice ghārat niyā bhoṭ bhiksār jhuli.

How many vote-mongers in disguise shall we see? They are going from house to house as friends of the poor. The leaders are out on the way asking for votes by preaching their own glories. Old leaders are giving new promises, moving from house to house with the begging bowls on their shoulders.

Uttarbanger kishak sābodhān,
Jadi māinser matan bācibār cān
Bhoṭ nibār bāde dyāśat nāgiche ḍheu
Congā phokeyā bhoṭ cāite kare hāu hāu.

The farmers of North Bengal! Be careful if you want to live like human being. There is a wave of vote mongers who have raised hue and cry on the canvassing pipes.

Bhāwāiyā songs have been composed on current economic and social programmes too. For example, they have composed songs on the recording of bargadars (sharecropper)

Oki O ore hāluyā
Dakhal rākh tui bhuin dakhal nyākheyā
Girigulār fāsār fusur tui jone śunis nā.
Kyāne tui dyākhiyāo dyākhis nā uār duśmani konā
Hāl tulibār buddhi kato toke māriyā.

O farmers! Establish your possession by taking hold of the land; do not listen to the whispering advises of the Giris (landowners). Why don't you see their enmity against you? They are playing the trick of evicting you.

Songs on adult education or literacy programme have also received due attention.

Janjālu kay Khānjālu-dā tui kyāman mānush
Hyār tin khan boi śyāsh karilek Nyālbhelur banus
Tor hyāskāri baro
Āijo paris A, Ā, kāilo je Ka Kha,
Dyāś swādhin hayyā kato iskul basichè
Grāme grāme hāi iskul ār pāṭhśālā haiche
Nām dastakhat kairbār nā pāy tāre bāde
Jāgāy jāgāy āro kato nāiṭ iskul haiche

Janjalu encourages Khanjalu by telling-what kind of man are you? Wife of Nyalbhyalu has completed reading three books already and you are still with ABCD. So careless a person you are! So many schools, pathsalas, high schools have been established in the villages after the independence. So many night schools have been established in different places to teach how to sign the names.

But the literacy programme cannot succeed because of some inherent problems and one of the reasons is abject poverty of the prospective scholars.

Pārāy pārāy iskul haice bhāi
Kyāmon kariyā chaoāk parāng kyārāsin tyāle nāi.
Kinibār nā pāong boi
Chaoāṭā mor iskul geiche khāyyā re māilor khoi.

There are schools established at different places. But how to give education to the children? They have no kerosene oil at home; no money to purchase book and the child is to go to school eating Milo (inferior food).

Even on a programme like family planning village composer has composed Bhāwāiyā.

Bocā kay ore buci hāṭ kyāne jāi Sitalkhuchi
Bujhi sujhi kari oprāsson
Ore sāt-ṭā byāṭā āṭ-ṭā byāṭi, kāmrā kāmri hiṭāhiṭi
Sagāy hāmāk kare jālāton.

Boca tells buci – let us go to Sitalkhuchi to have vasectomy operation. We are thoroughly harassed by seven sons and eight daughters.

Byāṭā gulār gosāgusi biāo dile sagāy khuśi
Gharat nāi mor ekṭāo ālo dhān

Sons are not happy and they want to marry.

Dhari māch nā chui pāni nāigbe nā ār ṭānāṭāni
Āgot thāki han sābodhān.

So, one can catch fish without touching water. There will be no hastle if we take care now onwards through family planning measures.

There are songs on the evil effects of dowry system too. One of them relates to the problem the boy is facing after marrying an ugly looking deaf girl simply on consideration of huge dowry money.

Ore ghaṭak śālār kathā dhariyā āgot nā bhābiyā
Biāo karnu ṭākār lobhe kainā nā dekhiyā
Daś hājār nagad ṭākā ryāḍio sāikel ghari
Lyāp tosok ār khāṭ pālong sonā daś bhari
Biāo thāki uṭhiyā bāsor gharat jāyyā
Mon-ṭā mor haṭṭu hailek kainār ḍhak dekhiyā.

Being lured by dowry of ten thousand rupees, radio, cycle, wristwatch, furniture, beddings and ten bhari of gold I married without bothering to see the bride. I got dejected when I saw the girl in the bridal room after the marriage was over.

It's therefore, found that changes in all the spheres of life of the folk community of North Bengal our getting reflected in present day Bhāwāiyā, although it is a fact that lots of old traditional Bhāwāiyā and Caṭkā songs are still popular and they are being sung with the new ones. But latest tendency is to go for newer and newer songs on new kinds of subjects of current importance.

Changes have taken place in the form of folk drama also. The traditional folk dramas were enacted in the manner so that songs, dance and dialogues got their due shares in the performance. In fact there was predominance of songs and dance, and very little use of dialogues and acting. Because of the non-availability of Chokrā dancers, efficient *Bairāgi* (jester) and sometimes efficient *Gidāl* (principal singer) as well as the influence of *jatra*, the folk drama form of Dotrā, Kuśān, Bishaharā, Chor-Chunni, Rang Pācāli, Khās Pācāli underwent massive changes.

In the new form there are hardly any songs and dances. Moreover, the hero, heroine or other actors, do the songs performed in course of acting. This folk drama has virtually become the mini form of '*Jatra*'; it is mainly dialogue based acting. The language of dialogue also has changed a lot. The mixed dialect (Kamrupi + Bangladesi) now prevailed in North Bengal has become the language of the dialogues of the folk dramas.

A major development taking place in the field was the popularity of a folk drama 'Maynār Cakur Jal', that is, the tears of Moyna. One Guneswar Adhikary of village Bhatibari in the district of Jalpaiguri composed this folk drama in jatra form with the dialogues mainly in Kamrupi dialect in 80's. The subject matter of the particular drama was the tragedy of Moynā, daughter of a poor Rajbanshi farmer.

Following the form composed by Guneswar Adhikary, some other *Pālā* (plays) were composed by other composers in the area. Guneswar Adhikary himself composed a few more plays on different themes. But the popularity of 'Maynār Cakur Jal' was so overwhelming that all such plays were named Moynār cakur jal to encash the advantage of its popularity. This form has rare similarities with the traditional folk drama. There are hardly four or five songs in the entire play performed for about two and a half hours. The traditional Chokrā dance has no place in it.

This is the state of affairs which the Bhāwāiyā-Caṭkā and Bhawiya-Caṭkā based other songs are going through. It is however, worthnoting that the popularity of 'Moynār Cakur Jal' is in the wane now. Music lovers, artistes and performers of some areas are now trying to revive the traditional form. We are to wait and see what form it takes in future.

Bhāwāiyā–Future

According to A.L. Lloyd, as old-fashioned rural population are urbanised and commercially organised practices supersede folk practices, the folk music is found to give way to a form of music commonly known as popular music. The socio economic cultural conditions prevailing currently in our country are similar to those in the West sometimes immediately after the Second World War, which can be termed the moment of 'pop culture', against the background of developing world market within a 'global' economy dominated by multinational corporations.

There are changes in technology, electronic systems taking over from the electro-mechanical mode typical of mass culture, with the potential of new production methods, magnetic tapes replacing music scores and the electric guitar and synthesizer replacing the existing professionalised instrumental skills. There are changes in relations of production too, with the opening of a new youth market, which is structurally a bit different from the older generation of music lovers. This group with its 'margin of rebellion' looks to new musical sources notably in rhythm to shun away the so-called feelings of oppression and frustration.

The new social patterns, technologies and musical styles are in the process of being substantially assimilated into a recognised music-industrial system; a transnational oligopoly of vast entertaining corporations, supplied to some extent by independent producers; served by mass audience radio and TV channels, by a symbiotically pliant music press and by related leisure-products businesses. This is a situation somewhat similar to that in 1960's in the West of new production methods, outrageous music, and independent operations. The culture was dominated by the elements of 'pop culture', with some elements of blues in it. The musical characteristics included can be summarised as below:

(*i*) Typical elements of lyric vocabulary, vocal patterns, both structural and intonational (rhythm, phrasing, melodic contour, rhetoric) borrowed from existing sources and performer – audience relationship.

(*ii*) Musical call and response, between singer and audience, and singer and instrument.

(*iii*) Very specific repertory with strong historical roots; styles which emphasize familiar and repeated elements and formulaic structures, performer's charismatic role in confirming group solidarity.

(*iv*) Most lyrics are concerned with sexual things and performances dramatize the situations and relationships.

(*v*) The music is valued for evidence of hard experience and work-rate, manifested in expressive explicitness, vocal effort and bodily exertion.

(*vi*) Lyric themes and vocabulary, sensuous vocal tone, paralinguistic effects and performance movements; strong connection between the musical style and dance style with a general sense of erotically understood rhythm.

In many ways this is a more sophisticated approach than Lloyd or Lomax's. Many of the homologies are seen not as innate but as associative that is, as product of historically informed social learning, cultural activity and conscious manipulation. They are the product of a particular part of dynamic, highly stratified and culturally pluralistic capitalist society.

The history of the evolution of Western folk suggests the course the evolutionary process the Indian folk song is likely to follow. With thè rapid development of the electronic media and easy contact and influence of Western pop, the folk forms of different regions of India are bound to be affected. This is quite evident from the recent history of Punjabi folk form *Bhāngrā*.

Punjab, the most developed state of India has a developed cultural form of *Bhāngrā*. People of Punjab are much more westernised in their attitude. Huge numbers of people from Punjab have settled in other states of India and in other countries of the world too. Their contact with U.K. Australia, France, Japan, Germany through their own people is worth noting. All these factors have contributed to the meteoric rise of the *Bhāngrā* form of music and dance mixed with western pop to a new height.

In fact, a few talented NRI artistes of Punjabi origin have first shown the prospect of *Bhāngrā*. Special mention may be made of Malkit Singh and Apache Indian who had shown that Punjabi *Bhāngrā* with its inherent quality of rhythm and tune could be well mixed with the western pop to make it acceptable to the tastes of the young generation.

The journey was started with 'Tutak, tutak, tootian' 'Gud nal isq mitha', of Malkit Singh, 'Dil da mamla hai' and 'Mamla gurbar hai' of Gurdas man. Things began to change radically with the advent of Apahe Indian who mixed Punjabi Bhangra with raggae and rap. With the remixes by Bally Sagoo the Punjabi music became up-market, and reached its zenith with 'Balle Balle' of Daler Mehandi, the most popular among them. What are the reasons for the boom in Punjabi music? Mr. Pawan Malhotra, Manager, Product development, HMV has aptly analysed them. According to him there are four main reasons:[6]

(*i*) affluence of the Punjabi community both in the country and abroad and their willingness to spend

(*ii*) their western way of living

(*iii*) popular numbers bearing western stamp and effervescence of the Punjabi music and finally

(*iv*) the advent of videos adding value to the songs. Videos and screen presence of artistes like Daler Mehandi have played tremandous role in making this music a very popular one.

When television is blasting something and somebody's face day in and day out, people have to recognise them. Daler Mehandi himself has ascribed a few reasons to the popularity of the present form of Punjabi music. According to him, this is the age of stress. At the end of the day, everybody wants to unwind and the better way of unwinding is to shake a leg to Punjabi music.

Moreover, the present day Punjabi music is in simplified form; it is easy-to-understand Punjabi, unlike earlier numbers. The tradition bound people like Charanjit Ahuja, a music composer however reacts that just by replacing ḍholak or ḍhol with drums does not make a Bhangra pop and it is nothing but a folk song. He is, however, angry at the way the language and its nuances have been sabotaged by the pop brigade.

In fact this is what is vital for every form of folk. With the coming of prosperity and affluence, easy contact with the global forms and change in tastes being affected by radio, T.V. and other media, folk forms are bound to go pop-way. Bhāwāiyā cannot be an exception. 'All folk forms of India are likely to be subjected to such changes sooner or later', comments the experienced Mr. Malhotra, because 'in this country nothing but folk tunes sell'. Folk tunes are more vulnerable to distortions because of their tonal and rhythmic quality and also because of the fact that there is none to prevent such distortions. There is no standard set for such tunes. Any body and every body can sing a folk song in whatever manner he or she likes. There is no institution worth naming for the training of folk songs.

The future of Bhāwāiyā and for that matter any form of Indian folk song can be guessed from the performance and observation of Pete Seeger, the American folk singer who happened to perform in a number of places in India including Calcutta in November 1996. In his repertoire he presented a number of songs—some of them his own compositions but some of them could hardly be included within the traditional definition of folk songs. In fact he is reported to have said

> "I do not see folk music as any particular group of folk songs or singers. I see it as an age-old process, which is present in many kinds of music where the old culture is changed by new people. It happens in all life. Old cooks change recipes for new ones".

He elaborated how cross-cultural contacts helped in making great music. In Calcutta he sang 'We shall overcome' 'If I had a hammer', 'Where have all the flowers gone', 'Satisfied mind', 'The Ross Perot guide to answer embarrassing question,' 'Guantanamera', etc. He sang Rabindra Sangeet 'Purano sei diner katha' and 'Raghupati Raghaba Raja Ram', the favourite song of Gandhiji and 'Abiyoyo', the legend of a giant. Rabindra Bharati University, Calcutta felicitated him with a D.Litt for his contribution to folk music. He has been described as a folk icon. He sang about working men who defended their rights, about the innocents who lost their lives in wars, about artists who suffered for their views, about fishermen who found that industrial pollutants have poisoned the fish and about the oneness of all religions. The life and performance of this great folk artist show how the concept of folk has changed over time.

An indication of the above evolutionary process is well caught in composer Hubert Parry's address (1899) to the inaugural meeting of the Folk Song Society.[7]

"In true folk-songs there is no sham, no got-up glitter, and no vulgarity...and the pity of it is that these treasures of humanity are getting rare, for they are written in characters the most evanescent you can imagine, upon the sensitive brain fibres, of those who learn them and have but little idea of their value. Moreover, there is an enemy at the doors of folk music which is driving it out, namely common popular songs of the day; and this enemy is one of the most repulsive and most insidious.... It is for... people who, for the most part, have the most false ideals or none at all—who are always struggling for existence, who think that the commonest rowdyism is the highest expression of human emotion; it is for them that the modern popular music is made and it is made with a commercial intention out of snippets of musical slang. And this product it is which will drive out folk music if we donot save it. For even in country districts where folk songs linger, the people think themselves behind hand if they do not know the songs of the seething towns.... But the old folk music is among the purest products of the human mind. It grew in the heart of the people before they devoted themselves so assiduously to the making of quick returns....[it is] characteristic of the race, of the quite reticence of our country folk, courageous and content, ready to meet what chance shall bring with a cheery heart. All the things that mark the folk music of the race also betoken the qualities of the race and are a faithful reflection of ourselves".

The Bhāwāiyā songs are in the same manner bound to be influenced by the changes in economic, social and political factors and the traditional Bhāwāiyā-Caṭkā songs are likely to be replaced by the newer ones in course of time. As in the case of *Bhāngrā*, the songs with faster rhythm and catchy tunes and words are likely to survive and be popular, while the ones with serious meanings and slow beat are likely to go out of the market. We can not however, say all these with certainty. It may so happen that talented singers and/or composers are born in this region as it happened with the coming of Abbas Uddin and Pyarimohan. Then the future of Bhāwāiyā might take new turn under the spell of that genius with right kind of vision and powers of innovation.

To get a proper reply to the query about the future of any form and style of folk music, one can take suggestion from the remark of the great classical singer C.R. Vyas, when asked about the future of classical music in the age of fusion and pop in an interview by Ratnottama Sengupta,[8]

"The basic structure of Yamon, Kafi or Bhupali is not changing. Only the speed is changing. Now people do not listen to music for peace of mind; they want music for excitement. They are bound to be tired of beat; sooner or later, change is natural. Bandishes will change; old bandishes will give way to new. The definition of bandish too may change. These changes will ensure the survival of classical music".

The priceless comment of C.R. Vyas, the classical maestro is equally applicable to any form of folk music too– Bhāwāiyā, Bhāṭiāli, Jhumur, Gambhirā, or Bāul – whatever it is.

REFERENCES

1. Alan Lomax, *Folk Song-Style and Culture*, New Branswick, N.J., 1968.
2. *Ibid.*
3. C. Keil, *Who needs – the 'folk ?* Journal of the Folklore Institute, 1978.
4. Pabitra Sarkar, *Lok Bhasa Lok Sanskriti,* Chirayata Prakashan, 2nd edn. Kolkata, 1997.
5. Verrier Elwin, *Folk Songs of Chhatisgarh,* Bombay, 1936.
6. Gazhala Wahab, 'The Balle Balle Brigade', *Graphiti of Telegraph*, 23rd August, 1998.
7. Hubert Parry, *Inaugural address to the Folk Song Society,* Journal of Folk Song Society, 1899.
8. Ratnottama Sengupta, 'The Ageless Maestro', published in *The Times of India*, March 11, 1999.

■■■

12

Trends of Distortions and its Remedies

In this chapter we would examine the issue raised about the remedies for the distortion of folk songs, dramas, etc. and the responsibility of the folk lovers under such circustances. There are tradition loving folklorists, performers and composers like Mr. Ahuja of Punjab in every society, every region and folk form, who are concerned with the authenticity and purity of the traditional form—the tune, language, rhythm and nuances. It is these people who have been trying with utmost efforts to maintain the purity of the forms.

One can probably take clue from the message of Dr. Heinz Mode expressed in an interview. The gist of his statement is given below:

> "After the first world war and much more after the second, great social changes have taken place. In my own country there is much esteem and regard for the old folk culture, although it had to be revived in some places. Because of the war and their consequences the folk tradition in Germany have become almost defunct, and so it had to be revived. Special schools and institutions have been founded to study and organize materials, publish books on folk dance, music and folklore or similar research works.
>
> The impact of social changes on folk traditions depends upon the social advancement and social situation of a country. In a country where old modes of living have been preserved to a great extent, one can gather sufficient materials through field works. But in a country which has been highly industrialised and where most of the village children are flocking to the town and where agriculture too is mechanised, there is hardly any scope for collecting field data for the old folk culture, folk tales, folk music, folk art and so on. There people have found other means of expressing their feelings and emotions".

Speaking about his own country, he stated that there are special institutions and large groups of folk dancers, folk musicians and others who try to recover and revive folklore and folk music because they constitute a great historical force. They contributed much to the evolution of the German people in the past.

It is no longer a living force but is a thing we are proud of. We are proud of our past, our folk culture, our tradition; but we have now come beyond the stage where folk culture could be continued as a living force in the old sense. Folk tales are not historical tales and so they cannot give direct evidence of history, but they contain elements which can be classified historically.

In this connection, I can not resist myself from mentioning the observations of Bihu Samrat Khagen Mahanta of Assam in an interview to the Statesman published on 12 June 1998.

> "The present trend of folk music is disturbing.... Even in remote village of the region one finds the younger generation swaying to tunes of Hindi film song. Even though they sing in their local dialects, the lyrics and music of folk have been modelled on the lines of popular Hindi numbers".

Regretting the gradual drifting of folk music from its roots, the Mahanta couple, Khagen and Archana pointed out the concept of globalisation of culture that has sounded the death-knell of traditional culture. Under such circumstances they confirm,

> "We are committed to preserve the rich musical heritage of Assam and if in the process we provide entertainment, it is a double achievement for us..... Both of us are striving to restore and preserve its originality and purity".

This is true for every form. Globalisation, onslaught of media have tremendous their influence on every folk form. Fortunately for us there are still some people fighting for the preservation of originality and purity of every such folk form.

This has happened in case of Bhāwāiyā too. There are still some people belonging to the older generation who perform in traditional songs and traditional ways of folk drama. Satis gidal performs Bishaharā in traditional form. Lalit Kuśani can enact and sing the Kuśan play in traditional form; similarly Fulti gidali still sings and dances on the traditional tunes of Kāti and Shāiṭal on the rhythm played on *ḍhāk*.

We should mention here the role played by some folk loving institutions and the Government. In this connection the part played by Paschim Banga Lok Sanskriti O Adivasi Sanskriti Kendra (West Bengal Folk & Tribal Cultual Centre) of the State Government of West Bengal deserves to be specially mentioned. The centre, originally named as Lok Sanskriti Parshad sponsored various folk programmes in the districts to encourage the regional forms of folk songs and folk dances. The centre organises workshops and seminars for discussions on originality, authenticity and purity of these traditional forms for creating awareness on the necessity of encouraging such forms and preserving them. The Parshad has played important role in encouraging performance of original Bhawiya in the region. It organised training courses in the pattern of 'gurukul' on Bhāwāiyā.

Workshops of folk drama—Dotorā, Kuśān and Bishaharā have also been organised in various places of North Bengal wherein emphasis has been given on the traditional way of presentation, but improvement in acting, mode of dialogue, improvement in application of *mudras* of dances at the same time. Lessons on the use of microphones, procenium stage, proportionate uses of songs and acting, etc. have been considered to be of tremandous effect in improving their overall performance to make it more acceptable to the audience while maintaining the traditionality.

Role played by the Backward Classes Welfare Department of the Government of West Bengal under the able leadership of Shri Dinesh Ch. Dakua, the then Minister-in-Charge of the Department for encouraging the performance of genuine Bhāwāiyā-Caṭkā through Annual competitions conducted throughout North Bengal is worth-mentioning in this connection.

Besides the State Government Departments, there are various other institutions working in the field to encourage performance of original and genuine forms of Bhāwāiyā-Caṭkā. Uttarbanga Bhāwāiyā Parishad and Abbasuddin Smaran Samity, Calcutta deserve special mention of such institutions. But for the sustained efforts of the State Government departments and the voluntary non-government institutes, Bhāwāiyā-Caṭkā would have lost much of its originality and traditionality by this time. It is however, high time that steps should be taken for organising preservation methods of the folk forms.

There are still some old performers in various parts of the country who can offer traits deserving preservation. Most of them are sufficiently old and aged and one cannot expect them to live longer. The State or any private institute should immediately take actions for recording those in audio and video for preservation. Proper arrangement for archives for this purpose is therefore, an urgent necessity. Folk and Tribal Cultural Centre, which has planned construction of archives for the folk and tribal arts and culture should give, focused attention to the early completion of their project. Recording of various forms of folk will, however, do yeoman's service in the mean time.

It may not be irrelevant to mention in this connection that the vast majority of Indians and so are the Bengalees, are ignorant of the value and significance of folk culture, tribal customs and art, ceremonies and festivals, rituals and rites. This is why we need a good number of trained and articulate anthropologists, sociologists, philosophers and educationists to educate us on the worth of our ancient folk and tribal culture. A majority of us would then see the need for their protection and preservation and make serious efforts for the same. State should play a leading role in this regard.

Sincere well-equipped training centers are also necessary for maintaining the tradition and preserving the folk traits. There is a general tendency found everywhere that the folk tunes attract the singers, particularly the folk singers and as such they would like to sing folk songs of all forms, having learnt the same from the teachers who themselves may not be knowing the form properly. A singer of Baul or Jhumur may have learnt Bhāwāiyā songs from the guru who is an expert of Jhumur but not of Bhāwāiyā. Or he may learn it from the C.D's, cassettes. Naturally the intonation, pronounciation and nuances of Bhāwāiyā cannot be expected from such singers. But nobody can resist such singers with good quality voice from singing Bhāwāiyā, although they may be causing damage to the form by performing the distorted versions.

The only remedy is therefore, to establish Training Centres with teachers from among the gurus who really know the form and can teach the genuine version of the form. Since the attraction and hence demand for the folk songs are found to be increasing day by day, there are no ways but to open properly equipped Training Centres for teaching genuine tunes of folk songs, if we want to prevent distortions and impositions in the name of folk. The Government or any non Governmental organisations should take this responsibility, along with the responsibility of archival works. Les us be optimistic about the fulfilment of this necessity some day in the intrest of our cultural heritage.

■■■

Glossary

Aesthetic	Concerned with beauty
Ahom	The dynasty that ruled Assam from the 15th Century
Anthropomorphic	Attributing human form or personality to god, animal etc.
Anuvadi	The note appearing more than Vivadi note but less than Samvadi note in classical raga of Indian music.
Bahe	A term used for addressing a person of paternal relation in Rajbanshi dialect.
Bargadar	Share cropper of agricultural produce.
Baudia	A term used for the word 'vagaband' in Rajbanshi dialect.
Baul	A person in search of 'self' within 'himself' through the path of an 'ism' mostly derived out of Vaisnavism. The mode of expression of a Baul through melody is "Baul song".
Bena	A stringed instrument used in folk drama 'Kushan' under the Bhawaiya form of folk songs of North Bengal.
Bhajan	A form of devotional song mainly based on classical musical format.
Bhadoi Khel	Song and dance connected with the worship of Teesta river in the district of Jalpaiguri.
Bhadu	A female deity worshipped by the rural people of western districts of West Bengal – Bardhaman, Bankura, Birbhum and Purulia.
Bhatiali	A form of folk song of the 'Bhati' area (low land) of the then East Bengal (present Bangladesh), associating boat and boatman.
Bhawaiya	A form of folk song of the then Kamrup, presently North Bengal, Northern Bangladesh and Western Assam.
Bishahara	A form of folk drama mainly based on musical melody glorifying Manasa, the snake goddess in Northern districts of West Bengal and Western districts of Assam.

Bodo	A tribe of Western Assam and West Bengal; the language spoken by the Bodo people.
Brahminisation	Adopting Brahminic ways of life in worship, manners, social rituals, etc.
Cadence	Rise and fall of the voice in reciting and singing .
Cantometrics	A modern method of studying and assessing various qualities of music.
Caryageeti	Music connected with Carya.
Catka	A form of folk music of North Bengal; it is the brisk form of Bhawaiya.
Chad petar gan	Songs sung by the labourers while hammering the roof casting.
Chilarai	The famous general Sukladhwaj of Kamrup nicknamed Chilarai as he fought like chila i.e. kite.
Chokra sance	A form of dance performed by boys cross dressed as girls in the folk dramas of North Bengal.
Constellation	Group of associated or similar people or things.
Deora	A term used in Rajbanshi dialect for devar, the younger brother of husband.
Dhak	Long cylindrical drum percussion (instrument) played with two sticks.
Dhamar	One of the oldest forms of classical song mainly on 'Hori or Holi' – the spring festival connected with Lord Krishna and Radha.
Dhan Katar gan	Songs sung by the farmers while harvesting paddy (dhan).
Dhol	Drum (percussion instrument)
Dhrupada	The oldest form of Indian classical song.
Dola	A term used for low lands/cradle in North Bengal.
Dotara/Dotorā	A string instrument essential for Bhawaiya, Bhatiali and other forms of folk songs of Bengal.
Dehatatwa	A dictum of devotional path to drive human body in reaching the almighty. The modious expression of this devotion is known as 'Dehatatwar Gaon' (song).
Ethnic	Racial/tribal group having common cultural tradition.
Ethnology	Science of different human races.
Ethnomusicology	Study of music with reference to the culture of the ethnic group of people.

Etymology	Study of origin and history of words and their meanings
Folk community	Community or group of people having same set of belief, faith, customs, manners and cultural ethos.
Folk dance	Dance performed by the rural common people, mainly based on rituals.
Folk song	Songs sung by common rural people in simple tune and rhythm expressing their feeling on different aspects of life and life style.
Fota	A piece of cloth used by the rural women for covering the upper part of the body; also known as 'patani'.
Gambhira	A form of folk drama of Malda district of West Bengal named after 'Gambhir' – the lord Shiva. The form centering Lord Shiva highlights contemporary problems.
Gorakhnather gan	Song eulogizing the glory of Gorakhnath, a deity worshipped by the Rajbanshi people of North Bengal.
Hexatonic	A composition with six musical notes.
Hinduised	Taken into the Hindu system of religion and belief.
Hudum Pujar gan	Songs associated with the deity Hudum worshipped by the women folk of Rajbanshi community of North Bengal.
Indo-Aryan	Family of languages spoken originally in Europe and parts of Western Asia by the Aryans.
Indology	Concerning ancient India.
Indomusicology	Study of the science of Indian classical music.
Interval	Difference in pitch between two notes.
Intonation	Quality of playing or singing in tune.
Jag gan	A form of folk drama of North Bengal pertaining to fertility cult performed for arousing kam (sexual urge).
Jhumur	A form of folk song prevalent in the western parts of West Bengal.
Kabigan	A form of duel between two poets who express their stand point through melody widely prevalent in rural Bengal.
Kamakhya	Kamakhya is goddess Kali in the temple of Kamakhya near Gouhati of Assam.
Kamrup	The ancient kingdom of Naraka and Bhagadatta – the area subsequently ruled by the Koch dynasty.
Kamtapur	A part of Kamrup, mainly Coochbehar district being ruled by the Khen Kings.

Kamtapuri	The dialect spoken by the people of the then Kamtapur.
Karam	A tribal festival observed with ritual as well as song and dance named after the twig of Karam tree which symbolizes the deity.
Kati nach	Kati is the local name of the Hindu god Kartika. The song and dance performed by the Rajbanshi women for Kati puja is called Kati nach.
Khemta nach	The form of dance performed by the cross-dressed boys in the folk dramas of North Bengal.
Khen	The dynasty which ruled Kamtapur in the 15th century.
Khol	The principal percussion instrument used for Kirtana, Bhawaiya songs and Bhawaiya based folk drama..
Khyayal	A very popular form of Indian classical music which has overtaken 'Dhrupad', the oldest form of Indian classical music.
Koch-Rajbanshi	The dynasty beginning with Biswasingha which ruled Kamrup and later on Cooch Behar from the 16th century to 1950 is known as Koch or Koch-Rajbanshi.
Kshatriya	Second from above in the ladder of the Hindu caste system – a military Hindu caste.
Kushan	The folk drama singing the glory of the main characters of Ramayana and Mahabharata.
Lalan award	The award introduced by West Bengal Government after the name of Lalan to be awarded to distinguished folk and tribal performers.
Laya	The speed of music-very slow, slow and fast.
Lingua franca	Language used by the people having different languages of an area for communication amongst them.
Mangala Kavya	The form of Bengali literature dealing with the Puranic gods and goddesses like Candi, Manasa, Dharma who are worshipped for the welfare (Mangala) of people.
Mahut	The elephant keeper and driver.
Maishal	The keeper of buffalo herds.
Manosiksha	The form of devotional music that is used for taming and putting restraint on the mind/feelings.
Matra	Count of beats in music to distinguish between talas-tala of 4 matras, 6 matras, 10 matras etc.
Mech	A tribe of bodo origin residing in Western Assam and North Bengal.

Mela	One of the arrangements of musical notes. Mela and Thata are two characteristics from which originated the concept "Raga" in classical music; also congregation of people.
Melody	Arrangement of musical notes in an expressive order; tunefulness.
Microtones	Expressing very small variations in musical tunes.
Mlechchas	Degraded in the Hindu caste system.
Mode	Any of several arrangements of musical notes.
Mongoloid	Belonging to Mongolian race.
Morpheme	Smallest meaning for unit in which a word can be divided
Morphology	Study of morphemes of a language and how they are combined to words.
Musicology	Academic scientific study of music.
Myth	Stories that originated in ancient times dealing with early beliefs, history of race etc.
Nachni	A form of dance with Jhumur form of folk song of western West Bengal.
Nada	Musical sound in early classical Indian music system.
Narayani Mudra	The coin which was in vogue during the reign of Naranarayana and later period in Kamrup.
Narayani Sena	The army of Kamrup under Naranarayana and Chilarai.
Natya Sastra	The book codifying different aspects of 'Natya', i.e. Sangeet (music), Nritya (dance) and Natya (drama). Natya Sastra of Bharata is the earliest document of Indian music.
Neo Indo-Aryan	Later form of Indo-Aryan ideas and thoughts.
Neo-Vaisnavism	Later form of Vaisnavism under Sankardeva of Assam.
North Bengal	Northern part of West Bengal and Bangladesh.
Nouka Baicher gan	Songs associated with boat rowing / boat race.
Notes	Swaras, viz. sa, re, ga, ma, pa, dha, ni.
Nuances	Subtle difference in meaning, colour, feelings etc.
Odava	Raga of five notes.
Pakad	Principal mode of a tune/music.
Palagan	Folk drama in ballad form.
Palligeeti	Folk Song/Song of rural people.

Pancali	Ballad form of music based on different deities of Hindus and Pirs of Muslims.
Paradigm	Set of all the different forms of a word.
Pentatonic	Composition of five musical notes.
Phonotactic	Derived from the system of sound.
Pitch	Set in a particular key / level e.g. high pitch / low pitch.
Poignancy	State of being sad or full of pity.
Polyphony Polyrhythm	Combination of several different melodic patterns to form a single piece of music/rhythm.
Pran Vayu	The vital force.
Psychic	Concerned with processes and phenomena that seem to be outside physical or natural laws.
Rabha	A 'tribe' of bodo-origin residing in western parts of Assam and north-east of West Bengal.
Raga	Combination of musical notes expressing different moods of human life and nature in Indian classical system.
Rajbanshi	The group of people who are supposed to be the original residents of Kamrup.
Resonant	Resounding; continuing to echo.
Samaganas	Recitation of hymns of Sama Veda.
Sampurna	Raga with all seven notes.
Samvadi	One of the classifying characteristic swaras of Indian classical music, used with second most frequency, in the raga.
Sarigan	Songs concerning boat race in southern part of Bengal.
Semi castes	A stage between the caste and tribes
Semi-tatsama	Words almost akin to Sanskrit.
Semi tribes	A stage nearing tribal attributes.
Shadava	Raga with six notes.
Shaitol Puja	Shaitol is deity of reproduction. Shaitol puja performed by the Rajbanshi women with the vow of having sons. The puja is associated with songs and dances.
Sonarai gan	Songs eulogizing the glory of Sonarai, the god of tiger.
Srooti	Hearing; The Vedas.
Sukati	Dried jute leaves used as food in Kamrup.

Toppa	Originated from Western India the form of Indian music now prevalent in North India and West Bengal.
Tarja	Form of folk song of competition between two composer singers.
Tatsama	Sanskritised words.
Terai	Geographical area in Himalayan foothills of North Bengal.
Thumri	Form of classical Indian music with certain characteristics – light in nature.
Tibeto-Burmese	One of the language groups of India.
Timbre	Characteristic quality of sound produced by a particular voice or instrument.
Tistaburir gan	Songs connected with the worship of Teesta river.
Tones	Quality or character of sound produced by a musical instrument.
Tonocolour	Timbre
Traditional music	Folk music
Tusu	Tusu is the deity worshipped in the western part of West Bengal where the folk song 'Tusu gan' becomes the major part of the Puja.
Vadi	The musical note appearing most frequently in the raga.
Vivadi	The musical note appearing with the least frequency in a raga of Indian classical music.
Vocabulary	Number of words that make up a language.
Vocalization	Singing.
Yodeling	Singing or uttering a musical call with frequent changes from the normal voice to high falsetto notes.

Bibliography

Bandopadhyay, Asit Kr., *Anchalik Bangla Bhasar Abhidhan*, Vol. I, Calcutta University, Kolkata, 1991.

Bandopadhyay, Krishnadhan, *Geeta-Sutrasar*, A.Mukherjee & Co., Kolkata, 4th edn. 1382 B.S.

Barma, Dharmanarayan, *A Step to Kamta Bihari Language,* published by Minati Barma Adhikari, Mokhada Pustakalaya, Tufanganj, 1991.

—, *Kamtapuri Bhasha Sahityer Rup Rekha*, Raidak Prakashan, Tufanganj, Cooch Behar, West Bengal, 1407 B.S.

Barma, H.K.Roy, *Kochbiharer Itihas*, published by the author, Magazine Road, Cooch Behar, West Bengal, 1977.

Barma, Sukhbilas, *Jag Gan, Abbasuddin Smaran Samity*, Kolkata, 1989.

—, *Bhawaiya*, Lok Sanskriti and Adivasi Sanskriti Kendra, I & C.A.Dept., Govt. of West Bengal, 1990.

Barua, Nihar, *Mahut Maishaler gan,* Parichay, Sharadiya, 1385 B.S.

Basu, Nagendra Nath, *The Social History of Kamrupa,* Vol. II, published by the author, 9, Viswakosha Lane, Bagbazar, Kolkata, 1926.

Bhaktisastri, Dharma Narayan Sarkar, *Uttar Banger Lok Sahitya O Bhasa*, published by the author, Lalmanirhat, Bangladesh, 1987.

Bhattacharjee, H.S. and Sudhishankar Bhattacherjee, *Kochbiharer Prachin Bratakatha,* Burdwan University, Burdwan, West Bengal, 1983.

Bhattacharya, Ashutosh, *Banglar Loka Sahitya (Folk-literature of Bengal)* Vol. III, Calcutta book House, Kolkata, 1996.

Bhattacharya, Sudhibhusan, Enthomusicology and India, Indian Publications, Kolkata, 1968.

—, Rhythm in Indian Music, Folklore (Kolkata), Vol. IX, No. 4, 1968.

—, Scales *in Indian Music,* Folklore, (Kolkata), Vol. IX, No. 6, 1968.

—, *Uncultivated Music of India,* Folklore (Kolkata), Vol. IX, No.2, 1968.

Bhattacharyya, Ajitesh (ed.), *Madhupurni-Cooch Behar Number and Special North Bengal Number,* Shibtali complex, Balurghat, West Bengal: 1396 B.S.(1990).

Bhowmik, Nirmalendu, *Pranta Uttarbanger Lok Sangeet,* Chirayata Prakashan, 2nd edn., Kolkata, 1997.

—, , *Pranta Uttarbanger Upabhasa,* Calcutta University, Kolkata, 1385 B.S.

Biswas, Hemanga (ed.), *Folk Music and Folklore-An Anthology,* Vol. I, Folk Music and Folklore Research Institute, Kolkata, 1967.

—, , *Lok Sangeet Samiksha – Bangla O Assam,* A. Mukherjee & Co., Kolkata, 1978.

—, , *Ujan Gang Baiya,* Anustup, Kolkata, 1990.

Bose, Nirmal Kumar, *Anthropology and some Indian Problems,* Institute of Social Research and Applied Anthropology, Kolkata, 1972.

Chattopadhyay, Bimal Chandra, *Uttarbanger Lok Sangeet,* Granthamandir Prakashan, Kolkata, 1992.

Chattopadhyay, Debiprosad, *Lokayata Darsana (Ancient Indian Materialistic Philosophy),* New Age Publishers, Kolkata, 1969.

Chattopadhyay, Suniti Kr., *Bangalir Sanskriti,* Paschim Banga Bangla Academy, I and CA Dept. Govt. of West Bengal; 2nd edn. Kolkata, 1991.

—, *ODBL, (Origin and Development of Bengali Language),* Calcutta University, Kolkata, 1926.

Choudhury, Khaled, *An interview with Surajit Ghosh in 'Prama',* Prama Prakashani, Special Art Number 2, 15th May, Kolkata, 1993.

Cook, Nicholas, *Music Imagination and Culture,* Oxford, Clarendon Press, 1990.

Danielou, A, *Ethnomusicology,* Journal of the Music Academy, Madras XXVII, 1956

Das Biswanath, *Joynath Munshir Rajopakhyan*, ed. Mala Publication, 2nd edn. Kolkata, 1989.

Das, Jogesh (ed.), Bishnu Prasad Rachana Sambhar, Rabha Rachanavali Prakashan Sangha, Tejpur, Assam, 1989.

Das, Nirmal, *Uttarbanga Bhasa Prasanga,* Sahitya Bihar, Kolkata : 2nd edn., 1997.

Das, Sukumar, *Uttar Banger Itihas,* Kumar Sahitya Prakashan, Kolkata, 1982.

Dasgupta, Kali, *Ethnic Songs,* Rabindra Sadan, Kolkata : 1977.

—, Lok Sanskriti, *Naya Ganatantric Sanskriti Andolan,* Prastuti Parva, Calcutta, 1991.

Deb, Chittaranjan, *Banglar Lok-Geet-Katha,* Purabi Dev 'Palligeeti', Kolkata, 1986.

—, *Banglar Palligeeti,* National Book Agency, Kolkata, 1372 B.S.

Deb, Ranjit, *Uttarbanger Chithi,* published by Ashit Baran Jana, Kolkata, 1382 B.S.

Deva, B.C., *Musical Instruments of India-their History and Development,* Firma K.L.M., Kolkata, 1978.

Dundes, Alan, *The Study of the Folklore,* Englewood Clliffs, N.J.: 1965.

East India Gazetteer, 2nd. edn., Vol. I, W.H. Allen & Co., London, 1828.

Elwin, Verrier, *Folk Songs of Chhatisgarh,* Bombay:1936.

Francis Buchanan Hamilton, *Account of the District of Rangpur 1810,* Appendix III of the District Census Handbook, Jalpaiguri and Cooch Behar : West Bengal, 1951.

Gait, Sir Edward, *A History of Assam,* Lawyer's Book Stall, Guwahati, Assam, 1905. 7th ed.1997.

Gangopadhyay, Binoy, *Rag Manjusha,* NAVANA, 47, G.C.Avenue, Kolkata: 1976.

Ghosh, Pradip Kr. (Tr.), *Sangeet Ratnakar of Sarangadeva,* Paschimbanga Rajya Sangeet Academy, Director of Culture, I & CA Deptt. Govt. of West Bengal, 1994

Gray Cecil, *The History of Music,* Reprint Services Corp., 1935.

Grierson, G.A. (ed.), "*Linguistic Survey of India*", Vol. V, Motilal Banarsidas, New Delhi, 1904.

Guha, Amalendu, *Medieval and Early Colonial Assam,* Centre for Studies in Social Sciences, K.P.Bagchi & Co., Kolkata, 1991.

Gurye, G.S., *Indian Costume,* Popular Prakashan, Bombay, 1966.

Haldar, Gopal, *Sanskritir Rupantar,* Muktadhara, Dhaka: Bangladesh, 1984.

Harker, Dave, Fakesong; the Manufacture of British folksong, 1700 to the present day, Milton Keynes, 1985.

Hocket, Charles F., *A Course in Modern Linguistics,* MacMillan & Co., New York, 1968.

Hood, Mantle, *The Ethnomusicologist,* McGraw Hill Text, 1971, rev. ed. New York, 1982.

Hunter, W.W., *Statistical Account of Bengal,* Vol. X, Turner and Company, London,1876; rpt. D.K.Publishing House, Delhi, 1974, rpt. West Bengal State Gazetteer, Higher Education Deptt.Govt. of West Bengal, Kolkata, 1997.

Hutton, John Henry, *Caste in India,* Cambridge University Press, Cambridge, 1951.

Islam, Mazharul, *A History of Folktale Collections in India and Pakistan,* Bangla Academy, Dhaka, Bangladesh, 1970.

John, Lovell Jr., *Black Song-The Forge and the Flame,* The MacMillan Company. New York.

Kakati, Banikanta, *Assamese-its Formation and Development,* 3rd edn., Lawyer's Book Stall, Guwahati, Assam, 1972.

Karan, Sudhir, *Simanta Banglar Lok Jan,* A. Mukherjee and Co., Kolkata, 1371 B.S.

Keil, C, *Who needs – the 'folk ?* Journal of the Folklore Institute, 1978.

Khan Choudhuri, Amanatulla, *Coch-Biharer Itihas,* Modern Book Agency, Kolkata, 1936; rpt. 1990.

Kothari, K.S., *Indian Folk Musical Insturments,* Sangeet Natak Academy, New Delhi, 1968.

Krishnaswamy, S. *Musical Instruments of India,* Publications Devision, Ministry of Information and Broadcasting, Govt. of India. New Delhi, 1965.

Lloyd, A, *Folk Song in England,* London, 1967.

Lomax, A, Cantometrics; an Approach to the Anthropology of Music, (Berkley, 1976)

—, *Folk Song-Style and Culture* (New Branswick, N.J.), 1968.

— (ed.), *The Penguin Book of American Folk Songs* (Harmondsworth), 1964.

Mahato, Pashupati Prasad, *The Performing Arts of Jharkhand,* B. B. Prakashan, Calcutta, 1987.

Majumdar, R.C., *History of Bengal,* The History of Bengal Publications Committee, Kolkata, 1948.

Majumdar, Sisir (ed.), *Uttarbanger Lok Natya,* Mom Prakashani, Kolkata, 1986; 2nd edn. 1990.

Mehta, R.C, *Value of Folk Music, Studies in Indian Folk Culture,* ed. S. Sengupta & K.D.Upadhyay, Calcutta, 1964.

Merriam, A. P., "The Anthropology of Music", (Evanston. IL), 1964.

Middleton, R. *Studying Popular Music, Open University Press* (Milton Keynes, Philadelphia) 1990.

Mitra, Sanat Kr., *Paschimbanga Lok Sanskriti Bichitra,* Biswas Publishing House, Kolkata, 1382 B.S.

Mukherjee, B.N. and P.K. Bhattacharjee (ed.), *Early Historical Perspective of North Bengal,* North Bengal University, Siliguri, Darjeeling, 1987.

Murdock, George P., "The Common Denominator of Cultures", Ralph Linton (ed.) *The Science of Man in the World of Crisis,* Columbia University Press, New York, 1945.

Nag, Hiten, *Uttarbanger Bhawaiya Gan,* Prakash Bhawan, Kolkata, 1998.

Narjinari, Hiracharan, *In Search of Identity-The Mech,* B.B.Prakashan, Kolkata, 1985.

Nath, D., *History of the Koch Kingdom : (1515-1615),* Mittal Publications, New Delhi, 1989.

Nettl, Bruno, *Folk and Traditional Music of the Western Continents,* (Englewood Cliffs, NJ), 1965.

Pal, Harish Ch. *Uttar Banglar Palligeeti-Bhawaiya Khanda,* ed. Chandrasekhar Pal, Kalika Press, Kolkata:1380 B.S. (1973).

Parry, Hubert, *Inaugural address to the Folk Song Society,* Journal of Folk Song Society, 1899.

Prajnanananda, Swami, *Historical Development of Indian Music*, Ramkrishna Vedanta Math, Calcutta, 1983.

Rajkhowa, J.P., *Generalissimo Chilarai and his Times,* Vikram Publishers, Guwahati, Assam, 2001.

Ranade, Asok D. Convenor, *Working Papers from the Seminar and Workshops on Documentation and Archiving for Ethonomusicology* Organised by Archives and Research Centre for Ethnomusicology, American Institute of Indian Studies. in Pune, Maharasthra, 1984.

—, *Indology and Ethnomusicology,* Promilla & Co., New Delhi, 1992.

Risley Herbert H., *The Tribes and Castes of Bengal,* Vol. I, Bengal Secretariat Press, Kolkata, 1892.

Roy, Sukumar, *Music of Eastern India,* Firma K.L.M., Kolkata, 1969.

Saha, Rebati Mohan, *Koch Rabha Bhasha,* Suravi Prakashan, Bilasipara, Assam, 1981.

Sanyal, Amiya Nath, *Ragas and Raginis,* Orient Longman, Calcutta, 1958.

Sanyal, Charu Chandra, *The Rajbanshis of North Bengal,* Monograph Series, Vol, XI, The Asiatic Society, Kolkata, 1965.

Sarkar, Pabitra, *Lok Bhasa Lok Sanskriti,* Chirayata Prakashan, 2nd edn. Kolkata, 1997.

—, *Lok Sanskritir Nandantattwa,* Bangla Academy, Paschim Banga, Kolkata,

Sarkar, Panchanan (ed.), *Rangpur Sahitya Parishad Patrika* (Part IV), Rangpur Sahitya Parishad, Rangpur, 1912-1919.

Schneider, M, *Primitive Music, New Oxford History of Music, Ancient & Oriental Music,* ed. E.Wellesz. London, 1957

Sen, Dinesh Chandra, *Brihod Banga Part I and II,* Calcutta University, Kolkata, 1935; rpt. Deys Publishing, Kolkata, 1993.

Sengupta, Pallab, *Lok Sanskritir Simana O Swarup,* Pustak Bipani, Kolkata, 1995.

Sengupta, Ratnottama, *The Ageless Maestro,* Published in The Times of India, March 11, 1999.

Sengupta, Sankar, *Cultural Instinct of Ethnomusicology,* Folklore, Vol. XVI, No.6, Kolkata, 1974.

Sharma Shibananda(ed), *Goalpara Zilla Sanskriti Sangrakshan Smriti Grantha,* Mahakuma Parisad, Dhubri, Assam, 1971.

Sharp, Cecil, *English Folk Song :* Some conclusions, Wakefield, Yorks, 1972, first published in 1907.

Siddique, Asraf, "Lok Sahitya", (Folk-Literature) *The Student Ways,* Muktadhara, 1963; 2nd edn. Dhaka, Bangladesh, 1980.

Sinha, Patiram, *Kamta Rajye Poundra,* Gayatri Sinha, Lily Cottage, Cooch Behar, West Bengal, 1379 B.S.

Sinha, Purnima, *An Approach to the Study of Indian Music,* Indian Publication, Kolkata, 1970.

Tagore, Raja S.M. *Shastriya Sangeet Vishayak Prastab,* Banga Sangeet Vidyalaya, Calcutta, 1871.

Udayraj, A. Gadnis, 'Tantra the exotic pathway to Spirituality', *Jetwings*, May, 1998.

Uddin, Md. Mansur, *Haramoni,* collected and ed. by Bangla Academy, 2nd edn., Dhaka, Bangladesh, 1978.

Wahab, Gazhala, 'The Balle Balle Brigade', *Graphiti of Telegraph*, 23rd August, 1998.

Weiner, Myron, *Sons of the Soil, Migration and Ethnic Conflict in India,* Oxford University Press, Delhi, Bombay, Calcutta, Madras.

Yehudi Menuhin & Curtis W.Davis, *The Music of Man, Macdonald Generals Books,* Macdonald & Jane's, London & Sydney, first ed. 1980.

■■■

INDEX

A

C

D

E

F

G

H

I

J

K

N

O

P

R

S

T

U

V

W

Y

T

U

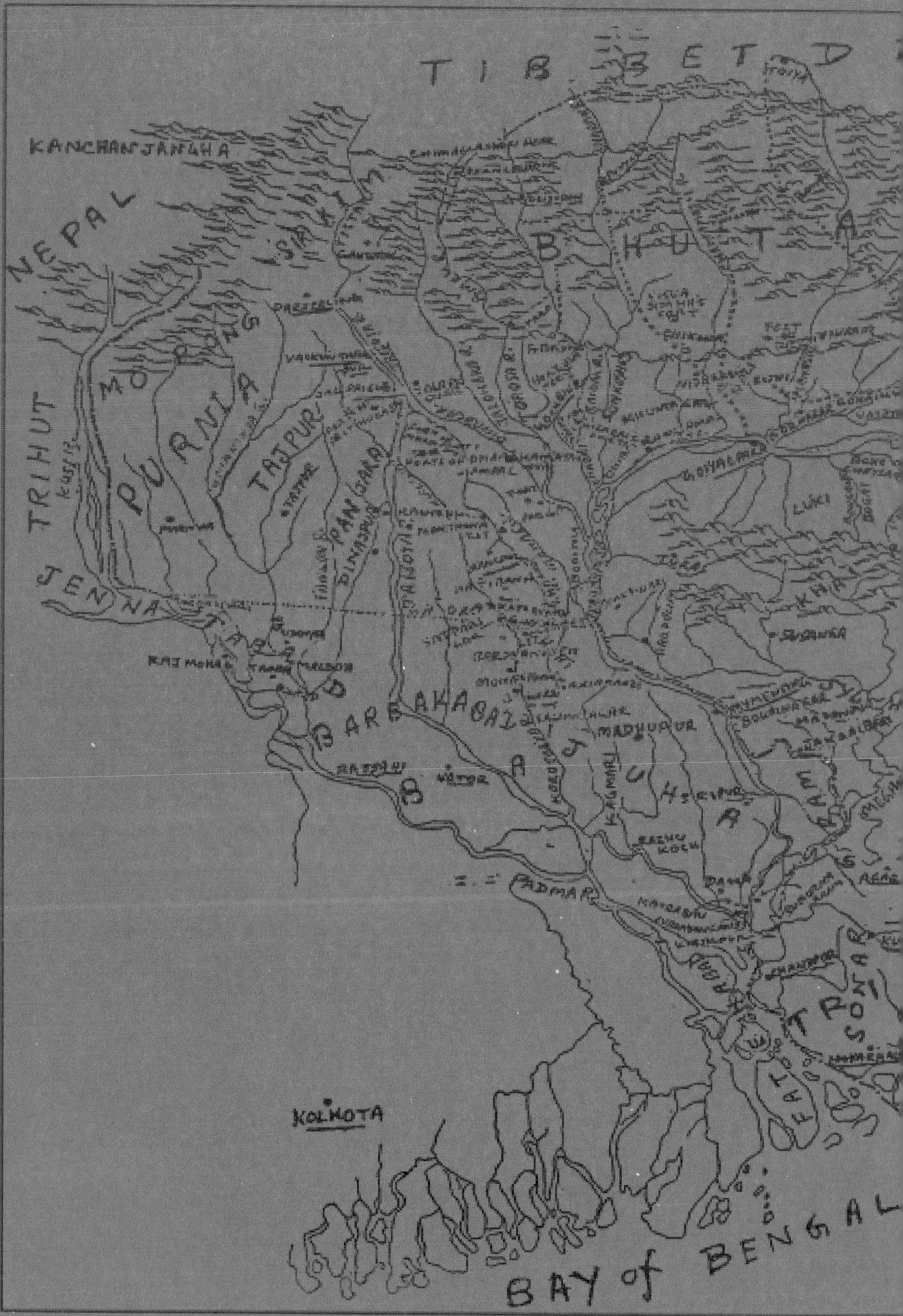
TIB BET
KANCHANJANGHA
NEPAL
MORANG
PURNIA
TRIHUT
TAJPUR
JENNA
RAJMOHAL
BARBAKABAD
MADHUPUR
PADMAR
LUKI
KOLKOTA
BAY of BENGAL